PORTAL

Connecting
God's
Word
to
Your Life

Also by Mark Witas:
Live Out Loud

PORTAL

Connecting
God's
Word
to
Your Life

Mark Witas

REVIEW AND HERALD® PUBLISHING ASSOCIATION
Since 1861 | www.reviewandherald.com

This book was
Edited by Rachel Cabose
Copyedited by Vesna Mirkovich
Designed by Emily Ford / Review and Herald® Design Center
Cover art by © Thinkstock.com
Typeset: Minion Pro 11/13

PRINTED IN U.S.A.

17 16 15 14 13   5 4 3 2 1

Library of Congress Cataloging-in-Publication Data

Witas, Mark, 1962-
 Portal : connecting God's word to your life [2014 teen devotional] / Mark Witas.
    pages cm
 ISBN 978-0-8280-2735-9
 1. Teenagers--Religious life. 2. Devotional calendars--Seventh-Day Adventists. I. Title.
 BV4531.3.W58 2013
 248.8'3--dc23

                         2013014569

ISBN 978-0-8280-2735-9

DEAR READER,

WHEN I CHOSE TO WRITE THIS YEAR'S YOUTH DEVOTIONAL, it wasn't a difficult decision to take my readers through a survey of the Bible, Genesis to Revelation. My passion for learning, knowing, and living the precepts of the Bible has taken me on a journey that I've been on for 29 years. Why not share it with friends?

Since my baptism in 1983 the Bible has been a close companion. I've discovered that Scripture isn't just ink on page—it's a living and breathing document full of insight about the character of God and the nature of humans.

The Bible is shockingly honest, brutally brash, and simply wonderful! Sometimes the Word of God is uncomplicated and easily understood. Sometimes it seems one needs a Ph.D. to "get it."

In this book I've taken portions of each book of the Bible and reflected on their meaning to me. Sometimes a passage of Scripture reminds me of something that's happened in my life. Sometimes it brings to mind a story that happened to someone else. Often I'll think of a song or a poem. And sometimes the passage of Scripture so overwhelms me (in a good way) that it needs to stand on its own without commentary.

I didn't cover every passage from every book of the Bible. A book like that would require more than a mere 365 pages. I just took what jumped out at me as I gleaned through the pages of Scripture. If I skipped a portion of one of your favorite books of the Bible, by all means read it, pray over it, let it wash over you, and be blessed by it.

Each daily reading in this book will take only a few short minutes. My challenge to you is to read the passage of Scripture that heads each daily reading. Get out your Bible and read the scriptures surrounding it to gather in good context and more meaning.

One thing you should know before you start reading this book is that I didn't skip the parts of Scripture that are uncomfortable. Some of the Bible is rated "R" for graphic violence and language (not swearing, but vividly descriptive yuck). I feel that if we're going to walk through the Bible, we can't be selective. So be warned: some of the subject matter we'll deal with may take a mature mind.

Finally, I hope you'll notice the thread throughout this book—that the Bible points to Jesus, because Jesus is the revealer of the Father. The Bible includes some tough stories that seem to call God's character into question. In those instances, and always, remember that Jesus said, "If you've seen Me, you've seen the Father" (see John 14:9). Filter all your questions about God through the person of Jesus. You can always depend on Him.

—MARK WITAS

War in Heaven

AND WAR BROKE OUT IN HEAVEN: Michael and his angels fought with the dragon. **REVELATION 12:7, NKJV.**

When I was in fifth grade, we had a substitute teacher who was more of a parent sent to babysit than a teacher. She was fun; I'm just not sure how much learning we accomplished while she was there. One day she decided to break us up into two teams to have the world's best rubber-band fight. She let us move our desks around and create barricades with all the furniture in the classroom. It was awesome—until the principal walked in and got hit by a projectile. We never had that sub again.

I think I've watched too many movies. When I see that word "war" in today's text, I think of explosions and machine guns and tanks and missiles. When I read in the Bible that there was war in heaven, I envision space-age laser swords with bright flashes of light and epic theme music playing in the background—a Star Wars battle on a much grander scale.

It's interesting that even though the word "war" is used to describe the battle that went on in heaven, it wasn't a war of physical violence. No light sabers, no laser guns—not even a rubber-band fight. It was a war of ideas and philosophy. It was a character assassination, a smear campaign. Satan was saying horrible things about God, and a bunch of heavenly beings bought into the lie. Satan actually convinced one third of heaven that God couldn't be trusted.

Has anyone ever said anything about you that wasn't true? What did you want to do about it? I'll bet you wanted to set the record straight! I'll bet you wanted everyone to know the truth about you. Well, so does God. He wants you to know who He really is and not who the devil has tricked people into thinking He is. God's way of clearing up the misconceptions about Himself was to send Jesus to earth. Jesus came to show us the Father. Jesus said, "If you've seen me, you've seen the Father" (see John 14:9).

Any time you have a question about who God is, look at Jesus. If your picture of God doesn't fit with who Jesus is, get to know Jesus. You won't be disappointed.

JAN 2

War on Earth

THE SERPENT SAID TO THE woman, "You will not surely die. For God knows that in the day you eat of it your eyes will be opened, and you will be like God." **GENESIS 3:4, 5, NKJV.**

W*aaaaaaa!*"
Bobby, a first grader, was brought into my office with tears streaming down his face, sore ribs, and a hurt neck. He couldn't talk; he could only cry and do those big intake breaths between siren calls. Finally, after he settled down, I heard the story.

It was winter, and the snowplows had made a huge mountain of snow on the edge of the school playground. Lots of the kids were playing on the top of the snow mountain. Bobby had almost made his way to the top when two of his classmates (both girls) shoved him down to the bottom of the hill and kicked him in the ribs and stomach several times for attempting his ascent.

When I brought the two little girls in and asked them what had happened, without any remorse they said, "He was trying to get to the top of the snow hill. We were the queens of the snow hill. So we shoved him off and kicked him." Both felt fine with the decision to defend their territory in such a violent way.

The Bible says that while in heaven Satan started the war because he wanted to take God's place as the ruler of the universe. When he couldn't succeed, he brought the war to earth.

Satan brought doubt into the mind of Eve. He had her thinking, *Maybe I really don't know God. Maybe He's not who He says He is. Maybe God is holding back from me. If I eat the fruit, maybe I can be a god too!*

The Bible describes Satan as someone who is self-promoting. Isaiah 14:12-14 says that he tried to ascend to the place of God. Compare that person to the person of Jesus, stooping down to wash the disciples' feet. See the difference?

In Philippians 2 it says that Jesus humbled Himself even unto death. People who act like the devil are self-centered, self-promoting. People who act like Jesus are others-centered. Devil followers will tear people down to make themselves look better. Jesus followers will lift others up to make others look better.

Fear This!

BUT THE LORD CALLED TO the man, "Where are you?" He answered, "I heard you in the garden, and I was afraid because I was naked; so I hid." **GENESIS 3:9, 10.**

Fear is the opposite of trust. My family just got a new cockatoo named Petri. A cockatoo is a big white bird that eats, screams, and makes bird droppings. That's my version of what a cockatoo is. The rest of my family would describe him as an intelligent, loving, curious, and fun bundle of love . . . who eats, screams, and makes bird droppings.

My son, Cole, wanted the bird. During the first couple of days we had Petri, it was *all fear* and *no trust*. My son would approach the cage, and Petri would puff up his feathers, raise the huge plumes on his head, and bounce up and down as if to say, "If you dare to put your hand in this cage to touch me, you'll end up with a bloody stump!" There was no way that Petri was going to let us touch him. He was too afraid. He didn't know us.

Three days later we left Petri's cage door open to let him come out on his own initiative. Pretty soon he crawled out of his cage, inched his way down to the floor, waddled across our family room, and poked around my son, just checking him out. Could he trust him or not? Within 20 minutes Petri was snuggled in my son's lap, chortling and cooing as Cole rubbed under his wings and massaged his little head. Fear was abolished, and trust cemented the relationship.

Adam and Eve didn't trust who God said He was. Their decisions caused them to fear instead. Anytime Satan can cause us to fear God, he's won the battle. He's caused humans to distrust God and blame Him for all kinds of things, hasn't he?

When there's a natural disaster, we often call it "an act of God." When tragedy strikes in our lives, we wonder why God would allow such a thing. Some Christians even portray God as a being who says, "Love Me and you can live forever, but if you don't, I'll roast you for eternity!" Humans have learned to fear God rather than trust Him.

The Bible sums up who God is in three words: "God is love" (1 John 4:8). Any other description of God is faulty at best. Remember, the more you know someone, the easier it is to trust them. And the more trust you have for a person, the easier it is to love them. Oh, and if you want to know God, get to know Jesus. You won't find fear there.

JAN 4

Not Pretty

THE LORD GOD MADE GARMENTS of skin for Adam and his wife and clothed them. **GENESIS 3:21.**

My wife has been a vegetarian all her life, and she will remain a vegetarian until she dies. Why? Is it because she has learned that her digestive system reacts better to fruits, nuts, and vegetables? Is it because she metabolizes a vegetarian diet more thoroughly than a diet with meat in it? Or could it be that she has realized some greater spiritual significance in a simpler diet of veggies and fruit? Nope. Not even close; none of the above.

In my wife's own words: "I could never eat anything that had a mother!" My wife loves animals, and animals love my wife. She grew up in a house that had a gibbon ape as a pet (more like a member of the family). Ferocious barking dogs will run up to us as we walk in our neighborhood, and she will bend down and start talking to them until they are licking her face (which is a total turnoff to me) and letting her rub their tummies.

Once we were watching a friend of mine participate in a triathlon. We were standing under a huge evergreen tree, cheering as the runners zoomed by. All of a sudden a baby bird fell out of the tree and landed on my wife's shoulder. It totally caught me by surprise. Not my wife. She acted as if it was supposed to happen. She walked around with this bird on her shoulder for the next 20 minutes, talking to it and petting it. When we had to leave, she took the little creature off her shoulder, said goodbye, and put it back in the tree as if this were something that happened every day. I think my wife is Doctor Doolittle.

God loves animals too. He gives them the breath of life, just as He does to humans. The Bible tells us that He notices every sparrow that falls from the sky.

Can you imagine the hurt it caused His heart when, because of sin, the first death ever recorded in the universe took place to clothe Adam and Eve? I'm really not sure how it happened, but I can imagine Adam and Eve watching as "the Lord God made garments of skin" for them. I think that's when they finally realized that sin is really ugly.

Snake Fright

SO THE LORD GOD SAID to the serpent, "Because you have done this, cursed are you above all livestock and all wild animals! You will crawl on your belly and you will eat dust all the days of your life. And I will put enmity between you and the woman, and between your offspring and hers; he will crush your head, and you will strike his heel." **GENESIS 3:14, 15.**

OK, I admit it: I think snakes are cool. Maybe it's their mysterious nature. Maybe it's the way they are designed. Maybe it's their colors. Maybe I like things that are a little bit dangerous. I don't know why, but I think snakes are cool.

Once on a trip to Kenya a large group from our mission team went caving. Just outside the cave my cousin Jed noticed some movement. That movement turned out to be a rock python about five feet long. Jed jumped on the python, captured it, and stuffed it into his empty backpack.

When everybody got back to camp, Jed motioned for a large group of Masai men to gather around. (Masai are the local people in the back country of Kenya.) They all thought that Jed was going to give them something out of the pack. They had no idea that there was a snake inside. Jed reached his hand into the pack and . . . I've never seen a group of men run faster in six different directions than I did that day. The locals were astounded to see even the girls in our group handling this huge, beautiful snake. They were very fearful of any snake that crawled on the ground.

The strife that God declared between the snake and the woman in the book of Genesis goes far beyond a natural fear of snakes. It speaks to the hostility that God's children have toward anything that the snake (dragon, serpent, devil, beast, or any other name for Satan) would have us believe about God. The snake that God was talking about would have us mistrust God and go our own way, just as he convinced Eve to do. Our enmity for the devil is matched only by our love for God and our desire to have Him lead our lives. I can't wait for the day when the head of the devil is finally crushed and we are home with the God who loves us.

JAN 6

Devil Versus Angel

SIN IS CROUCHING AT YOUR DOOR; it desires to have you, but you must rule over it. **GENESIS 4:7.**

When I was a kid, I loved cartoons. The cartoons that I used to watch were quite different from the cartoons that are on today. They were less complicated in their story lines and a lot more violent. Popeye, Elmer Fudd, Yosemite Sam, Wile E. Coyote, Tom and Jerry . . . all of them had the uncanny ability to fall off a cliff, be hit in the head by a frying pan, or be hit by a train, and instead of dying they could miraculously come back for the next escapade that had them chasing after whatever they were chasing after.

One thing all of these cartoons had in common was how they portrayed temptation. The cartoon characters would see a situation that tempted them, and all of a sudden a little angel and a little devil would appear, one on each shoulder of the cartoon character. The little devil and the little angel would have a conversation with the character and each other. Usually the little devil would win, and the cartoon character would do something naughty.

I'm pretty sure that Cain didn't have a little devil and a little angel on his shoulders as he struggled with temptation, but the above text clearly shows that there was a battle raging in Cain's mind over a decision that he, and only he, could make.

Cain was struggling with the same thing that Lucifer struggled with in heaven: my way or God's way? It was the same struggle that Cain's mom had faced in the garden. Should I believe and trust in God's way, or should I take matters into my own hands and do things my way?

Our ultimate struggle with sin boils down to the same question: Do I want to let God be the leader, or do I want to lead? Do I trust God enough to give Him control over every aspect of my life, or do I not trust Him to do a good job with my future?

The way to rule over the sin that is crouching at our door, the way to flick that little devil off our shoulder, is to hand control of our everyday life to the God who desires our good. So flick the devil off and listen to that angel today!

Mystery Man

ENOCH WALKED FAITHFULLY WITH GOD; then he was no more, because God took him away. **GENESIS 5:24.**

The age-old Bible trivia question that always stumps the experts is Who is the oldest man who ever lived? Most good Bible students would enthusiastically answer, "Methuselah!" At which point those of us who like to pretend we are clever would answer, "Nope! It's Enoch! He was born and never died!"

The Bible doesn't say very much about Enoch. He's listed in several genealogies in Scripture with no reference to who he was. It's too bad we don't know more about this man, because he and Elijah share the distinction of being the only two people who ever got to heaven without having to pass through death.

I guess if you were to pick just *one* of the few words written about Enoch in the Bible that describe who he was, maybe the word *walked* would be a good one. Enoch *walked* with God.

There is something special about walking, especially if you are walking *with* somebody. I've been on some pretty cool walks in my life—walks that really meant something to me. Maybe the best walk I've ever been on was on a warm spring evening in Victoria, British Columbia. I was walking along the bay between the city and the water, hand in hand with the girl I wanted to marry. It was on that walk that we shared the intimate details of our lives, gained each other's trust, and secured each other's love. It was on that walk that I got my first kiss! And the rest (as they say) is history!

Walking with God is an experience similar to the walk I had with my future soul mate. When we walk with God, we experience an intimacy with Him that we could have with no other. We share with Him our hopes and dreams. We spend time with Him and Him alone, not letting anyone or anything else distract us from the attention we are paying to each other. As you walk with God, He will gain your trust and secure your love. That love and trust will prepare you to be His bride and get you a seat at the wedding feast someday soon.

JAN 8

Very, Very Naughty

THEN THE LORD SAW THAT the wickedness of man was great in the earth, and that every intent of the thoughts of his heart was only evil continually. **GENESIS 6:5, NKJV.**

I'm not sure I could do any one thing *all the time.* I like playing ping-pong, but I couldn't do it all the time. I like playing golf, but after three days in a row I'd rather do something else. I like hanging out with friends, but after a while I'm pretty sure they'd need some separation from me!

I've tried to do things for long periods of time. Once I decided to try eating only foods that grew out of the ground. I saw a TV show in which a bunch of unhealthy people switched to this diet of vegetarian uncooked or unprocessed foods. The results on the TV show were remarkable. The people lost weight and were healthier than they had ever been. Now, I'm not obese or unhealthy by most standards, but I thought the diet looked like something I'd like to try, just to see what kind of effect it would have on my body and my mind. So I committed to eating only raw things that grew from the ground for the next two weeks. Fruit, nuts, and veggies. Raw. All the time. I lasted a day and a half.

I learned that the only thing I can do continually, all the time, is breathe. Yet the Bible says that during Noah's time people in this world had gotten so depraved that they were planning and scheming in their hearts to do evil things *all the time.* How twisted is that? It became like *breathing* to them. They did two things all the time: breathe and think of evil things to do. Can you imagine surviving in a world like that?

God had to do something to save the crown of His creation. He had to do something to save humans. And in all the earth (and I'm not sure how many people were on the earth by this time) He found one man and his family who weren't thinking of evil things to do with all their spare time. Noah stood out in the crowd.

Think of your life. Think of the people you hang around. Do you stand out in the crowd as someone God would choose to start things in a new direction?

JAN 9

Crazy Big Waves

NOW THE FLOOD WAS ON the earth forty days. The waters increased and lifted up the ark, and it rose high above the earth. **GENESIS 7:17, NKJV.**

I've guided whitewater rafting adventures down the Wenatchee River in central Washington State for more than 20 years. I love whitewater rafting. There's something about the thunderous sounds of giant frothy waves that gets my blood pumping and my heart racing! And I'll admit that part of the thrill is the danger factor. I like being a little afraid as we go through a series of crazy enormous waves that could flip our raft in the blink of an eye.

I had guided that river more than a hundred times. I had never flipped a raft. Never. On each trip I safely guided my group through the series of rapids. They come in succession down the Wenatchee River: Satan's Eyeball, Rock and Roll Rapids, Drunkard's Drop, Snowblind, Granny's Rapids, and, of course, The Suffocater.

On this particular Sunday the river was running higher than it had in 70 years. A group of people from Seattle had hired us to take them down the river. I gave them all a waiver to sign stating that they understood that the river was at flood stage and that I had never guided a raft in water this big. They all signed on the dotted line and jumped into the raft. And, of course, when we hit Rodeo Hole, the whole raft flipped, and everyone went in. I've never seen nine people with more frightened eyes in my life. We got everyone back in the boat, and all of them were very cautious for the rest of the trip.

Can you imagine what it would have been like in the ark during the Flood? I imagine very little light, all the animals terrified and making their noises, and that group of eight faithful people not knowing which direction the wind and waves were going to take them. It must have been terrifying. Or was it?

If all eight people had enough faith to get in the boat at God's bidding, maybe they knew that God was with them in the midst of the storm. Maybe Noah and his family were experiencing peace in the storm—a peace that passes all understanding.

JAN 10

Promises, Promises!

THE RAINBOW SHALL BE IN the cloud, and I will look on it to remember the everlasting covenant between God and every living creature of all flesh that is on the earth. **GENESIS 9:16, NKJV.**

There is nothing like the feeling of a broken promise. Maybe even worse is the feeling of being the one who breaks a promise.

In my first year as a pastor I was asked to speak for an eighth-grade graduation for our local junior academy. It was the school I had attended from the fourth through the tenth grade, and it was now in the district of my first church. I would often go to the school and enjoy visiting with the kids and teachers, so when they asked me to be the speaker for their special day, I gladly said yes.

One Thursday about 6:45 p.m. I was at my mom's house installing a new refrigerator. I was kind of grubby and had no idea that graduation was to start in 15 minutes. My mom's phone rang. It was the principal of the school, who had just called my house and had been directed by my wife to call my mom's home.

"Where are you?" the caller asked without any introduction.

"Um, I'm right here. Who is this?"

"This is the principal. Why aren't you here to speak for graduation?"

My heart sank. I told the principal that I didn't know what to do. I'd completely forgotten about my promise to speak there. It would be at least an hour before I could make it. He hung up in disgust (rightfully so), and I felt like a toad.

There's nothing worse than a broken promise.

God's promises are true. He never breaks them. The Bible is full of promises for God's children. There are promises for us in times of trouble. There are promises for us in times of success. There are promises of salvation and promises for our future.

At the end of the Flood God promised that the earth would never again be destroyed by a flood. So put away your life jackets. He'll keep that promise, too.

Confusion Can Be Fatal

COME, LET US GO DOWN and confuse their language so they will not understand each other. **GENESIS 11:7.**

I've never been more disoriented than the time I decided to have a somersault contest with Maddie Miller in her swimming pool. Maddie is my good friend's daughter. During the summer of 2008 she was 14 years old and a very good swimmer. It was a hot summer day, and we were all enjoying the pool, when Maddie challenged me to a swim race. I knew full well that Maddie could beat me in a race, so I challenged her to another contest. I said, "Let's see who can do the most somersaults in the pool. You start."

Maddie is not one to back down from any challenge, so she grinned her approval, took a deep breath, and began. One, two, three, four. *Oh, no, she's going to do a lot more somersaults than I was planning on!* Nine, 10. *Maybe I should just get out of the pool and run into the house while she's still under water.* Eleven, 12. She came up gasping for air.

"Twelve!" she announced. "Try and beat 12!"

I was not about to let a 14-year-old girl beat me in anything. I took a deep breath and went under. One, two, three, four. *Ha! This is easy!* Six, seven, eight. *I wonder how it's going to look in the newspaper when everyone sees that I died in a somersault contest?* Ten, 11, 12, 13! I was done! I'd won! Oh, but one problem—I was so dizzy I had no clue which way was up and which way was down. I was completely out of breath and couldn't find the surface of the water to get precious oxygen!

I panicked for a quick second. Then I remembered just to relax and let my body float up so I could get my bearings. I came up out of the water gasping for air, victorious.

I was confused, very confused. The Tower of Babel ended up being a place of confusion. Later on in the Bible Babylon is described as a place where confusion about God runs rampant. Maybe that's why the book of Revelation calls us out of Babylon. If you want clarity about God, look at Jesus. He's the antidote to confusion. He's the clearest picture of the Father you'll ever see. No confusion there.

JAN 12

Moving Day

THE LORD HAD SAID TO ABRAM, "Go from your country, your people and your father's household to the land I will show you." **GENESIS 12:1.**

How many times have you moved in your life? I've moved 18 times in 48 years. Eighteen times! That means that I'm averaging a move every three years or less. In 1962 I started off in West Covina, California, and now I live in Burlington, Washington.

I know a lot of people hate to move, but I love it! I love it because it gives me a chance to go through all my stuff and see what I've been missing while living where I've been living. Each precious acquisition is found, wrapped up, and boxed for the move. I can't believe all the stuff my wife and I have acquired after 25 years of marriage that we never see and never use!

Each time I've moved (with the exception of my childhood years), I made an informed decision on where to go and where to live. I went early to scout out homes and make plans so I would know what I was getting into. At no time in my life did I pack up the moving van, throw my family into the cab, and start driving, not having an idea of where we'd end up. I always had a plan.

Not so with Abram. God said, "Abram, pack up your stuff, gather your family, and go where I will lead you."

"Where am I going?" Abram might have wondered.

"You are going where I will lead you," God may have answered.

"OK, I'll do it" was Abram's reply.

That, my friends, is amazing faith. To leave all that you know, to leave friends and family, to leave the comfort of what seems to have been a rich lifestyle for an uncertain adventure with God would take some pretty amazing faith.

Can you imagine the conversation between Jesus and His Father? Jesus was about to embark on an adventure that would take Him away from all the comforts of home. His trust in the Father would lead Him to earth to live a life totally dependent on His Father—kind of like Abram. What would it be like to depend totally on God for each move we make in our lives?

Spineless Man of God

WHEN THE EGYPTIANS SEE YOU, they will say, "This is his wife." Then they will kill me but will let you live. Say you are my sister, so that I will be treated well for your sake and my life will be spared because of you. **GENESIS 12:12, 13.**

When I think of a superhero, I think of a guy in a mask and tights running, flying, or jumping to the rescue of a damsel in distress. When I was a kid, I really liked Superman. He was clean-cut, had that magnificent S on his chest, and had a pretty cool cape. In each episode of those black-and-white TV shows that I watched as a kid, one thing was certain: Superman would sacrifice his own safety to make sure that the girl was saved in the end.

When we read the story of Abram, we really have to scratch our heads, don't we? There is no doubt that this great hero of faith has God on his side. He has shown his great faith by leaving his family and traveling at God's leading. And then faith gives way to fear.

Can you imagine the look on Sarai's face as Abram explains his plan? It would be like Superman saying, "Do what you want with the girl, but leave me alone!" Rather uncharacteristic for a hero of any kind! I'm sure Sarai was at least a little disappointed in her husband.

In this story things go from bad to worse when Pharaoh takes Sarai as his wife. Abram seems to be getting off easy on this one—in fact, he receives all kinds of wealth and gifts from Pharaoh because of Sarai! But then God intervenes.

When Pharaoh finally figures out what's going on and returns Sarai to Abram, the pagan king chastises the man of God for being dishonest and deceitful. Can you imagine?

Yet even in this story we see a mini-picture of the grace of God. Do you see it? Here Abram does a horrible thing and gets rewarded despite his poor behavior. Just like us. We give God our sin, and He takes it and gives us eternal life. Doesn't quite seem fair, does it? That's why grace is so amazing. Thank You, God, for grace.

JAN 14

Family Is Family

SO ABRAM SAID TO LOT, "Let's not have any quarreling between you and me, or between your herders and mine, for we are close relatives." **GENESIS 13:8.**

My sister and I fought like cats and dogs. If she said it was white, I said it was black. If it was her idea, it was a bad idea. If I could get her in trouble with the parents, I would. We just didn't get along.

On the way to school one day my sister was commenting on how nice her new dress was. She couldn't wait to show it to all her friends at school. Of course, I started making fun of the new dress, getting her all riled up in the car. My mom had to separate us more than once.

As the school day went on, I was walking back from the playground toward the school when I looked up and saw my sister. She had tears in her eyes and mud all over her new dress. I thought she had fallen on the playground and was ready to rub it in, but she blurted out, "Artie pushed me into the ditch and got my dress all dirty!"

I ran over to Artie and asked him what had happened. He confirmed my sister's story and followed it up with a snide remark about her . . . so I punched him in the nose.

A teacher came to separate us. We ended up in the principal's office. Artie ended up with tissue stuck up his nose. I told the principal, "Nobody messes with my sister."

I'm not sure how Abram felt about Lot after they parted ways. I'm guessing that it stung more than a little bit. Lot seemingly chose better land for his flock and his people. Yet when Lot was captured by the enemy, Abram, as old as he was, went after them with the fury of a big brother.

Have you ever wondered why God is described as *jealous*? It's because no matter how we treat Him, He's always willing to jump in and protect us from the bullies of this world. And anytime He can, He will.

And What Was Your Name?

BUT ABRAM SAID TO THE king of Sodom, "With raised hand I have sworn an oath to the Lord, God Most High, Creator of heaven and earth."
GENESIS 14:22.

Jack attends my church. He's a cool old guy—80-plus years old with a keen mind, a sharp wit, and a twinkle in his eye. People in our community have known him for years.

I was teaching in our midweek meeting when Jack raised his hand. I gestured to him and said, "Jack, would you like to make a comment?"

"John. My name is John."

I didn't know what to say. Had I forgotten his name? But the other people in the room looked as confused as I did. I said, "I thought your name was Jack. Everyone's been calling you Jack since I met you several months ago. You even filled out your information for our church records as Jack—but you're telling me your name is really John?"

"That's right. My name is really John."

After the meeting Jack came up to me and said, "My name really *is* John, and that's what I want to be called from now on."

I wondered aloud, "How is it that for the past 40 years people have been calling you Jack?"

"Well, to tell you the truth, someone called me Jack in front of some other people, and I didn't have the heart to correct them. People have been calling me Jack ever since. I've just now gotten up the courage to tell everyone they were wrong."

It seems that there's a lot in a name.

When Abram came back from the battle to save Lot, the king of Salem (later renamed Jerusalem) came out to meet him. This king was a priest to "God Most High," and he praised God Most High in front of Abram and his friends for giving them victory. The only problem was that God Most High was also a term for a Canaanite god who was generally viewed as the good creator. Abram wanted to make sure that there was no question about which God he and Melchizedek served, so he introduced the whole group to the true God of the universe: "*The Lord*, God Most High." He used the name Yahweh (the Lord) as an introduction to his God, the God of love and grace.

JAN 16

Pinky Swear

HE TOOK HIM OUTSIDE AND said, "Look up at the sky and count the stars—if indeed you can count them." Then he said to him, "So shall your offspring be." **GENESIS 15:5.**

When I was a kid, there were varying levels of honesty among my neighborhood friends that warranted the need for verbal covenants to "prove" the story that was being told. We would always start off with a "pinky swear," and if that didn't seem to do the trick, we'd move to the expression "Do you swear on a stack of Bibles?" And if there was still a little doubt, we'd resort to the mother of all verbal covenants: "Do you Charlie swear?" Nobody outside my neighborhood knew what this meant. But if you "Charlie swore" on a story and we found out it wasn't true, everyone in the group got to hold you down and give you a charley horse in your thigh. Pretty foolproof system, if you ask me.

God had been promising Abram a son for quite some time, and Abram kept doubting God's ability to fulfill the promise. So God made a covenant with him—a weird one.

In Genesis 15 God has Abram get a heifer, a goat, and a ram, along with two birds. He has Abram cut the heifer, goat, and ram in half and lay the halves opposite each other (gross, right?). He lays the two birds opposite each other, too.

Then God puts Abram to sleep and gives him a vision of a smoking pot and a blazing torch passing back and forth through the middle of the carcasses.

Weird, huh? What most people don't know is that in Abram's culture this covenant would not have been unusual. To seal a serious agreement, people would actually do this with animals. As the person making the promise passed through the corridor of carcasses, they would say, "If I don't keep my covenant, may what happened to these animals happen to me."

Abram was wavering in his faith. God saw that, and even though God never needs to pinky swear, He increased Abram's faith by this visual covenant that Abram would understand. God loves us so much that He'll come down to our level to increase our faith. God always provides.

Be Sure:
Your Sin Will Find You Out

NOW SARAI, ABRAM'S WIFE, HAD borne him no children. But she had an Egyptian slave named Hagar. **GENESIS 16:1.**

Have you ever had a time in your life when your past came back to haunt you? How many times have we seen family or friends try to fool themselves by making excuses for behavior that usually leads to bad consequences?

When I was 19 years old, I had a 1978 Toyota Celica that wouldn't start very well. I'm as much of a mechanic as I am an astrophysicist, so I didn't know what was wrong. I just knew that if I kept turning it over, eventually the car would start.

On one occasion in downtown Seattle I was parked in a public parking lot, and my car wouldn't start. I kept turning the engine over, but nothing happened. Getting frustrated, I lost my focus for a split second as my foot slipped off the clutch . . . while the car was in first gear . . . as I was turning it over. My car lurched forward and put a nice-sized dent in the car in front of mine.

Now I was mad. And scared.

I jumped out of my car and surveyed the damage done to the VW in front of me. I quickly realized that nobody else was around. It was my lucky day! Being the pillar of moral ineptness that I was, I jumped into my car and drove off without leaving a hint that I'd ever been there.

It wasn't more than a few days later that the owner of the VW found out what had happened and discovered that I was the culprit. My attempt at covering up my mistake came back to bite me hard.

In Genesis 15 we see that Sarai gives Hagar to Abram to bear her a child. Did you notice where Hagar is from? Go back to the January 13 reading (specifically, Genesis 12:16) to find out. That's right—Abram's sin in Egypt brought about another heap of trouble for him down the road.

Sin can be like a rock thrown into a still pond. The ripple effect of it can come back to damage us long after we thought the event was over. We need to learn that living life with integrity and always taking the high road gives us a life with no regrets.

JAN 18

I've Got This

SO SHE SAID TO ABRAM, "The Lord has kept me from having children. Go, sleep with my slave; perhaps I can build a family through her." **GENESIS 16:2.**

Yesterday we learned that trying to cover up our mistakes instead of owning up to them can (and usually does) come back to hurt us. As we ponder the sixteenth chapter of Genesis, there's another lesson we can draw from it: when God says He'll do something, He'll do it. He doesn't need our help.

My wife and I bought our Maytag washer and dryer in 1985. At the writing of this book, it's 2011. We still have our washing machine, and it works fine. We have a new dryer, but I'm not happy about how we got it.

At some point in 2010 our dryer started to make a deep rumbling noise while it ran. It still got all our clothes dry, but it sounded like a cement mixer. I did what most intelligent men would do in this situation: I shut the laundry room door while we were using the dryer so we didn't have to hear it.

One Sunday afternoon I decided to (my wife made me) take a look at the problem and see if I couldn't fix it myself. A friend and I took the dryer apart, and I found that the belt on the unit was about ready to give up the ghost. I figured a new belt would cost $25 or so—no big deal. While I was looking at that problem, my friend was fiddling around with a switch in the electronic part of the machine. As he fiddled, a spring popped, a lever broke, and the whole part crumbled in his hands.

"What did you do?" I snapped.

"Nothing; it just broke!" he said in a panic.

The next day I had to spend $400 on a new dryer.

Why is it that we have the insatiable need to meddle with things that are not our business to meddle with? God told Abram, "I'll give you a son." Abram tried everything in his power to make God's promise happen, which messed things up for himself and for generations to come.

When God makes a promise, let Him fulfill it. Your efforts to help Him out may just complicate things for you and those around you.

The God Who Sees Me

SHE GAVE THIS NAME TO the Lord who spoke to her: "You are the God who sees me," for she said, "I have now seen the One who sees me." **GENESIS 16:13.**

To be seen by someone for who you really are can be both liberating and terrifying. I once knew a girl who refused to look anyone in the eye. As I got to know her, I finally got up the nerve to ask her why. Her answer really surprised me. She said, "I don't want anyone to *see* me. You can look at me, but I'm afraid if you look into my eyes you might see what happened to me."

As I counseled this person, I found that she had experienced considerable pain and suffering at the hands of her parents and other family members—unspeakable things that are too heavy to share in this book.

I *can* share that as this girl was finally able to talk with me about her pain, she began to experience a freedom that she had never felt before. Eventually she began to have more confidence, even braving eye contact with people for the first time in a long time—all because somebody took the time to understand her, to *see* her.

There is nothing like the freedom and acceptance of being seen by someone you can trust, someone who clearly loves you.

Can you imagine the pain that Hagar must have felt? Going from slavery in Egypt into Abram's care, she was taken from her land to live with people of a different language and culture. At a presumably young age, she was asked to sleep with the old patriarch to bear him children—no love involved, just a means to an end. And then after Hagar did everything that Abram and Sarai had asked, she was mistreated by Sarai and driven by desperation to flee from their camp into the wilderness.

In the midst of her distress something beautiful happens in the wilderness. God sees her. He doesn't just see her body—He sees her heart. He sees her situation. He sees her trouble, and He intervenes. God embraces her with care and direction.

God sees you. He understands you. He hurts when you hurt. He smiles as you experience joy. God sees *you*.

JAN 20

A Done Deal

NO LONGER WILL YOU BE called Abram; your name will be Abraham, for I have made you a father of many nations. **GENESIS 17:5.**

Notice that God tells Abraham that He has "made" him a father of many nations. Abraham has not had Isaac yet. Ishmael is not the "great nation" that God has promised all along. Yet Abraham is told that God *has made* him a father of many nations. God's idea of time and promises is different from our idea of time and promises.

Those two little words in italics give us an idea of how great our God really is. *Has made*. Isaac, the child of promise, hadn't been born yet. Sarai wasn't even pregnant! But God still considered His promise a done deal. God was sure of what was going to happen, even though Abraham was still apprehensive.

We are much more like Abraham than we are like God, at least in this respect. The Bible tells us that we were chosen in Christ before the foundation of the world (Ephesians 1:4). We are literally born with the work of our salvation done. God is planning to have us in the kingdom. We have nothing to do but say, "Thank You for saving me." Yet somehow we get the mistaken idea that we have to convince God to let us into heaven by demonstrating good behavior or avoiding bad actions. We think we have to somehow find something we can *do* to "get saved."

Second Timothy 1:9 says that God gave us His grace "before the beginning of time." The act of forgiveness and acceptance toward us happened in the heart of God before we were born—even before He created the world! His saving grace was applied to us before we drew our first breath.

It is true that we can choose to have our names blotted out of the book of life (why would anyone want to do that?), but unless our words and actions convey that we are not interested in God's gift, we are a people who are bound up in the benefits of His grace.

I'm so glad that God thinks of me in those terms rather than in terms of what I deserve. I'm so glad that we have a God who doesn't hold our sins against us. I'm so glad that God sees where we will be and counts us as being there already.

JAN 21

God's Embarrassing Idea

THIS IS MY COVENANT WITH YOU and your descendants after you, the covenant you are to keep: Every male among you shall be circumcised. **GENESIS 17:10.**

To speak of certain things—even though they are in the Bible—in any detail would make us blush, avoid eye contact, and feel very uncomfortable in mixed company. Yet in this case, if we were to avoid this teaching of Scripture, we'd be missing out on one of the greatest lessons in the Bible.

God made a new covenant with Abraham, the covenant of circumcision. Have you ever wondered what this was all about?

Twenty-four years earlier God had told Abraham that he was going to become a great nation. God made a promise. Abraham got busy right away trying to fulfill that promise. He and Sarah hadn't had any children up to that point in their marriage, so *just in case God couldn't deliver*, Abraham brought Lot, a male relative, with him when he left his home country. That didn't work out too well, so Abraham told God that he was going to make his servant Eliezer his heir. God said no to that proposal, so Abraham ended up sleeping with the servant girl he got in Egypt and getting her pregnant, which messed up all kinds of things.

Abraham did everything in his power to make God's promise come true. Abraham didn't realize that his efforts to fulfill God's promises were getting in the way of the faith that God wanted from Abraham.

I imagine God saying something like this: "Abraham, you trust Me with *almost* everything. You trusted Me enough to move from your homeland. You trust Me with your money. You trust Me with your time. Abraham, there is one part of your body that you don't trust Me with, so the new covenant I'm going to make with you will be a constant reminder that you need to trust Me with that, too."

God made this new covenant with a 99-year-old Abraham. The covenant of circumcision was a reminder to Abraham and his descendants that they were to trust God with *everything*. God doesn't need our help to fulfill His promises. We can trust that He'll deliver. God wants our everything. Not most us—all of us.

JAN 22

ROFL

ABRAHAM FELL FACEDOWN; he laughed and said to himself, "Will a son be born to a man a hundred years old? Will Sarah bear a child at the age of ninety?" **GENESIS 17:17.**

Some things just seem impossible. My family joined several people from my church to see Cirque du Soleil one Sunday afternoon. I'm not sure that I've ever seen anything stranger or more curious in my life. I would have to describe some of the things that the acrobats did as simply "impossible." If I hadn't seen them contort and stretch their bodies to do those amazing feats, I don't think I would have said it was possible.

I've seen other things in my life that seemed impossible. I've seen people who were supposed to survive less than six months living in perfect health 10 years later. I've seen self-destructive, nasty people have their lives completely rejuvenated by the power of Christ. I've even seen the Red Sox win a World Series.

Jesus told His disciples that nothing is impossible with God. Jesus said it, but sometimes we don't act as if we believe it.

When God announced that His plan was to use Abraham's old, worn-out DNA and Sarah's tired and barren body to produce a child of promise, the absurdity of the idea hit Abraham so hard that he hit the deck in an uncontrollable giggle. He laughed. At God. The Creator.

I find it very interesting that God instructs Abraham that when he and Sarah finally do have this child, they should name him "He Laughs." That's what the name Isaac means in Hebrew. The "he" in "he laughs" has always been attributed to Isaac. I think God is looking back at Abraham's response to His declaration and teaching him a lesson.

It's as though God is telling Abraham—telling us—that when He says He's going to do something, He's going to do it. We may doubt His power. We may insert our will into God's plans, making things messier than they need to be, but in the end God wins.

God's made you some promises. Is He able to accomplish them in your life?

Ready for Company

ABRAHAM LOOKED UP AND SAW three men standing nearby. When he saw them, he hurried from the entrance of his tent to meet them and bowed low to the ground. He said, "If I have found favor in your eyes, my lord, do not pass your servant by. Let a little water be brought, and then you may all wash your feet and rest under this tree. Let me get you something to eat, so you can be refreshed and then go on your way—now that you have come to your servant." **GENESIS 18:2-5.**

My friends Ron and Joyce are the most gracious hosts I know. They have ridden the rollercoaster of financial disaster and success and found themselves doing well in their retirement years. Consequently, they have three beautiful homes in three beautiful places that anyone would want to vacation in.

What's amazing about Ron and Joyce isn't their financial success. What's amazing about Ron and Joyce is that they have never met a stranger. They open their homes to just about anybody anytime, whether they are home or not. As a pastor, I've called them several times and asked to use their homes for spiritual retreats. Not only would they always say yes, they would make sure everything was set up perfectly to accommodate our needs. And they always refused to accept any kind of payment for their kindness.

I'm pretty sure that if the Lord and His companions were standing on the edge of Ron and Joyce's yard, they would be ushered in and fed one of Joyce's famous meals. And then Ron would take them golfing.

I believe that this sort of kindness puts God's people in a unique place in which God can reveal Himself in their lives. When we make a practice of going out of our way to treat God's children as if they matter, God will show Himself in ways that will amaze and surprise us.

Remember Hebrews 13:2. Entertaining strangers could turn out to be something more than we could ever imagine. And remember Jesus' words: "Inasmuch as ye have done it unto one of the least of these my brethren" (Matthew 25:40, KJV).

JAN 24

Laugh It Up

SO SARAH LAUGHED TO HERSELF, saying, "After I am worn out, and my lord is old, shall I have pleasure?" **GENESIS 18:12, ESV.**

Wes is 82 years old. Wes has lived for about 30,000 days. Wes has survived the Great Depression, World War II, and the invention of the cell phone. Wes should be at home sitting on the porch sipping lemonade. Instead, Wes is flying to Mozambique this fall to put on a series of evangelistic meetings for people who don't know about Jesus. Wes is our church janitor who moves things by himself when most people would find a helper (or two) to save their back. Wes is also the head elder in my church.

Wes has somehow decided that advancing in years isn't going to keep him from becoming and doing whatever the Lord calls him to do. Wes hasn't taken the position—ever—that would take him out of the game.

Sarah had given up. She was worn out and wrung out and tapped out. God's promise meant nothing to her because she couldn't see past her wrinkles. She had every reason to doubt. She'd passed her child-producing years (biologically speaking) long before. She and Abraham had tried and tried and tried to somehow fulfill the promise that Abraham would have an heir, and that had just become an exercise in frustration. And now, after all that, she was supposed to believe that God was going to pull off some sort of miracle and make her fruitful again? Fat chance. So she laughed.

When you look in the mirror, what do you see? Pimples? Hair that won't cooperate? Crooked teeth or thin lips? A person who's too fat or too skinny, too short or too tall? Do you see a person who has tried and tried and tried to be who they think God wants them to be but seemingly fails every time they attempt to live up to God's promises?

I think the first thing we all have to do is approach life as Wes does. Refuse to give in to self-doubt or negative expectations. See yourself as God sees you—as someone who is a conqueror in whatever He has called you to do. God's ideal for you is more than you can even dream. So let's not laugh off His calling as if it's something trite. Let's live our lives as though His promises were already fulfilled in us.

The Great Interrogation

AND THE LORD SAID, "The outcry of Sodom and Gomorrah is indeed great, and their sin is exceedingly grave. I will go down now, and see if they have done entirely according to its outcry, which has come to Me; and if not, I will know." **GENESIS 18:20, 21, NASB.**

When I was a chaplain at Mount Pisgah Academy in North Carolina, one of my jobs was to sit on "ad council." Ad council was a group of staff members who had as one of their responsibilities the discipline of students who had made wrong choices. Often this meant that we had to bring students in and inquire (interrogate them) about some misdeed that we had heard about but weren't sure of.

This all became interesting, because much of the time the students wouldn't know how much we knew, so they would come in holding their cards very close to their chest, not wanting to give away anything that could incriminate them.

I hated that game of cat and mouse, especially when the staff had confirmed the whole story (we knew everything and everybody that was involved in the crime), but the student didn't know that we knew everything.

But for each case we wanted to find out from the persons involved what they knew. We also wanted to give them a chance to tell their story.

It would have been much easier for us to skip calling the student in and just execute judgment. It would have been easier for us, but not for the student *or the student body.*

You will notice a pattern in the Bible. Before God is forced to turn His back on a person or a group of people, before He "executes judgment," He investigates. Why? Doesn't He already know what's going on?

God doesn't investigate for Himself. He does it for our benefit. God is love. God is fair. And because God is love, He does not control us. We have freedom to love Him back or to ask Him by our words or actions to butt out of our lives. When this happens, He will regretfully honor our choice. But before He does, He will show His children that He is fair by investigating for Himself and for our benefit. This is true of God in the past, and it is true till the end of time.

JAN 2b

The Big Negotiation

THEN HE SAID, "Oh may the Lord not be angry, and I shall speak only this once; suppose ten are found there?" And He said, "I will not destroy it on account of the ten." **GENESIS 18:32, NASB.**

That the Lord would have this conversation at all with a human being demonstrates His patience and gentleness. He could have looked at Abraham and said, "Hey, Abe! Why don't you just mind your own business! I know what I'm doing!"

Instead, the Lord patiently listens to Abraham as he whittles down his numbers so that the people of Sodom (especially his nephew and family) would stand the best chance of surviving God's withdrawal of His Spirit from that place.

Abraham's negotiation for souls shows me that he had a godly love for sinners. He wasn't negotiating with God to save his own soul; he was worried about others.

The people of Sodom were so debased that they were evil all the time. The Bible describes people like those who lived in Sodom as people who spent their time inventing new ways to do evil. What's remarkable to me is that Abraham's attitude seems to reflect how the Lord feels about all of His children, wicked or righteous.

When Jesus came to earth, He demonstrated the Father's perspective by saying that God treats and loves all of His children equally and that we should strive to act the same way. He asked us to love our enemies and pray for them. Paul said that we should repay contempt with love, thereby heaping hot coals on the heads of those who treat us poorly.

I once knew a college student who gave a drunk guy on the street $20 after the drunk told him he needed the money for bus fare. When I heard about this, I chastised the student and told him not to be so gullible.

Jerry, my college-aged friend, said, "What's that to me? One of God's children asked for $20. I gave it to him. What he does with it is between him and God." Jerry had a love for souls a lot like Abraham's. I think we could all stand to look at lost souls more as Jesus did. And Jerry. And Abraham.

Sickos

BEFORE THEY LAY DOWN, the men of the city, the men of Sodom, surrounded the house . . . and they called to Lot and said to him, "Where are the men who came to you tonight? Bring them out to us that we may have relations with them." **GENESIS 19:4, 5, NASB.**

I'm not sure that there could be anything more terrifying than being surrounded by a group of people, full of hate (and probably alcohol), threatening to tear you limb from limb if you don't do as they ask.

Without going into great detail, I've seen what happened when a combination of poor values and alcohol devastated the life of a young girl. The sickness of the acts that a group of young men participated in against the will of this young woman can be described only as something you'd read about in an Old Testament account of debauchery.

How do people get to the place where they can take part in such heinous activities? How can a person become so wicked that they would join a gang of people, stand outside the house of a neighbor, and demand that the guests of the home be released into their hands so they could have "relations" with them? How can a person get that mentally and spiritually deranged?

Well, the answer I have for you is . . . I don't know. It's beyond me. But it happens. There are people who traffic in human slaves, sell young girls into prostitution, and participate in child pornography with seemingly no struggle of conscience. I don't know how a person can become so devoid of love.

But I do know that when people sink that low, they have likely banished the Holy Spirit from their lives so thoroughly that God will be forced to leave them with their sin, and the sin they cling to will bring the wrath of God—either in their lifetime or, if not on this earth, at the end of time. In the case of Sodom it was sooner rather than later. And the natural result of God's Spirit being completely withdrawn, leaving a group of people to their sin, is frightening to see.

God's wrath can be described as the wages of sin. When He is forced to turn His back and leave a person to their sin, it's a pretty scary thing.

JAN 28

What a Deal!

BUT HIS WIFE, FROM BEHIND HIM, looked back, and she became a pillar of salt. **GENESIS 19:26, NASB.**

When I was a kid in school, my classmates and I would sit around at lunchtime and trade items that our moms had packed in our lunches. Most of the time I'd trade a sandwich for a sandwich or a dessert for a dessert. But every once in a while I'd pull off a trade that made my friends jealous. Every once in a while I could convince a kid to trade my little baggie of celery and carrot sticks for a Hostess Twinkie or Cupcake.

Of course, as soon as the swap was made, I downed the delicious dessert as fast as I could, lest my unfortunate classmate were to get buyer's remorse.

Since then I've learned that the old adage is true: "One man's junk is another man's treasure." I've given stuff that I couldn't have cared less about to people who gave me some great stuff in exchange. Once I even traded a bunch of old baseball cards for a tricked-out mountain bike! (I still kind of wonder if one of those cards wasn't worth a pile of money.)

It's been said that "everybody has their price." And for some things I suppose that's true. But at what price would you trade your salvation? What earthly thing would you trade heaven for?

The Bible clearly teaches that your salvation has been secured and is yours for the taking. Your name is written in the book of life. What would the devil have to offer for you to want your name blotted out of that book?

For some it's a relationship with the wrong person that drags them away. For others it's the pursuit of money. For still others it may be how they are treated by someone in the church. And for many it's the allure of the glitz and glamour of the world.

Lot's wife had her priorities so out of whack that she just couldn't bring herself to leave the bright lights and the lush lifestyle of Sodom. Even before she left that city, she'd traded in her crown of life for a pile of salt.

What would the devil have to offer *you* to convince you to trade in your crown?

JAN 29

Oops, I Did It Again!

ABRAHAM SAID OF SARAH HIS WIFE, "She is my sister." So Abimelech king of Gerar sent and took Sarah. **GENESIS 20:2, NASB.**

Does this story sound familiar? Just eight chapters earlier in Genesis Abraham (then still Abram) did the exact same thing when he went to Egypt. *The exact same thing!* Now, I have a hard time seeing a guy shove his wife off to some other guy one time—but really, Abraham? You did it again?

And to make matters more frustrating, the first time he did this the trouble it eventually brought him was so stingingly painful that it almost broke up his whole family! Remember his first time around? He ended up leaving Egypt with a maid-servant who would eventually become a second wife and give birth to Ishmael.

When I see that Abraham gives his wife away to another king, I want to reach into my Bible, grab Abraham by the beard, and shake him!

And then I take a look in the mirror. How many times have I promised the Lord that if He'd just get me out of a jam, "I'll never ever do that again"? Well, I'm not going to tell you how many times I've made that promise, because it's none of your business! Suffice it to say, I've promised God many times that I was going to leave a particular sin in my life behind, only to be found doing that same thing again.

Somehow sin cons us into taking the easy way out so that we get into a habit of sinning. And the more we do it, the less we want to come back to the God we vowed we wouldn't have to come back to again for the same thing we said we weren't going to do just two weeks earlier.

It's a vicious cycle. So how do we get out of it?

I have found that every time I'm tempted to sin, I have to make one of two choices: (1) keep God around and not commit the sin or (2) ask God to leave so I can sin.

My suggestion? Keep God around. Don't push Him away so you can sin. Instead, bring Him all the closer so He can give you the victory over that bad habit when it creeps up on you.

JAN 30

Something's Missing

THEN THE LORD TOOK NOTE of Sarah as He had said, and the Lord did for Sarah as He had promised. So Sarah conceived and bore a son. **GENESIS 21:1, 2, NASB.**

I want you to read the above verse one more time and look for something that's not there. Go ahead, I'll wait . . .

Notice it? See what or who isn't a part of this wonderful equation? That's right. Abraham isn't there, at least in the first part of these verses.

I find it interesting that as human beings we think it's important to "help" God out by trying to do for God what only He can do.

God proclaims in Scripture that He loves us unconditionally, so we go out and try to do all kinds of things to somehow earn His love. The Bible tells us that Jesus died for the sins of the whole world and purchased our salvation. So what do we do? We try to earn our salvation by doing all kinds of things to impress God enough to save us.

I recently sat with a man who was dying of an incurable disease. He had served the Lord faithfully and had done more to give his church a great name in the community than anyone could have imagined.

On his deathbed he asked his family to leave the room so he could talk with me. He began to tear up as he said, "Pastor, I don't know if I'm saved or not. I'm not sure that I've done enough."

"What else do you think you could have done to make God love you enough to bring you to heaven?" I asked.

"Well, I don't know," he admitted.

God promised Abraham a son. Abraham did everything he could to fulfill that promise and in the process botched everything up. Finally, when Abraham just got out of the way and let God work, God delivered what He said He would deliver.

God has promised you that salvation is yours if you want it. Do you want it? Are you walking with Him? Then there is no condemnation for you. Let God be God.

The Best-Laid Plans . . .

NOW SARAH SAW THE SON of Hagar the Egyptian, whom she had borne to Abraham, mocking. Therefore she said to Abraham, "Drive out this maid and her son, for the son of this maid shall not be an heir with my son Isaac." **GENESIS 21:9, 10, NASB.**

Once when I was in my later teens, I had a friend who had a really bad cold. He was sneezing, snorting, and coughing to the point where I really felt sorry for this miserable character. So I did what I thought at the time was a good deed. I gave him some of my prescription allergy medicine. It had always helped me with my runny nose and sneezing during allergy season, so it stood to reason that it would help my friend, too. Right?

He took the medicine. Two hours later I had to take him to the hospital. Something in the medicine caused an allergic reaction, and he developed hives all over his body. So much for my good intentions.

I'm sure that Abraham thought he was doing the sensible thing when he took Hagar as his wife and had a son with her. I'm also sure that Abraham loved his son Ishmael very much. Yet because he had presumed to fulfill the promise of God through his own strength, Abraham had created a mess that was just now coming back to bite him.

Sarah's insistence that Hagar and Ishmael be kicked out of camp won the day, and Abraham had to say goodbye to a wife and a son. How that must have broken his heart! And can you imagine the hurt that Abraham's own son must have felt as his own father rejected him? That hurt would last for generations, even into to-day's world with the strife that continues between Ishmael's offspring (the Arabs) and Isaac's offspring (the Jews.)

I don't want to beat a dead horse here, but I have to say it again: When we presume to take the place of God in our own life or in the life of someone else, we will reap a sorry reward in the end. God can forgive us for our mistake, but the earthly repercussions may last a lifetime. Once again, we need to let God be God.

FEB 1

Voices in the Night

HE SAID, "TAKE NOW YOUR SON, your only son, whom you love, Isaac, and go to the land of Moriah, and offer him there as a burnt offering on one of the mountains of which I will tell you." **GENESIS 22:2, NASB.**

Seriously? After all that Abraham has been through, after all the mistakes he has made, after God has allowed him to send his firstborn son off into the wilderness, now God wants Abraham to take his only other son, tie him up, put him on a pile of rocks, cut his throat, and burn him? Seriously?

I want you to take a moment here and make this relevant to your situation. I want you to imagine your father waking you up at 3:00 a.m. When he is finally able to rouse you, he informs you, "God just woke me out of a dead sleep and told me I'm supposed to cut your throat and burn you on an altar as a sacrifice to Him."

How would that sit with you? Would you run? Would you call 9-1-1? Or would you say, "OK, Dad, I trust you. Let's go do what the Lord wants you to do"?

I've had many people ask me, "How did Abraham know that it was God talking to him and not Satan?"

My answer is simple. Jesus said that sheep recognize their shepherd's voice (John 10:4). Abraham had talked with God many times before. He knew God's voice.

I've always been amazed at the faith of Abraham *and* Isaac in this situation. Notice that there is no struggle between the old man Abraham and his young son Isaac. Isaac seemingly lays down his life in agreement with his father, Abraham. In this simple but extremely challenging act of faith, Abraham and Isaac demonstrate what God the Father and God the Son had done and would do for the salvation of all humankind.

A lot of people assume that God *demanded* that Jesus come to earth and die for us horrible sinners—or maybe that Jesus had to talk His Father into saving us instead of wiping us out of existence. The Bible paints a different picture. It says that the Lamb (Jesus) was slain from the foundation of the world (Revelation 13:8). This tells me that Father and Son acted on our behalf as a team, like Abraham and Isaac, to rescue us and forgive us before we ever sinned. What a story! What a God!

A Time to Die

NOW SARAH LIVED ONE HUNDRED and twenty-seven years; these were the years of the life of Sarah. Sarah died in Kiriath-arba (that is, Hebron) in the land of Canaan; and Abraham went in to mourn for Sarah and to weep for her. **GENESIS 23:1, 2, NASB.**

My dad used to tell me that the only two things you can rely on are death and taxes. And while I'm sure that these are not the only two things I can rely on, death and taxes both happen reliably all over the earth. Of the two, I prefer taxes.

As a pastor I've had to preside over too many funerals. I've had to bury young, middle-aged, and old people. I've been to funerals that were so sad that people had to be carried because they couldn't walk. As many funerals as I've attended, I never get used to them. They never become routine. They always feel wrong—none more so than the funerals of people in my family.

My grandmother died in her early 90s. She lived a wonderful life that was filled with joy and adventure. Although she had lost her husband years earlier, she had three loving children who took good care of her and included her in many of their adventures. Grandma Velda's funeral was a mix of fun memories and tears. Still, it didn't feel right to say goodbye to such a bright light.

Sarah lived a long life with Abraham. She experienced the ups and downs of marriage, laughed at God, and bore a son. She lived her life, and then she died. She didn't know it, but Sarah died the mother of the nation that would see the birth of the Messiah.

Death is a tough subject to talk about. You'd think it would be easy, since it happens so often. But when a grandpa or grandma, a mother or father, a brother or sister, a friend or classmate passes away, it always leaves us with an empty feeling that is hard to explain.

The great hope of Christianity is that there is more to this life than this life. First Corinthians 15:26 tells us that "the last enemy that will be abolished is death" (NASB). The reason we don't like death is because it's our enemy. But praise God, one day death will be defeated once and for all!

FEB 3

Matchmaker God

SWEAR BY THE LORD ... [that] you will go to my country and to my relatives, and take a wife for my son Isaac. **GENESIS 24:3, 4, NASB.**

Now, be honest here: If your parents were to approach you and say, "Don't worry about finding a spouse; we'll arrange a marriage with a good family and get you a life mate . . . without any input from you . . . and you won't see him/her until your wedding day . . . but we've asked God to lead us, so it'll be OK," how would you react?

Marriage in North America and most of Europe doesn't work this way anymore, does it? In our culture we see our lovely daffodil across the room for the first time and take notice. They haven't seen us, but we see them. Somewhere along the line we get the idea that we should talk to our newly found daffodil. From there we go on dates, meet each other's families, and experience each other in various situations that tell us what we could be getting into if we were to marry this person.

After repeating this cycle dozens of times with several different people, with any luck at all we get engaged, announce it to our friends and family, and then get married. Generally the wedding costs lots of money and is a joyous occasion.

Then we tell people that "God brought us together." How much "God" actually went into the process?

Isaac lived in different times. Abraham didn't even consult Isaac when he sent his servant to find him a wife. Dad was sure that none of the girls in Canaan were fit for his one and only son. Instead, he wanted to get someone from his family back toward Mesopotamia in the city of Nahor to be the life mate for his chosen son.

Abraham's servant had to make a choice relying entirely on God's leading. Isaac had no input. Do you think you could ever have the kind of faith in your God (and in your parents) that would allow God to have the only input into selecting the person you spend the rest of your life with?

Your Top Five

O LORD, THE GOD OF MY MASTER ABRAHAM, please grant me success today, and show lovingkindness to my master Abraham. Behold, I am standing by the spring, and the daughters of the men of the city are coming out to draw water; now may it be that the girl to whom I say, "Please let down your jar so that I may drink," and who answers, "Drink, and I will water your camels also"—may she be the one whom You have appointed for Your servant Isaac; and by this I will know that You have shown lovingkindness to my master. **GENESIS 24:12-14, NASB.**

If I were to ask you to list the most important qualities of a future spouse—maybe your top five—what would you write on that list? Go ahead, write them down. If you are reading this with someone else, share your top five right now.

Now look at the qualities of Rebekah.

1. She wasn't afraid of hard work. She was performing the task of hauling water from a spring to her home in the city. I'm not sure how many trips she was planning on making, but I'm fairly sure that most people I know wouldn't be able to make even one trip with a clay jar that holds five gallons of water.

2. She was attractive. I'm not sure if Rebekah was necessarily a beauty queen, but it seems that she took care of herself so that she presented nicely—something we can all appreciate.

3. She was a virgin. Rebekah had been faithful to her belief that she was meant for one man with whom God would unite her. She stayed pure.

4. She was considerate. When a complete stranger (Abraham's servant) asked her for water, she didn't hesitate to offer it to him.

5. She went the extra mile. Rebekah didn't just give Abraham's servant a cup of water. She watered his camels until they had finished drinking. She had no obligation to do that. It was her nature to do things until they were finished.

Now let's turn the spotlight on *you*. What qualities are you developing to be a great person? What qualities are you developing to be a great spouse? Are you letting God develop you into the person He'd like you to be?

FEB 5

Born That Way

WHEN THE TIME CAME for her to give birth, there were twin boys in her womb. The first to come out was red, and his whole body was like a hairy garment; so they named him Esau. After this, his brother came out, with his hand grasping Esau's heel; so he was named Jacob. Isaac was sixty years old when Rebekah gave birth to them. **GENESIS 25:24-26.**

There's a guy at my church who is one of the brightest people I know. He's got it all. He's good-looking, he's talented, he's very good at his job, and he's got an amazing family. And he and I don't get along at all.

If I think something is awesome, he thinks it's awful. If I think we ought to go this direction with the church, he thinks we need to go the opposite. I like certain kinds of music, and he thinks my music is inappropriate.

For a long while he and I were debating (arguing) by e-mail and just getting more upset with each other. Finally I sent an e-mail expressing my frustration. "Do you just not like me or something?" I asked.

The response from this person was so true. He explained that we were both wired up by God to have extreme personalities that are opposite of each other. Our job is to try to work together on things that will benefit the church and not waste our time on things that we will never agree on.

Jacob and Esau were born wired up differently. But that doesn't mean that they were pegged as good and evil—or both evil, with one bent on deception and the other on violence. Yes, they were born with certain tendencies and certain inclinations; their genetic makeups gave them that. But every person, no matter how they are wired up, has the gift of freedom to choose good or evil, love or hate.

Later in life Jacob chooses to deceive; Esau chooses to let his stomach rule his brain. But neither of them had to make those poor choices. They both could have chosen to honor God in every situation.

No matter how you are wired up, you can choose to take the right road in life and honor God with your relationships and your choices.

My Kingdom for a Meal!

ONCE WHEN JACOB WAS COOKING STEW, Esau came in from the field, and he was exhausted. And Esau said to Jacob, "Let me eat some of that red stew, for I am exhausted!" (Therefore his name was called Edom.) Jacob said, "Sell me your birthright now." Esau said, "I am about to die; of what use is a birthright to me?" Jacob said, "Swear to me now." So he swore to him and sold his birthright to Jacob. Then Jacob gave Esau bread and lentil stew, and he ate and drank and rose and went his way. Thus Esau despised his birthright. **GENESIS 25:29-34, ESV.**

There is nothing quite as motivating or powerful as our appetite. I have been known to plan road trips around the places we would stop to eat the food I was craving. I've also been known to get exceedingly grumpy when food I was looking forward to and expecting was somehow unavailable or, worse yet, had been eaten by someone else.

Food is an obsession for more than just me. A couple of years ago a medical journal released a study showing that 68 percent of Americans were overweight. Appetite is a powerful thing. I once heard a preacher say that our stomach is the only god that gets bigger when worshipped!

Our appetites can get the best of us. Appetite certainly didn't do Adam and Eve any favors in the Garden of Eden. That fruit on the tree of the knowledge of good and evil must have looked pretty tasty. Maybe that tree grew candied apples.

I can imagine that Esau was famished after being out hunting. Apparently he hadn't been able to shoot or snare anything to eat, so when he came back into camp, the smell of what Jacob was cooking triggered the off switch in his brain and the on switch in his salivary glands.

Whatever the case, Esau traded his right to lead the family and be in charge of the family's land and possessions after his father's death—for a pot of red stew.

Acting out of impulse rarely produces the positive long-term results that acting from your values will. God is looking for a people who have Jesus' values and will act on those values rather than on the impulse of appetite or any other kind of strong urge. What are your values, and how do you live your life by them?

FEB 7

Daddy Made Me Do It!

SO ISAAC STAYED IN GERAR. When the men of that place asked him about his wife, he said, "She is my sister," because he was afraid to say, "She is my wife." He thought, "The men of this place might kill me on account of Rebekah, because she is beautiful." **GENESIS 26:6, 7.**

One part of the Ten Commandments has always bothered me. It's in the second commandment. It says that God punishes people for the sins of their ancestors a couple generations up the line from them. How is this fair? Should I be punished for something my great-grandpa did?

I'm pretty sure that God is expressing a prophecy here more than He is being mean or unfair. Study after study shows that parents pass on habits and tendencies—good or bad—to their children. Many of the bad habits we acquire can be traced back to our parents and their parents and their parents' parents. Character traits are hard to change, especially if we don't even notice how harmful they are.

Isaac is in a land where his father once lived. The king's name is the same. And the situation seems to be the same too. Isaac's wife is what some today would call a hottie. He's afraid that the men of the country he lives in will see her and want her so badly that they'll kill him to get her. So he lies and says, "She's my sister."

If you look a few chapters back in your Bible, you'll see that in Genesis 20 Abraham did the *same* thing with the *same* king before Isaac was born. A chip off the old block! It seems that our parents' bad habits can become our bad habits!

But the good news in this is twofold: (1) it's also true that you may pick up all the good habits your parents have instilled in you, and (2) you don't have to make the same mistakes your parents did. Second Corinthians 5:17 says that when you reside with Christ, you are a new creation. The old will go and the new will come.

You don't have to succumb to history. Break the cycle! Take the good and leave the bad. Become the person God has called you to be. Start a new story with good things that you can pass on to your children—habits that will bless them and not lead them to make mistakes that could hurt their chances at a successful life.

Sneaky Little Devil

JACOB WENT CLOSE TO HIS FATHER ISAAC, who touched him and said, "The voice is the voice of Jacob, but the hands are the hands of Esau." He did not recognize him, for his hands were hairy like those of his brother Esau; so he blessed him. "Are you really my son Esau?" he asked. "I am," he replied. **GENESIS 27:22-24.**

I think lying is the worst thing ever. I hate being lied to. Once I was at a car dealership to get my oil changed. Before I paid my bill, I was informed that during their routine checkup they had found several things on my vehicle that needed to be fixed or replaced. The recommended repairs added up to hundreds of dollars that I wasn't about to spend on the spot. So I paid for the oil change and left.

On the way home I stopped at a local mechanic shop owned by some people I know. I showed them the list of things that the dealership had said I needed to have repaired.

My mechanic friend crawled under the vehicle and checked one of the items that the dealership had said should be fixed right away. When he crawled back out, he said, "I don't know why they would tell you that this needs to be fixed. There is nothing wrong with it. And I can't see any evidence that they actually looked at it, either. They were just lying to you to get you to pay them money."

I hate being lied to! In Revelation 12:9 the Bible describes the dragon (the devil) as someone who "deceives the whole world" (NKJV). Liars, people who intentionally mislead people to gain some sort of advantage, are just like the devil.

John 1 tells us that Jesus came to give us truth. People who practice telling the truth are just like Jesus.

Jacob and his mother were not acting like Jesus. They were exhibiting a lack of faith that God's will would be done in Jacob's life.

Lying to get our way, even if we think what we are getting is ultimately God's will, is always wrong. Take the high road and be like Jesus. Be a truth teller, not a deceiver. God loves it when His children represent Him in truth. Jacob's lie got him in a world of trouble. And as you will see, he passed this habit down to his sons too.

FEB 9

God's Not Mad

JACOB LEFT BEERSHEBA AND WENT TOWARD HARAN. And he came to a certain place and stayed there that night, because the sun had set. Taking one of the stones of the place, he put it under his head and lay down in that place to sleep. And he dreamed, and behold, there was a ladder set up on the earth, and the top of it reached to heaven. And behold, the angels of God were ascending and descending on it! And behold, the Lord stood above it and said, "I am the Lord, the God of Abraham your father and the God of Isaac. The land on which you lie I will give to you and to your offspring. Your offspring shall be like the dust of the earth, and you shall spread abroad to the west and to the east and to the north and to the south, and in you and your offspring shall all the families of the earth be blessed. Behold, I am with you and will keep you wherever you go, and will bring you back to this land. For I will not leave you until I have done what I have promised you." **GENESIS 28:10-15, ESV.**

Have you ever felt as if God was mad at you for something? When I was a kid, I used to think that if something bad happened to me, it was because I had done something wrong and God was either "getting me back" or withholding His favor from me.

I wonder how Jacob felt as he fled the wrath of his brother, Esau, toward his uncle Laban's house. He had stolen the birthright. He had deceived his father. He had deceived his brother. He was running for his life. How happy could God be with him?

I'm so glad we don't worship and serve a fickle God. Our God loves us no matter what our behavior. And He wants us to know that. In Jacob's case God shows up in a way that indelibly stamps His love on Jacob's life.

In this wonderful dream Jacob is reassured that he is chosen by God to be His agent to populate the world with people who will share His glory throughout the whole earth. The promise that God had originally made to Abraham is reconfirmed, and Jacob wakes up loved and reassured.

In fact, Jacob's experience is so vivid and moving that he names the place Bethel, which means "House of God." This is a place where Jacob has a sort of conversion experience. Where is your House of God?

Sight for Sore Eyes

WHEN JACOB SAW RACHEL daughter of his uncle Laban, and Laban's sheep, he went over and rolled the stone away from the mouth of the well and watered his uncle's sheep. Then Jacob kissed Rachel and began to weep aloud. He had told Rachel that he was a relative of her father and a son of Rebekah. So she ran and told her father. **GENESIS 29:10-12.**

Do you believe in love at first sight? How about love at first sound? I hadn't been dating anyone for about a year. I had promised God that I was *not* going to get mixed up with any women. I had been baptized and attending church for only about a year when she happened to me.

The first time I saw her, I noticed that she was pretty. The next time I saw her, I noticed that she was with another guy. But the clincher, the one thing about her that got my heart beating fast and led me to pursue her, was her voice. I heard her sing, and that was it. I was in. Head over heels in love. Five months later we were married!

Can you imagine poor unsuspecting Rachel as she is minding her own business, guiding her sheep to the well? Love is probably the last thing on her mind. She's too busy making sure she doesn't become like Little Bo Peep, who lost her sheep.

Before she knows it, this strange man from another neighborhood gallantly rolls the stone from the well, grabs her and kisses her, and then starts to cry! What would you do if that happened to you? I'm guessing you might do what she did—run and tell your daddy!

Romantic love is one of those gifts from God that at times sweeps us off our feet and makes us act so irrationally that even *we* may not understand what we are doing! Yet it's a gift from above that, when used responsibly, can provide a life of fulfillment.

Jacob's love for Rachel seems to leap the bounds of logic and enter the realm of the unrealistic. Yet Jacob's love for his future wife is rock solid, so strong and lasting that he is willing to work seven years for her hand in marriage. Have you ever met anyone so impressive that you'd work seven years for them—for free?

FEB 11

What Goes Around Comes Around

FINALLY, THE TIME CAME for him to marry her. "I have fulfilled my agreement," Jacob said to Laban. "Now give me my wife so I can sleep with her." So Laban invited everyone in the neighborhood and prepared a wedding feast. But that night, when it was dark, Laban took Leah to Jacob, and he slept with her. (Laban had given Leah a servant, Zilpah, to be her maid.) But when Jacob woke up in the morning—it was Leah! "What have you done to me?" Jacob raged at Laban. "I worked seven years for Rachel! Why have you tricked me?" **GENESIS 29:21-25, NLT.**

The phrase "the pot calling the kettle black" is used to accuse a person of being guilty of the very thing of which they accuse another.

I grew up with a stepfather whose moral compass didn't work. He abused his body with drugs, alcohol, and tobacco. He used foul language. His temper got him into physical altercations. He was also the most verbally abusive and critical person I think I've ever met.

When my mom married him (right out of a federal prison in which he'd resided for 18 years), she dragged him to church for several weeks. Finally he stopped going, announcing that he didn't want to go anymore because the people were too critical and were all a bunch of hypocrites. Talk about the pot calling the kettle black!

After the celebration of the wedding feast, Jacob, with no lights or electricity, went to his tent on a honeymoon of sorts with his new bride. When he woke up in the morning, it wasn't Rachel lying next to him; it was her older sister, Leah.

Jacob had been deceived. And he was indignant. He couldn't believe that anyone could be so deceptive!

Um . . . Jacob? Ever heard that saying about the pot and kettle?

One of the great rules of life is spoken of in Scripture: what you sow, you will reap (see Galatians 6:7). In other words, if you deceive others, don't be surprised when you are deceived. If you are kind to people and treat them well, you can expect many people to return that action.

What kind of seed are you sowing? What kind of life garden can you expect to grow from the seeds you have sown?

Crazy Love

"IT'S NOT OUR CUSTOM HERE to marry off a younger daughter ahead of the firstborn," Laban replied. "But wait until the bridal week is over, then we'll give you Rachel, too—provided you promise to work another seven years for me." So Jacob agreed to work seven more years. A week after Jacob had married Leah, Laban gave him Rachel, too. (Laban gave Rachel a servant, Bilhah, to be her maid.) So Jacob slept with Rachel, too, and he loved her much more than Leah. He then stayed and worked for Laban the additional seven years. **GENESIS 29:26-30, NLT.**

I was in love. At least my 19-year-old brain thought I was in love. I was going out with a girl that I really enjoyed being around. In an act of kindness I volunteered my truck and myself to drive her from Seattle to South Dakota to pick up a bunch of things that she had left there when her family had moved out west. We drove straight through without stopping.

When we arrived in South Dakota, we walked into the home of a friend of my girlfriend's family. Not 15 minutes after we sat down in the living room, the doorbell rang. It was a guy about my age. My girlfriend looked at me and said, "This is my ex-boyfriend Keith. I'm going to walk around the block with him to say hi." Two hours later she came back to the house and told me that she loved Keith and that she and I were no longer boyfriend and girlfriend.

I had gone through a lot of work to get to South Dakota for my girlfriend. I thought I deserved to be her number one. I was heartsick when I couldn't have her as my girlfriend anymore.

Can you imagine how Jacob felt after he had worked for seven years to gain the hand of the one he loved, only to wake up next to somebody whom he not only didn't love but also hadn't really even noticed much? He must have been furious. Jacob was starting to experience a little of what his family must have felt when he deceived them. Yet Jacob loved Rachel so much he did another seven years of free labor so he could have her too. Can you imagine someone loving you that much? That's crazy love! And God loves you more than that. He'd give up more than seven years of His life for you. He'd give up eternity.

FEB 13

I'll *Make* You Love Me!

LEAH BECAME PREGNANT and gave birth to a son. She named him Reuben, for she said, "It is because the Lord has seen my misery. Surely my husband will love me now." She conceived again, and when she gave birth to a son she said, "Because the Lord heard that I am not loved, he gave me this one too." So she named him Simeon. Again she conceived, and when she gave birth to a son she said, "Now at last my husband will become attached to me, because I have borne him three sons." So he was named Levi. **GENESIS 29:32-34.**

I've seen some pretty sorry things in my life, but none quite as sorry as a desperate teenager who isn't loved by the one they love.

I was sitting in my office one day when a 15-year-old boy came bursting in, throwing himself on my office couch in tears. This guy was a mess. Every hole on his face was leaking as he blurted out his hurt. The pain that drove this leaky-faced young man into my office was a breakup (after three weeks of dating) with a girl who he was sure was going to be his forever. Oh, the drama.

After he settled down and stopped dripping on my couch, he started to come up with all kinds of ideas to *make* this girl love him. He was going to send her flowers, ask to carry her books from class to class, change his cologne, and get a different haircut.

When he finished talking, he asked my opinion about his plans to *make* this girl love him. I told him that he was going to end up looking like a creepy stalker and that he needed to respect her wishes.

"But how am I going to *make* her love me if I don't do all this stuff?" He started crying again.

I explained to him that love cannot be forced. Love is never controlled but always comes from a place of freedom and choice.

Poor Leah had a broken heart. She tried to *make* Jacob love her by bearing him children. It didn't work.

I know all kinds of people who try to *make* God love them by doing all kinds of things that He wants them to do. It's sad, really. We can't earn God's love. But when we fall in love with Him, we'll want to do all the right things anyway.

Get Me Out of This Family!

WHEN LABAN HAD GONE to shear his sheep, Rachel stole her father's household gods. Moreover, Jacob deceived Laban the Aramean by not telling him he was running away. So he fled with all he had, crossed the Euphrates River, and headed for the hill country of Gilead. **GENESIS 31:19-21.**

How would you like to be part of Laban's family? Can you say *dysfunctional*? I suppose I shouldn't talk. My family wasn't the most functional group in the neighborhood. My mom and dad were in a perpetual argument until they divorced after 22 years of marriage. My mom got remarried to a guy she met while he was still in prison serving a sentence of 20 years to life. That relationship was a disaster. My dad married a woman who worked in the film industry. Their marriage lasted for a few years before it came to a bitter end. My sister and I didn't really have any model for how a healthy, productive family should behave, so we had to figure it out on our own.

Looking to the Bible doesn't seem to help much either. It seems that all the families in the Bible were dysfunctional too! Adam and Eve, Abraham and Sarah, Isaac and Rebekah, Jacob and Rachel and Leah . . . where do the cycles of deception and brokenness stop? When do things get *normal,* whatever that is?

The good news about God is that we don't have to stay in the cycle of dysfunction if we don't want to. The Bible says that we have the opportunity to become a "new creation" when we follow God's will for our lives. And that's something you can start now, even before you marry and have your own family.

The first thing you can do to have a functional family is to be a functional person! Take an inventory of your own life. Do you live by your values, or do you let your feelings dictate your actions? Do you communicate honestly, or do you find yourself having to be deceptive to get your way?

One reason Jesus came to this earth is to show us how to live. He loved, He told the truth, He was honest (even when it hurt), and He was merciful. He honored His mother and Father. Our task is to strive to live like Him. Living like Jesus gives us the best shot at having a family that will bring joy to ourselves and those around us.

FEB 15

Looking Fear in the Face

WHEN THE MESSENGERS RETURNED TO JACOB, they said, "We went to your brother Esau, and now he is coming to meet you, and four hundred men are with him." **GENESIS 32:6.**

When I was a kid, I idolized a guy in my neighborhood who was four years older. His name was Gordon. Gordon had cool clothes. He knew all kinds of stuff that I hadn't discovered yet. The bedroom in his house was decorated with all the latest posters of the coolest bands. He was really good at basketball. And sometimes he was nice to me; more often than not, he'd pick on me. It was quite a dilemma. I was afraid of him, but I really wanted to be his best friend!

Time after time I would come running into my house crying because "Gordon hit me" or "Gordon made fun of me" or "Gordon took my bike." Each time my dad would look over his newspaper and say, "Hit 'im over the head with a stick!"

Hit him over the head with a stick? That didn't seem like a great idea.

One day after a negative episode with Gordon, my dad sat me down and had a talk with me. He said, "As long as Gordon knows you're afraid of him, this will keep happening. Just hit him over the head with a stick one time, and he'll never bother you again."

I decided to act. Just a few days later Gordon was picking on me again. He took one of my shoes and held it away from me so I couldn't reach it. Getting more and more angry, I looked around. There was no stick. So I closed my eyes and punched Gordon in the stomach as hard as I could. He dropped my shoe. I ran home. And Gordon never picked on me again.

Now, I'm not suggesting that violence is the answer. But I *am* saying that facing your fears with honest integrity is the only way to get past them. Jacob was terrified of Esau. It took a resolute heart to take God's hand and walk toward that fear. But it was a necessary step in Jacob's evolution as a follower of God. What fear do you need to overcome so that God can use you more effectively? Take His hand and walk through the storm. You won't be disappointed.

Oh, by the way, Gordon and I are still good friends 40 years later!

Heavenly Wrestling

THEN THE MAN SAID, "Your name will no longer be Jacob, but Israel, because you have struggled with God and with humans and have overcome."
GENESIS 32:28.

Jacob's parents gave him a name that meant "deceiver." Can you imagine being out in the neighborhood as a kid and having your mom call you in to eat: "Deceiver! Time for dinner!" Jacob certainly lived up to his name.

We still do this kind of thing, don't we? Maybe people don't name their children "Deceiver" or "Liar" or "Stupid," but I've seen oodles of parents who treat their kids in such despicable ways that I can almost predict how the children will turn out.

If you grow up in an environment that tells you that you are stupid or unattractive or good-for-nothing, what do you think your self-opinion will be? How do you think you will act as you grow up? People still name their kids bad names.

Jacob didn't like it that he had deceived his brother. He didn't like it that he had deceived his father. He didn't like it that he had snuck out on Laban, either. Jacob wanted to change. He wanted to have God's blessings in his life. His first step toward that was to reconcile with Esau, his brother. God recognized his effort.

The night before Jacob was to meet Esau, he was alone, contemplating his fate, when a stranger appeared out of nowhere and began to wrestle with him. This wrestling match lasted all night, until Jacob held on and begged the mysterious Hulk Hogan to bless him before He left. The divine visitor blessed Jacob with a better blessing than Jacob ever could have asked for: a name change. Jacob went from "Deceiver" to "Prince of God."

Now, some of your Bibles will say that the word *Israel* means "he struggles with God." But the word *Israel* is broken up into two Hebrew words, *sara* and *el*. *El* is the short term for God in the Old Testament. *Sara* and its relative, *sarar*, mean to prevail or rule as a prince. God changed Jacob's name. With his new name, "Prince of God," and his new attitude, Jacob started on a remarkable journey.

What's your name? Who gave it to you? Revelation 2:17 says that God will give us a "new name" if we overcome with Him. Care to wrestle?

FEB 17

Sweet Reconciliation

THEN JACOB LOOKED UP and saw Esau coming with his 400 men. So he divided the children among Leah, Rachel, and his two servant wives. He put the servant wives and their children at the front, Leah and her children next, and Rachel and Joseph last. Then Jacob went on ahead. As he approached his brother, he bowed to the ground seven times before him. Then Esau ran to meet him and embraced him, threw his arms around his neck, and kissed him. And they both wept. **GENESIS 33:1-4, NLT.**

Adi and Rudolf Dassler were brothers who decided to go into the shoe business together. One loved to design shoes, and the other was a natural-born salesman. As their business grew, the brothers began to bicker about small things that eventually turned into big things. It wasn't long before the siblings argued about everything from politics to religion. Neither brother could put down his pride and attempt reconciliation. Finally Rudolf decided he'd had enough. He moved across the river from his brother and opened up his own shoe company. Both brothers eventually died estranged from each other.

Jacob and Esau had plenty of reasons to dislike each other. They were different in so many ways. And the things that they had done to each other, from the threats to the deception, gave them even more reason to continue a pattern of hate and irreconcilable differences.

Yet both brothers laid down their pride and decided to do the godly thing, to reconcile. The Merriam-Webster dictionary defines the word *reconcile* this way: "to restore to friendship or harmony."

The Bible tells us that Jesus came to reconcile us with the Father. Not that God had any hard feelings toward us, but we had some ideas about God that needed straightening out. The Son came to give us a clear picture of a loving Father who would sacrifice everything for us. Jesus is the great reconciler.

I suppose you may be wondering about Adi and Rudolf . . . what companies did they start? Adidas and Puma. Two shoe companies that remind us of the importance of reconciliation.

FEB 18

Two Wrongs Don't Make a Right

THEN JACOB SAID TO SIMEON AND LEVI, "You have brought trouble on me by making me obnoxious to the Canaanites and Perizzites, the people living in this land. We are few in number, and if they join forces against me and attack me, I and my household will be destroyed." **GENESIS 34:30.**

In today's story Jacob and his family have moved close to the city of Shechem. One of Jacob's daughters, Dinah, goes into the city and introduces herself to the local girls. As they are cavorting around, Shechem, the son of the local ruler, sees Dinah, takes her, and rapes her. In the process, the Bible says, he falls deeply in love with her.

Well, anyone who knows anything about love knows that it cannot be forced. Whatever Shechem was feeling for Dinah certainly wasn't love. But he did want to possess her, that's for certain.

Shechem and his dad approach Jacob and ask for Dinah's hand in marriage. But more than that, they attempt to make a treaty with Jacob and his clan. They want Jacob to stay in their area and to trade goods, cattle, and daughters in marriage.

Jacob's sons agree to the treaty, but with a condition: that every male in the city of Shechem be circumcised as they all are. The townspeople agree.

After the men of the city have all been circumcised and are lying around in pain, two of Jacob's sons sneak in and kill the unsuspecting men as revenge for the rape of their sister. The rest of his sons steal all of their cattle and their money and capture their children and their wives, bringing them back to Jacob's camp. This, of course, upsets Jacob and makes him fearful that the other cities in the region will hunt him down and kill him and his family.

Fighting hurt by inflicting more hurt is a response that seems natural. When someone hits us, we hit back. If someone insults us, we insult back. If someone dislikes us, we try to add to their pain by mistreating them in word or in action.

Jesus challenges His followers to break the natural cycle by responding unnaturally. He asks us to treat our enemies with love. After all, that's how God treats us. The Bible says that while we were enemies of Christ, He still died for us (see Romans 5:8).

55

FEB 19

My Go-to Place

JACOB SET UP A STONE PILLAR at the place where God had talked with him, and he poured out a drink offering on it; he also poured oil on it. Jacob called the place where God had talked with him Bethel. **GENESIS 35:14, 15.**

When I was a teenager, there were times I just had to get away. Because of the stress of life, conflict with my family, or confusion about relationships, I just couldn't handle being around people or staying where I was. I had to get away and get some perspective. Every time this happened in my life, I would end up in the same place—on top of Widow Maker Hill. I suppose you may be wondering why I chose such a morbid-sounding spot!

When I was in tenth grade, a guy from my mom's church took an interest in me and started challenging my spiritual direction. I really liked him and for a short period of time acted on his request to start communicating with God and reading my Bible. I couldn't do this very well at home, so I'd get on my motorcycle, ride up to Poplar Street, take a right into the woods, and ride the trails all the way to a huge hill that was very difficult to navigate. My friends and I had named it the Widow Maker because it took us several attempts to get to the top of the hill the first time we tried to ride up it. On many occasions we lost traction and fell off our motorcycles, tumbling back down the hill with our motorcycles following close behind. When we finally figured out how to conquer the hill, the view from the top was spectacular. This is where I would go to read my Bible. It was serene.

Later in life when problems would arise, even though I wasn't connected to God as I should have been, I'd find myself on this hill, my go-to place, to gather perspective and take a deep breath.

Bethel, which means "House of God," was Jacob's go-to place. This was where he and God had met previously (remember the ladder to heaven?). This was where Jacob was reminded of God's blessings on his life. This was where Jacob could remember that everything would be OK.

Do you have a go-to place?

See You Later

ISAAC LIVED A HUNDRED AND EIGHTY YEARS. Then he breathed his last and died and was gathered to his people, old and full of years. And his sons Esau and Jacob buried him. **GENESIS 35:28, 29.**

Pastors experience death a lot more than most people. It comes with the job. When a loved one starts to slip away, many church members ask the pastor to come and pray with the dying person and their family. It's a sacred time, full of God's presence. Psalm 116:15 says, "Precious in the sight of the Lord is the death of his faithful servants."

I was living in North Carolina when my sister gave me the call. "Mom isn't doing too well. I think you'd better come."

My mom had been diagnosed with a brain tumor 20 years before this phone call. After surgery and radiation therapy, the next 20 years brought a steady decline in her mental health. The last four years of Mom's life she was unable to speak. We were looking at a slowly sinking ship, and we knew it.

I traveled out to Washington State, where my sister took care of our mom. When we took Mom to the hospital, the neurologist told us there was really nothing we could do. Our options were to feed and hydrate Mom through tubes to sustain her life or else "allow her to die." Keeping Mom alive through tube feedings just so she could lie there and exist didn't seem like something she'd want us to do. So we made the decision.

The doctor told us Mom would last about eight days without food and water. She lasted 14. Mom died on Thanksgiving Day. She wanted to be cremated and have her ashes sprinkled in the little town of Beverly, Washington, where she grew up. I think my sister still has our mom's ashes—couldn't bring herself to say goodbye.

I can imagine that Isaac's family mourned his passing too. I'm not sure if they quite understood the prospects of eternal life, but I know that they felt the sting of death just as we do. I'm looking forward to the day that death is defeated and sorrow is no more. I'll bet you are too.

FEB 21

You Won't Believe This One!

JOSEPH HAD A DREAM, and when he told it to his brothers, they hated him all the more. He said to them, "Listen to this dream I had: We were binding sheaves of grain out in the field when suddenly my sheaf rose and stood upright, while your sheaves gathered around mine and bowed down to it." **GENESIS 37:5-7.**

I've had some weird dreams in my life. When I was young, I'd have a recurring nightmare in which I would be playing in a yard with all my best friends. I remember the feeling of having more fun and experiencing more joy than I had ever known. All was bliss. And then I'd look over and see a brick wall. On that brick wall was a metal bracket with a big red button in the middle of it. In my dream everybody knew that if someone pushed the red button, some sort of catastrophe would come upon us, and we'd all die. So everyone stayed clear of the button . . . until a kid I didn't recognize would go over, give an impish smile, and press the button. At that point I'd wake up screaming, and my mom would rush in and put me back to sleep. Weird dream.

Joseph had a weird dream. He may not have had it repeatedly, but it was weird enough to stay with him in his waking hours. I don't know if Joseph was ignorant or just arrogant, but you'd think he would have known that if he told his family members about his dreams, it would upset them. I mean, what else could a dream like that mean—either the one in our text above or the dream of the sun, moon, and 11 stars bowing down to him?

Couple his dream-sharing with the fact that his brothers already thought he was a snot-nosed brat whom Daddy loved more than everybody else, and you've got a recipe for disaster. I wish I could jump into the story and tell him, "Joseph! Keep the dream to yourself. Don't share it! You're acting like a spoiled brat!"

But he didn't follow my imaginary advice. He shared his dream and offended his brothers and his dad. What they didn't know was that these revelations weren't rooted in Joseph's arrogance. They were all God's doing. He was showing His hand ahead of time so that later on the faith of Jacob's family would be increased by looking back to see that God had been guiding through the good and the bad.

How can you look back and see God's working in your life?

The Green-eyed Monster

"HERE COMES THAT DREAMER!" they said to each other. "Come now, let's kill him and throw him into one of these cisterns and say that a ferocious animal devoured him. Then we'll see what comes of his dreams."
GENESIS 37:19, 20.

When I was a kid, I had a dog named Ginger. She was a very intelligent mix of about a thousand breeds. When asked what kind of dog she was, my dad would say, "She's a Heinz 57!"

Ginger had a hilarious trait that enabled me to exploit the green-eyed monster within her. I would get my cat and place her on my lap. If Ginger was looking, she'd sit up very quickly and stare. Then I'd start to pet the cat and talk to it. "You're my favorite animal in the house. I love you so much. Aren't you just so pretty?"

Ginger would start to growl. The more I'd fawn over the cat, the more upset Ginger would become. Finally, she'd let out a bark, jump up on my lap, nose the cat away, and start to lick my face. The jealousy was too much. She couldn't handle letting someone else garner the attention that only she deserved.

Jealousy is one of the most hideous human responses known on earth. It has caused grief and regret and jail time for centuries. Jealousy is the source of junior high girls' gossip and mean-spirited jokes; it's the genesis of junior high guys' black eyes and fat lips. Jealousy can be a rotten thing.

Joseph's brothers were jealous. Jacob didn't help the situation by making his son that coat of many colors. Jealousy ate away at Joseph's brothers every day until they hated their brother so much that they wished him dead.

When we act out of jealousy, we presume that God cannot be trusted to do what needs to be done. We presume that we should possess what is not ours. Jealous acts steal freedom, making them the antithesis of love. Jealousy is a green-eyed monster that has no business in the life of someone who is committed to Christ.

Are you willing to allow those around you the freedom to choose you or not choose you for who you are? Are you willing to trust God to work in your situation?

FEB 23

Um, Yuck!

MEANWHILE JUDAH SENT THE YOUNG GOAT by his friend the Adullamite in order to get his pledge back from the woman, but he did not find her. He asked the men who lived there, "Where is the shrine prostitute who was beside the road at Enaim?" "There hasn't been any shrine prostitute here," they said. **GENESIS 38:20, 21.**

When I started to write this book, I decided not to gloss over the parts of Scripture that are uncomfortable. Sometimes stories in the Bible are not rated G. This is one of those stories.

Genesis 38 tells us the story of a young woman, Tamar, who was married to one of Judah's sons (Jacob's grandsons). She was a Canaanite girl. Unfortunately her husband—one of God's people—was so wicked that he died in his own sin.

The custom was that if a man died, his wife would go to the next brother in line so that she could still have children. So Judah gave her his next son. That son didn't want to have children with her, so when they slept together, he didn't finish the process; instead "he spilled his semen on the ground" (verse 9). For this he also dies.

Now Judah has only one son left. He's afraid that Tamar is some sort of man killer, so he refuses to give him to her in marriage.

This bums Tamar out, so she disguises herself as a prostitute and entices her father-in-law, Judah, to sleep with her. She gets pregnant with her father-in-law's twin babies.

When Judah finds out that his daughter-in-law is pregnant, he threatens to have her put to death for being an adulterer—until he finds out that the kids are his. Then he repents of his sin and reconciles with Tamar and the rest of the family.

I don't think Hollywood could come up with a story this sick and twisted. Yet here it is in the Bible. Real life, gritty, no holds barred. Yuck.

So what can we do with such a story? We look at it and learn such lessons as (1) don't take a wife who's not of your faith; (2) don't try to manipulate God to suit your own desires; (3) don't deny people the things that are rightfully theirs; and (4) when you get busted for your sin, repent and make peace with the people around you. Now, back to our regularly scheduled program . . .

Why I Got Fired

THE LORD WAS WITH JOSEPH so that he prospered, and he lived in the house of his Egyptian master. When his master saw that the Lord was with him and that the Lord gave him success in everything he did, Joseph found favor in his eyes and became his attendant. Potiphar put him in charge of his household, and he entrusted to his care everything he owned.
GENESIS 39:2-4.

I haven't always worked to the best of my ability. When I was in boarding academy, we had an industry on campus that made furniture. This business was there to aid students in their tuition so they could afford a private education. Students could do all kinds of jobs at the factory, from sorting cut wood to sweeping sawdust.

The furniture factory had an agreement with the school that they would train the students and teach them the value of hard work. This agreement was struck before they met me.

I was fired four times from Harris Pine Mills. I was fired for not showing up to work. I was fired for safety violations. I was fired for throwing small blocks of wood up through the rafters in the building and hitting another worker in the head . . . You get the picture. I wasn't really putting a lot of pride into my work.

Then I got a car. Of my own. I had to afford the gas and insurance. I applied at a Wendy's restaurant and was the best worker there. I came early and left late. I learned that much of my reputation as a person revolved around my work ethic. People started to think well of me because of how hard I worked.

This is what Joseph discovered while he was in captivity. He was able to look past his situation and do everything diligently to the glory of God. He made himself invaluable in every situation, even if he didn't particularly enjoy what he was doing.

Would you hire you?

One of the most valuable lessons that any young person can ever learn is the value of working hard, of finishing well, of taking pride in their work. Doing your best in your work not only helps you to represent God in your daily life; it also gives you a leg up on those around you who are satisfied with mediocrity.

FEB 25

Caught on Camera

JOSEPH WAS A VERY HANDSOME and well-built young man, and Potiphar's wife soon began to look at him lustfully. "Come and sleep with me," she demanded. **GENESIS 39:6, 7, NLT.**

I've heard people say that the definition of *integrity* is how you act when nobody is around to judge your actions.

I enjoy watching television shows in which hidden cameras observe people who have no idea that they are being watched. In one TV show the police place an unlocked car with keys in the ignition in different parts of the city. The car is fully equipped with hidden cameras and microphones to record everything that happens to the unsuspecting car thieves who can't refuse the prospects of a free car.

After the thieves get in the car and start down the road, the car is remotely turned off and the doors lock, trapping the thieves. When they are interrogated by the police, they come up with the funniest excuses as to why they got in the car, started it up, and drove away. Of course, they don't realize that the hidden microphones and cameras have already recorded their true motives.

Joseph was a red-blooded teenager who had the same drives and interests as most. His master's wife was making advances that many people would fall to.

Add to these temptations the fact that Joseph had been betrayed by his family, and he could have reasoned that God had betrayed him too. What would it hurt to fall to temptation this one time? Nobody would know. Nobody would see. Why not do it just this once? After all, his master's wife was kind of his boss too. He'd just be obeying her orders.

It's evident that when Joseph was young, he made a decision to live by his values and not make decisions based on his feelings. He knew the difference between right and wrong, and even if he felt abandoned by his family and possibly by his God, Joseph was going to remain faithful.

When temptation comes knocking on your door, how do you respond? Do you look both ways to see who's watching? Or have you already set your values and determined to act on them?

Remember Me

BUT WHEN ALL GOES WELL WITH YOU, remember me and show me kindness; mention me to Pharaoh and get me out of this prison. **GENESIS 40:14.**

One of the most frightening situations a school administrator faces on a regular basis is traveling with a group of students. Keeping track of a large group of young people takes the kind of skill, precision, and organization that can be gained only by advanced degrees from institutions of higher education!

When I was the principal of a K-12 school in central Washington, I would occasionally drive the big tour bus for trips. On one such occasion I was driving a bus full of high school students about three hours to Spokane, Washington, to see a life-size replica of the Old Testament sanctuary. About halfway there we stopped at a rest area for a bathroom break. After 10 minutes I blasted the horn, and everyone got back in. I got on the microphone and asked, "Is everyone back on the bus? Do you see anyone missing?"

The response was resounding: "Everybody's on board; we can go!"

We were about 35 miles down the road when someone said, "Hey, where are Brandi and Addie?"

I'm not sure if this was the first time I left students at a rest stop, but it was the only time that such a mistake was brought to my attention. We turned around and rescued the flustered young women with many apologies and bribes not to tell their parents!

Joseph had a simple request of his fellow prisoner: If I do you this favor, remember me when you get out of this horrible place. Rescue me.

Of course, when this inmate got sprung, he didn't remember Joseph. He just went on living his life until much later when knowing Joseph served to his advantage.

Loyalty goes a long way with me. Remembering the favors people have done for us along the way is important. Why not take a moment today to make a phone call, send a note, or write an e-mail to someone who has helped you along life's road?

FEB 27

Stick Around and See

THEN PHARAOH SAID TO JOSEPH, "Since God has made all this known to you, there is no one so discerning and wise as you. You shall be in charge of my palace, and all my people are to submit to your orders. Only with respect to the throne will I be greater than you." **GENESIS 41:39, 40.**

I've been a fan of Seattle sports teams ever since my family moved there in 1965. I've watched them on TV, listened to them on the radio, and seen them live. Admittedly there has been little to cheer about in Seattle sports, but we've had our moments. Much to my chagrin, I missed one of those moments not too long ago.

I had driven three hours to Seattle with my son and his friend to watch a Mariners baseball game. The day was filled with wonderful ballpark food and lots of souvenirs. But the game was horribly lopsided in favor of the visiting team. The Mariners were down by six or so runs by the middle of the eighth, and we had a three-hour drive ahead us. So we left.

On the way home I turned on the radio to catch the rest of the game, only to hear the announcers going crazy as the M's scored seven runs in the ninth to win the game. I hate missing a good ending.

Joseph's life was heading nowhere good. His brothers hated him so much that they sold him into slavery; his master's wife got him thrown in jail because he wouldn't sleep with her; and he was stuck in an Egyptian jail for years. As far as Joseph could see, there was no light at the end of the tunnel. And if there was, it was a train.

Yet Joseph remained faithful to the values his God had instilled in him through his father, even through the tough times. And guess what? It paid off.

Joseph could have thrown in the towel at any time. He could have given up on God or even on life. But he didn't. He endured and overcame.

The Bible tells us over and over that the person who overcomes will receive a reward. How about you? Have you ever felt that you just wanted to throw in the towel? Have you ever wondered if being faithful was worth it? Have you ever seen the wicked prosper and wanted to join their ranks? Don't do it. Be an overcomer. Stay faithful, and you will see your reward.

Who's to Blame?

WHEN JACOB LEARNED THAT there was grain in Egypt, he said to his sons, "Why do you just keep looking at each other?" He continued, "I have heard that there is grain in Egypt. Go down there and buy some for us, so that we may live and not die." **GENESIS 42:1, 2.**

I have a friend who does not believe in God. In a wonderful moment of debate he asked me this poignant question: "If there is a God, why are there so many starving children in the world?"

This was a good question. My response was "I suppose that God would ask us a similar question: Why do we allow so many children to starve? God has supplied us with more than enough food. He's given us the technologies and resources to distribute this food worldwide. He's provided us with every opportunity as a human race to take care of each other. So why don't we do God's bidding and feed all the starving children?"

My friend admitted to me that he hadn't lifted a finger to relieve the suffering of any starving child. My point was Why blame God?

Each year 2.6 million children die because they don't have enough to eat. Those are just the ones under age 5. Can you imagine what it would be like to starve to death? How horrible to ebb away into a needless death.

Jacob's family was experiencing famine to the point that he thought their lives were in danger. He had heard that Egypt had grain to sell, so he sent his boys to get some life-saving food. He didn't know that this was all part of God's plan to preserve the family line that would eventually produce Jesus. Jacob's long-lost son, Joseph, was going to be the key to saving the lives of thousands around the world because he was willing to be used by God.

You may not end up saving thousands, but consider what you could do to provide relief for just one in this world who is starving for food and for Jesus. You could be somebody's Joseph!

MAR 1

This Is a Test . . .
This Is Only a Test

JOSEPH GAVE ORDERS TO FILL their bags with grain, to put each man's silver back in his sack, and to give them provisions for their journey. After this was done for them, they loaded their grain on their donkeys and left. **GENESIS 42:25, 26.**

Trust. That word is just a strong word, isn't it? Trust.

Trust is everything in our personal relationships. If business partners don't trust each other, it's a disaster. Married couples who don't trust each other often end up in divorce. And in a faith relationship—well, what kind of faith can survive without trust?

We trust blindly all the time, don't we? We drive down the highway at 60 miles per hour, trusting that the person driving the other way won't steer their vehicle into ours. We get in elevators, airplanes, and boats, trusting that the people responsible for their upkeep have done their job. If we knew that any of the maintenance people in charge of our airplane had shown up for work drunk the day we were to fly, we wouldn't get on the plane—at least I wouldn't.

I've had students in school who had a track record of stealing from their classmates. They had repented of each of their crimes, but any time something went missing, guess whom my thoughts turned to?

Joseph needed to know. He needed to know that his little brother was actually alive and that his brothers hadn't killed Benjamin or sold him into slavery. He needed to know that they had repented and that they meant it. In the words of a recent U.S. president: "Trust, but verify."

So Joseph secretly returned the silver they had paid for their grain and demanded to see Benjamin, his little brother. Would they come back for more food and return their silver? Would they produce evidence that his brother was safe? That was the only way he could know their true heart.

It's amazing to see the kind of trust that Jesus placed in His Father while He was on this earth. He trusted God's faithfulness and love for Him, and you can have that same trust too.

The Revealing

JOSEPH SAID TO HIS BROTHERS, "I am Joseph! Is my father still living?" But his brothers were not able to answer him, because they were terrified at his presence. **GENESIS 45:3.**

When I lived in North Carolina, my house frequently ended up looking like a CSI murder scene. Oh, maybe I should have started the paragraph with this statement: I own cats.

Sometimes my cats would bring in creatures of all shapes and sizes—alive—and let them go. These animals would fly, scamper, hop, or slither for shelter, trying to get away from my murderous felines. My wife would start screaming and throwing cats in the bathroom so that they couldn't do more damage.

My job was to capture the little critters and escort them outside so that they could live another day. This was not an easy task, because these animals were terrified of me! I was their friend. I wanted to save them. Yet the closer I got to them, the more terrified they became.

Can you understand why Joseph's brothers were afraid? Can you imagine how their minds were whirling when Joseph revealed his identity to them? Do you think Judah instantly remembered every hate-filled word he had screamed as Joseph was trapped in the pit they had thrown him into so many years ago? The sin that they had committed against their brother was so grievous, so personal, that they were terrified when they heard him say, "Hey, guess what? I'm your brother!"

What Joseph's brothers didn't know, at least at that moment, was that Joseph had no malice in his heart toward them. He didn't hate them. He loved them and wanted to save them from the famine that was threatening their family.

The Bible promises that Jesus is going to come back to save His friends from this sin-sick world. One of the most tragic verses in the Bible says that some people are going to respond to Jesus' second coming with terror instead of open-armed joy. Why? Because they don't really know Him. They consider Him an enemy, when all along He's had no malice toward them. He just wants to save them. To be afraid of God makes sense only if you don't know Him.

MAR 3

God's Got Plans

AND NOW, DO NOT BE DISTRESSED and do not be angry with yourselves for selling me here, because it was to save lives that God sent me ahead of you. . . . But God sent me ahead of you to preserve for you a remnant on earth and to save your lives by a great deliverance. **GENESIS 45:5-7.**

I love how God works. Usually it's in unseen ways that would confound the brightest of minds. Sometimes we can look at our current situation and see a huge mess, when all along God is using a bad situation to prepare us for something great.

Imagine Joseph's life. As a young man he was hated by most of his family. When attempting to obey his father, he was thrown into a pit, wondering if his brothers would ever let him out. He was sold into slavery. He was sold in an Egyptian auction as if he were a cow or a goat. He was falsely accused of the same hideous crime that Shechem had committed against Joseph's half-sister. And his reward for remaining faithful to God? He was thrown into an Egyptian prison, where he was punished and ridiculed for his faith.

Joseph could have been a bitter man bent on revenge. Instead, he chose to allow God to soften his heart and use him as an instrument of forgiveness and peace. Instead of whining, Joseph praised. Instead of revenge, Joseph chose reconciliation. Instead of dwelling in the pain of the past, Joseph chose to stand up and look toward a brighter day, allowing God to make all things good.

It's easy to let our circumstances get us down. It's easy to live in the past. But that's not what we are called to do. We are called to understand that God has good things in store for us. We are called to recognize that He wants us to succeed, no matter the circumstance.

Are there obstacles in your path today? Are there seemingly impossible situations that you don't think can ever be resolved? Stay faithful. Hope for the future. And most important, cling to the promise that all things work together for those who love God.

Sweet Reunion

JOSEPH HAD HIS CHARIOT MADE READY and went to Goshen to meet his father Israel. As soon as Joseph appeared before him, he threw his arms around his father and wept for a long time. **GENESIS 46:29.**

Allow my imagination to be spilled out on this page.

Times have been dark. The world seems to have gone crazy in the past couple of years. My country is no longer a bastion of freedom. Economic chaos enables the few to control the many. Natural disasters have become normal rather than occasional. My family and I have lost our home; we've lost our ability to make a living; and now we are on the run, being chased by those who would have us imprisoned—yes, even killed—for our allegiance to God's Word.

We are not afraid, because we know that we are on the precipice of what we've hoped and longed for our whole lives. And then we see it. A cloud half the size of a man's fist. It's not a normal-looking cloud. It seems to be alive with activity. It springs toward the earth with power and speed. The ground starts to shake at the sound of a great trumpet blast, and we know that He is here to rescue us.

We join the throngs of people in the air in the most surreal event any human has ever experienced. Heaven ends up being more spectacular than anything I can imagine. The sights and sounds cannot be described.

As I'm absorbing the immensity of the moment, I hear my name called. It's Jesus motioning for me to come near to Him. As I draw near, I notice that He is also beckoning toward another. It's my mother. She is now restored to full health in a body that will never give up on her. We embrace, and our reunion is filled with tears of joy and satisfaction. All is well. We are reunited again.

I think that what we see in the reunion of Joseph and his father, Jacob, is a precursor to what we will soon experience in heaven. In Jacob's mind Joseph had been dead, and now he was alive. That reunion in Goshen was all that Jacob needed to complete his life. What a beautiful moment.

If you're reading this with someone, tell him or her what person you are looking forward to seeing again when you get to heaven.

MAR 5

How Soon They Forget

EVENTUALLY, A NEW KING came to power in Egypt who knew nothing about Joseph or what he had done. He said to his people, "Look, the people of Israel now outnumber us and are stronger than we are. We must make a plan to keep them from growing even more. If we don't, and if war breaks out, they will join our enemies and fight against us. Then they will escape from the country." **EXODUS 1:8-10, NLT.**

I like to be liked. I think everybody does. I think I like to be liked because if people like me, then I like them. And if they like me and I like them, well, that means I have more friends. And I like having friends; my Facebook account would testify to that.

A trait that is related to my liking to be liked is my desire to do a great job wherever I am called to serve. I want to do such a good job at whatever church or school I'm serving that I leave some sort of legacy. I think this desire is steeped more in an unhealthy sense of pride than in anything else, but I'll admit: I want to be remembered after I leave.

It wasn't too long ago that I visited an institution that I used to be a part of. When I was there, I did my best to start programs and lay down traditions that would leave the lasting stamp of Mark Witas all over them.

To my chagrin, nothing that I had started was still being practiced. Nobody really remembered who I was, because all the people working there had changed. It was almost as if I had never been there.

One of the hard lessons I learned that day is something that the Bible talks about often. I need to have a healthy perspective on who I am in the great scheme of things. Not only does Jesus emphasize an attitude of humility (the last will be first; the greatest among you will be the least), but the Bible reminds me that I am like the grass of the field, flourishing one day and gone the next.

This isn't to take away from our duty to impact our world for Jesus to the best of our ability, but it is a reminder that when we are gone, a new pharaoh will be in town. Let's not think too highly of ourselves. Instead, let's think highly of Jesus and the calling He has placed on our lives. Let's do our best for Him, not for our egos.

A Deliverer Is Born

"YES, GO," SHE ANSWERED. So the girl went and got the baby's mother. Pharaoh's daughter said to her, "Take this baby and nurse him for me, and I will pay you." So the woman took the baby and nursed him. When the child grew older, she took him to Pharaoh's daughter and he became her son. She named him Moses, saying, "I drew him out of the water." **EXODUS 2:8-10.**

Moses' story is a remarkably familiar one.

God's people are steeped in slavery. They have been that way for many years. Once a proud people, the descendants of the patriarchs Abraham, Isaac, and Jacob have now been reduced to a people of forced labor—second-class citizens.

God's people need to be saved from their slavery. So what does God do? He sends a deliverer. It's interesting how He chooses to do this. He sends a baby to be born in the midst of God's people. Of course, the king isn't interested in the Jews' need to have a leader born to save them, so he orders the death of all the Jewish male children. Of course, this doesn't work, because Moses is put in a basket and floated down the Nile to save his life.

In the end God delivers Moses to the very home of the enemy of God's people. Moses is brought up and trained in the courts of the most powerful nation on earth, all before he goes out into the wilderness for 40 years to learn what it means to be a servant leader.

Does any of this sound familiar?

About 1,400 years later we find God's people in slavery again—this time to sin. God sends a Savior in the form of a baby. A king gets upset by this news and tries to kill all the Jewish male children in one area of his kingdom. God saves that child by bringing Him to Egypt. This child, named Jesus, spends 40 days in the wilderness before He begins His ministry to call His people out of the slavery of sin.

Moses and Jesus share quite a beginning. That's one reason Moses is one of the most pivotal figures in the Bible. His life will be poured out in the service of God and His people. How can God use you to serve Him and His people today?

MAR 7

Bad Decision

MANY YEARS LATER, when Moses had grown up, he went out to visit his own people, the Hebrews, and he saw how hard they were forced to work. During his visit, he saw an Egyptian beating one of his fellow Hebrews. After looking in all directions to make sure no one was watching, Moses killed the Egyptian and hid the body in the sand. The next day, when Moses went out to visit his people again, he saw two Hebrew men fighting. "Why are you beating up your friend?" Moses said to the one who had started the fight. The man replied, "Who appointed you to be our prince and judge? Are you going to kill me as you killed that Egyptian yesterday?" Then Moses was afraid, thinking, "Everyone knows what I did." And sure enough, Pharaoh heard what had happened, and he tried to kill Moses. But Moses fled from Pharaoh and went to live in the land of Midian. When Moses arrived in Midian, he sat down beside a well. **EXODUS 2:11-15, NLT.**

When I was 14, I was in a Fred Meyer department store and in the area that displayed all the vinyl music albums. (For those of you under 50 years old, a vinyl album was how we used to listen to music—just after we invented electricity.)

I had no money, but I really wanted two of the albums that were for sale. So in a moment of sheer stupidity I found an empty Fred Meyer bag, slid the albums into it, and walked out of the store.

I had just hit the sidewalk outside when I felt a large hand on my shoulder. It was the store manager. I ended up in the manager's office being scolded and ordered not to come into that particular store for at least a year. They didn't call the police, for which I'm still thankful.

It turns out that while I was being sneaky, three young women in the store observed me stealing the records. They told the manager, and the rest was history.

Moses let his temper get away from him. He had the chance to be a Joseph. He had the chance to live a righteous life no matter what the situation. Instead, he chose to take matters into his own hands and exact revenge. To react violently out of anger is never God's way.

The decision to act with violence sent Moses on a trip that God would use to train him in tactics that he hadn't learned back in Pharaoh's palace.

Make your decision today to live a humble life based on the values of Christ.

Desperate Slaves

DURING THAT LONG PERIOD, the king of Egypt died. The Israelites groaned in their slavery and cried out, and their cry for help because of their slavery went up to God. God heard their groaning and he remembered his covenant with Abraham, with Isaac and with Jacob. So God looked on the Israelites and was concerned about them. **EXODUS 2:23-25.**

I was longing for help. I wasn't even sure what kind; I just knew that my life wasn't turning out the way I'd thought it would. I was a slave to a bad relationship, a slave to some bad habits, and a slave to a job I didn't enjoy.

I didn't really pray about it. I didn't even complain out loud about the haunting feeling that my life was much less than it should be. I was 21 years old, living with a girl I didn't love and having no spiritual sense about me. I was a slave, the chains of bad decisions holding me down.

The children of Israel were steeped in slavery. They had become mentally and spiritually deprived. To make matters worse, many of them didn't even know how bad their condition was.

The one thing they did know was that they didn't like being slaves.

The Bible says that they cried out about their condition. Notice that it doesn't say that they cried out to God. It says that their cries for help "went up to God." In other words, they probably weren't even crying out to Him. They were probably just complaining a lot—something that the children of Israel got really good at in the wilderness. Yet God responded to their need.

This is all reminiscent of the New Testament text that tells us that "while we were still sinners, Christ died for us" (Romans 5:8).

God's grace is a constant force in this world. He doesn't extend it just to His friends. He extends it to all. Always. Even when we don't know we need it.

I'm so glad that God sent an irritating little pastor to my door one Sunday morning. That was the beginning of my exodus from sin into the promised land of God's grace.

MAR 9

Are You Listening?

ONE DAY MOSES WAS TENDING the flock of his father-in-law, Jethro,the priest of Midian. He led the flock far into the wilderness and came to Sinai, the mountain of God. There the angel of the Lord appeared to him in a blazing fire from the middle of a bush. Moses stared in amazement. Though the bush was engulfed in flames, it didn't burn up. "This is amazing," Moses said to himself. "Why isn't that bush burning up? I must go see it." When the Lord saw Moses coming to take a closer look, God called to him from the middle of the bush, "Moses! Moses!" "Here I am!" Moses replied. **EXODUS 3:1-4, NLT.**

Once upon a time there was a reporter from New York City who was assigned to write a story about an old Native American chief who lived on a reservation in the central plains of the United States. When the story was finished, the reporter couldn't help wondering what this man of the open prairie would think of New York City. So he asked the chief if he would like to travel there and visit.

It wasn't long before the elderly chief and the reporter were walking down a bustling street in the middle of the city. The reporter tried to catch every glance and facial expression as the old man gazed at the skyscrapers and all the people in the city. At one point the old man stopped and said, "H'mmm. A cricket."

The reporter said, "What? How can you hear a cricket with all this busyness around us?"

The old man walked another few feet, bent down, and picked up a cricket that was near a tree planted in a box on the busy sidewalk. The reporter couldn't believe it. "How did you hear that?"

The chief pulled a handful of change out of his pocket and threw it on the ground. Immediately 50 people stopped and looked to see where the money was. "It all depends on what you are listening for," he said.

Moses had been in the wilderness and had regained his spiritual perspective. And when God showed up, Moses turned and experienced it.

Do you give yourself the time and the opportunity to watch and listen for God in your life? Do you give yourself time to be quiet?

Ask God for the gift of noticing Him today.

Who, Me?

"AND NOW THE CRY of the Israelites has reached me, and I have seen the way the Egyptians are oppressing them. So now, go. I am sending you to Pharaoh to bring my people the Israelites out of Egypt." But Moses said to God, "Who am I that I should go to Pharaoh and bring the Israelites out of Egypt?" **EXODUS 3:9-11.**

I've never felt worthy of the profession that I'm in. To stand up and deliver weekly messages about the most powerful Being in the universe to a congregation of people who want to know more about Him is humbling.

I think one of the reasons I feel unworthy is that I haven't always made the right decisions in life. Folks who knew me as a young man in academy and my early college years know that I didn't choose behaviors that would make God smile.

These feelings of inadequacy were heightened one day when I was speaking at a camp meeting. It had been a good week. I felt that God was moving in the messages He had given me to speak. I felt that I was doing what I was called to do, until . . .

A person attending the camp meeting, whom I recognized from my teen years, approached me after a sermon and said (with a somber expression), "I knew you in high school. I don't think it's right that you are a minister now."

I didn't know what to say. This person was right. I was not voted "most likely to become a preacher" in academy. I'm actually not quite sure how I ended up being a pastor. It just kind of happened.

When I shared this conversation with my wife on the phone that night, she reassured me that God, not a human being, calls people into the ministry.

Moses felt pretty inadequate for the job God was calling him to do. After all, he was a murderer on the lam. He was no longer a prince in Pharaoh's house. He was a lowly shepherd. What qualified him to lead God's children out of Egypt?

The answer to that question is: God qualified him.

Have you ever considered yourself "less than"? Have you ever turned down an opportunity because you didn't feel worthy? Well, join the club. And then realize that your calling is not from people but from God. Fear not—God is calling *you*!

MAR 11

The God Who Has No Name

MOSES SAID TO GOD, "Suppose I go to the Israelites and say to them, 'The God of your fathers has sent me to you,' and they ask me, 'What is his name?' Then what shall I tell them?" God said to Moses, "I AM WHO I AM. This is what you are to say to the Israelites: 'I AM has sent me to you.'" **EXODUS 3:13, 14.**

My mom wanted to name me David Timothy Witas. My dad was shooting for Oscar David Witas. They settled for Mark Andrew Witas. I'm glad my dad didn't win. In my time I would have been followed around in school with kids singing the Oscar Mayer Weiner song all the time.

It was Israel's tradition that a person's name would somehow describe their character. The names Jacob, Israel, Moses, Joshua, and so on all have significant meanings attached to them.

This becomes a dilemma for Moses, because what are you supposed to name God? All the gods in Egypt have names. What about this really powerful God who shows up in a burning bush? What is Moses supposed to call Him?

The ancient Hebrew name of God is what we would write as *Yahweh*. We pronounce this word out loud, but Jews never do. They have avoided saying this name for so long—hundreds of years—that no one today knows what the actual pronunciation is! One legend says that this is because the word *Yahweh* was meant to be breathed, not spoken. Thus every time a person breathes in and out, they breathe the sacred name of God. Too sacred to say, God's name must only be breathed.

Moses wants to place a label on God. He wants to name Him. And God's response? I AM.

In other words: "You can't put Me in a box. You can't name Me! Don't even try! I'm not like the gods you learned to bow down to in Egypt. I have no limitations. I simply AM. I exist. That's all you need to know."

One of the bad habits that believers fall into is to somehow create God in their own image. We gather together all of the best qualities in us and then crown them God. But God is bigger than our imaginations. He just IS!

I Need a Sign

BUT MOSES PROTESTED AGAIN, "What if they won't believe me or listen to me? What if they say, 'The Lord never appeared to you'?" Then the Lord asked him, "What is that in your hand?" "A shepherd's staff," Moses replied. "Throw it down on the ground," the Lord told him. So Moses threw down the staff, and it turned into a snake! Moses jumped back. Then the Lord told him, "Reach out and grab its tail." So Moses reached out and grabbed it, and it turned back into a shepherd's staff in his hand. "Perform this sign," the Lord told him. "Then they will believe that the Lord, the God of their ancestors—the God of Abraham, the God of Isaac, and the God of Jacob—really has appeared to you." **EXODUS 4:1-5, NLT.**

I've never been an asker of signs. I just figure that if I take a job or make a big decision that I've prayed about, God will go along with me and bless me. If He didn't want me to go, He wouldn't have opened the door for me in the first place.

I have a pastor friend who likes to have a sign before he makes a big decision. His wife likes to ask for signs from God too. One of the times that this philosophy worked out in a really interesting way was the time they received a call to pastor in another district. They both asked God for a sign to help them know whether this was His will.

At the time they were living in the house of a church member who had moved out of town for work. The church member was kind enough to let the pastor and his wife live in the house rent-free. The pastor decided to call his landlord (if you could call a person who doesn't charge you rent a landlord) and tell him he was pondering a move.

The landlord replied, "Huh. That's a coincidence. My former employer just called me and offered me a job with a higher salary and more benefits than I'm getting here. I'm coming back to town, and I didn't know how I was going to call and tell you that you had to move out of my house!" *There's your sign.*

Moses seemed to need some convincing. God turned a staff into a snake and a healthy hand into a leprous one, and Moses was convinced.

I think God likes it better when His kids just believe and act on what He tells them rather than demanding a sign. But sometimes He provides one for those of us who need a little boost to our faith.

MAR 13

Misplaced Blame

THE ISRAELITE OVERSEERS REALIZED they were in trouble when they were told, "You are not to reduce the number of bricks required of you for each day." When they left Pharaoh, they found Moses and Aaron waiting to meet them, and they said, "May the Lord look on you and judge you! You have made us obnoxious to Pharaoh and his officials and have put a sword in their hand to kill us." **EXODUS 5:19-21.**

My stepdad would have been an interesting case study for anybody doing research on how a brain works.

While in prison he picked up several bad habits that followed him for the rest of his life. One of those habits was smoking cigarettes. He smoked so much that my mom's relatives would wrap cartons of cigarettes and give them to him for Christmas.

When the doctors told my stepdad that he had throat cancer, he was actually surprised! He'd never had a steady job, so he and my mom were poor. His options were limited, so he accepted the help of a teaching university in Seattle and had surgery and radiation to clear up his cancer. Despite the doctor's strong suggestion that he quit smoking, he didn't.

After the radiation treatments had finished and the cancer was all gone, we were sitting at dinner one evening when my stepdad announced, "I'm going to sue the doctors who worked on me. Those radiation treatments made it so I can't taste food anymore!" Then he got up and went outside for a smoke.

Misplaced blame. Sometimes when we're upset, we tend to blame the wrong people.

When Pharaoh made life even more difficult for Israel, they blamed Moses and Aaron. It reminds me of the times I've heard people say, "Why is God doing this to me?"

Misplaced blame happens when we point the finger at God for the things Satan does to us or the problems caused by living in a world of sin. Remember, God is good. All the time. He's not the cause of our trouble. He's the solution to our trouble. Blaming God for our problems is like blaming the teacher when we don't turn our homework in. It makes no sense.

Hope for the Future

"THEREFORE, SAY TO THE ISRAELITES: 'I am the Lord, and I will bring you out from under the yoke of the Egyptians. I will free you from being slaves to them, and I will redeem you with an outstretched arm and with mighty acts of judgment. I will take you as my own people, and I will be your God. Then you will know that I am the Lord your God, who brought you out from under the yoke of the Egyptians. And I will bring you to the land I swore with uplifted hand to give to Abraham, to Isaac and to Jacob. I will give it to you as a possession. I am the Lord.'" Moses reported this to the Israelites, but they did not listen to him because of their discouragement and harsh labor. **EXODUS 6:6-9.**

It's really hard to see past a bad situation. I can't tell you how many times I've sat with people who have been the victims of broken relationships as they sob out their true feelings: "I will never be able to love or trust anybody ever again!" The future looks bleak when your hopes have been shattered.

When Moses and Aaron came to town, the Israelites caught a glimpse of possible deliverance from their bondage. Moses came in speaking big words about how the Lord was going to bring them out of Egypt. Their hopes were high. And then those who lorded it over them crushed their hopes.

All they could see was that they had to find their own straw to make an impossible number of bricks. All they could feel was the whip of the taskmaster. All this talk of deliverance sounded like empty promises.

Throughout my life I've heard people say that Jesus is going to come and deliver His people. I've heard people say, "The Promised Land is right around the corner!"

When I look around me and measure things from my own experience, I can get discouraged. Is Jesus ever going to come?

I would like to encourage you today. Don't lose hope. Your God will deliver you just as surely as He delivered the Israelites from their bondage. Stay faithful and place your hope in the promise of His soon return.

MAR 15

You Can't Prove It!

THEN THE LORD SAID TO MOSES, "Pay close attention to this. I will make you seem like God to Pharaoh, and your brother, Aaron, will be your prophet. Tell Aaron everything I command you, and Aaron must command Pharaoh to let the people of Israel leave his country. But I will make Pharaoh's heart stubborn so I can multiply my miraculous signs and wonders in the land of Egypt. Even then Pharaoh will refuse to listen to you. So I will bring down my fist on Egypt. Then I will rescue my forces—my people, the Israelites—from the land of Egypt with great acts of judgment. When I raise my powerful hand and bring out the Israelites, the Egyptians will know that I am the Lord." **EXODUS 7:1-5, NLT.**

One of the most frustrating character traits of human beings is our ability to dig in our heels and stubbornly resist in the face of overwhelming evidence and unyielding pressure.

I was working at a school when some students were brought into a discipline committee for drinking alcohol on a school trip. Four people had been involved in the incident. The first three came in and gave an honest review of their involvement. The fourth person, whom the other three had all indicted in their confessions, denied any involvement.

The three confessors were suspended from school, while the fourth person just got more and more stubborn in his denial. The committee didn't feel that they could suspend him without concrete evidence, so while the other three went home, this young man stayed on campus. Everybody knew he was guilty, but he maintained his innocence.

Then a videotape of the trip turned up. On this tape was certain evidence that this young man was drinking. When he was shown the tape, he said, "You can't prove that it was alcohol in that bottle!"

I believe that God wanted Pharaoh to repent. When the Bible says that God hardened Pharaoh's heart, we might more accurately understand it to mean that when God tried to reach Pharaoh's heart, it got harder. That makes sense because the Bible says that God does not lead people into sin; the devil does.

Pray that your heart will be pliable today. And as we continue through the story of Moses and Pharaoh, remember that God's desire is that all will come to Him and experience His love and grace.

Gods Versus God

NOW THE LORD HAD SAID TO MOSES, "I will bring one more plague on Pharaoh and on Egypt. After that, he will let you go from here, and when he does, he will drive you out completely." **EXODUS 11:1.**

Hapi, Heqet, Thoth, Apis, Imhotep, Seth, Nut, Kheper, and Ra—these are the names of some of the Egyptian gods that the plagues of Egypt attacked.

Water turning to blood; infestations of frogs, gnats, and flies; dying livestock; and boils, hail, locusts, and darkness were all messages to the Egyptian people that their gods of the earth and sky were no match for the power and influence of the living God, Yahweh.

Each of these plagues also attacked the Egyptians' livelihood. Their whole economy depended on the things that were being ruined by these disasters. If you want to get people's attention, hit them in the pocketbook!

Plague by plague, the Egyptians' faith in their own gods eroded to the point that, Exodus 11:3 tells us, "the Lord made the Egyptians favorably disposed toward the people, and Moses himself was highly regarded in Egypt by Pharaoh's officials and by the people."

The people were convinced. Many of them would even leave Egypt with the Israelites. But there was one person who wasn't going to let go of his power. There was one person who would not give in. Pharaoh's heart was as hard as stone. Against the advice of his presidential cabinet, Pharaoh refused to let God's people go.

The tenth and final plague would be the plague that broke Pharaoh's will, at least temporarily: the death of the firstborn sons of Egypt.

What a price to pay for stubborn pride. Each time God withdrew His blessings and protection from Egypt, disaster struck. And now, on this last dark night, God would withdraw His blessings and protection from Egypt one last time. This is one of the saddest stories in the Bible. It reminds me of how folks at the end of time will choose to hold on to their sins rather than hold on to the love of God. Their sins will destroy them as surely as Egypt suffered because of its pride.

God desires humility in His followers, not pride. Let's strive for a soft, teachable heart and spirit.

MAR 17

Scary Night

THEY ARE TO TAKE SOME of the blood and smear it on the sides and top of the doorframes of the houses where they eat the animal. That same night they must roast the meat over a fire and eat it along with bitter salad greens and bread made without yeast. Do not eat any of the meat raw or boiled in water. The whole animal—including the head, legs, and internal organs—must be roasted over a fire. Do not leave any of it until the next morning. Burn whatever is not eaten before morning. "These are your instructions for eating this meal: Be fully dressed, wear your sandals, and carry your walking stick in your hand. Eat the meal with urgency, for this is the Lord's Passover. **EXODUS 12:7-11, NLT.**

When I was a kid, my friends and I thought we were clever. We weren't; we just thought we were. We'd get a kick out of pulling pranks on unsuspecting people as they drove down Winesap Road. Often we'd hide in the bushes on the side of the road, hurl uprooted ferns or weeds at passing cars, and then run.

One night we were hiding on the side of the road with some eggs that Kenny had stolen out of his mom's refrigerator. The first two cars gave us no reaction. The third car screeched to a stop, and four large adult males jumped out and started chasing us. They were larger and faster than we had anticipated, so instead of being able to run out of the field into Kenny's neighborhood, we had to hide in the weeds.

I hunkered down in the weeds as these angry men yelled and thrashed around, hoping they could get their hands on us to wring our necks. One of them almost stepped on me as I sat there and held my breath. I was never found, they left, and I had survived another episode with my idiot friends.

That night I was afraid. I wonder what thoughts went through the brains of God's people on Passover night. Were they afraid? Were they confident that the blood of the lamb on their doorframe would shield them from death?

I know a lot of people who are afraid of the Second Coming. They don't want it to take place because they are afraid of what might happen to them when Jesus comes back.

Remember, Jesus is our Passover lamb. When we have His blood painted on the door of our hearts, we have passed over from death to life. When Jesus is in our lives, there is no reason to doubt His power to save us from death.

Freedom Thief

ALL THE ISRAELITES DID JUST what the Lord had commanded Moses and Aaron. And on that very day the Lord brought the Israelites out of Egypt by their divisions. **EXODUS 12:50, 51.**

What a day it must have been for Israel to be free at last! They had been without a country of their own for 400 years. There were people in that exodus group who had known nothing but slavery. Can you imagine what it would have been like to gather all your earthly belongings and join the big procession as the Israelites began to march out of Egypt toward the Promised Land?

Freedom. It's a word that packs a lot of power and a lot of promise. Freedom. I'm sure whatever country you are currently living in—if it is free—has paid for its freedom in blood. We don't take kindly to people or things that rob us of our freedom.

Next to murder, kidnapping carries some of the stiffest penalties a person can face for a crime. Stealing someone's freedom is serious business in North America.

I remember what I felt like when my parents would take my freedoms away because of something I had done wrong. I didn't like it. I can't tell you how many times I have been "grounded for life"! I'm 50 years old now. I can't help wondering if I'm still grounded . . . I'll call my dad and ask him.

We don't like it when people take our freedom, yet many willingly hand it over to the devil every day. Sin is the great freedom thief. It robs us of everything good that we can become. It lures us in with promises of fun and excitement, only to leave us with the handcuffs of bad habits and unshakable regret.

I've talked with too many young people who wanted to quit a smoking habit but couldn't. They were in chains, and they knew it. This can be said for all kinds of habits that we develop because of the allure of sin.

Jesus is the great freedom provider. He is able to break the chains of slavery that clasp around us. When we willingly obey His calling in our lives, He provides a way for us to be free indeed! And that, my friend, is a sure ticket to the Promised Land!

MAR 19

The Scenic Route

WHEN PHARAOH LET THE PEOPLE GO, God did not lead them on the road through the Philistine country, though that was shorter. For God said, "If they face war, they might change their minds and return to Egypt." So God led the people around by the desert road toward the Red Sea. The Israelites went up out of Egypt ready for battle. **EXODUS 13:17, 18.**

My best buddy, Alex Bryan, and I were driving across the country from Michigan to Seattle. This was before the days of GPS devices and cell phones with the nice woman inside who tells you when to take a left and when to take a right.

We were all packed for the journey and had a bunch of music lined up to listen to. We had also done our research and found all the sports stations of the major cities we were going to pass through so we could keep up with the news from our favorite teams.

As we entered Illinois, we began to get into Chicago traffic. We were fine. In fact, we made a covenant not to get all stressed out about the traffic, because we were bound to have a good time. So we turned up the music and started to talk about the problems of the world and how if we were president, we'd solve them all.

Even though we were having a great time traveling and talking together, it seemed as if we had been in the car for a really long time. Then we saw it: a sign that said, "Next Exit Wisconsin". *Wisconsin!* We weren't supposed to go through Wisconsin! One of us (I'm very sure it was Alex) didn't see the signs for the highway we were supposed to stay on. We ended up taking the scenic route to Seattle.

Sometimes God takes us to places we would never have chosen had we been in charge. I love that about God. Often we find ourselves in a place that requires us to look up and say, "I don't know why I'm here, but I am. Lord, I will trust Your lead in my life. Please make this journey a worthwhile one."

I don't know where He's led you today, but trust Him to keep leading. And while you're on the journey, don't forget to enjoy it! After all, you get to make it only once!

MAR 20

The Great Wall of Fish

THEN MOSES STRETCHED OUT his hand over the sea, and all that night the Lord drove the sea back with a strong east wind and turned it into dry land. The waters were divided, and the Israelites went through the sea on dry ground, with a wall of water on their right and on their left. **EXODUS 14:21, 22.**

One of my favorite places in the whole world is the basement of Ripley's Aquarium of the Smokies in Gatlinburg, Tennessee. I could sit there for hours in front of the huge window that lets me look into a tank filled with the creatures that God created to thrive in the great seas of the world. Their beauty is beyond compare. The patterns they move in as they make their rounds in the huge display astound me. The show I see in the darkness of that one area in the aquarium is second to none.

This fascinating place makes me wonder what the view was like for God's people as they filed through the middle of the Red Sea. I can't imagine how exciting it would have been to look into what was possibly the world's first aquarium. Did they see a whale? Did they find Nemo? (Maybe they didn't even know he was missing!)

Kidding aside, I wonder if in the midst of one of God's mightiest miracles the children of Israel were able to take a deep breath and take in the majesty. Or did they think they had to hurry through the Red Sea before Pharaoh could figure out a way to get around God and get them?

One of the most wonderful things about our God is His attention to detail. Had I been there, I would have had to sit on a slimy rock in the middle of the Red Sea and just watch, the way I end up doing in Gatlinburg. I would have wanted to take in the wonder of God's creative power. Maybe I would stand up, approach the wall of water, and stick my hand into it to see if I could pet a curious dolphin.

If you are experiencing the blessings and deliverance of God in your life today, take time to slow down and look around. Look at the details that God has so artfully painted onto the canvas of your life. Thank Him for His creative beauty and imagination. Take time right now to notice the details of God in your life and share them with a friend.

MAR 21

Wrong Way on a One-Way Street

THE EGYPTIANS PURSUED THEM, and all Pharaoh's horses and chariots and horsemen followed them into the sea. During the last watch of the night the Lord looked down from the pillar of fire and cloud at the Egyptian army and threw it into confusion. He jammed the wheels of their chariots so that they had difficulty driving. And the Egyptians said, "Let's get away from the Israelites! The Lord is fighting for them against Egypt." **EXODUS 14:23-25.**

When I was 16 years old, I had about as much sense as a bag of hammers. Can you imagine how surprised I was that the government actually let me have a driver's license? By the time I was 17 years old, I had acquired 11 tickets. Most of those tickets were for speeding. However, I was soon to discover that the Department of Licensing has their limits on these things.

The final straw came shortly after I turned 17. I owned a 1968 Pontiac GTO (a dangerous weapon in the hands of an idiot!) that just seemed to attract the attention of local law enforcement. My friends and I were cruising up and down a strip in Everett, Washington, called Colby Avenue. It was a weekend cruising spot for teenagers at the time. The music was loud, another car was revving its engine, and I was off! I made a quick turn in the confusion of the moment and found myself going the wrong way on a one-way street. The first vehicle I met up with was—you guessed it—a police car. It turns out that it's illegal to drive the wrong way down a one-way street. I lost my license for a year. I've been a pretty responsible driver since then.

It amazes me that Pharaoh was so filled with hate that he pursued the Israelites down what turned out to be a one-way street. After the plagues, after the pillar of fire, his hatred and pride led him and his armies into a very bad place. Our passions and emotions can do that to us. That's why it's so important for us to live by our values and not by our emotions. We can make horrible decisions in the heat of the moment. It's so much wiser to step back from the heat, collect ourselves emotionally, and pray. Ask God to lead.

Acting out of principle and our God-given value system will never lead us down a one-way street to destruction.

Partying for the Lord

THEN MOSES AND THE ISRAELITES sang this song to the Lord: "I will sing to the Lord, for he is highly exalted. Both horse and driver he has hurled into the sea." **EXODUS 15:1.**

Booooorrrrriiiiiinnnnnggggg! There is nothing more disconcerting to me than a boring church service. Don't get me wrong. I love church. I'm a church guy! I can sit through almost anything and find a tremendous blessing from the Lord in it. But every once in a while I visit a church that confirms my belief in our doctrine of the state of the dead.

For some reason we have confused the word *reverence* with the word *quiet*. Reverence actually has its roots in the word *revere*. To revere someone is to appreciate and laud them. I'm not sure how revered God can feel if all He gets from a worship service is half-dead saints whispering "amen" when the pastor says, "And in closing . . ."

In Luke 15 there are three stories that illustrate God's victory over Satan in people's lives. All three times when the lost is found, there is rejoicing, feasting, and celebration!

In Revelation 4 the throne room of heaven is filled with activity that celebrates the holiness of God. Loud thunder, singing, and praise fill His presence.

Sometimes we need to break out of our silence and SHOUT to the Lord!

In today's scripture God has finished doing a mighty thing. He's parted the Red Sea with a "blast" from His "nostrils." (I'm not sure that God actually has nostrils, but the anthropomorphism is cool . . . Google that word if you don't know what I mean.) He's delivered His people from the enemy. And they celebrate. They sing and dance and play instruments to honor the Lord. When was the last time any of us appreciated God like that?

I'm not advocating chaos here. I'm just saying that God deserves better than silence from us. He is worthy of more than just an occasional "amen."

Speak to your youth leader and plan a party to honor God. Make it lively and wonderful, every part of it directed at our amazing God to celebrate His deliverance in our lives.

MAR 23

The World's Most Annoying Noise

WHEN THEY CAME TO MARAH, they could not drink its water because it was bitter. (That is why the place is called Marah.) So the people grumbled against Moses, saying, "What are we to drink?" **EXODUS 15:23, 24.**

In the movie *Dumb and Dumber* one of the characters, while riding in a truck with his friends, asks, "Wanna hear the most annoying noise in the whole world?" He proceeds to scream this horribly loud and obnoxious sound that drives the fellow sitting in the middle seat crazy. It was a really annoying sound, but not as annoying as the sound in our verses today.

I can't think of a sound that is more irritating than whining. Conversely, I can't think of a more beautiful sound than thanksgiving, praise, and adoration.

I've led out in dozens of overseas mission trips. Before each trip I meet with the group of people who intend to go and lay out my rules for the trip. At the very top of the sheet of rules it reads, "Thou shalt not be a whiner."

Nothing can ruin a perfectly good trip like a couple of whiners who can't be pleased. It's worse than fingernails running down a chalkboard. (For those of you who are 21 and younger, a chalkboard is what classrooms used to have on the walls instead of the whiteboards and SMART Boards you have now. I miss chalkboards.)

Israel had just witnessed the most miraculous rescue event in history. How magnificent it must have been to walk through the Red Sea on dry ground. This was a huge piece of evidence that God had good things in store for His people. He was going to take care of them, right? Still they whined.

It must have grieved the heart of God to hear this from the people He had just saved. I wonder if He felt like saying, "Hey, let's go back into the Red Sea!" (Everyone should be glad that I'm not God.)

Instead, He patiently solved the problem, reminding them through Moses that if they didn't rebel, if they just did what He led them to do, He would continue to be the God of blessings in their lives. I'm glad God is God even when I'm a whiner. Let's be the kind of people who recognize God's blessings in all circumstances.

Honey-Nut Potato Chips

THE ISRAELITES ATE MANNA FORTY YEARS, until they came to a land that was settled; they ate manna until they reached the border of Canaan. **EXODUS 16:35.**

One of the basic attributes of God that Scripture reveals to us is that He is our provider. That's why we thank God for our food before we eat it, or at least we should. He provides.

The Israelites were just getting settled into the journey in the wilderness when they noticed that food was going to be an issue. As usual, they complained as only they could, and once again God came through with an amazing blessing for their lives. Each morning He gave them honey-nut potato chips to eat. I call this miracle food honey-nut potato chips; they called it manna.

God heard their cry and responded. He gave them instructions on how much manna to collect each day. When the people did as they were instructed, everything went swell. When they didn't . . . maggots.

Israel had long since forgotten about the seventh-day Sabbath established at Creation, so God reminded them. On Fridays they were supposed to collect twice as much manna as on the other days. Only this time when they kept it overnight, the manna wouldn't be maggot-filled. On Sabbath it would taste as yummy as before.

Of course, there were people who decided to ignore God's invitation to take a Sabbath off. They wandered around looking for manna and found none on the seventh day. I know people who still do this. They ignore the rest God freely offers them so they can pursue their own interests. Seriously, people, when was the last time your boss had to tell you twice to take a day off? Take the Sabbath and chill!

God provided Israel with honey-flavored bread that would sustain them. God has provided us with His Son, the Bread of Life.

Each day we can still gather the Bread of Life and "taste and see that the Lord is good" (Psalm. 34:8). There is just enough of the Bread of Life for all God's people who will take and eat. Thank You, Jesus, for being our nourishment in a world starving for true bread.

MAR 25

My Thirsty History

I WILL STAND THERE BEFORE YOU by the rock at Horeb. Strike the rock, and water will come out of it for the people to drink. **EXODUS 17:6.**

My thirst has evolved since I was a little tyke. When I was in my teens, there was nothing I liked better than an ice-cold glass of 2 percent milk. My mom threatened to buy a cow because I went through so much milk as a youngster.

Then I graduated from milk to orange juice. If I had played a couple hours of basketball with friends, there was nothing like a cold glass of orange juice to quench my thirst.

And now? I haven't drunk milk in 10 years, and I'm not sure I would like the taste of it anymore. Lately I've found that nothing can soothe my parched throat and lips like a lukewarm glass of water. I know that sounds horrible to most people, but room-temperature water just does it for me now!

Israel was wandering in the wilderness in temperatures that I'm sure made them very thirsty. So they complained . . . again . . . as they always did . . . because they were a stiff-necked people.

I love God's solution for this one. He told Moses to go up to a rock and hit it, and water would come out. I'll bet Moses hit the rock really hard. When he did, water came out, and the Israelites' thirst was quenched.

Jesus tells us that if we want it, He will give us living water, and we will never thirst again. I like the thought of that: living water from the Rock of our salvation.

When we spend time with Jesus on a daily basis, we get bread from the Bread of Life and living water from the Rock of our salvation. He supplies our needs.

All of this points forward to a day when we will sit at the banquet table together in heaven, reunited with our God and our human friends. I hope we will be able to drink the water that flows from the throne of God. I'm sure this water is the best, even better than the water that came out of that rock in the desert.

MAR 26

God's House
Is a House of Salvation

THEN HAVE THEM MAKE a sanctuary for me, and I will dwell among them. Make this tabernacle and all its furnishings exactly like the pattern I will show you. **EXODUS 25:8, 9.**

The earthly sanctuary was an amazing place. It didn't just look cool; it *was* cool. Why? Because it was a place where faith in God's mercy and grace took center stage.

If a person needed forgiveness from sin, they would take a spotless lamb from their herd or purchase one from someone else and approach the entrance to the sanctuary. They would meet up with a priest there.

The innocent lamb would then be placed on its side and tied to some stakes in the ground. When the lamb was secured, the sinner would place their hands on the head of the lamb and confess their sins. As they did this, their sins would symbolically be transferred to the lamb. Symbolically that lamb would now be guilty for that sinner's sins. The lamb's throat would be cut. The sinner would walk away forgiven.

Doesn't that sound horrible? My wife would have been a terrible Israelite. She likes animals more than she likes most people! Killing an animal would be almost unthinkable for her.

As awful as the sacrificial system sounds, it was a reminder that sin kills. Sin is the opposite of life; it is death. And that little innocent lamb, that baby sheep, reminds us of Jesus.

It was the sin of the world—more specifically, my sin—that killed Jesus, the Lamb of God, on the cross. He took the shame, the guilt, and the ultimate penalty for my sin so that I wouldn't have to. Forgiveness has been extended, and our salvation has been secured.

Everything in the earthly sanctuary pointed to Jesus. Every article of furniture, every ritual, every little lamb. Jesus was the fulfillment of it all. And now He stands in heaven as our high priest, forgiving, purifying, and preparing for the day that God will tabernacle with His people once again. I'm looking forward to that day, aren't you?

MAR 27

The Least You Can Do

WHEN THE LORD FINISHED SPEAKING to Moses on Mount Sinai, he gave him the two tablets of the covenant law, the tablets of stone inscribed by the finger of God. **EXODUS 31:18.**

The Ten Commandments are probably the most recognized set of laws on the planet. We have replicas of them in our courthouses, we hear them mentioned in church on the weekends, and they just make sense. After all, would you want to live next to somebody who did the exact opposite of the Ten Commandments? I wouldn't.

The Seventh-day Adventist Church lifts up the Ten Commandments in the world and preaches that all believers should observe all 10—and I agree. But I want you to notice something about the Ten Commandments that many people overlook: the Ten Commandments describe the very least we can do for God and for others. Have you ever noticed that?

The least I can do for you is not murder you. The least I can do for you is not steal your possessions. The least I can do for you is not steal your wife/husband.

In regard to God, the least you can do for Him is to remember Him one day per week. The least you can do for Him is not use His name inappropriately. The least you can do for God is to avoid making a big ceramic animal and bowing down to it.

When you look at it that way, the Ten Commandments aren't really very hard to keep. I mean, do you really want to murder somebody today? Do you really want to bow down to a stuffed animal and call it God? Me neither.

Jesus challenges us to do more than the minimum for God and for the people around us. He challenges us to have an everyday, living faith that does more than just avoid sin; He challenges us to be proactive in our faith and do good.

The Ten Commandments are just the starting point for those who are babies in the faith. Jesus challenges us to grow from babies into mature believers who will change the world by being the hands and feet of Christ.

Not-So-Quiet Riot

SO ALL THE PEOPLE TOOK off their earrings and brought them to Aaron. He took what they handed him and made it into an idol cast in the shape of a calf, fashioning it with a tool. Then they said, "These are your gods, Israel, who brought you up out of Egypt." **EXODUS 32:3, 4.**

There is an old expression that rings true in many cases: "When the cat's away, the rats will play."

Israel had seen the mighty hand of God in Egypt. They had walked on dry land through the middle of the Red Sea. They had seen the miracle in Marah of the bitter water turned sweet. They had drunk water that had come out of a rock. So what did they do when Moses went up the mountain to receive their moral and civil laws? They made a baby cow out of gold and bowed down to it.

Mind you, they had already received the verbal law and had heard the Ten Commandments. So they knew that what they were about to do was something that God was very opposed to. Why did they do it? And why did Aaron allow them to do it?

I love Aaron's response when Moses came down and asked what was going on. "Well, they gave me all their gold; I put it in the oven; and *bam!* This golden calf jumped out!" Really? I used that kind of logic on my mom when I was 4. Aaron was a grown man! Is that the best he could come up with?

It baffles me to think of how quickly we can lose sight of the Lord. Even in times of blessings we are quick to look to created things to comfort us. We fall into the trap of letting the television or video games entertain our troubles away. Or we become dependent on something even more harmful. Like a dog coming back to its vomit, we end up trusting in ungodly things instead of trusting in the One who delivered us from all that garbage in the first place.

I love the example Jesus set for us. In everything He did He leaned heavily on the Father and put His hope and trust in Him. Never did He trust in the created. Always He trusted in the Creator.

MAR 29

At One With God

ON THIS DAY ATONEMENT WILL be made for you, to cleanse you. Then, before the Lord, you will be clean from all your sins. **LEVITICUS 16:30.**

All year long people would approach the sanctuary and receive forgiveness for their sins. All year long the priest would take the blood from those innocent lambs and sprinkle it on different articles of furniture. So symbolically the forgiven sins would leave the lamb and enter the holy place of the sanctuary. There they would stay throughout the year, until . . .

Once a year there was a special celebration called the Day of Atonement. This day gives us a glimpse of how things will be played out at the end of time. On this day (among other things) two goats were brought into the sanctuary, one called the Lord's goat and one called the scapegoat. The Lord's goat was sacrificed as a sin offering. The scapegoat had a very different fate.

The high priest would place his hands on the scapegoat and confess all the sins that all of God's people had committed all year long. Remember how the sinner's sins were transferred onto the innocent lamb? Well, now all of those sins that had come into the sanctuary all year were symbolically transferred onto the head of the scapegoat. Then the scapegoat was led out into the wilderness to be left all by itself until it died there.

The Day of Atonement was always good news for God's people. They looked forward to that day like no other holiday, because on that day they were pronounced one with God. They knew that God was faithful in His grace and forgiveness. And they knew that ultimately the scapegoat was going to suffer for all of their sins.

The book of Revelation points to a time that God's people will truly be at one with Him—forgiven and clean. It points to a time that the devil will get what he deserves and that we will get what we don't deserve: a place next to our Deliverer forever.

No Prejudice Allowed

MIRIAM AND AARON BEGAN TO talk against Moses because of his Cushite wife, for he had married a Cushite. **NUMBERS 12:1.**

As you may know, Moses married Zipporah, a woman from Midian. He had at least two children by her, and up until this point he apparently hadn't heard a word of complaint from Aaron or Miriam (his brother and sister) about his wife.

So what brought on these complaints? Some people think Aaron and Miriam started to worry that Moses was going to die and leave one of his kids (not full-blooded descendants of Abraham) in charge. Others think Aaron and Miriam didn't like the fact that Moses had married someone of another nationality. Many believe the complaint came because Moses had married a dark-skinned woman. I'm not sure which of these theories is correct, but if Aaron and Miriam were complaining about Zipporah being a Black woman, I love how God chose to handle it.

Here's His response: "The anger of the Lord burned against them, and he left them. When the cloud lifted from above the tent, Miriam's skin was leprous—it became as white as snow" (Numbers 12:9, 10).

I know this isn't supposed to be funny, but I kind of think it is. It's almost as if God says, "You don't like Zipporah's dark skin? Fine; I'll make you as white as you could possibly want to be." In the words of one of the young people in my church, "Oh, snap!"

There is no place for prejudice in the kingdom of God. None. Judging people by the color of their skin, their national heritage, or the straightness or curliness of their hair is the opposite of how God judges a person. The Bible tells us that God looks at the heart, not the skin—and we should too.

Are there prejudices in your life that you need to give to God? Ask Him to make you the kind of person who looks for people's potential rather than putting them in a box based on their outside appearance.

MAR 31

Giants in the Land

BUT THE MEN WHO HAD GONE UP WITH HIM SAID, "We can't attack those people; they are stronger than we are." And they spread among the Israelites a bad report about the land they had explored. They said, "The land we explored devours those living in it. All the people we saw there are of great size. We saw the Nephilim there (the descendants of Anak come from the Nephilim). We seemed like grasshoppers in our own eyes, and we looked the same to them." **NUMBERS 13:31-33.**

One of the saddest things I've ever seen happened just after I had gone skydiving with my youth group and a bunch of their parents. Dozens of us traveled about two hours over the border into British Columbia to go skydiving. We all signed waivers, took four hours of training, paid our (nonrefundable) money, and got suited up for the big jump.

After the jump we were all sitting around on a deck outside the skydiving offices, laughing and telling our stories. On the outskirts of our group were half a dozen people who had no stories. Why? Because they had ended up being too afraid to follow through with the jump.

Israel had wandered in the wilderness for 40 years. Finally they got to the border of the Promised Land. Finally they could see the end of their journey. This was it! They were almost home! But then 10 of the 12 men sent to spy out the land gave their report.

"They're really, really big! And tall! And mean-looking! And some of them don't comb their hair! Be afraid! Be very afraid!" OK, even though I put it in quotes, that's not quite what they said, but they might as well have.

Did they forget who was on their side? Did they forget that when God is with us, no one can stand against us? Were they really going to let fear steal the Promised Land away from them? Yup.

Sometimes our lives can seem as if they are full of big, scary enemies. Sometimes we can be paralyzed by fear when God asks us to step out in faith. But remember, when God is for us, who can be against us? He says, "Do not fear, for I am with you" (Isaiah 41:10).

Snake on a Stick

SO MOSES MADE A BRONZE SERPENT, and put it on a pole; and so it was, if a serpent had bitten anyone, when he looked at the bronze serpent, he lived. **NUMBERS 21:9, NKJV.**

I like snakes. I think they are really fun to look at and play with. Of course, I grew up in the Seattle area, where, in contrast to many other parts of the world, we have no poisonous snakes. We just have garter snakes: black snakes with a couple of yellow stripes down their backs. These snakes eat slugs and mice, not people. Or that's what I thought until one tried to eat me!

I was 14 years old. It was a Sabbath afternoon at Hawthorne Park. I loved Hawthorne Park because it was the best of two worlds. The parking lot was next to huge grassy fields with swings, slides, and monkey bars. At the end of the grass was a forest that had trails leading to a beach on Puget Sound. It was always beautiful there. On this particular day I was running to catch up with some friends who had hit the trail toward the beach, when I saw it—a beautiful garter snake about a foot long slithering across the trail.

I scurried over, picked it up, and started to play with it. I decided that I'd bring it down to the beach to show my friends. I ran down the trail, keeping my eyes on the path lest I trip on a root or step in some mud.

When I got down to the beach, my friend Brett saw that I had a snake in my hand and ran over to see it. He looked down and started laughing. "Hey, that snake is eating you!"

I looked down, and sure enough, the snake had most of my left thumb in his mouth and down his throat, and I didn't even feel it. I yanked my thumb out and let the serpent go.

The Israelites weren't so lucky. They were being bit by venomous snakes. God used an unusual means to cure them of their ailment. He had Moses put a snake on a pole so that if they looked up and gazed at the snake, they would be healed.

That snake on the pole represented Jesus, who took our sin and was hung on a pole so that when we look at Him, we can live. Thank You, Jesus, for healing us.

APR 2

Shrek's Inspiration

THIS TIME WHEN THE DONKEY saw the angel, it lay down under Balaam. In a fit of rage Balaam beat the animal again with his staff. Then the Lord gave the donkey the ability to speak. "What have I done to you that deserves your beating me three times?" it asked Balaam. "You have made me look like a fool!" Balaam shouted. "If I had a sword with me, I would kill you!" "But I am the same donkey you have ridden all your life," the donkey answered. "Have I ever done anything like this before?" "No," Balaam admitted. **NUMBERS 22:27-30, NLT.**

King Balak, son of Zippor (insert junior high joke here) hires a prophet named Balaam to curse Israel. Balaam accepts the job, which turns out to be more difficult than he bargained for.

On the way to do the devil's work, the prophet Balaam has some transportation problems. His donkey keeps running off the road. The donkey has never done this before. Maybe it's getting old. Maybe it's just acting like a donkey! Either way, Balaam starts to beat the poor animal to get it to cooperate.

What Balaam *can't see* is what I'm convinced animals *can see* more than we realize. Balaam's donkey sees an angel barring the way. Each time the donkey sees the angel, it takes a quick evasive action, perhaps almost throwing Balaam off the donkey and onto his backside.

During Balaam's last beating, the donkey has had enough. The Lord opens the donkey's mouth, and it talks to its owner. The thing that amazes me is that Balaam doesn't even blink. He doesn't seem astonished that a donkey is talking! He is so mad that he stands there and argues with his donkey. I find this comical and tragic.

The tragedy here is that when we decide to stand on the side of evil instead of good, we leave behind the better part of our nature and sometimes find ourselves in a senseless, defensive rage that no one can reason with.

I believe that's where the devil is in his frame of mind. Senseless rage. He would love to have you join him. That's why it's so important to flee from evil and cling to good.

Are You Blessed or Cursed?

IF YOU FULLY OBEY THE LORD your God and carefully keep all his commands that I am giving you today, the Lord your God will set you high above all the nations of the world. You will experience all these blessings if you obey the Lord your God: Your towns and your fields will be blessed. Your children and your crops will be blessed. The offspring of your herds and flocks will be blessed. Your fruit baskets and breadboards will be blessed. Wherever you go and whatever you do, you will be blessed. **DEUTERONOMY 28:1-6, NLT.**

I hope I'm not going out on too much of a theological limb here to say that both the blessings and the curses pronounced in these verses are not as much acts of God—positive or negative—as they are natural consequences of the decisions that the people of earth make every day for good or for bad.

For instance, if I choose to lie around in a sedentary life and eat Oreo cookies and chips all day, I will get fat and out of shape. God didn't curse me to be fat. I became fat because I didn't pay attention to the food He provided me instead of the products supplied by the good people at Nabisco and Frito-Lay.

Through Moses, God gave the children of Israel a huge code of conduct that told them how to treat one another and how to treat God. If they ignored that code of conduct and lived without it or the law of God, the natural consequence would be disaster. If they complied with the law God gave them, blessings would be a natural occurrence; they would be a naturally healthy, wealthy, and happy people.

Does that mean that rebellious people won't experience happiness or that righteous people won't experience pain in life? No. It does mean that people who obey God will have a better quality of life than they would have if they didn't obey—even through the hard times.

APR 4

No Time to Wimp Out

BE STRONG AND COURAGEOUS, because you will lead these people to inherit the land I swore to their ancestors to give them. Be strong and very courageous. Be careful to obey all the law my servant Moses gave you; do not turn from it to the right or to the left, that you may be successful wherever you go. Keep this Book of the Law always on your lips; meditate on it day and night, so that you may be careful to do everything written in it. Then you will be prosperous and successful. Have I not commanded you? Be strong and courageous. Do not be afraid; do not be discouraged, for the Lord your God will be with you wherever you go. **JOSHUA 1:6-9.**

Being strong and courageous isn't an easy task to pull off when it seems everything and everybody is against you. The temptation to give up or give in is strong—it seems like the logical thing to do.

I once had a church member who went through a painful separation and divorce. Her husband dragged her through court and tried to take the kids, the house, and all their assets.

Prior to the divorce I had counseled the couple as they tried (she tried much harder than he did) to save their crumbling marriage. During this counseling I learned that he had cheated on his wife multiple times, he was dishonest about money, and he was verbally abusive to her and their children.

Yet during the divorce proceedings she decided not to bring up any of the things that would indict her husband and expose him for the person he truly was.

When I asked her to explain, she said, "I have two reasons not to drag him through the mud: 1. He's my children's father. I don't want them to see their father in a bad light. 2. I've already forgiven him. I'm going to go on with life and let God be the judge." That is "strong and courageous" personified.

As we take a walk through the Bible, we now find ourselves in the book of Joshua. Joshua's calling is to be strong and courageous in the face of a stubborn people and hostile enemies. He found the strength he needed in God, just as my friend in the above story did. Root yourself in God. Be strong and courageous!

And the Walls Came a-Tumblin' Down

WHEN THE TRUMPETS SOUNDED, the army shouted, and at the sound of the trumpet, when the men gave a loud shout, the wall collapsed; so everyone charged straight in, and they took the city. **JOSHUA 6:20.**

There is nothing like being the new guy. In every church where I've pastored and in every school where I've been principal I have heard the familiar cry, "That's not how the person before you did things!"

There is nothing worse than hearing those words, because they conjure up instant comparisons to someone who lives large in the minds of the people you are working with—an image you cannot battle. As hard as we might try, we are not anybody but who we are.

Moses had led Israel for 40 years, and now Joshua, the new kid on the block, is given the mantle of leadership. Can you imagine the first meeting he has with his military generals, in which he lays out his plan for the conquest of Jericho?

I can hear it now: "OK, fellas, what we're gonna do here is silently march around the city for six days. During those six days nobody is to make a sound; we're just going to march. Then on the seventh day we'll march around the walls of the city seven times. At the end of our seventh trip around Jericho, we're going to make as much noise as we can, and the huge stone walls of the city will crumble. That's the plan."

I can see the generals of Israel's army glancing across the table at one another. Crickets chirp in the long pause. Finally: "Um, really? This is your plan?"

"Yup, this is my plan—well, it's God's plan. He told me this is the plan."

God's ways are not our ways. He will lift us up into positions of leadership that will defy human sensibilities. Our job is not to be like the person we've replaced. Our job is to be who God calls us to be and to do what He calls us to do, no matter how unorthodox or bizarre that may seem to those who knew another leader.

Joshua's—er, God's—plan was weird, but it worked. One by one cities fell, and Canaan became the Promised Land of God's people.

APR 6

Bad Lemon

ACHAN REPLIED, "IT IS TRUE! I have sinned against the Lord, the God of Israel. This is what I have done: When I saw in the plunder a beautiful robe from Babylonia, two hundred shekels of silver and a bar of gold weighing fifty shekels, I coveted them and took them. They are hidden in the ground inside my tent, with the silver underneath." **JOSHUA 7:20, 21.**

Have you ever heard the old adage "One bad apple will spoil the whole barrel"? The thought is that one rotten piece of fruit will infect the rest of the fruit around it. I've never seen a barrel of apples before, but I have had a bad experience with a bag of lemons.

Every morning I do something that many of my friends find disgusting: I make a green power drink. I get out my juicer and put a head of romaine lettuce, a bunch of kale, three apples, a carrot, and a lemon in it. The concoction gives me energy and nutrients that sustain my mornings much better than a bowl of Lucky Charms.

One morning I juiced my lettuce, kale, carrot, and apples, but I didn't have any lemons left in my fruit basket in the kitchen. I knew I had some lemons in the pantry, so I went in (without turning the lights on . . . big mistake) and reached into the bag where the lemons were. I felt a lemon, grabbed it, and yanked it out of the bag.

Poooof! Something exploded all over the front of me. I turned on the light. My lemon was so rotten that it had sprayed powdered lemon mold all over the front of my suit (I was already dressed for church). It was ghastly. I looked in the bag and saw that the rest of the lemons had also given up the ghost. One bad lemon did all that damage!

Israel was like a big bag of lemons that needed to be protected from anything that could infect the whole community. That's why they had their health laws. That's also why open defiance had to be dealt with in such a harsh way. Israel had to be protected from bad lemons. Achan turned out to be a bad lemon.

When I was a school principal, it was my duty to remove students from the school who were dragging the other students into bad behavior. One bad lemon could infect the whole school. God was kind of like the principal of the children of Israel.

Pray that you will be a person who bears good fruit. This world has enough bad lemons in it already.

Long Day

ON THE DAY THE LORD GAVE the Amorites over to Israel, Joshua said to the Lord in the presence of Israel: "Sun, stand still over Gibeon, and you, moon, over the Valley of Aijalon." So the sun stood still, and the moon stopped, till the nation avenged itself on its enemies, as it is written in the Book of Jashar. The sun stopped in the middle of the sky and delayed going down about a full day. There has never been a day like it before or since, a day when the Lord listened to a human being. Surely the Lord was fighting for Israel! **JOSHUA 10:12-14.**

I'm trying to think of the longest day in my life. My first thought is that anytime I have to go into a cell phone store or the Department of Motor Vehicles, I'm in for a long day. But those are not the longest days I've ever experienced.

I think the longest period of time I've experienced in a 24-hour day (at least it seemed horribly long) was when I flew to Kenya with a group of 60 to participate in a mission trip. We took off from Atlanta on a flight that at the time was the longest nonstop flight in the world, more than 17 hours in the air from Atlanta to Johannesburg, South Africa. That was miserable. As far as I recall, God didn't perform any miracles during that flight to make my backside any happier.

Joshua and his warriors were fighting against the Amorite kings to protect Israel's friends the Gibeonites. The battle was fierce, and Joshua needed more time to be victorious. So he asked God for a little more time in his day. It appears, from what the Bible says, that God gave Joshua an extra 24 hours of daylight to finish the task.

I have no idea how God did this. I do know that the earth revolves around the sun, and the moon revolves around the earth. So the author's description of what happened that day may not be the scientific way to explain it, but we do that all the time. We say, "Oh, look! The sun is going down!" If we were going to be scientific about it, we would say, "Oh, look! The earth is rotating, so that we can't see the sun anymore!"

However it happened, the miracle is one more example of God's standing up for His children when they need Him to. I'm so glad I serve a God who will stand up for me. And I'm glad that even after a good long day, I can rest in the knowledge that God is fighting my battles right alongside me.

APR 8

Refuge

THE LORD SAID TO JOSHUA, "Now tell the Israelites to designate the cities of refuge, as I instructed Moses. Anyone who kills another person accidentally and unintentionally can run to one of these cities; they will be places of refuge from relatives seeking revenge for the person who was killed. "Upon reaching one of these cities, the one who caused the death will appear before the elders at the city gate and present his case. They must allow him to enter the city and give him a place to live among them. If the relatives of the victim come to avenge the killing, the leaders must not release the slayer to them, for he killed the other person unintentionally and without previous hostility. But the slayer must stay in that city and be tried by the local assembly, which will render a judgment. And he must continue to live in that city until the death of the high priest who was in office at the time of the accident. After that, he is free to return to his own home in the town from which he fled." **JOSHUA 20:1-6, NLT.**

I grew up in a neighborhood that was filled with kids. As young people we loved to play all kinds of games together. We played the traditional sports, such as baseball, football, and basketball, but we also loved to play hide-and-seek, tag, and capture the flag.

Several of the games we played had a place called "home base," where the enemy couldn't tag you. If you were standing on home base, you were safe. But the moment you stepped away from home base, you were fair game to be tagged, hit with a ball, or deemed "it."

God saw the need in Israel's judicial system to provide a kind of home base for His children. The penalty for murdering someone in that culture was death. But what if you did something accidentally that caused someone's death? What happened to you then?

In that culture a family member was allowed to avenge the death of their beloved by taking your life. It doesn't seem like a great rule, but that was the rule. So God provided cities of refuge for people who were the victims of unfortunate circumstance. As long as the perpetrators of negligent homicide stayed in the city, they were safe. But if they stepped out of "home base," they were fair game to the avenging family.

Jesus is our refuge. As long as we dwell in Him, the enemy cannot steal our eternal life. But when we venture out on our own, we may become victims of the avenger.

Stick a Needle in Your Eye

BUT IF YOU TURN AWAY and ally yourselves with the survivors of these nations that remain among you and if you intermarry with them and associate with them, then you may be sure that the Lord your God will no longer drive out these nations before you. Instead, they will become snares and traps for you, whips on your backs and thorns in your eyes, until you perish from this good land, which the Lord your God has given you. **JOSHUA 23:12, 13.**

I was visiting the playground of the school across the street from my church the other day when I heard a familiar sound. The sound came from a little girl who was making a solemn oath to one of her little friends. The promise went something like this: "Cross my heart, hope to die, stick a needle in my eye."

Where do we come up with these things? I stood there and wondered, *Has there ever been a time in human history when a child broke a promise and this oath was fulfilled?* "I'm sorry, Johnny, but you promised to share your dessert with little Freddy at lunch, and you didn't. We have to hold you down and poke a needle in your eye. And then we have to kill you, as per the agreement you swore on the playground."

In a way, the parting words of General Joshua to his people were an oath. At least they were a good predictor of what was going to happen. He warned the Israelites to stay away from the cultural influences of the nations around them, because these influences would lead the Israelites away from God and toward the bad things that caused the eventual downfall of these nations.

I love Joshua's vivid descriptions of the pain Israel would suffer if they were to fall in this way: "Whips on your backs and thorns in your eyes." Joshua was describing the natural consequences of sin to the people of God. Sin becomes a burdensome taskmaster that blinds you to the reality of God. Joshua's warning: stay away from it.

Of course, as you will see in the book of Judges, Israel didn't stay away from sin. They played with it and got burned again and again. But God was faithful to His people, as He always is. Sin is bad. God is good. Joshua knew that and reminded his people of it just before he died.

APR 10

NC-17

THEN THE LORD RAISED UP JUDGES, who saved them out of the hands of these raiders. Yet they would not listen to their judges but prostituted themselves to other gods and worshiped them. They quickly turned from the ways of their ancestors, who had been obedient to the Lord's commands. **JUDGES 2:16, 17.**

I'm not much of a movie guy. In fact, I tend to fall asleep during movies. My wife, on the other hand, loves anything that has to do with a good story. She's a voracious reader. And on Sunday mornings I usually find her watching some sort of story on DVD or on the Hallmark Channel. She just loves a good movie. Me, not so much.

When viewing a movie I always like to look at what it's rated and then look at some reviews to help me understand its content. I don't want to waste two hours of time watching something that's going to drag me further away from God and detract from my relationship with Him. (Maybe that's why there aren't many movies that hold my attention.)

Movies move from mild to extreme by these ratings: G, PG, PG-13, R, and NC-17 (formerly X). Movies with an NC-17 rating are considered "adult entertainment." I think it's ironic that things no adult should ever watch are called adult entertainment.

One of the assignments I used to give in Bible class was for my students to write a movie script from any of the stories in the book of Judges. They had to write the script, choose actors to play the parts (the actors had to be people who attended their school), and then rate the movie G, PG, PG-13, R, or NC-17, according to the story the Bible detailed.

One of the things that I like and don't like about the book of Judges is how honest and gritty it is. The stories in this book are entertaining and horrifying at the same time. It seems that whoever wrote this book of Scripture wrote it with an honest heart. They didn't want to paint a picture that was anything but real. As we go through portions of this book together, we will take an honest look at the story of the people of God.

APR 11

The Southpaw

EHUD THEN APPROACHED [EGLON] while he was sitting alone in the upper room of his palace and said, "I have a message from God for you." As the king rose from his seat, Ehud reached with his left hand, drew the sword from his right thigh and plunged it into the king's belly. Even the handle sank in after the blade, and his bowels discharged. Ehud did not pull the sword out, and the fat closed in over it. Then Ehud went out to the porch; he shut the doors of the upper room behind him and locked them. **JUDGES 3:20-23.**

As you will see, there's a pattern to Israel's behavior in the book of Judges. When they behave as the Lord wants them to, they don't suffer the effects of sin. When Israel disobeys the Lord, essentially ignoring God, the effects of sin and disobedience make them subject to the nations around them.

Today's chapter describes how for 18 years Moab has ruled over Israel. Moab's king (described as a very fat man) is named Eglon. King Eglon demands taxes and tribute from Israel. The Israelites don't like this, so they call out to the Lord and promise to obey Him . . . again.

God sends Israel a deliverer named Ehud. Ehud is left-handed, and this plays to his advantage in the story. He and an entourage from Israel bring tribute to the Moabite king. After the group leaves, Ehud runs back and says, "I forgot that I have a secret message for the king that is only for his ears."

The king claps his hands and sends all his guards and attendants out. Ehud approaches the king, takes the sword from the sheath on his right thigh (when the king's men searched him, they likely would have checked his left thigh, where right-handed people keep their weapon), and drives it into the king's gelatinous belly. The Bible becomes vivid as it tells us that the fat on the king's belly engulfed the sword and made it disappear.

Why go through this part of the Bible? Shouldn't we skip all the R-rated stuff? I believe each story in the Bible is there for a reason. In this case we see again how God will use any means He can to protect His children when they call out His name. Ehud was a man of war and a man of God.

APR 12

God Calls Whom
He Wants to Call

DEBORAH, A PROPHET, THE WIFE OF LAPPIDOTH, was leading Israel at that time. She held court under the Palm of Deborah between Ramah and Bethel in the hill country of Ephraim, and the Israelites went up to her to have their disputes decided. She sent for Barak son of Abinoam from Kedesh in Naphtali and said to him, "The Lord, the God of Israel, commands you: 'Go, take with you ten thousand men of Naphtali and Zebulun and lead them up to Mount Tabor. I will lead Sisera, the commander of Jabin's army, with his chariots and his troops to the Kishon River and give him into your hands.' " **JUDGES 4:4-7.**

What do the countries of Mongolia, Argentina, Bolivia, Iceland, China, the Philippines, Nicaragua, Ireland, Sri Lanka, Israel, Great Britain, Latvia, Finland, Chile, India, Costa Rica, and Brazil have in common? Here's a hint: the United States does not share what these countries have in common. Have you figured it out?

What do the above countries share in their history that the United States has not seen to date? All of them have had a woman as their head of state (president, prime minister, etc.).

Romans 13 tells us that the leaders of the world are placed in authority by God's direction. So in essence God ordained all of these women to be the leaders of their countries. Whether they did God's bidding while in leadership is another story.

In our story today God called a female to lead His people in a desperate time of need. Deborah must have been wired up by God with gifts of wisdom and courage. She also must have been devoted to seeking God's will for her people, because when she instructed her general to go into battle, she didn't do so in a timid way.

In the Seventh-day Adventist Church we look to Ellen White as a leader and a prophet who was called and ordained by God to her special ministry. He called her to a task that wasn't pleasant at times, but she did her work anyway.

God's call in your life has nothing to do with gender. He is looking for willing people who are gifted as He sees fit to finish His work here on earth. Don't let any human being put a limit on what God has called you to do.

When Less Is More

THE LORD SAID TO GIDEON, "With the three hundred men that lapped I will save you and give the Midianites into your hands. Let all the others go home." So Gideon sent the rest of the Israelites home but kept the three hundred, who took over the provisions and trumpets of the others. **JUDGES 7:7, 8.**

Gideon's story involves some heavenly math. Equation 1: 32,000 men minus 22,000 men equals too many men. Equation 2: 10,000 men minus 9,700 men equals glory to God and no possibility of pride and self-congratulation.

Our world is full of chest-thumping, I'm-better-than-you, me-first arrogance. Hip-hop music in pop culture celebrates rappers and singers who proclaim their dominance over women, money, and one another.

We love to give ourselves props. We love to have people notice how good we are at the things we are good at. Professional football players who score touchdowns because of a total team effort make a spectacle by drawing all the praise and attention to themselves, much to the embarrassment of the offensive linemen who made their touchdown possible. We love to take credit where credit is (or isn't) due.

God knows our nature. He knows that in times of trouble we call out to Him, and in times of deliverance we "thank our lucky stars" and give ourselves credit for being brave through a hard situation.

That's why the story of Gideon is so wonderful. God knew that if 32,000 Israelites marched out against the Midianites and won the battle, they would think very highly of their efforts, leaving God as an afterthought in their victory celebrations.

So God defeated thousands with only a few hundred men. Acknowledging His working and giving Him glory are unavoidable in a situation like this. Humans can claim no praise. It's distinctly a "God thing."

Think back on the blessings in your life. Who do you think bestowed those blessings on you? Your lucky stars? No, God has blessed you. Take a moment today to recognize and thank God for the victories and blessings in your life.

APR 14

Talking Trees and a King-killing Woman

ABIMELECH FOLLOWED THEM TO ATTACK the tower. But as he prepared to set fire to the entrance, a woman on the roof dropped a millstone that landed on Abimelech's head and crushed his skull. He quickly said to his young armor bearer, "Draw your sword and kill me! Don't let it be said that a woman killed Abimelech!" So the young man ran him through with his sword, and he died. **JUDGES 9:52-54, NLT.**

King Abimelech was a piece of work. He was from the town of Shechem. His father, Gideon, ruled the Israelites and fathered Abimelech, adding him to 70 other brothers (his father was active with multiple wives and at least one girlfriend). At some point Abimelech convinced himself that he needed to be the king of Israel, so he rallied the people to help him get his bothersome brothers (who ruled as a group of judges) out of the way.

In an act considered the exact opposite of brotherly love, Abimelech murdered all 70 of his brothers on the same rock—all but Jotham, the youngest brother.

When the people gathered to proclaim Abimelech king, young Jotham stood up on a hill and told a parable/prophecy about some trees who were asked to rule the other trees. None of the trees wanted to be king because they had more productive things to do. Finally, a thornbush said yes to the agricultural coronation. In the parable Jotham likened his brother Abimelech to the thornbush and said, in essence, "If you citizens are doing the right thing here, I hope you all live happily ever after. But if not, you and Abimelech will destroy each other."

Abimelech faced nothing but problems with the people and ended up trying to rule through military force. As he attempted to storm a tower in one city, a woman dropped a millstone on his head, cracking it open. Just before he died, he had his armor bearer run him through with a sword so that "no one can say a woman killed me." The end.

Abimelech serves as a great example to us that when we run ahead of God and do things our way, we can miss His will and His blessings for us and the people around us. Our plans may not be His plans. Our ways may not be His ways. Our job is not to run ahead of God with our own agenda. Our job is to seek His lead and follow His plan, no matter our role.

Jephthah and His Band
of Merry Men

JEPHTHAH THE GILEADITE was a mighty warrior. His father was Gilead; his mother was a prostitute. Gilead's wife also bore him sons, and when they were grown up, they drove Jephthah away. "You are not going to get any inheritance in our family," they said, "because you are the son of another woman." So Jephthah fled from his brothers and settled in the land of Tob, where a gang of scoundrels gathered around him and followed him. **JUDGES 11:1-3.**

The first few verses of Judges 11 always make me think of the legend of Robin Hood. There's something that appeals to my masculinity in the thought of a macho man leading a band of other macho men fighting for justice. And I love it that God chooses another underdog to do His bidding: Jephthah, an outcast who's unwanted by his people. This is a guy who has no chance of becoming anything in life.

As it turns out, Jephthah is good at something: fighting. In fact, he's very good at fighting. He gets with some other nasty characters in the Land of Tob (my favorite place name in the Bible) and becomes the ultimate bad boy.

Some local Israelite leaders hire Jephthah to fight for them and promise him the moon if he will. Jephthah agrees. As he goes into battle, Jephthah makes a promise to a God he barely knows. "If You give us a victory, I'll sacrifice the first thing that walks out of my house when I get home."

Jephthah wins the battle, goes home, and looks up to see his daughter walking out the door. He gives his daughter some time to mourn with her friends, and then "he did to her as he had vowed" (Judges 11:39).

This story starts off with a great macho theme and ends with what sounds like a brutal promise kept. I don't know for sure what happened to Jephthah's daughter, but I do know that promising God things when we want His help shows a deficient understanding of how He operates and how He wants us to operate toward Him.

God loves us all the time. He will help us whenever we ask. We don't need to make promises to convince Him to help us—especially ones that could blow up in our faces.

APR 16

Messed-up Hero

SAMSON SAID, "LET ME DIE WITH THE PHILISTINES!" Then he pushed with all his might, and down came the temple on the rulers and all the people in it. Thus he killed many more when he died than while he lived. **JUDGES 16:30.**

Here's another proof that God can use anybody in any culture at any time to save His people. Samson is a child of promise who grows up like many kids—with long hair and an attitude.

Samson does everything he's not supposed to do. He sleeps with Philistine prostitutes, wanders into vineyards (as a Nazirite, he's supposed to stay away from wine and all other grape products), tries to marry a Philistine woman (someone not of his faith or his people), and seemingly yells at God for water after he kills 1,000 people with the jawbone of a donkey.

Yet in spite of this behavior, the Bible tells us, he is equipped with the "Spirit of the Lord" on several occasions. The Spirit of God inhabits Samson, even though Samson is not any kind of positive role model for young Israelites in his town. In fact, I don't know a whole lot of parents today who would want their children to act as Samson acted. Yet God used him anyway.

God is truly amazing. He can use anything or anybody to accomplish His will, especially when it comes to protecting His children—even when His children don't act like they're His children.

After reading the story of Samson, I ask myself, *What is it that qualifies him to be listed with God's faithful in Hebrews 11?* He prays only twice (at least as recorded in the story). Once he begs God for water because he's thirsty. The second time is just before he dies, when he asks God to give him revenge because the Philistines poked out his eyes.

It's good to remember that God's faithfulness is a much bigger factor in our lives than our faithfulness. His goodness outweighs our goodness. His love is bigger than our failures. Even in a spiritually stunted state, when we call out to God, He will always answer us and take us back into His arms.

The Sickest Story
in the Whole Bible

EVERYONE WHO SAW THIS SAID, "Nothing like this has ever happened before, not since the people of Israel came out of Egypt. Think about it. Tell us what to do." **JUDGES 19:30, NCV.**

OK, I admit it: I can't wait to get done with the book of Judges. If you have read chapter 19 in preparation for this devotional thought, you know why. What a sick bunch of people lived in the Promised Land during this time of Israel's existence! It really speaks to God's patience as His people learn to become more like Him and less like the enemy.

In this horrible story a man is traveling with two other people, one of whom is his concubine (a female servant that a man can have physical relations with). As evening comes, they pass by a Canaanite city to get to a city that is part of Israel; it would be safer there, right?

They get to that city so late that they find an empty city square, so they plan to sleep in the street overnight. A kind gentleman finds the travelers in the city and insists that they come and spend the night in his home.

After they wash their feet and eat some food, there's a knock on the door. It's a rowdy group of people who want the man to send out the travelers so the townspeople can have sex with them. The host offers them his virgin daughter, but they won't have her. Finally the men give these perverts the concubine, whom they abuse all night and leave for dead on the front porch. The travelers go home, where the master of the house cuts the dead woman's body into 12 pieces and sends one to each tribe of Israel.

All the Israelites then say to one another: "Nothing like this has ever happened before, not since the people of Israel came out of Egypt. Think about it. Tell us what to do."

Tell us what to do? Take an inventory of your cities and country. Take an inventory of yourselves. You are becoming more and more evil, and it's getting out of control. Don't wink at sin. Call it by its right name and deal with it! When a group of people shuns God and embraces evil, the moral decay that comes as a result is nothing less than heinous and ugly.

APR 18

Finally—Some Good Stuff!

BUT RUTH REPLIED, "DON'T URGE me to leave you or to turn back from you. Where you go I will go, and where you stay I will stay. Your people will be my people and your God my God. Where you die I will die, and there I will be buried. May the Lord deal with me, be it ever so severely, if even death separates you and me." When Naomi realized that Ruth was determined to go with her, she stopped urging her. **RUTH 1:16-18.**

Every once in a while there is a story in the Bible that just makes me want to weep for joy. This is one of those stories.

Ruth was a person who for much of her life probably had not even heard about the true God of the universe. She came from a part of Canaan in which people worshipped gods made of stone. Ruth was an unlikely hero in the Bible for sure.

It's easy to judge people when their background doesn't match our idea of "God's people." It's easy to think that God's people are identified by where they live or where they go to church. We need to remember that God has people tucked in every corner of this world. Jesus once told a group of Jews, "I have sheep that you don't know anything about."

Ruth was one of God's people. She may not have even known at this point that she was one of God's people, but she was. The deeply Spirit-led decision she made to take care of her mother-in-law instead of looking out for her own self-interest demonstrates the spirit of Christ like few other stories in the Bible. Ruth demonstrates a depth of character that every believer should have.

When push comes to shove, do you look out for your own interests or for the interests of others? I believe that when we are buried deep in the life, death, and resurrection of Jesus, we will bear the kind of fruit that Ruth did.

Ruth's mother-in-law felt abandoned by God. What she didn't realize was that God was using His daughter Ruth as His agent of soothing love on her behalf.

Hard Work Works

BOAZ REPLIED, "I'VE BEEN TOLD all about what you have done for your mother-in-law since the death of your husband—how you left your father and mother and your homeland and came to live with a people you did not know before. May the Lord repay you for what you have done. May you be richly rewarded by the Lord, the God of Israel, under whose wings you have come to take refuge." **RUTH 2:11, 12.**

The saying "Be sure your sin will find you out" is paralleled by the idea that "good deeds will follow you."

Somehow word of the commitment that Ruth had made to Naomi, her mother-in-law, got around. People took note of Ruth because of the godly decision she had made. The text also indicates that Ruth was a determined and hard worker. People noticed that too.

One of the secrets of success in this world is hard work. Many times hard work trumps talent or natural ability. In fact, some of the least successful people I know possess all kinds of talent that they are too lazy to do anything with.

Indira Gandhi, the former prime minister of India, once said, "My grandfather once told me that there were two kinds of people: those who do the work and those who take the credit. He told me to try to be in the first group; there was much less competition."

Natural talent comes sparingly, but hard work is a trait that anyone can develop. And it pays off.

Ruth had her back to the wall. She and Naomi needed food and shelter. She could have folded under the pressure and faded away into her situation. Instead, she took matters into her own hands and worked hard to reverse her situation. She got out in the field and started to glean. People noticed her determination. I think God also smiles on good effort. I'm not talking about effort toward salvation; I'm talking about good old-fashioned hard work—doing the best you can, given your situation.

What kind of work reputation are you developing with your parents, friends, and teachers? Just for today, take some pride in what you do and work hard. You'll like the results.

APR 20

Matchmakers

ONE DAY NAOMI SAID TO RUTH, "My daughter, it's time that I found a permanent home for you, so that you will be provided for. Boaz is a close relative of ours, and he's been very kind by letting you gather grain with his young women. Tonight he will be winnowing barley at the threshing floor. Now do as I tell you—take a bath and put on perfume and dress in your nicest clothes. Then go to the threshing floor, but don't let Boaz see you until he has finished eating and drinking. Be sure to notice where he lies down; then go and uncover his feet and lie down there. He will tell you what to do." **RUTH 3:1-4, NLT.**

I will admit my last foray into the world of arranged romance. It was a Saturday night. We had several people in our living room playing table games and eating heartburn-inducing food. As our evening was winding down, I was on my Facebook account, surfing for who knows what, when an idea popped into my head. I looked up and said to Rachel, a single friend who was visiting, "Hey, I'm going to Facebook all my single male friends and hook you up!"

Without blinking an eye, she called my bluff. "Go for it!"

So I did. That very night Aaron sent Rachel a Facebook message. They "friended" each other, and—well, the rest is history. They have fallen in love and are headed toward marriage (as of the writing of this book). I tell everybody that if they live happily ever after, I should get the credit; if they end up in a messy breakup, it was just a joke and I get none of the blame!

Naomi loved Ruth as she would her own daughter. She wanted nothing more than for Ruth to find the comfort and security that a good husband could give. So she arranged romance in a way that only two conniving females could! She made sure Ruth was dressed to a T and all perfumed up—a trap that no man could resist!

Actually, Ruth had it all. She was the kind of person that any single man would be attracted to. She was a person of integrity. She was a hard worker. She was caring. And now that she was all prettied up and smelling good, Boaz didn't stand a chance!

What qualities are you looking for in a future spouse? Take a hard look at Ruth. If you strive to develop a character like that in yourself and look for those traits in a future mate, you will likely have a great marriage someday.

Hand Me That Sandal

(NOW IN EARLIER TIMES IN ISRAEL, for the redemption and transfer of property to become final, one party took off his sandal and gave it to the other. This was the method of legalizing transactions in Israel.) So the guardian-redeemer said to Boaz, "Buy it yourself." And he removed his sandal. **RUTH 4:7, 8.**

The thought of a guardian-redeemer is a really cool one. In the time of Ruth a guardian-redeemer was a kind of superhero to a widow. At that time women weren't normally allowed to own property. They needed a husband to legitimize their existence, in human eyes. When a woman's husband died prematurely and she had no sons to carry on the family name, her options were few. She could beg, she could sell herself into prostitution, or she could be taken care of by a guardian-redeemer.

The guardian-redeemer would examine the case of the widow. If he decided to manage the widow's property and take her on as a wife, the widow would be *redeemed*. If the man refused to redeem her, the widow could bring him before the local elders, take one of his sandals, and spit in his face (see Deuteronomy 25:9)!

Young Ruth caught the eye of the much older Boaz, not because she was gorgeous (we don't get any indication of whether she was pretty or not), not because she was rich (she wasn't), and not because of any other shallow reason. Boaz noticed Ruth because of her outstanding character traits. He saw her as a kind, loyal, hardworking young woman. Those qualities made her attractive to Boaz, so he became her guardian-redeemer.

Ruth's amazing journey doesn't end with her fairy-tale marriage to Boaz. Yes, it is a stirring story of quality character and true romance, but that is just the beginning.

Ruth's child became King David's grandfather. Ruth became an ancestor of our guardian-redeemer, Jesus. Her character and her faithfulness to the Spirit's lead in her life were used by God as a link in the human chain of events that would eventually give us Jesus. What an honor! And to think that none of this would have happened if Ruth hadn't listened to the Holy Spirit and had an unselfish heart.

APR 22

Feeling Lower Than
a Snake's Belly

WHENEVER THE DAY CAME for Elkanah to sacrifice, he would give portions of the meat to his wife Peninnah and to all her sons and daughters. But to Hannah he gave a double portion because he loved her, and the Lord had closed her womb. Because the Lord had closed her womb, her rival kept provoking her in order to irritate her. This went on year after year. Whenever Hannah went up to the house of the Lord, her rival provoked her till she wept and would not eat. **1 SAMUEL 1:4-6.**

It seems that the Bible is rife with examples of women who are picked on because they can't have kids. Usually this is complicated by the fact that the woman's husband has another wife who *can* have kids. And, of course, the wife who can have kids makes life difficult for the wife who can't have kids.

In this story Hannah becomes so overwhelmed with despondency that she acts like a drunk homeless person.

Have you ever been so emotionally drained that you walked around like a zombie? Have you ever been so devalued by the people around you that you weren't sure where to turn or how to act? I have. When this happened to me, nothing could get me out of my funk like a good friend used by the Lord.

While I was a principal, there was a period of time I felt about as worthless as a bag of stale air. My life was out of balance. I was working too many hours trying to fix all the things that I thought were wrong in the school and in my life. But my many hours just complicated things more. Eventually I began acting much more like a zombie than a vibrant believer in God's leading in my life.

During this discouraged phase I had a friend who would spend time with me on the golf course, over lunch, or on the phone. He would tell me lies (that's how I viewed them) about what a wonderful person I was. He would remind me of my calling to leadership. He would blow sunshine my way when all I could see was darkness.

Are you open enough to allow God to use you to bring hope into the life of another? I have found that when I allow God to use me to minister to others, the blessings that flow back to me are overwhelmingly good.

Bad Boys

NOW ELI'S SONS WERE EVIL MEN; they did not care about the Lord. This is what the priests would normally do to the people: Every time someone brought a sacrifice, the meat would be cooked in a pot. The priest's servant would then come carrying a fork that had three prongs. He would plunge the fork into the pot or the kettle. Whatever the fork brought out of the pot belonged to the priest. But this is how they treated all the Israelites who came to Shiloh to offer sacrifices. Even before the fat was burned, the priest's servant would come to the person offering sacrifices and say, "Give the priest some meat to roast. He won't accept boiled meat from you, only raw meat." If the one who offered the sacrifice said, "Let the fat be burned up first as usual, and then take anything you want," the priest's servant would answer, "No, give me the meat now. If you don't, I'll take it by force." The Lord saw that the sin of the servants was very great because they did not show respect for the offerings made to the Lord. **1 SAMUEL 2:12-17, NCV.**

What makes a person wicked? Do they just wake up that way on a certain day? Can you identify an evil tendency when they're toddlers? Is it how they're raised?

I grew up next to a family that had nine children. They all had the same parents. They all lived in the same house and in the same neighborhood. Yet one of them ended up being a moral wreck and dying a horrible death after taking a deadly mixture of illegal drugs. Why him? How did the other eight kids turn out to be great people with balanced lives?

I suppose a wicked life could come from any number of places. I've seen some people who just seemed to have a brain defect that eliminated their moral compass. I've seen people who ended up wicked because they made a series of choices that became a way of life and so clouded their perspective that they didn't even know they had become amoral people.

In the case of Eli's sons it seems that a lack of parental backbone contributed to their demise. Parents who nod and smile at their children instead of guiding them with appropriate discipline don't realize what they are doing to their children.

Eli's sons were driven by greed and selfishness and used their power in the temple for their own gain. If only they had humbled themselves and obeyed, God could have blessed them immeasurably.

APR 24

Growing in the Right Direction

AND THE BOY SAMUEL CONTINUED to grow in stature and in favor with the Lord and with people. **1 SAMUEL 2:26.**

Don't you just love the balance of today's text? Samuel grew in physical height, in favor with God, and in favor with people. Nice balance, don't you think? So how does one go about growing like that?

I've always grown physically. Some of my growing was good and some of it not so good. The good part (at least I've always enjoyed it) is that I was born tall. My birth mother tells me that when I was born, the doctor measured me at 22 inches long. From there I was always the tallest in my class, except for about four months in sixth grade. Jeanine Wedel shot right past me for those few humiliating months until I regained my rightful title as the tallest in the class. I stopped growing when I reached six feet six inches at 18 years old. I consider that good stature growth.

When I became an adult, I didn't realize that my teenage eating habits needed to change. I gained weight and started to get chunky. I found that exercise and a good plant-based diet did a lot to shed the extra "stature" I had added in the wrong direction.

If you want to grow up as Samuel did, in a way that God and people can admire, here's some of my advice:

1. Eat a balanced plant-based diet and try to stay away from all those processed and sugary foods.

2. Learn good hygiene. Take care to clean your body and look nice.

3. Be a positive person. Look people in the eye when you talk to them. Be confident in who God made you to be.

4. Be a well-read person. People who read are people who are informed about life and can contribute to an intelligent conversation.

5. Spend time in the Word and in prayer each day. Center your life in Jesus and let Him be your guide.

6. Forgive others as Jesus has forgiven you. Some people will hurt you on purpose. Your forgiveness renders their attacks meaningless and useless in your life.

Using God

AT THAT TIME ISRAEL WAS AT WAR with the Philistines. The Israelite army was camped near Ebenezer, and the Philistines were at Aphek. The Philistines attacked and defeated the army of Israel, killing 4,000 men. After the battle was over, the troops retreated to their camp, and the elders of Israel asked, "Why did the Lord allow us to be defeated by the Philistines?" Then they said, "Let's bring the Ark of the Covenant of the Lord from Shiloh. If we carry it into battle with us, it will save us from our enemies." . . . When all the Israelites saw the Ark of the Covenant of the Lord coming into the camp, their shout of joy was so loud it made the ground shake! "What's going on?" the Philistines asked. "What's all the shouting about in the Hebrew camp?" When they were told it was because the Ark of the Lord had arrived, they panicked. "The gods have come into their camp!" they cried. "This is a disaster! We have never had to face anything like this before! Help! Who can save us from these mighty gods of Israel? They are the same gods who destroyed the Egyptians with plagues when Israel was in the wilderness. Fight as never before, Philistines! If you don't, we will become the Hebrews' slaves just as they have been ours! Stand up like men and fight!" So the Philistines fought desperately, and Israel was defeated again. The slaughter was great; 30,000 Israelite soldiers died that day. The survivors turned and fled to their tents. The Ark of God was captured, and Hophni and Phinehas, the two sons of Eli, were killed. **1 SAMUEL 4:1-11, NLT.**

The text for today's devotional is longer than usual for a reason. I think it's important for us to recognize how dangerous it can be to "use God" without His consent. Being presumptuous in our faith can get us into all kinds of trouble.

I've known many people who have told me things such as "God really wants me to enter into this business arrangement" or "God led me to this man or woman and wants us to be together." And then when the business falls apart or the relationship isn't something that God has truly blessed, *KA-BLAM!*—everything blows up in their faces. Then they blame God.

God did not instruct Israel to go into this battle or to bring the ark into it. But Israel's leaders were corrupt and did what they wanted. And it blew up in their faces. God will not be mocked. Honor Him, and He'll honor you. But don't try to use Him to get what you want out of life. Instead, follow His lead. He knows what's best.

APR 26

The Story of
the Golden Hemorrhoids

AND IT WAS SO, THAT, after they had carried it about, the hand of the Lord was against the city with a very great destruction: and he smote the men of the city, both small and great, and they had emerods in their secret parts. **1 SAMUEL 5:9, KJV.**

If you want to read an entertaining story in the Bible, read the three-chapter account of the convincing affliction that God used to bring the ark of the covenant back to Israel.

When the Philistines initially captured the ark of the covenant from the Israelites, they brought it back to the town of Ashdod to their temple of worship. One of their gods was named Dagon. Dagon, according to some descriptions, was a weird-looking god whose stone image looked like a man with the bottom half of a fish. Dagon was the Philistines' fertility god—a deity they worshipped in hopes that they would be productive in their sex life and in their crops.

The ark of the covenant was set in front of Dagon and left there overnight. In the morning, when the Philistine priests came in to check on their fish-man god, they found that he had fallen facedown in front of the ark.

They propped Dagon back up, secured the statue in place, shrugged their shoulders, and left. The next morning they came in to check on Dagon again. This time he had fallen over facedown and broken his head and hands off. How embarrassing for Dagon!

You would think that the Philistines would get the hint and give the ark back to Israel. But they didn't. So God gave them another hint. He afflicted the people in the region with "tumors." That's how the New International Version puts it.

The King James Version tells it a little differently. It says they were afflicted with "emerods in their secret parts." That's right, hemorrhoids. Capturing the ark of the covenant became a real pain in the rear.

Read the rest of the story in 1 Samuel 6 to see the miraculous way that the ark found its way back home to Israel. Even though they didn't deserve Him, God demonstrated in the return of the ark that He will never leave or forsake His people.

Be Careful What You Ask for;
You Just Might Get It!

SO ALL THE ELDERS CAME TOGETHER and met Samuel at Ramah. They said to him, "You're old, and your sons don't live as you do. Give us a king to rule over us like all the other nations." When the older leaders said that, Samuel was not pleased. He prayed to the Lord, and the Lord told Samuel, "Listen to whatever the people say to you. They have not rejected you. They have rejected me from being their king. They are doing as they have always done. When I took them out of Egypt, they left me and served other gods. They are doing the same to you. Now listen to the people, but warn them what the king who rules over them will do." **1 SAMUEL 8:4-9, NCV.**

Walking through a pet store, my wife and I were cooing over all the little kitties and puppies in their little kitty and puppy prisons when I noticed him. It seemed that anywhere I walked along the viewing window, he followed along in his cage. I'd never really paid attention to anything with feathers before, but this little Jenday conure caught my eye. He had a bright-yellow head, an orange breast, and blue-tipped green feathers.

The pet store pusher asked me if I'd like to hold him. "Sure!" I said, not realizing that this was a part of the pet store's evil scheme.

A half hour later we were going home with a $500 bird. This parrot stayed in our family for 10 years and became the bane of my existence. He went to the bathroom everywhere, bit people, and destroyed my wife's wardrobe. And I was the one who really wanted him!

Instead of staying faithful to God and reaping His blessings, the Israelites looked at the kingdoms around them and wanted to be like them. That was Israel's prayer. "Give us a king!"

God had warned Israel in the book of Deuteronomy about having a king. He had prophesied what would happen to them. And they asked for it anyway. Be careful what you ask for! You just might get it.

I think it would be better to walk in the blessings of the Lord and let Him lead in our life than to demand things that we want because everybody else has them. May God lead you, and may you be satisfied with His blessings in your life.

APR 28

Saul the Great, Saul the Sad

KISH HAD A SON NAMED Saul, as handsome a young man as could be found anywhere in Israel, and he was a head taller than anyone else. **1 SAMUEL 9:2.**

SAUL SAID TO HIS ARMOR-BEARER, "Draw your sword and run me through, or these uncircumcised fellows will come and run me through and abuse me." But his armor-bearer was terrified and would not do it; so Saul took his own sword and fell on it. When the armor-bearer saw that Saul was dead, he too fell on his sword and died with him. So Saul and his three sons and his armor-bearer and all his men died together that same day. **1 SAMUEL 31:4-6.**

Israel's first king started off with such promise. He seemed to be a strong leader who had a passion for God's will and a love for his country. And then the one temptation that has been known to corrupt good, strong people began to ensnare him.

Saul was overwhelmed by the lure of power. As he gained success after success in his domestic and military tasks, he began to rely more on himself and less on God. Instead of glorying in the success of others, he felt threatened when people did well.

Saul began to compromise in what he knew the Lord wanted of him. He still believed in God. He still went through the motions of worshipping God. Any casual observer would have thought he was a believer. But Saul started to drift, and his power-hungry heart started to take over.

It wasn't long before Saul lost control of his emotions. His outbursts were violent at times. He even went against a direct command of the Lord and consulted a spirit medium to call up a demon for advice on how to run the country.

Saul was a great man of promise for Israel who turned out to be a sad, moody, defiant, desperate man.

King Saul could have been the greatest king in the history of Israel. Had he submitted to God's lead in his life and paid attention to God's desire for Israel instead of his own desires, his could have been a much different story.

Unfinished Business

"DON'T BE AFRAID," SAMUEL REASSURED THEM. "You have certainly done wrong, but make sure now that you worship the Lord with all your heart, and don't turn your back on him. Don't go back to worshiping worthless idols that cannot help or rescue you—they are totally useless! The Lord will not abandon his people, because that would dishonor his great name. For it has pleased the Lord to make you his very own people. "As for me, I will certainly not sin against the Lord by ending my prayers for you. And I will continue to teach you what is good and right. But be sure to fear the Lord and faithfully serve him. Think of all the wonderful things he has done for you. **1 SAMUEL 12:20-24, NLT.**

Carpenters work on a house until it's done. When they're finished, they can look back at their handiwork, smile at their accomplishments, and go on to the next project. Not so with a pastor.

When has a church ever reached a point where its growth and work are finished? When have church members ever reached a point where they need no more spiritual growth and maturity? A pastor's work is never done.

That's why it's so difficult for me as a pastor to say goodbye to a church or school when I move to another district. To leave something before it's finished goes against my nature. I like to finish things. I don't have things in my home that are halfway done. If I start a project, I complete it. Yet each time I leave a church or a school campus where I've worked, I look at all the possibilities still left in that place and wonder . . .

I think that's how Samuel felt as he gave his retirement speech in 1 Samuel 12. He saw all the progress God's children had made in Canaan. But he also took note that there was much work to be done in their hearts and minds, and he couldn't see who was going to step up to the task. His sons were a joke. He'd already warned the Israelites how their experiment with having a king would turn out. What would happen to Samuel's people?

One of the things we sometimes forget is that even though God gives us a task, that task is not ours alone. God's plans are His plans. We are involved in them only because He has called and we have answered. He will finish what He starts. That includes the work He's doing on us!

APR 30

Little Big Man

BUT THE LORD SAID TO SAMUEL, "Do not consider his appearance or his height, for I have rejected him. The Lord does not look at the things people look at. People look at the outward appearance, but the Lord looks at the heart." **1 SAMUEL 16:7.**

He is five feet 10 inches tall. He weighs 180 pounds. The average weight for a person in his profession is 248 pounds. The average height is more than six feet tall. Yet somehow this little guy was able to reach the pinnacle of success in the National Football League.

His name? Doug Flutie. His talent? Playing quarterback. All his life people told Doug Flutie he was too little to be a quarterback. Yet after playing quarterback for Boston College, he won college football's most prestigious award: the Heisman Trophy. Despite such success, he wasn't selected in the draft by an NFL team until the eleventh round—284 players were picked in front of him.

Nobody would give him a chance in the NFL, so he ended up in the Canadian Football League, where he won the Grey Cup for the Calgary Stampeders and was named the CFL's most outstanding player a record six times.

In 1998 Doug Flutie played for the NFL's Buffalo Bills and earned a Pro Bowl selection and the NFL Comeback Player of the Year award—at five feet 10 inches and 180 pounds. Whodathunk?

"The Lord does not look at the things people look at. People look at the outward appearance, but the Lord looks at the heart."

When God chose David, it was almost as if He was choosing the anti-Saul. King Saul had it all going on. He was a tall, good-looking, self-confident man. David was a young, smaller, overlooked shepherd boy. He had bigger, more talented, more noticed brothers, all fit to be king—in human eyes.

When you look in the mirror, what do you see? Maybe that's the wrong question. When you look in the mirror, what does God see? He sees His beloved son or daughter. He sees all the potential that others may not.

The Power of Music

WHENEVER THE SPIRIT FROM GOD came on Saul, David would take up his lyre and play. Then relief would come to Saul; he would feel better, and the evil spirit would leave him. **1 SAMUEL 16:23.**

When I was young, I was not a converted person. I didn't exercise good discretion in choosing my relationships, my diet, or my entertainment. I was a spiritual train wreck. And from my very early years music played a part in my development as a person—not necessarily a good part, as you can imagine.

At 19 I purchased tickets to a concert being put on by a then-popular heavy metal group named Quiet Riot. (Even the name of the group might give you a hint that this was not an event where I was likely to find spiritual benefit.) As my girlfriend and I went into the Seattle Center Arena for the concert, our senses were overstimulated by the sights and sounds of people doing and saying things that glorified wrong and not right.

When the music started, my girlfriend and I worked our way to the front of the coliseum through the throngs of people. The music was ear-splittingly loud. Then the crowd surged toward the stage, trapping us in the massive throng. At one point I actually lifted my feet off the ground and didn't fall, held up by human flesh pressing in on all sides.

Eventually the fans became so rowdy that my girlfriend got a black eye, and we ended up sitting in the back for the rest of the event.

Music can affect people in a powerful way, for good or for evil. God has given us the gift of music to benefit us and to praise Him. David found a way to use music to calm and soothe. Other places in the Bible describe loud, rhythmic music designed to praise God and elevate a mood of joy.

When you put the earbuds in your ears, what are you filling your body (heart and brain) with? Is it music that will make you a better person? Is it music that heightens lasting joy? Would you put a splitter in your iPod and share the tunes with Jesus as He sits next to you?

Remember, what you put in will come out.

MAY 2

Watch Out for Falling Giants

AS GOLIATH MOVED CLOSER TO ATTACK, David quickly ran out to meet him. Reaching into his shepherd's bag and taking out a stone, he hurled it with his sling and hit the Philistine in the forehead. The stone sank in, and Goliath stumbled and fell face down on the ground. So David triumphed over the Philistine with only a sling and a stone, for he had no sword. Then David ran over and pulled Goliath's sword from its sheath. David used it to kill him and cut off his head. When the Philistines saw that their champion was dead, they turned and ran. **1 SAMUEL 17:48-51, NLT.**

The story of David and Goliath is one of the epic stories in Scripture. Everybody loves the story of the underdog beating up the odds-on favorite. I love the story because God seems to make a habit of choosing the insignificant to take down the significant.

Every day Goliath stands on the top of a hill across from God's army and insults the soldiers, their mothers, their pets, and their God. And every day the hosts of Israel's army look at each other and wonder what they should do. They don't like what's going on, but the giant is bigger, stronger, and better at insults than they are.

When David shows up to give his brothers some food to sustain them for the battle they aren't fighting, he hears the Philistine's insults, and he becomes indignant.

He starts to complain, "Whoa! Did you hear what that guy is saying about our mamas? And did you hear what he's saying about our God? Why isn't anybody doing something about this?" The big people, the important people, the people who matter, try to shut him up.

Finally David gets an audience with his king. King Saul is as much of a coward as everyone else. But after an unsuccessful attempt to armor David up, he gives David his blessing to go fight the mean giant.

I love how bold David is as he approaches Goliath and takes him down. He even puts an exclamation point on his victory by using the giant's sword to lop off Goliath's head. (Then he carries it around with him for a few days!)

David had a fierce faith in God, and he acted on it. He didn't know for sure what the outcome would be, but he boldly went into battle to defend his friend, his God.

Evil Spirits and Jealous Kings

AFTER DAVID HAD KILLED THE PHILISTINE, he and the men returned home. Women came out from all the towns of Israel to meet King Saul. They sang songs of joy, danced, and played tambourines and stringed instruments. As they played, they sang, "Saul has killed thousands of his enemies, but David has killed tens of thousands." The women's song upset Saul, and he became very angry. He thought, "The women say David has killed tens of thousands, but they say I have killed only thousands. The only thing left for him to have is the kingdom!" So Saul watched David closely from then on, because he was jealous. The next day an evil spirit from God rushed upon Saul, and he prophesied in his house. David was playing the harp as he usually did, but Saul had a spear in his hand. He threw the spear, thinking, "I'll pin David to the wall." But David escaped from him twice. **1 SAMUEL 18:6-11, NCV.**

I want to talk about jealousy in this chapter, but first I need to address two other things.

1. These verses say that Saul was prophesying. The original word here means "to speak by inspiration," which is what prophets do. Obviously, though, whatever Saul said was "inspired" by the evil spirit that possessed him and not by the Holy Spirit.

2. The text speaks of an "evil spirit from God." If you are a believer, this should make you a little uncomfortable. It flies in the face of what the New Testament teaches —that God is light, and in Him there is no darkness at all (see 1 John 1:5). Just remember, many people in Old Testament times apparently didn't know who the devil was. Satan is mentioned only a few times in these books; God usually gets all the credit and all the blame. As we look at Jesus as the representation of God on earth, we can conclude that God does not tempt, He does not harm, and He does not send evil spirits to torment or deceive.

Now, about jealousy . . . Saul was jealous of David because he saw in David the blessings of God that he used to see in himself. One of the telltale ways you can know if you're falling into the trap of jealousy is this: When you see your peers succeed, do you feel a genuine gladness for them, or do you secretly wish they would fail? Can you be happy for the success of others, or do you wish you were in their place?

Jesus celebrates our successes. He loves it when we achieve. We should try to be like Jesus when it comes to the success of others.

MAY 4

The Amazing Gift of Friendship

AFTER THE BOY HAD GONE, David got up from the south side of the stone and bowed down before Jonathan three times, with his face to the ground. Then they kissed each other and wept together—but David wept the most. Jonathan said to David, "Go in peace, for we have sworn friendship with each other in the name of the Lord, saying, 'The Lord is witness between you and me, and between your descendants and my descendants forever.'" Then David left, and Jonathan went back to the town. **1 SAMUEL 20:41, 42.**

I think the best friend I have ever had was Jeff Bently. I'm not sure he would feel the same about me as I do about him, but there was a time in my life that I loved him as much as any human being on earth.

Jeff and I were eighth-grade classmates and spent a lot of time hanging out at school, on the weekends, and during the summer. We shared secrets that junior high boys would never utter to a parent. We enjoyed the same music. We just liked being together.

I'll never forget the moment he broke the news that his family was moving from Seattle to Boise, Idaho. I felt as if I had been punched in the gut. I felt like crying. When I told my mom the news at home that night, I was barely able to speak without breaking down.

There's something special about finding a kindred spirit—a best friend. To this day I place a high premium on the godly men in my life who are closer than a brother. When they are joyful, I am joyful. When they hurt, I hurt. Friendship is truly a gift from God.

David and Jonathan were thrown into a tumultuous situation. Jonathan's dad was horribly jealous and full of hate toward David. Yet Jonathan and David discovered that they were kindred spirits—closer than a brother. And this relationship was a faith-building one.

To be a good friend you have to be selfless, thoughtful, kind, and loyal. A good friend will make you a better person; they will not drag you away from God. A good friend will have your back, even when you do foolish things. God calls us to be good friends. He also asks us to have the wisdom to choose good friends.

Respect or Revenge?

HE CAME TO THE SHEEP pens along the way; a cave was there, and Saul went in to relieve himself. David and his men were far back in the cave. The men said, "This is the day the Lord spoke of when he said to you, 'I will give your enemy into your hands for you to deal with as you wish.'" Then David crept up unnoticed and cut off a corner of Saul's robe. **1 SAMUEL 24:3, 4.**

Saul had given up on the Lord and had gone his own way. The Lord wanted to work with him, but God never forces people to follow Him. Israel was going to need a new champion, a new king, and that champion was David. Saul knew this in his heart of hearts, so he hated David and wanted to kill him. In fact, Saul was so consumed by hatred for David that at times he ignored the threats of the nations around him so he could pursue and kill the former shepherd boy.

When I was young, my dad instilled in me the idea that violence was OK as long as it was in self-defense. If someone broke into my house, I figured I'd use my baseball bat and hit a home run with the intruder's kneecaps.

What about David? King Saul was threatening David's life each day, so any action David took against Saul would be in self-defense. Besides, David had already been anointed by Samuel, making him the rightful king—so wouldn't he be justified in getting rid of his rival?

Finally the opportunity came. Saul entered a cave, not knowing that David and his companions were hiding there. David's chance to eliminate his greatest threat was right in front of him. God had even told David that he could do as he pleased in this case. And what did David do? Instead of cutting Saul's throat, he cut a little piece of cloth to show both Saul and his own men that leaders deserve respect, even if they aren't doing all they should do.

Jesus exhibited the same kind of respect for the corrupt spiritual leaders of His day. He didn't like what they were doing, but He still encouraged people to give to the church and to present themselves to the priests after they were healed.

Honor your parents and your pastor and your teachers and the leaders of your community by being a good citizen and a Christlike person—even if they aren't.

MAY 6

What's in a Name?

NABAL ANSWERED DAVID'S SERVANTS, "Who is this David? Who is this son of Jesse? Many servants are breaking away from their masters these days. Why should I take my bread and water, and the meat I have slaughtered for my shearers, and give it to men coming from who knows where?" David's men turned around and went back. When they arrived, they reported every word. David said to his men, "Each of you strap on your sword!" So they did, and David strapped his on as well. About four hundred men went up with David, while two hundred stayed with the supplies. **1 SAMUEL 25:10-13.**

David was on the run from Saul and had to rely on the kindness of people he had helped in the past. He banked on people returning good for good. So when he heard from his men that Nabal had badmouthed him and sent them away without any food, he lost his temper and decided to go and take care of the matter like a soldier.

As he was riding in to take care of business, Nabal's wife, Abigail, ran out to meet him and begged for her husband's life. She also brought a ton of really good food (the secret to any man's heart) to thank him in advance for sparing her family.

During this point in Israel's history, babies wouldn't receive a name until several days after they were born. Parents wanted to see what their children's character traits were, even at an early age, and they would choose a name based on what they thought their child's character was projecting.

Nabal, in Hebrew, means "fool" or "idiot." As I write this, I'm sitting in a ski lodge on Mount Baker. The person next to me is someone I'm studying with to prepare her for baptism. On hearing this story, she asked, "Why would anyone name their child 'idiot'?" I don't know, but it seems that they got the name right.

Nabal became what they named him. His faithful wife saved him from the wrath of David, but not from the eventual fate of every idiot. Nabal died of a heart attack when he found out how close he had come to dying by the sword of David.

If people were to give you a name after observing your character, what would they call you? Let's hope your life would give you a name that speaks well of you and the God you serve. If not, why not strive for a name change?

Bewitched

THE WOMAN ASKED, "Whom do you want me to bring up?" He answered, "Bring up Samuel." When the woman saw Samuel, she screamed. She said, "Why have you tricked me? You are Saul!" The king said to the woman, "Don't be afraid! What do you see?" The woman said, "I see a spirit coming up out of the ground." Saul asked, "What does he look like?" The woman answered, "An old man wearing a coat is coming up." Then Saul knew it was Samuel, and he bowed facedown on the ground. Samuel asked Saul, "Why have you disturbed me by bringing me up?" Saul said, "I am greatly troubled. The Philistines are fighting against me, and God has left me. He won't answer me anymore, either by prophets or in dreams. That's why I called for you. Tell me what to do." **1 SAMUEL 28:11-15, NCV.**

While the list of major no-no's found in the Bible is long, right up toward the top would be "Don't play around with the devil and his angels."

When my wife was in college, she and a group of friends were at a pastor's house having worship and prayer one Friday night. The pastor had to leave on a call, but before he left he introduced a young woman named Amy to the group. As he was heading out the door, he whispered to one of the guys, "Keep an eye on Amy. She's going through a real battle right now."

It turned out that the "real battle" was over her involvement in a satanic cult. She was wavering on whether to follow through with the rites of membership in this cult and was exploring Christ as an option for her life.

Before they knew it, ten 18-year-olds were holding down a fully possessed young woman who was writhing on the floor with guttural voices coming out of her. After they'd prayed frightened prayers for a while, the pastor walked in the door. He took in the scene and said, "Amy, your time of confrontation has not yet come. In the name of Jesus Christ, leave her." The demon left, Amy recovered, and to our knowledge she is still a follower of Christ today.

Don't mess with Satan. Don't watch movies, listen to music, or play games that dabble in the occult. Stay away from the devil's playground. Wrap yourself in Jesus.

MAY 8

A Sad End to a Once-Great King

THE PHILISTINES CLOSED IN ON Saul and his sons, and they killed three of his sons—Jonathan, Abinadab, and Malkishua. The fighting grew very fierce around Saul, and the Philistine archers caught up with him and wounded him severely. Saul groaned to his armor bearer, "Take your sword and kill me before these pagan Philistines come to run me through and taunt and torture me." But his armor bearer was afraid and would not do it. So Saul took his own sword and fell on it. When his armor bearer realized that Saul was dead, he fell on his own sword and died beside the king. So Saul, his three sons, his armor bearer, and his troops all died together that same day. **1 SAMUEL 31:2-6, NLT.**

I'm not impressed with the fate of tall people in the Bible. It seems as if each one of them turns out to be some sort of wretch. Goliath was no prize, and now Saul ends up dead on his own sword. I'm concerned about the tall people in the Bible because I'm six feet six inches, and I don't want to turn out like any of them!

The message in Saul's tragic story isn't about the dangers of being tall. The message in this story is all about unrealized potential.

When Saul was first anointed as king, he had all the potential in the world. He was mighty in war, and in the beginning he gave credit to God for his victories. Through Samuel, King Saul brought the people of God back to the law of God, which they had been ignoring for decades.

So what happened to Saul? He got comfortable with the gifts God had given him and relied on them instead of on the Giver of those gifts. Saul depended on himself and his wisdom. Saul became proud of the person God had chosen him to be. And when people become proud, they get so full of themselves that there is no room for God.

Saul's story should serve as a sobering reminder to everyone who professes to be a God follower. Remember, this walk with Christ is not a sprint; it's a marathon. Receive the good gifts and talents that Jesus gives you and then ask Him to be the Lord of all of them. Don't get so puffed up that there isn't room for Jesus in your heart.

MAY 9

"Burn in Hell, Osama!"

DAVID TOOK UP THIS LAMENT concerning Saul and his son Jonathan, and he ordered that the people of Judah be taught this lament of the bow (it is written in the Book of Jashar). **2 SAMUEL 1:17, 18.**

I remember where I was when I first heard that Osama bin Laden had been killed by American forces. I heard it on the radio on my way home from a meeting. I raced into the house and turned on the TV news to learn the details about the demise of the terrorist mastermind who had eluded American military intelligence for more than 10 years. As I took in the coverage of the brave Navy SEAL operation, the scene flashed from the diagrams of Bin Laden's safe house in Pakistan to video from the streets of Washington, D.C., and other cities in the United States.

People were cheering in the streets and chanting "U-S-A, U-S-A!" It was exhilarating to see such national pride spontaneously bursting out in the streets. Then I started to read the signs that people were holding up to the news cameras. "Burn in hell, Osama!" was one of the more tame ones. And, to be honest, I started to feel uncomfortable with the sentiment behind them. If you read today's chapter, maybe you'll see why.

David had every reason in the world to hate King Saul. King Saul not only despised David; he tried on several occasions to murder him. David spent the better part of his young adult life running away as Saul hunted him like a dog on a foxhunt.

So you would think that when David heard of Saul's death, he'd throw a huge party and hold up a sign that said "Burn in hell, Saul!" But he didn't. No. David was filled with the Spirit of God and not the spirit of this world. David was like Jesus, who said, "Love your enemies and pray for those who persecute you" (Matthew 5:44). David somehow grasped the concept that forgiving our enemies is what God calls us to do.

When God watches the destruction of the wicked at the end of time, do you think He'll be throwing a party and holding up a sign? What do you think His reaction will be as He sees the destruction of those who would rather die than spend eternity with Him? I think that's what our reaction should be whenever anybody chooses death over life—even when justice is served.

MAY 10

The Lust of the Eyes

ONE EVENING DAVID GOT UP from his bed and walked around on the roof of the palace. From the roof he saw a woman bathing. The woman was very beautiful, and David sent someone to find out about her. The man said, "She is Bathsheba, the daughter of Eliam and the wife of Uriah the Hittite." Then David sent messengers to get her. She came to him, and he slept with her. (Now she was purifying herself from her monthly uncleanness.) Then she went back home. **2 SAMUEL 11:2-4.**

The evolution of sin in the human mind is a curious and deadly thing. It starts with the senses. We see something. We smell something. We hear something. We feel something. We taste something.

After our senses take notice, we process the information that has just entered our brains. Do I look again? Do I listen more intently? Or do I walk away right now?

If we choose to dwell on what our senses first perceived, that's usually when the hook is set. It's just a matter of time before the desires of our flesh become louder than the still small voice shouting for us to flee.

Look at David's example. One night he couldn't sleep. He went out onto his balcony and saw her, bathing on her roof (they didn't have indoor plumbing back then—this would have been a normal thing). He should have turned away. She was not his wife (and he had more than one, plus concubines, to sleep with). But he didn't. He entertained the thought.

At his command Bathsheba was brought to David, and for all intents and purposes, he raped her. She may not have screamed for help; she may not have yelled "No!" But if you define rape as using one's power to inflict one's sexual desire on another, then this was rape.

The deed was done. He sent her home. His sinful lusts were satisfied. She was left with the walk of shame down the corridors of the palace and back to her house.

Anytime we dive into the desires of our sinful selves, our actions damage us and those around us. The better choice is to flee from temptation. God always gives us a way out. Hang on to Jesus and turn away from the tempter. If you do, you will avoid the kind of mess David brought upon himself.

Bob and Weave

THE WOMAN CONCEIVED and sent word to David, saying, "I am pregnant."
2 SAMUEL 11:5.

One of the responsibilities I had when working on academy campuses was to sit on discipline councils. During these meetings at one academy I sat next to a faculty member who had a good sense of humor and knew human nature. Often when a student came in and was confronted with whatever they had done that deserved discipline, my associate would lean over and whisper, "Now watch him bob and weave."

The expression "bob and weave" comes from a technique that boxers use to avoid being hit by their opponent. King David starts to bob and weave when he finds out that his sin has gotten a married woman pregnant.

King David sends for Bathsheba's husband, Uriah, and tries to get him to go and sleep with his wife. Uriah is so loyal to his fellow troops that he refuses to go home to his wife until all his friends can have the same luxury.

So David gets Uriah drunk, figuring drunken people don't hold to their convictions very well. Still Uriah doesn't go home to his wife.

Finally King David arranges for Uriah to be killed in battle. That's right—David murders someone so he can save face. He tries to cover up his sin by destroying the evidence.

That's what sin does. Sin causes us to act in shameful ways. The only way to avoid these shameful behaviors after we sin is to confess those sins and let God heal our self-inflicted wounds.

Yes, it would be great if we could just not sin in the first place. But as strong as all of us would like to be, we all fall short of our desired faithfulness. Sometimes we fall little. Sometimes we fall big, like David.

God understands. He knows you. He knows your struggles. And He's already forgiven you for your sin. All you need to do is confess it and thank Him for His grace. When you confess that sin, He is ever faithful to forgive your sin and cleanse you from all the icky stuff you've gotten yourself into. After we sin, the big battle is with our pride. Can we admit our failures, and can we accept His forgiveness?

MAY 12

The Relentless Pursuer

THEN DAVID SAID TO NATHAN, "I have sinned against the Lord." Nathan replied, "The Lord has taken away your sin. You are not going to die." **2 SAMUEL 12:13.**

One of the most common ways for people to deal with their problems is to ignore them. Like the proverbial ostrich sticking its head in the sand, if I don't see the problem, then maybe it will go away.

People do this with their health—sometimes until it's too late. People do this in relationships. I know somebody who is 28 years old and is married for the fourth time. Each time a problem arose in their marriage, this person would make it go away by getting rid of the relationship.

Of course, this common way of dealing with problems never works. The only way to truly deal with a problem is to deal with the problem! If I have a problem with my health, I need to find out what it is and treat it. Ignoring it won't make it go away. If I have a problem in a relationship, I need to figure out what it is. Ignoring it or covering it up doesn't make the problem go away.

And if I have sin in my life . . . well, you know the drill.

David tried to cover up his problem (impregnating a married woman and then killing her husband), thinking it would just go away. I'm so glad we serve a God who in His heart desires our health and welfare. When we sin and try to cover it up, God pursues us to help us confront our sin. He knows that if we are allowed to bury it or sweep it under a rug, it never really goes away.

God sent the prophet Nathan to David. When David was confronted with his sin, he confessed and repented in tears. Notice the difference between David and Saul. David acknowledged and accepted responsibility for his sin, and God saved him. Saul swept his sins under the rug and ended up falling on his own sword.

It's easy for us to get defensive when somebody points out our sin. But wouldn't it be better for us to "man up" (as my dad would say) and take responsibility for what we've done? The cleansing power of Jesus' blood can take away the sting of sin and cleanse us from the guilt that burdens us.

Love Never Forces

TAMAR SAID TO HIM, "No, brother! Don't force me! This should never be done in Israel! Don't do this shameful thing! I could never get rid of my shame! And you will be like the shameful fools in Israel! Please talk with the king, and he will let you marry me." But Amnon refused to listen to her. He was stronger than she was, so he forced her to have sexual relations with him. After that, Amnon hated Tamar. He hated her more than he had loved her before. Amnon said to her, "Get up and leave!" **2 SAMUEL 13:12-15, NCV.**

This Bible story has an all-too-familiar theme. One of David's sons falls in lust with one of his half-sisters, Tamar. He's so in lust with her that it consumes his every thought. He actually starts to get physically sick because he's so bothered by his emotions for her. So he and a friend devise a plan to trick Tamar into being in the same room with Amnon, the sicko.

Amnon tricks Tamar and forces her to be intimate with him. The whole time she is screaming and begging him not to do it. But he is so consumed with sick emotion for her that he rapes her anyway.

Notice what happens after he is done satisfying his lust. "Then Amnon hated her with intense hatred. In fact, he hated her more than he had loved her." This radical swing in emotion may surprise some of you. But let me tell you, it's no surprise to me.

I can't tell you how many sobbing young women I've had in my office through the years who have allowed a young man to satisfy his lust with them, only to be dumped for the next hot little thing to come along. Lust had quickly turned to disgust.

Young men and young women, don't give your body away. And until you are old enough to do so, don't give your heart away, either. Your body and your heart are sacred things that belong to God, not to somebody who wants to smooth-talk you into actions of regret. Don't let somebody's clever arguments convince you to act on lust in an attempt to fulfill what only God can give you. Live your lives without regret.

And remember, love doesn't force, and it doesn't coerce. If somebody has to talk you into giving your body or your heart away, get out of that situation as fast as you can!

MAY 14

Rumors and Revenge

ABSALOM NEVER SAID A WORD to Amnon, either good or bad; he hated Amnon because he had disgraced his sister Tamar. **2 SAMUEL 13:22.**

So Absalom, David's son, decides to get revenge on Amnon, David's other son, for raping Absalom's sister, who is also David's daughter. Does this sound like an afternoon soap opera or what? The point is, Absalom didn't like it that Amnon got away with raping Tamar. No punishment, no discipline. It seemed as if King David didn't even care that it had happened. So Absalom was going to take matters into his own hands.

Two years later Absalom was planning to throw a huge party during a big sheep-shearing event. Absalom approached David and said, "I'd like all my brothers to be there at the party!" David acquiesced and allowed all his sons to go.

When Amnon the rapist was drunk on wine, Absalom had his men slaughter him. By the time the news of Amnon's death reached the palace, the story had blown up, and the rumor was spreading that Absalom had killed all of David's sons. This had King David and his officials in mourning. Finally the news was corrected, and David found out that only Amnon had been killed.

Absalom fled the scene and went to live in a place where he would be protected from any kind of justice or revenge that might come his way.

There are so many things wrong with this story that it's hard to know where to start. First of all, where was King David when his daughter got raped? Why didn't he punish Amnon? When we overlook justice, bad things can happen. People can take matters into their own hands, and then things can get really ugly.

Second, when we take justice into our own hands by resorting to physical violence, we end up lowering ourselves to the same level as those we are trying to punish. There's a part of me that applauds Amnon's fate. I think anyone who treats a young woman the way Amnon treated his half sister deserves what Amnon got. But the Bible is pretty clear about using violence to exact revenge. It's not a recommended course of behavior. "Vengeance is mine; I will repay, saith the Lord" (Romans 12:19, KJV).

Isn't it amazing how one sin starts an avalanche of sins?

Looks Aren't Everything

IN ALL ISRAEL THERE WAS NOT A MAN so highly praised for his handsome appearance as Absalom. From the top of his head to the sole of his foot there was no blemish in him. Whenever he cut the hair of his head—he used to cut his hair once a year because it became too heavy for him —he would weigh it, and its weight was two hundred shekels by the royal standard. **2 SAMUEL 14:25, 26.**

The entertainment world was steeped in controversy in 2011 when Bradley Cooper was named "Sexiest Man Alive" by *People* magazine. As Cooper was accepting his award, movie fans around the world petitioned *People* to take back their announcement and proclaim Ryan Gosling as the winner of this prestigious (lame) award. People, get a life!

If there had been a *People* magazine in Jerusalem during the time of David and Absalom, they wouldn't have even needed a contest. Absalom was cut. His muscles had their own muscles. When he walked past the ladies, they would call out such cheesy pickup lines as "If I were a stoplight, I'd turn red every time you passed by just so I could stare at you a bit longer."

But as the saying goes, looks aren't everything. Absalom had a problem. His problem was very similar to the problem Lucifer had in heaven. He wanted the throne, even though it wasn't his to possess. Absalom began to subvert his father's authority. As the silver-tongued young man flattered the people with favor, they started to wonder if Absalom wouldn't make a better king than David.

With the support of the people and his incredible good looks, Absalom's head got big, and he made his move. He declared war on his father and tried to forcibly take the kingdom from him.

Good looks are a curse that I have never had to deal with! Yet we all have gifts from God that we can use for His glory or for our own. Absalom let his gifts override his character and destroy him.

Remember, every perfect gift is from God, and, when used and appreciated as such, can bring us joy and Him glory. Let's give our pride a break and use our gifts to honor God instead of using them to make ourselves look good in the eyes of others.

MAY 16

How to Treat a Dead Dog

AS KING DAVID CAME TO Bahurim, a man came out and cursed him. He was from Saul's family group, and his name was Shimei son of Gera. He threw stones at David and his officers, but the people and soldiers gathered all around David. Shimei cursed David, saying, "Get out, get out, you murderer, you troublemaker. The Lord is punishing you for the people in Saul's family you killed! You took Saul's place as king, but now the Lord has given the kingdom to your son Absalom! Now you are ruined because you are a murderer!" Abishai son of Zeruiah said to the king, "Why should this dead dog curse you, the king? Let me go over and cut off his head!" But the king answered, "This does not concern you, sons of Zeruiah! If he is cursing me because the Lord told him to, who can question him?" David also said to Abishai and all his officers, "My own son is trying to kill me! This man is a Benjaminite and has more right to kill me! Leave him alone, and let him curse me because the Lord told him to do this. Maybe the Lord will see my misery and repay me with something good for Shimei's curses today!" So David and his men went on down the road, but Shimei followed on the nearby hillside. He kept cursing David and throwing stones and dirt at him.
2 SAMUEL 16:5-13, NCV.

As you've noticed, today's text was longer than most in this book. I wanted you to read it all because it contains one of the most valuable lessons in all of Scripture.

How you deal with criticism may well dictate how fully you achieve in life. Notice that David doesn't order one of his archers to shish-kebab Shimei. Instead he tells his entourage that this criticism, as harsh as it sounds, may be from the Lord; it may be true. Now, *that* is spiritual maturity.

When people criticize me, I tend feel threatened and give a knee-jerk response. I want to defend my actions, even if they are wrong. David realized that the best way to deal with criticism is to take it in, think about it, and weigh the evidence.

The next time someone criticizes you—friend or foe—don't react in a negative way. Take the criticism in. Approach some trusted friends and ask them if the criticism is true. If it is, repent and make appropriate changes in your life. If it's not, then let it go. Either way, criticism is fuel to make you a better person. And it could be God's way of getting your attention in an area of your life that needs it.

Just Hangin' Around

NOW ABSALOM HAPPENED TO MEET David's men. He was riding his mule, and as the mule went under the thick branches of a large oak, Absalom's hair got caught in the tree. He was left hanging in midair, while the mule he was riding kept on going. **2 SAMUEL 18:9.**

Absalom had made David's life miserable. In no particular order of importance, he had murdered his brother, taken over the throne of Jerusalem by force and intimidation, had an immoral physical relationship with David's concubines on the roof of the palace in view of the inhabitants of the kingdom (to demonstrate his dominance over David), and pursued David and his troops to kill his father. Absalom was probably not a candidate for the annual Son of the Year award.

And now Absalom the handsome, Absalom the warrior, Absalom the proud, is suspended between heaven and earth—by his beautiful hair. The powerful general of the rebel army is stranded by 100,000 follicles on his handsome head.

One has to wonder if Absalom had a knife to free himself but didn't want to do damage to those stunning locks of hair. All we know is that in the end David's men did him in with some throwing knives.

The most amazing part of this whole story isn't the end of Absalom; it's the reaction of David. You would think that David would be overjoyed at the news that his enemy is dead. Instead he mourns, "O my son Absalom! My son, my son Absalom! If only I had died instead of you—O Absalom, my son, my son!" (verse 33).

A lot of people think that at the end of time when the wicked are destroyed by the sin they cling to, God is going to get some sort of perverse satisfaction from their death. Instead, I think God is going to act as David did—even though His children were His enemies.

When David expressed his sorrow, he lamented, "If only I could have died instead of you." Jesus *did* die instead of us. He allowed our sin to crush the life out of Him so that we wouldn't have to suffer the punishing weight of our sins. What a heart-wrenching experience it will be for Him to watch many of His children crushed by the guilt of their sins when they didn't have to suffer such a fate.

MAY 18

The Stone Thrower Returns

WHEN SHIMEI SON OF GERA crossed the Jordan, he fell prostrate before the king and said to him, "May my lord not hold me guilty. Do not remember how your servant did wrong on the day my lord the king left Jerusalem. May the king put it out of his mind. For I your servant know that I have sinned, but today I have come here as the first from the tribes of Joseph to come down and meet my lord the king." Then Abishai son of Zeruiah said, "Shouldn't Shimei be put to death for this? He cursed the Lord's anointed." David replied, ". . . Should anyone be put to death in Israel today? Don't I know that today I am king over Israel?" So the king said to Shimei, "You shall not die." And the king promised him on oath. **2 SAMUEL 19:18-23.**

The power of forgiveness was once presented to me this way: If you own a puppy and it waddles up to you and rolls onto its back, you have three choices: (1) you can scratch its belly and make its legs quiver from happiness, (2) you can ignore it, or (3) you can lift your foot and crush the puppy with your heel. The choice is yours, but scratching the puppy's belly will be best for the puppy, and it will make you feel good too.

Remember Shimei? He's the one who was cursing King David and throwing rocks at him a few chapters earlier. At the time David took the criticism and weighed it. As it turned out, Shimei's criticism was wrong, and David was the chosen king of Israel. Now David has the opportunity to forgive, to ignore, or to crush. David chooses the correct way: he forgives. Why?

Consider this quote:

"Forgiveness means refusing to make them pay for what they did. However, to refrain from lashing out at someone when you want to do so with all your being is agony. It is a form of suffering. . . . You are absorbing the debt, taking the cost of it completely on yourself instead of taking it out on the other person. It hurts terribly. Many people would say it feels like a kind of death. Yes, but it is a death that leads to resurrection instead of the lifelong living death of bitterness and cynicism."*

This is the forgiveness Jesus offers to us. This is the forgiveness Jesus calls on us to offer to those who offend us. When we practice forgiveness, we come as close to being like God as any of us will ever get.

---

* Timothy Keller, *The Reason for God: Belief in an Age of Skepticism* (New York: Penguin, 2008).

MAY 19

The Devil Made Me Do It

ONCE AGAIN THE ANGER OF the Lord burned against Israel, and he caused David to harm them by taking a census. "Go and count the people of Israel and Judah," the Lord told him. . . . But after he had taken the census, David's conscience began to bother him. And he said to the Lord, "I have sinned greatly by taking this census. Please forgive my guilt, Lord, for doing this foolish thing." **2 SAMUEL 24:1-10, NLT.**

Sometimes the Bible can seem a little confusing when it comes to who God really is. In this story God tells David to count his soldiers (something that the Law forbade) and then gets mad at David for counting his soldiers. David feels guilty for counting the soldiers, even though God is the one who told him to do it!

That's like your mom asking you to steal cookies from the cookie jar. So you steal the cookies. Then your mom punishes you for stealing the cookies she told you to steal. And on top of it all, you feel guilty for doing what your mom told you to do! Make sense?

To clear up the confusion, I would like to posit a theory that I mentioned briefly once before. It seems that many of the Old Testament writers didn't have a clue that the devil existed. In fact, he is mentioned only a few times in the Old Testament. So in the Old Testament God gets all the credit for the good things that happen, and He gets all the blame for the horrible things that happen.

Take a look at the same story in a book written many years after 2 Samuel: "Satan rose up against Israel and incited David to take a census of Israel. So David said to Joab and the commanders of the troops, 'Go and count the Israelites from Beersheba to Dan. Then report back to me so that I may know how many there are'" (1 Chronicles 21:1, 2). See the difference? Same story, only this time the author of the story knows who Satan is.

One of the fundamental reasons that Jesus came to earth was to show us the Father. He needed to do this because human beings have had a muddled view of God from the beginning. Let us always remember that "every good and perfect gift is from above, . . . from the Father" (James 1:17) and that Satan is the author of sin, death, lying, and suffering. God is love. And Jesus came to show us the Father. In fact, Jesus said, "If you've seen me, you've seen the Father" (see John 14:9).

MAY 20

Anything You Want

NOW, LORD MY GOD, you have made your servant king in place of my father David. But I am only a little child and do not know how to carry out my duties. Your servant is here among the people you have chosen, a great people, too numerous to count or number. So give your servant a discerning heart to govern your people and to distinguish between right and wrong. For who is able to govern this great people of yours? **1 KINGS 3:7-9.**

Once upon a time three men were walking along a beautiful sandy beach. One of them saw something shiny glimmering in the sand. He bent down to pick it up and saw that it was an old gold lamp. As he started to rub the sand off it, a genie popped out (this is not a true story) and said, "Thank you for freeing me from this lamp! I'll now grant each of you one wish!"

The first man said, "I'd like to be twice as smart as I already am." The genie crossed his arms, nodded, and said, "Your wish has been granted."

The second man said, "I'd like to be 10 times smarter than I already am!" The genie crossed his arms, nodded, and said, "Your wish has been granted."

The third man said, "I'd like to be 100 times smarter than I already am!" The genie crossed his arms, nodded, and turned the third man into a woman. Old joke.

OK, so the genie appearance isn't going to happen, but if God came to you and told you He would give you anything you wanted—anything in the world—what would you choose? An unlimited bank account? The ability to read minds? The ability to breathe underwater? (I think I might be tempted to choose that one.)

Solomon had this very option, and he chose to ask for wisdom to guide God's people in the right way. This was an indication that Solomon had a good character. He asked for a gift that would bless others and not just himself.

What are your desires in life? When Jesus had the option to give up on the human race or give up heaven so that we could know the Father—when He was faced with safety in heaven versus death on earth—He chose the gift that would bless others.

Blessing others with our gifts takes a commitment of self-sacrifice. But it pays off big-time!

MAY 21

A Place to Find God

IN THE FOUR HUNDRED and eightieth year after the Israelites came out of Egypt, in the fourth year of Solomon's reign over Israel, in the month of Ziv, the second month, he began to build the temple of the Lord. **1 KINGS 6:1.**

It seems there are lots of "homes" for God in the world. Some would say that Rome is a good place for God. Others might say that their church is where God is on any given weekend. Pantheists say that God is alive in everything, such as my computer desk or my hat.

And then there are places in the world where God seems to be absent. I've heard people say He's not in places where there is war and strife—or at Chicago Cubs games.

I'd like you to consider an interesting quote from a book called *The Ministry of Healing:* "Many feel that it would be a great privilege to visit the scenes of Christ's life on earth, to walk where He trod, to look upon the lake beside which He loved to teach, and the hills and valleys on which His eyes so often rested. But we need not go to Nazareth, to Capernaum, or to Bethany, in order to walk in the steps of Jesus. We shall find His footprints beside the sickbed, in the hovels of poverty, in the crowded alleys of the great cities, and in every place where there are human hearts in need of consolation" (pp. 105, 106).

God is where His people are. Solomon did a wonderful thing in building a place set aside for worshipping and giving to God. But God's people seemed to sequester Him in a temple. They needed to realize that God desires to live in our hearts.

I've been to some pretty spectacular places that made me feel as if God was there. Cathedrals in Europe, wilderness mountains I've hiked, and quiet rooms where several friends knelt together in prayer have all given me the sense that God was there. I suppose He was.

As I thought about all these places I've experienced God's presence, I noticed one thing they had in common. I was there. God was there because I was there and He was in my heart. God doesn't reside in buildings or on mountains. He sides in you, if you invite Him to.

MAY 22

Credit Where Credit Is Due

WHEN THE QUEEN OF SHEBA HEARD about Solomon, she came to test him with hard questions. She traveled to Jerusalem with a large group of servants and camels carrying spices, jewels, and much gold. When she came to Solomon, she talked with him about all she had in mind, and Solomon answered all her questions. Nothing was too hard for him to explain to her. The queen of Sheba learned that Solomon was very wise. She saw the palace he had built, the food on his table, his many officers, the palace servants, and their good clothes. She saw the servants who served him at feasts and the whole burnt offerings he made in the Temple of the Lord. All these things amazed her. So she said to King Solomon, "What I heard in my own country about your achievements and wisdom is true. I could not believe it then, but now I have come and seen it with my own eyes. I was not told even half of it! Your wisdom and wealth are much greater than I had heard. Your men and officers are very lucky, because in always serving you, they are able to hear your wisdom. Praise the Lord your God, who was pleased to make you king of Israel. The Lord has constant love for Israel, so he made you king to keep justice and to rule fairly." **1 KINGS 10:1-9, NCV.**

Before I became a pastor, I worked for a television and radio station in downtown Seattle. It was a local ABC affiliate that broadcast to most of the great state of Washington. I did everything from sorting mail to holding microphones for live shows.

One evening while I was at the station after work to meet a friend for dinner, the radio producer and technician came out of the booth in a heated discussion about a crisis with their technology. A live guest who was being wired into the show had been cut off, and they had to reconnect pronto. I quickly figured out how to fix their technology problem, and the news interview with a prominent politician went on uninterrupted.

The next day the head of the news department had a huge meeting to congratulate the producer and technician for their hard work in solving this issue. He gave them both bonuses as they smiled and accepted the accolades. Not once did the two guys acknowledge that I was the one who had fixed their problem.

Today's text shows the opposite. God got all the glory as the queen of Sheba saw what Solomon had attained. Let's remember to point to God as the power behind our successes.

MAY 23

Love Is Blind (Sometimes)

KING SOLOMON LOVED MANY WOMEN who were not from Israel. He loved the daughter of the king of Egypt, as well as women of the Moabites, Ammonites, Edomites, Sidonians, and Hittites. The Lord had told the Israelites, "You must not marry people of other nations. If you do, they will cause you to follow their gods." But Solomon fell in love with these women. He had seven hundred wives who were from royal families and three hundred slave women who gave birth to his children. His wives caused him to turn away from God. As Solomon grew old, his wives caused him to follow other gods. He did not follow the Lord completely as his father David had done. Solomon worshiped Ashtoreth, the goddess of the people of Sidon, and Molech, the hated god of the Ammonites. So Solomon did what the Lord said was wrong and did not follow the Lord completely as his father David had done. **1 KINGS 11:1-6, NCV.**

One of the smartest and most successful businessmen I know has been through four marriages and is going on his fifth. He tells me that this is the one! (The woman he's marrying is 20 years his junior.) I can't help thinking that maybe my friend isn't very good at picking life mates.

I know other people who have relatively high IQs when it comes to most things in life, yet as soon as they get into relationships with the opposite sex, their IQ drops about 20 points. Some people just have a knack for picking the wrong person to fall in love with.

Solomon had everything going for him. He had the splendor of a glorious kingdom. He was wise beyond human understanding. He built a beautiful Temple for his God. His palace was luxurious. But all of that couldn't prevent him from falling in love with 700 women who would become his wives, plus 300 concubines (housekeepers that he could be intimate with). *One thousand women!* Are you kidding me?

When it came to love, the wisest man on earth became about as smart as a bag of hammers! And as he married these women from other countries, they started to pollute Israel with their gods. This would become the downfall of the nation.

A word of advice: Don't get into relationships that you *hope* will one day honor God. Let Him match you up with people who will strengthen your walk with Him.

MAY 24

My Advice About Advice

BUT REHOBOAM REJECTED THE ADVICE of the older men and instead asked the opinion of the young men who had grown up with him and were now his advisers. "What is your advice?" he asked them. "How should I answer these people who want me to lighten the burdens imposed by my father?" The young men replied, "This is what you should tell those complainers who want a lighter burden: 'My little finger is thicker than my father's waist! Yes, my father laid heavy burdens on you, but I'm going to make them even heavier! My father beat you with whips, but I will beat you with scorpions!'" **1 KINGS 12:8-11, NLT.**

I like the story of the emperor's new clothes because it illustrates the importance of getting advice from people who will be honest with you and not flatter you. You know the story, right?

There's an arrogant emperor who loves to look at himself in the mirror. A couple of scam artists approach him and tell him that they have created a new set of clothes that only smart, good-looking, and gifted people can see. They pretend to hold the outfit up (there's nothing there to see), and, not wanting to be ignorant, ugly, and ungifted, the emperor says, "I'll take one!"

The emperor holds a parade to show off his new set of clothes. The word goes out that only the smart, good-looking, and gifted people can see this avant-garde attire. So the emperor walks down the street in the nude as his adoring subjects cheer his new clothes—until a little kid who doesn't care what anybody thinks says, "Hey! Why is that guy naked?"

If you're going to seek advice, don't seek it only from close friends your own age. Often they will hold back vital advice for fear of alienating you or hurting your feelings.

When I need to seek wisdom, I try to get it from a variety of people whom I give permission to give me honest feedback. Often I will seek out someone older than I am who I know is good with God. A true friend can tell you the painful truth and still be your friend.

Rehoboam was a hotheaded young man who took advice from other hotheaded young men. His kingdom did not last.

Caught in the Crazy Cycle

AFTER SEEKING ADVICE, THE KING made two golden calves. He said to the people, "It is too much for you to go up to Jerusalem. Here are your gods, Israel, who brought you up out of Egypt." One he set up in Bethel, and the other in Dan. And this thing became a sin; the people came to worship the one at Bethel and went as far as Dan to worship the other. **1 KINGS 12:28-30.**

It's been said that the definition of insanity is doing the same thing over and over and expecting a different result each time. I don't know if that would mark a person as insane, but it certainly would speak to their stupidity!

I've experienced déjà vu in more than just my mind. I've actually done some things again and again and each time acted a bit surprised that it always turns out the same. If I'm drinking a soft drink with crushed ice in it, when the soft drink is gone and I want some ice in my mouth, I will be the guy who tilts the cup up and taps the bottom of it to get one piece of ice to fall into my mouth. Of course, every single time all the ice slides down at an alarming speed, hits me in the nose, and goes down my shirt. This has happened about 38 times in my life. It will probably happen again tomorrow.

As you remember, Israel had tried the golden calf idea at the base of Mount Sinai while Moses was receiving the law. Moses was not pleased, God was not pleased, and people suffered. What would make King Jeroboam believe that somehow this time God would bless bowing down to a golden calf? Did the king think that God had changed His mind?

Sometimes it's hard to get out of the habit of doing things that are self-destructive. Whether it's a chemical habit such as smoking, an emotional habit such as an eating disorder, or a social habit such as gossiping, the repeated cycle of self-destruction can be frustrating, to say the least.

If this chapter speaks to you and reminds you of something you keep going back to that is robbing you of an excellent life, take courage. Jesus will give you strength to overcome the burden you are carrying. Tell somebody you trust. Have them cheer you on and hold you accountable. Trash that golden calf and live an abundant life!

MAY 26

A Good Egg

AND ASA DID WHAT WAS RIGHT in the eyes of the Lord, as David his father had done. He put away the male cult prostitutes out of the land and removed all the idols that his fathers had made. He also removed Maacah his mother from being queen mother because she had made an abominable image for Asherah. And Asa cut down her image and burned it at the brook Kidron. But the high places were not taken away. Nevertheless, the heart of Asa was wholly true to the Lord all his days. **1 KINGS 15:11-14, ESV.**

If you have been reading through the Bible along with this devotional, or even if you have a general knowledge of the history of Israel, you know that by this time in our story Israel had split into two different countries: Judah and Israel. Both of these countries had a succession of kings who did horrible, awful, downright icky things that grieved the heart of God.

Yet every once in a while there was a king who stood out, did the right thing, and made God proud. Asa was one of those kings. We don't have a huge list of all his conquests, we don't know what kind of wealth he amassed, and we don't even know if the people in his kingdom liked him—we just know that when it came to being faithful to God, Asa stood out like a tree in a forest of shrubs.

When I was in high school, I didn't make great choices, and I remember times I stood out for the wrong reasons. I also remember seeing classmates stand up for the good. Even though I wasn't always standing with them, I admired them for being bold enough to do what was right, even if people were laughing at them at the time.

Ellen White wrote these great and true words: "The greatest want of the world is the want of men—men who will not be bought or sold, men who in their inmost souls are true and honest, men who do not fear to call sin by its right name, men whose conscience is as true to duty as the needle to the pole, men who will stand for the right though the heavens fall" (*Education*, p. 57).

King Asa stood up for the right, even though it may not have been popular to do so. What about you? Is it time to take a stand today? Is it time to let the world know through your actions that Jesus is Lord of your life?

I Don't Want Your Job

NOW ELIJAH THE TISHBITE, of Tishbe in Gilead, said to Ahab, "As the Lord the God of Israel lives, before whom I stand, there shall be neither dew nor rain these years, except by my word." And the word of the Lord came to him, "Depart from here and turn eastward and hide yourself by the brook Cherith, which is east of the Jordan. You shall drink from the brook, and I have commanded the ravens to feed you there." So he went and did according to the word of the Lord. He went and lived by the brook Cherith that is east of the Jordan. And the ravens brought him bread and meat in the morning, and bread and meat in the evening, and he drank from the brook. **1 KINGS 17:1-6, ESV.**

I've had some jobs that I didn't particularly enjoy. When I was a teenager, I worked for a fish-and-chips restaurant. My job was to stand in a kitchen all day cutting and filleting fish. I had a hard time getting rid of the fish smell from under my fingernails after work. One summer I had to work in 90-degree weather tearing down the upper floor of a house. One of my tasks was to remove the insulation. That was pretty yucky. (Should a grown man use the word *yucky*?) There was a period of time one day that I had to work on a septic tank. I'll not go into detail, but let's just say it was hard not to vomit from the fumes I had to inhale. These were all pretty bad jobs, but I wouldn't trade any of them for the job of a prophet.

This story marks the beginning of a long battle between King Ahab; his queen, Jezebel; and the prophet Elijah. It is an epic battle between good and evil, between God and the devil. Elijah was called into a pretty tough profession.

Yet, as we see throughout the Bible, God doesn't call us to anything that He doesn't give us the strength and ability to handle.

In this case God used a part of His creation—ravens—to deliver meals to Elijah. I don't know if you've ever noticed, but ravens aren't the most giving of all birds. They're usually fighting over roadkill or over french fries in the McDonald's parking lot. Yet God used these selfish birds to feed the prophet. I love how God takes care of His children. I love how He calls *and* He provides.

Listen today for the call of God in your life. Answer that call, and He will provide!

MAY 28

He Wants It All

SO ELIJAH WENT TO ZAREPHATH. When he reached the town gate, he saw a widow gathering wood for a fire. Elijah asked her, "Would you bring me a little water in a cup so I may have a drink." As she was going to get his water, Elijah said, "Please bring me a piece of bread, too." The woman answered, "As surely as the Lord your God lives, I have no bread. I have only a handful of flour in a jar and only a little olive oil in a jug. I came here to gather some wood so I could go home and cook our last meal. My son and I will eat it and then die from hunger." "Don't worry," Elijah said to her. "Go home and cook your food as you have said. But first make a small loaf of bread from the flour you have, and bring it to me. Then cook something for yourself and your son. The Lord, the God of Israel, says, 'That jar of flour will never be empty, and the jug will always have oil in it, until the day the Lord sends rain to the land.'" So the woman went home and did what Elijah told her to do. And the woman and her son and Elijah had enough food every day. The jar of flour and the jug of oil were never empty, just as the Lord, through Elijah, had promised. **1 KINGS 17:10-16, NCV.**

Here is a woman so destitute that she's about to make her last meal. God asks her to exhibit enough faith to use the last little bit of food in her cupboard on Him rather than on herself and her only son. "Oh, and if you do, I'll make sure you never go hungry again."

I wonder if she thought, *What kind of gall does God have to ask for my last bite of food? Where was He when my husband died? Where has He been as my son and I have gone to bed hungry each night? And now He wants my last meal? That's some demanding God.*

It must have taken an amazing amount of faith for that widow to mix that last batch of bread, bake it, and hand it to the prophet of God. But she did it. And she was rewarded for her faith.

Have you ever wondered, *What does Jesus want from me?* Here's my simple answer: Jesus wants your all. He wants everything. He doesn't want a part-time lover; He wants a full commitment. Jesus wants your money and your body and your time and your relationships and your hobbies and your heart. Jesus wants it all.

"Love the Lord your God with all your heart and with all your soul and with all your strength" (Deuteronomy 6:5). What does Jesus want from me? He wants everything.

Battle of the Gods

AT THE TIME OF SACRIFICE, the prophet Elijah stepped forward and prayed: "Lord, the God of Abraham, Isaac and Israel, let it be known today that you are God in Israel and that I am your servant and have done all these things at your command. Answer me, Lord, answer me, so these people will know that you, Lord, are God, and that you are turning their hearts back again." Then the fire of the Lord fell and burned up the sacrifice, the wood, the stones and the soil, and also licked up the water in the trench. **1 KINGS 18:36-38.**

I can just hear an announcer with a microphone in the middle of a boxing ring: "In this corner, weighing in at infinity, with an undefeated record, all by knockouts . . . Yahweh!

"And in this corner, the challenger. He's a god made up in the imaginations of the Canaanites—the supposed lord of rain, thunder, fertility, and agriculture. He weighs in at whatever his wood and stone idols weigh in at. This should be a good match! Let's get ready to rumble!"

OK, you and I know that this isn't going to be much of a fight, but it sure is one of the most entertaining battles recorded in Scripture. Elijah, standing alone, representing the God of the universe, confronts the prophets of Baal—all 450 of them. Elijah lays down the gauntlet: whoever can get their god to rain fire down from heaven on their altar wins.

The prophets of Baal sacrifice their animal, lay it on the altar, and dance around, cutting themselves and yelling out to their god. Silence.

Elijah doesn't flinch. In fact, he even goads them along, asking if maybe Baal can't hear their yelling because he's taking a nap.

Wanting to make his point loud and clear, Elijah has the people dump gallons of water over his offering until the trenches around the altar are full.

All eyes are on Elijah and that altar. Will he dance around and cut himself to appease his God? Nope. One simple prayer, and the blast from heaven is so powerful that it licks up the whole sacrifice, the wood, the stones, and the water! The prophets of Baal who have led God's people astray are destroyed, and God's name is vindicated in Israel—at least on that day.

MAY 30

Rottweiler Versus Chihuahua

AHAB TOLD JEZEBEL ALL THAT ELIJAH HAD DONE, and how he had killed all the prophets with the sword. Then Jezebel sent a messenger to Elijah, saying, "So may the gods do to me and more also, if I do not make your life as the life of one of them by this time tomorrow." Then he was afraid, and he arose and ran for his life and came to Beersheba, which belongs to Judah, and left his servant there. But he himself went a day's journey into the wilderness and came and sat down under a broom tree. And he asked that he might die, saying, "It is enough; now, O Lord, take away my life, for I am no better than my fathers." And he lay down and slept under a broom tree. And behold, an angel touched him and said to him, "Arise and eat." **1 KINGS 19:1-5, ESV.**

My friend had a rottweiler. A rottweiler is a large, intimidating dog that weighs as much as a small horse. This rottweiler was so big that when I'd drive up to my friend's home, the dog would stand and look into my car window and bark. I usually had to call my friend with my cell phone to have him call off the dog.

One of the funniest things I've ever seen was when a mutual friend came to visit with his little Chihuahua, a dog small enough to fit in my front pocket. When the Chihuahua was set on the living room floor, he made a beeline for the huge rottweiler. I thought, *This little Chihuahua must look like an appetizer to the rottweiler.* But then the strangest thing happened: the Chihuahua attacked the rottweiler! And the rottweiler yelped and ran away from the Chihuahua! For some reason the rottweiler didn't realize that with one snap of its massive jaws the little dog would have been history.

Elijah had just called fire down from heaven. He had just boldly killed 450 prophets of Baal. He was riding high! And now? We find Elijah running like a scared rabbit from a wicked queen. What made the difference?

Elijah was experiencing what all of us experience in life—highs and lows. In our highs it seems that nothing can touch us. In our lows we feel as vulnerable as that rottweiler being attacked by the Chihuahua.

The constant in this whole equation is that God will never leave us or forsake us. Jesus is constant. His mood doesn't go up and down. He always loves, always protects, and always forgives—even when we are scared and weak.

MAY 31

Shhh—Do You Hear It?

AND HE SAID, "Go out and stand on the mount before the Lord." And behold, the Lord passed by, and a great and strong wind tore the mountains and broke in pieces the rocks before the Lord, but the Lord was not in the wind. And after the wind an earthquake, but the Lord was not in the earthquake. And after the earthquake a fire, but the Lord was not in the fire. And after the fire the sound of a low whisper. And when Elijah heard it, he wrapped his face in his cloak and went out and stood at the entrance of the cave. And behold, there came a voice to him and said, "What are you doing here, Elijah?" **1 KINGS 19:11-13, ESV.**

One cold January morning a man stood at a Metro station in Washington, D.C., and started to play the violin. He played six classical pieces for about 45 minutes. During that time, since it was rush hour, approximately 1,100 people went through the station, most of them on their way to work.

In the 45 minutes that the musician played, only seven people stopped and listened for a while. Twenty-seven gave him money, most without even pausing in their normal pace. He collected roughly $32. When he finished playing and silence took over, no one applauded.

The busy commuters didn't know that the violinist was Joshua Bell, one of the most talented musicians in the world, carrying out an experiment organized by the Washington *Post*. He had just played some of the most intricate pieces ever written, using a violin worth $3.5 million. Three days before playing in the subway Joshua Bell had played to a packed concert hall in Boston, where typical seats cost $100.

Life is loud. Life is busy. We have things to do. We have places to go. We have earphones in, listening to music and anything else to occupy our time. When we get home, we run to our computer or flick on the television to see what's wrong with the world or to be entertained.

I fear that sometimes we get so wrapped up with the noise of life that we can't hear the still small voice of God. What if He's been trying to say something, but we've been too busy to listen? "Be still, and know that I am God" (Psalm 46:10). Turn the noise off and let God speak to you today. You never know what you might hear.

JUNE 1

Up, Up, and Away!

AS THEY WERE WALKING ALONG and talking together, suddenly a chariot of fire and horses of fire appeared and separated the two of them, and Elijah went up to heaven in a whirlwind. Elisha saw this and cried out, "My father! My father! The chariots and horsemen of Israel!" And Elisha saw him no more. Then he took hold of his garment and tore it in two. **2 KINGS 2:11, 12.**

Two. That is the number of people who have gotten off this rock without dying. Two. Enoch and Elijah. Out of the billions of people who have been born and lived on this earth, only two (that we know of) have escaped without dying. That's a pretty amazing statistic to me. So why them? Why Enoch and Elijah? Why not me?

The answer to that question is . . . I don't know. Did Enoch and Elijah somehow earn the right to bypass death and take an instant trip to heaven? Probably not. Both of them were human beings who likely had the same struggles in faith that everyone else has. I don't know why God chose them, but I'm glad He did.

There were others who got to go to heaven. Moses did. In fact, in the Gospels Moses and Elijah show up at the transfiguration of Jesus. Elijah represents those of us who will be alive when Jesus comes again. Moses represents those of us who will die and be resurrected at His coming.

When Elijah was carried away by the fiery chariot, Elisha mourned the loss of his friend. I'm not sure that Elisha understood fully where Elijah had gone; he just knew that he wasn't coming back. Yet the work of God needed to continue in Israel, so Elisha took the cloak of Elijah and moved on. He must have been in a daze as he walked away from that place. But as he was soon to find out, the spirit of his master Elijah (the Spirit of God, actually) was now resting on him to do mighty things for God.

Sometimes it's not easy to move on when we've experienced a spiritually powerful event. We want to savor that feeling, that high, for just a little bit longer. Yet after our spiritual highs we are called back into the real world to do God's work.

It's good to remember that after a spiritual high the world still needs to see Jesus in us. Our highs and our lows need to be filled with Jesus' touch for others.

JUNE 2

Don't Hug the Bears

FROM THERE ELISHA WENT UP TO BETHEL. As he was walking along the road, some boys came out of the town and jeered at him. "Get out of here, baldy!" they said. "Get out of here, baldy!" He turned around, looked at them and called down a curse on them in the name of the Lord. Then two bears came out of the woods and mauled forty-two of the boys. **2 KINGS 2:23, 24.**

In 1988 I was the dean of boys at a school 300 miles north of Vancouver, British Columbia. This school was situated in Canada's coastal mountains, a five-hour drive from the nearest town of any consequence. Jagged snowcapped mountains surrounded the valley we lived in, and cascading waterfalls hung like drapes everywhere we looked. If it sounds like paradise—well, it kind of was.

In this valley lived lots of deer, bears, cougars, eagles, salmon, and other critters that God created. Some afternoons we would go and admire the animals at the local zoo. OK, there was no local zoo, but we would go to the dump to watch the bears. It was always comical to see them climb in and out of the old cars dumped there, eat garbage, and play around like a bunch of kids in a toy store. They looked cute and cuddly. But each time I took kids to the dump I reminded them all, "You may want to hug the bears, but remember, if you run up to a bear to hug it, it will hug back."

There were a few times that a bear felt threatened by our presence and began to charge us. They were bluffing, and I knew it, but each time it happened I realized that no human would stand a chance against the claws, teeth, and ferocity of a charging bear.

The story of the disrespectful youth and their close encounter with a couple of big, furry bears serves to remind me how critical it is for us to respect those whom God has called into ministry.

My mama taught me a few things: Take your hat off when you enter a church; always say "please" and "thank you"; be kind to people when others are putting them down; respect your elders and ministers. She would say, "These things make God smile." Take a moment today to pray for your pastor.

JUNE 3

Controlled Chaos

THE WIFE OF A MAN from the company of the prophets cried out to Elisha, "Your servant my husband is dead, and you know that he revered the Lord. But now his creditor is coming to take my two boys as his slaves." Elisha replied to her, "How can I help you? Tell me, what do you have in your house?" "Your servant has nothing there at all," she said, "except a small jar of olive oil." **2 KINGS 4:1, 2.**

Our God is a compassionate God. He realizes that sometimes life on this sin-sick earth is going to kick us in the teeth pretty hard. Folks like to say that God is in control. I look around me and think, *If God is in control of this world, then I'm a little worried about heaven.*

God doesn't even say that He's in control of this earth. The psalmist tells us that "the highest heavens belong to the Lord, but the earth he has given to mankind" (Psalm 115:16). The fact that God has chosen to step back and not control everything that happens on this earth is why life kicks us in the teeth from time to time; it's why we get cancer, car accidents, tornadoes, and zits. A God-controlled place doesn't have these things.

Yet God does control some things. He hasn't let go of the winds of strife; if He had, we'd be living in *complete* chaos. And most important, He allows human beings the choice of whether to give Him control of their lives. He won't take control, but He invites us to hand Him control.

What do people look like when they give God control of their lives in a chaotic world? Well, the Bible says that those people practice true religion. And what is true religion? That's when God-controlled people look after widows and orphans in their distress (James 1:27). It's when we become the hands and feet of Jesus to those who are poor, when we see those who need a hand up and we offer it as appropriate.

Elisha allowed God to have control of his life. He saw the distress of the widow and had compassion on her. He directed her to get a bunch of empty jars and pour the oil from her jar into them. Her oil never ran out. She got enough extra-virgin olive oil to pay off her debts, save her sons from the slave market, and live her life without fear.

Have you chosen to give God your life in the middle of this chaotic world?

JUNE 4

Serial Sneezer

WHEN ELISHA ARRIVED, the child was indeed dead, lying there on the prophet's bed. He went in alone and shut the door behind him and prayed to the Lord. Then he lay down on the child's body, placing his mouth on the child's mouth, his eyes on the child's eyes, and his hands on the child's hands. And as he stretched out on him, the child's body began to grow warm again! Elisha got up, walked back and forth across the room once, and then stretched himself out again on the child. This time the boy sneezed seven times and opened his eyes! **2 KINGS 4:32-35, NLT.**

Sneezes are funny things. I don't know this for a fact, but I'll bet our sneezes are like fingerprints or voices—each person's sneeze seems to be unique to them. Some people have sneezes that would rival a sonic boom. Others work up to a thunderous sneeze like everybody else, but when they finally let it out, you can barely hear a thing. I call those "almost sneezes." They can't really be satisfying, can they?

Sandy Smith, my sister-in-law, sneezes three times in a row every time she sneezes. I want somebody who knows about these things to e-mail me and tell me why she always sneezes three times. Whenever she shows signs of a sneeze, I think, *One, two . . . wait for it . . . annnnnnd three!* As regular as clockwork. Happens every time.

I don't have a clue why the boy in this story sneezed seven times after he was raised from the dead. I'm going to ask God about that someday. But I do have a clue why God's prophet was given the power to raise this precious gift from the Lord up from death's gloomy grip.

Can you imagine the joy of the mom and dad as their little guy raced into their outstretched arms? The happy tears must have flowed that day, and God received the glory.

There will be a day when this kind of thing happens worldwide. Moms, dads, kids, grandparents will fly into the arms of long-lost loved ones and experience joyful reunion. On this day God will receive the glory, and all will be well. But I can't help wondering: when my family members are raised imperishable, will they sneeze seven times before we all go to heaven?

JUNE 5

Death in the Pot

ONE OF THEM WENT OUT into the fields to gather herbs and found a wild vine and picked as many of its gourds as his garment could hold. When he returned, he cut them up into the pot of stew, though no one knew what they were. The stew was poured out for the men, but as they began to eat it, they cried out, "Man of God, there is death in the pot!" And they could not eat it. **2 KINGS 4:39, 40.**

All the stories of Elisha and his prophetic calling fascinate me, but I especially like this one. It reminds me of eating at my grandma's house.

My grandma had many fine qualities. She was good with money, she was a faithful church member, and she always made me feel good about praying. Whenever she'd babysit my sister and me, we'd kneel down and say our evening prayers before bed. When I had finished my prayer, no matter what I'd said, Grandma would comment, "Now, that was a nice prayer, Mark."

My grandma had several God-given gifts, but one of those gifts was *not* cooking. Grandma was a horrible cook. One time we went to her house for Easter dinner. We sat around the table and started to dig in. When she cut into the meat loaf she had made for us, we saw that the middle of it was all raw and pink. I think I heard a cow moo as she made the first cut! It turned my stomach, and I had to excuse myself from the table.

Another time we were there for Thanksgiving dinner. I had a plate full of all kinds of food (mostly stuff my mom had made). I picked up my fork, speared the ranch-soaked salad, and chomped away. As I ate, one piece of crunchy lettuce didn't seem to respond like the others in my mouth. I couldn't quite break it down. Finally I spit it out to see why. It was a Band-Aid. With a little blood spot in the middle of it. From my grandma's finger.

Can you imagine how horrible the cook for the school of the prophets felt when everybody was eating his stew? He was probably eating it, too, when he heard someone yell, "There's death in the pot!" This was a saying I almost yelled on several occasions at my grandma's house.

I can't wait to sit at the promised banquet table when we get to our heavenly home. No Band-Aids. No raw meat loaf. No death in the pot. Just great food with Jesus.

Get the Bread Out

"HOW CAN I SET THIS before a hundred men?" his servant asked. But Elisha answered, "Give it to the people to eat. For this is what the Lord says: 'They will eat and have some left over.'" Then he set it before them, and they ate and had some left over, according to the word of the Lord. **2 KINGS 4:43, 44.**

One of the things I've noticed about the Bible is that somehow everything always plugs into, points to, or otherwise speaks of Jesus and His ministry on earth. This short story in 2 Kings is no different.

In the story a man comes from a place called Baal Shalishah to bless Elisha and his ministry with 20 loaves of bread freshly baked from the first of the harvest. Elisha receives the man graciously, but instead of putting all the bread in his pantry, he asks his servant to distribute the bread to the 100 people who are gathered there.

Now, I don't know how big these loaves were, but it seems that 20 loaves of bread ought to feed 100 people. If you split each loaf between five people, they would have enough food to sustain them for the day. But the servant looks at the men and assesses very quickly that this is not going to be enough for all of them to eat. These loaves must have been miniloaves.

Elisha takes in the problem and does a Jesus thing. He says, "Give it to the people to eat. For this is what the Lord says: 'They will eat and have some left over.'"

The men all ate, and there was bread left over (maybe 12 baskets of it?).

This is a story that not many people know about. Most of us remember Jesus feeding the 5,000. Far fewer have heard of Elisha feeding the 100. But I'd like to take note here of Elisha's food distribution skills. Actually, I'd like to take note of how God takes care of His children. In this story He uses a willing giver (the man who brought the bread) and a willing servant (Elisha) to feed His people.

I believe God is looking for willing givers in His church today. And I believe God is looking for willing servants to make sure those gifts are distributed as He would have them distributed. God can do miracles when He has these two ingredients in His church and on His earth.

JUNE 7

White Spots Gone

THE KING OF ARAM had great admiration for Naaman, the commander of his army, because through him the Lord had given Aram great victories. But though Naaman was a mighty warrior, he suffered from leprosy. At this time Aramean raiders had invaded the land of Israel, and among their captives was a young girl who had been given to Naaman's wife as a maid. One day the girl said to her mistress, "I wish my master would go to see the prophet in Samaria. He would heal him of his leprosy." **2 KINGS 5:1-3, NLT.**

This is one of those stories that gets a lot of play for all sorts of reasons. Usually, when people write about or preach on this story, they emphasize Naaman's stubbornness or his dipping seven times in the muddy waters of the Jordan. I heard one preacher do a pretty nice job with this story when he emphasized God's willingness to heal a Gentile at a time that Naaman wasn't necessarily friendly with Israel. All these are good aspects of the story, but I can't help noticing an often overlooked part: the little servant girl.

Imagine with me what it would be like to be sitting in your living room one evening with your family when all of a sudden the door is kicked down, your parents are killed, and you are dragged off to be a slave in the house of someone from another country. The spite in my heart would be almost overwhelming. The anger toward my captor would be all-consuming. And if I were to hear that my master had gotten leprosy? I'd jump for joy! I certainly wouldn't try to help him!

Yet here is this little woman of God who has the Spirit of Jesus in her. She hears the bad news and gives Naaman the good news that God is in the business of restoring and healing people. Naaman listens to her and ends up being cured of the dreaded disease.

When Jesus was on the side of a mountain speaking truth, He said, "Love your enemies and pray for those who persecute you" (Matthew 5:44). When we hear those words, we nod our heads and say to ourselves, *Yes, we should love our enemies and be nice to people we don't like.* Yet when the rubber meets the road, are we willing to be so like Jesus that we would do what the servant girl did? Sometimes faith isn't easy. Yet this little girl demonstrated her faith in a Christlike way.

JUNE 8

It's a Floater!

THE GROUPS OF PROPHETS SAID to Elisha, "The place where we meet with you is too small for us. Let's go to the Jordan River. There everyone can get a log, and let's build a place there to live." Elisha said, "Go." One of them said, "Please go with us." Elisha answered, "I will go," so he went with them. When they arrived at the Jordan, they cut down some trees. As one man was cutting down a tree, the head of his ax fell into the water. He yelled, "Oh, my master! I borrowed that ax!" Elisha asked, "Where did it fall?" The man showed him the place. Then Elisha cut down a stick and threw it into the water, and it made the iron head float. Elisha said, "Pick up the axhead." Then the man reached out and took it. **2 KINGS 6:1-7, NCV.**

I t's hard for me to wrap my mind around incidents that seem to defy the laws of nature. God made the universe to operate a certain way, right? Gravity works. Rocks sink. Wood floats. The Cubs lose. That's the natural order of things.

And then, just when you get used to things happening the way they are designed to happen, *boom*, God comes in and radically shifts our reality. The sun stands still, manna shows up on the ground, a storm is calmed by a Rabbi who yells, "Peace, be still," and a sunken axhead floats. (The people who finally found the *Titanic* could have used Elisha to throw a stick into the Atlantic and raise that sunken ship up. It would have been a lot easier than using all those subs and cameras.)

God sometimes acts in surprising ways to ensure that His work gets done. Raising up this school for His workers was important to Him. So the axhead floated.

Can you think of times when things "should" have happened one way, but for some unseen reason they worked another way? Take a moment or two to share some of your "God moments" with a family member or a friend. If you are alone, take a moment to journal some of the stories you can remember in which God showed up in a miraculous way. In this world of scientific law it's good to remind ourselves that God is bigger than our understanding.

JUNE 9

Retaining an Enemy Versus Winning a Friend

AS THE ENEMY CAME DOWN toward Elisha, he prayed to the Lord, "Make these people blind." So he made the Aramean army blind, as Elisha had asked. Elisha said to them, "This is not the right road or the right city. Follow me and I'll take you to the man you are looking for." Then Elisha led them to Samaria. After they entered Samaria, Elisha said, "Lord, open these men's eyes so they can see." So the Lord opened their eyes, and the Aramean army saw that they were inside the city of Samaria! When the king of Israel saw the Aramean army, he said to Elisha, "My father, should I kill them? Should I kill them?" Elisha answered, "Don't kill them. You wouldn't kill people whom you captured with your sword and bow. Give them food and water, and let them eat and drink and then go home to their master." So he prepared a great feast for the Aramean army. After they ate and drank, the king sent them away, and they went home to their master. The soldiers of Aram did not come anymore into the land of Israel. **2 KINGS 6:18-23, NCV.**

One of the certainties in life is that there will be people who don't like you. As charming and good-looking as you might think you are, somebody someday will think you're a toad. They will treat you poorly (usually behind your back) and make life difficult. They will be your enemy. So how should you treat your enemies?

I love how the above story illustrates God's treatment of His enemies. Elisha was surrounded by people who wanted him dead. His request wasn't that God strike down his enemies and kill them. No, his request was that they be blinded.

Elisha led his now-blinded enemies into the capital of Israel. You'd think the slaughter would be on, right? But in a strange twist, instead of having the king of Israel wipe out his enemies, Elisha had him prepare a huge feast and treat the invaders like honored guests. This act did more to strike down the enemy than any war could have done. This act defeated an enemy by making an ally.

I think it's natural for us to wish our enemies harm. It's natural but not godly. The narrow road is for us to try to turn an enemy into a friend. Paul says that when we treat our enemies with kindness and love, it's like heaping hot coals on their heads.

Did you know that God has prepared a feast for His enemies (us), and He invites them all to attend? Maybe we should consider doing the same.

Pedal to the Metal

THE LOOKOUT REPORTED, "He has reached them, but he isn't coming back either. The driving is like that of Jehu son of Nimshi—he drives like a maniac." **2 KINGS 9:20.**

Jack Zapara was a friend I idolized growing up. He was a year older than I and a hundred times more daring. He was good-looking and funny, and he loved adventure. Jack was a talented motorcycle rider and drove fast cars fast.

One weekend he and I decided to head over to the Olympic Mountains in western Washington to do some trail bike riding up Mount Townsend. We loaded up his truck with motorcycles and food and headed for the hills. It was a gorgeous day, and we spent it riding through mountain meadows where wildflowers scattered their beauty across the scenery.

After we were done riding, we put the bikes back into the truck, fastened them down so they couldn't move, and started down the long dirt road to suburbia. When he'd come up the road, Jack had taken his time. On the way back down Jack drove like Jehu. He put the pedal to the metal and flew down the mountain. Zipping down the hill about 40 miles per hour too fast, we slid around the dirt corners with the back end of the truck fishtailing toward the edge of the cliff (on my side of the vehicle). I was so scared I got welts on my arm! I knew Jack was a good driver, but I just about fainted on the way down that hill.

Jehu drove like Jack. All the time. He had a reputation for it. But Jehu was much more than a wild driver. He was passionate about defending the cause and character of God. He knew that God's people were in a world of hurt and would be as long as Jezebel and her son Joram were in charge. Jehu did his best to make sure that these two leaders bent on evil were taken out of office so that God's people could have relief from their evil ways.

God uses all kinds of people with all kinds of characteristics to achieve His goals in this world. He can use a peaceful shepherd as well as a stunt driver. And He can use you, too. Even if you have lots of speeding tickets. Even if you give your friend welts because you're a wild driver.

JUNE 11

The Young King's Turnaround

HEZEKIAH TRUSTED IN THE LORD, the God of Israel. There was no one like him among all the kings of Judah, either before him or after him. **2 KINGS 18:5.**

Hezekiah. His name literally means "Yahweh has strengthened." Nobody really knows why Hezekiah decided to do the right thing. He certainly didn't get that tendency from his family tree—he came from a succession of wicked people interspersed with halfhearted worshippers of God. His daddy definitely didn't raise him right.

Maybe it was his great-grandfather Uzziah who inspired him. Many years earlier Uzziah had started to clean up Israel but had stopped short of the task, leaving many of the high places and shrines for people to worship false gods.

Maybe Hezekiah had heard one of the prophets say, "If my people, which are called by my name, shall humble themselves, and pray, and seek My face, and turn from their wicked ways; then will I hear from heaven, and will forgive their sin, and will heal their land" (2 Chronicles 7:14, KJV).

Whatever the cause, after coming to the throne the young king started a reformation in Judah greater than any the country had seen before. He set out to destroy all the public shrines and meeting places that were meant for worshipping gods of stone and wood. Hezekiah even had to destroy something that was once good but that the people had begun using for evil.

Do you remember the story in the Bible about the children of Israel wandering in the wilderness and being bitten by venomous snakes? If you remember, God instructed Moses to make a bronze snake and put it on a tall pole. Everyone who looked at the bronze snake was cured of their poisonous snakebite and lived. Neat story, right? Well, the people of Judah had found that snake on the pole and were worshipping it along with their other false gods, so Hezekiah had to destroy it, too.

Hezekiah made following Yahweh cool again in Judah. I think this world could use a few more Hezekiahs. What kind of influence can you have on the people in your home, school, or workplace by doing right and standing up for truth?

JUNE 12

Do Right, Get Attacked

HEZEKIAH RECEIVED THE LETTER from the messengers and read it.
Then he went up to the temple of the Lord and spread it out before the
Lord. **2 KINGS 19:14.**

When you do what's right, everything in your life becomes easy, you have no personal tragedies, and all your plans work out great—correct?

I can't tell you how many times I've seen people come out of the world, give their hearts to the Lord, make huge changes in their lives to follow Jesus, and be baptized as a symbol of their commitment to Him, only to be attacked and smacked down on every side. It is almost a guarantee that when a person takes a step toward a godly life, they are going to face challenges as Satan tries to make them question that decision.

Soon after Hezekiah made sweeping back-to-God changes in Judah, he was attacked by the same country that had previously sacked and ruined Israel. The Assyrian armies surrounded Jerusalem and posted an army to the south to hold off help from Egypt, a country with which King Hezekiah had formed an alliance. Things looked grim.

The message from the surrounding army of the Assyrians was tough: "We have conquered bigger and badder countries than you—countries with bigger and badder gods than the invisible one you worship. You have two choices: you can surrender, or we will keep you surrounded, cutting off the food and water supply until you are so desperate that you will eat and drink your own body waste. The choice is yours." Strong language from a strong opponent—ancient trash talk.

I love King Hezekiah's response to the Assyrians: he and the prophet Isaiah laid out their lament to the Lord in the Temple. Hezekiah understood that when life throws a wrench into your happiness, all you can do is go to the Lord and ask for deliverance.

God's response to King Hezekiah's pleading? He dispatched an army of angels to conquer the Assyrians and sent the attackers back to their country with their tails between their legs. God's name was vindicated, and Hezekiah was looked on with huge favor in heaven and on earth.

JUNE 13

Not Ready to Push Daisies!

THEN THE PROPHET ISAIAH called on the Lord, and the Lord made the shadow go back the ten steps it had gone down on the stairway of Ahaz. **2 KINGS 20:11.**

At the height of his service to God, after cleaning up all the idolatry in Israel and seeing the defeat of Assyria, King Hezekiah gets sick. The Bible doesn't say exactly what kind of illness he gets; it just says he's at death's door. The disease produces some kind of open sore or boil on Hezekiah's body.

The prophet Isaiah, son of Amoz, goes to him and says, "This is what the Lord says: 'Put your house in order, because you are going to die; you will not recover'" (2 Kings 20:1).

Can you imagine? After all your effort to do the right thing, this is your reward? Well, to be honest with you, sometimes, yes.

"I have seen something else under the sun: The race is not to the swift or the battle to the strong, nor does food come to the wise or wealth to the brilliant or favor to the learned; *but time and chance happen to them all*" (Ecclesiastes 9:11). Nobody is immune to the effects of sin in this world. Nobody. There is no such thing as a charmed life.

As long as we live here on this earth, we are living in enemy territory. We are all going to bask in good times, and we are all going to be touched by evil. All of us. Living a righteous life gives us no guarantee that we will somehow avoid the touch of sin and evil in our lives. But it does mean that we will inherit a life beyond this one, a life that will be filled with joy and love and goodness.

Hezekiah cries out to the Lord and asks to be healed. Lying in his bed, he turns to the wall in his room and prays for God to deliver him from yet another peril. And the Lord answers His prayer. The prophet Isaiah comes back in, puts a lump of crushed-up figs on the king's boil, and tells him that the Lord has granted him 15 additional years to live. What a gift. Hezekiah probably cherished each day after that.

Each day is a gift from God. Let's make the best of today, shall we?

JUNE 14

I Did It by Myself

HEZEKIAH RECEIVED THE ENVOYS and showed them all that was in his store-houses—the silver, the gold, the spices and the fine olive oil—his armory and everything found among his treasures. There was nothing in his palace or in all his kingdom that Hezekiah did not show them. **2 KINGS 20:13.**

Hezekiah's deliverance came with a sign. He asked God to make the shadow on the stairway of Ahaz go backward as proof that he would survive his disease and live 15 more years. Now the sun moving backward is something that doesn't go unnoticed. All the way over in Babylon the soothsayers of that great nation noticed the phenomenon too.

When word got out that the Lord had done this for Hezekiah, the Babylonian king was so intrigued that he sent envoys to visit with King Hezekiah to hear the story.

Here was a perfect opportunity for Hezekiah to introduce these foreign dignitaries to the wonders of Yahweh, to the great God of the universe. This was his chance to be a gospel witness, to be the salt of the earth. Hezekiah had a golden opportunity to be a great evangelist and introduce the country of Babylon to the worship of the one true God.

So what does Hezekiah, the great reformer, do? He says, "Look at all my stuff! Look at all my gold! Look at my huge bank account! Look at all my boats and cars and big-screen TVs!" Not a mention of the God who gave him everything.

The Babylonians went back to their country impressed. In fact, they were so impressed that they told their king, "Hey, there's a lot of loot down there in Judah. We should invade and take it all for ourselves."

It wasn't long after Hezekiah's reign that Nebuchadnezzar did just that. He carried off all of Hezekiah's gold and even some of Hezekiah's relatives to Babylon—young men such as Shadrach, Meshach, and Abednego.

How many opportunities have we missed by focusing on our things instead of on the God who lavishes good things on us? Give God the credit for the blessings in your life today.

JUNE 15

Bring On the Haters

NOW WHEN THE ADVERSARIES of Judah and Benjamin heard that the returned exiles were building a temple to the Lord, the God of Israel, they approached Zerubbabel and the heads of fathers' houses and said to them, "Let us build with you, for we worship your God as you do, and we have been sacrificing to him ever since the days of Esarhaddon king of Assyria who brought us here." But Zerubbabel, Jeshua, and the rest of the heads of fathers' houses in Israel said to them, "You have nothing to do with us in building a house to our God; but we alone will build to the Lord, the God of Israel, as King Cyrus the king of Persia has commanded us." Then the people of the land discouraged the people of Judah and made them afraid to build and bribed counselors against them to frustrate their purpose, all the days of Cyrus king of Persia, even until the reign of Darius king of Persia. **EZRA 4:1-5, ESV.**

You probably know that the books of the Bible are not in chronological order. The stories in Ezra and the next couple of books take place after the Israelites were allowed to come back from captivity in Babylon to rebuild their country. This was good news to all the people of Israel who had a deep desire to go home.

One of the heads of the building committee was named Zerubbabel (one of my favorite names in Scripture). He and several other leading families were excited about rebuilding the Temple of God. So what happens when God asks you to complete a task that the devil has no interest in you completing? You face opposition.

Satirical artist Jack Levine said, "Ah, but it's nice to be in the opposition, nice to be a bone in somebody's throat." In other words, some people in this world thrive on making life difficult for those around them. This is a reality in life. Your job is (1) to make sure you are never a stumbling block to godly progress and (2) to stick with the life God has asked you to live, despite opposition from the haters around you.

If Noah had given up because of opposition, the ark never would have been built. If David had listened to the scoffers, Goliath never would have been slain. If Ezra and Zerubbabel had given in to the haters, the Temple never would have been rebuilt.

You're going to have scoffers in your life—people who don't want you to succeed. Choose to listen to God's encouraging voice and let the scoffers babble on.

JUNE 16

Can't Stand It

WHEN I HEARD THIS, I tore my tunic and cloak, pulled hair from my head and beard and sat down appalled. **EZRA 9:3.**

What wrecks you? What is it that when you hear it, your heart skips a beat, your spirit is moved, and you just have to say something or do something? Injustice? Bigotry? Racism? Religious intolerance? Abuse?

Candy Lightner was mad. When Candy's daughter Serena was 18 months old, their car was hit from the rear by a drunk driver. The accident caused minor injuries to her daughter. Six years later her son, Travis, was run over and seriously injured by a driver who was high on tranquilizers. He suffered numerous broken bones and other injuries, was in a coma for a while, and suffered permanent brain damage. The driver received no ticket.

On May 3, 1980, Candy Lightner's 13-year-old daughter, Cari, was walking in her neighborhood to a church carnival when she was struck from behind by a drunk driver. He drove off after having killed the young girl. This was the drunk driver's fifth offense in four years. Under the laws of the land at the time, the drunk driver likely would not serve any jailtime. Candy Lightner was wrecked. She started MADD (Mothers Against Drunk Driving) the day after Cari's funeral.

Candy Lightner was moved by her experience. She just couldn't stand by and do nothing. She had to make a difference.

As odd as this might sound, Ezra was wrecked by the news that many of the refugees who were coming back home to Israel had intermarried with women from the countries surrounding Israel. This would ruin the revival and reformation that Israel was experiencing, and he knew it. It so upset him that he pulled his hair and beard out. He knew that drastic things needed to happen to bring Israel back to a place where they could serve God without any reservation. So, in a strange act, all the husbands sent their wives away, back to the countries they came from.

What wrecks you? What have you seen that needs to be changed? Maybe this feeling you have is a call to do something that will make this world a better place.

JUNE 17

A Longing for Home

THE WORDS OF NEHEMIAH THE son of Hacaliah. Now it happened in the month Chislev, in the twentieth year, while I was in Susa the capitol, that Hanani, one of my brothers, and some men from Judah came; and I asked them concerning the Jews who had escaped and had survived the captivity, and about Jerusalem. They said to me, "The remnant there in the province who survived the captivity are in great distress and reproach, and the wall of Jerusalem is broken down and its gates are burned with fire." When I heard these words, I sat down and wept and mourned for days; and I was fasting and praying before the God of heaven. **NEHEMIAH 1:1-4, NASB.**

For most people the word *home* brings feelings of comfort and a smile. All the smells, the sounds, the people, and the pets, combined with the feeling of the bed you've slept in for most of your life, add up to that wonderful feeling that we call *home*.

I was born in southern California but raised in Seattle. Seattle is where I spent my childhood and teen years. It's where I attended high school and college. I was married in the Seattle area. I grew up as a fan of Seattle sports teams and know all the hot spots in the city. Each time I return from out of town, my heart skips a beat as the jet plane banks hard over the city and gives me a view of the Space Needle, Elliott Bay, and Lake Washington. No matter where I live, Seattle is and always will be my home.

This is how Nehemiah felt about Jerusalem. It broke his heart to find out that his home was in disrepair. So he fell at the feet of the Lord, fasted, prayed, and started planning for a way to rebuild the broken walls of home.

Nehemiah's passion to restore the walls of Jerusalem is a mini-illustration of what Jesus must feel about the damage done to His heavenly home. The Bible tells of a spiritual power that has damaged the sanctuary in heaven by spreading lies about God (Daniel. 8:11-13). You can almost hear in Jesus' voice the anticipation of having heaven repaired when He tells His disciples in John 14:1-3 that He is going to prepare a place for them.

Nehemiah repaired the walls of Jerusalem. We can help repair the heavenly sanctuary by telling the truth about God, dispelling the lies the devil has spread.

JUNE 18

Be Kind to the King

IN THE MONTH OF NISAN in the twentieth year of King Artaxerxes, when wine was brought for him, I took the wine and gave it to the king. I had not been sad in his presence before, so the king asked me, "Why does your face look so sad when you are not ill? This can be nothing but sadness of heart." **NEHEMIAH 2:1, 2.**

When my wife, Wendy, was in high school, she was with a couple friends in the Portland, Oregon, area, enjoying a park on a sunny Sunday afternoon. As they were driving around a one-way loop in the park, a police officer shot them with his radar and pulled them over. Before the officer even reached the window, the driver of the car started complaining about the "lowlife police officer who would stake out a park and pull people over."

My wife's friend barely had the window down before he started to cop an attitude with the middle-age officer. As my wife tells the story, her friend was very rude to the officer and then sat in the car fuming after receiving a ticket. It kind of ruined an otherwise pleasant day at the park.

It wasn't long before the driver started to feel bad about how he had acted. He apologized to Wendy and her friend and then said, "I need to apologize to that police officer, too."

They drove around the loop one more time, pulled up behind the police officer, got out of their car, and sang to him. (I know this sounds weird, but they were all part of the same singing group.) The officer didn't give any reaction.

After they pulled away, the police officer again turned on his lights and pulled them over. He walked up and said, "You are the strangest kids I've ever met, but you made my day." Then he handed the driver the original of the ticket he had previously written and said, "Have a nice day."

The Bible admonishes believers to treat their leaders with obedience and respect. Nehemiah had such a good relationship with the king of Persia that the king noticed a change in his mood. Nehemiah probably didn't agree with everything the king did, but he always kept a pleasant attitude around his boss and treated him with respect. This attitude played to Nehemiah's favor when the time was right.

JUNE 19

Many Hands Make Light Work

THE SONS OF HASSENAAH REBUILT THE FISH GATE, laying its boards and set-ting its doors, bolts, and bars in place. Meremoth son of Uriah, the son of Hakkoz, made repairs next to them. Meshullam son of Berekiah, the son of Meshezabel, made repairs next to Meremoth. And Zadok son of Baana made repairs next to Meshullam. The men from Tekoa made repairs next to them, but the leading men of Tekoa would not work under their supervi-sors. **NEHEMIAH 3:3-5, NCV.**

Whether something is heavy or not is relative to the number of people do-ing the lifting. This is true of literal weight or mental weight. I remember watching the movie *Apollo 13*, which depicts a disaster that almost took the lives of three brave astronauts on their way to the moon. The spacecraft was running out of water and power, and it would have if a large group of people hadn't come to the table and collectively figured out a way to save the day. It took everybody's ideas to make that mission a success.

In my life I see this happen after every large program at the church or school where I work. If after the spring concert everybody just got up and left, the prin-cipal or the PE teacher or a lonely janitor would have a full day's work ahead of them. Instead, dozens of people work together to put the metal chairs in the racks, move the bleachers back to where they belong, sweep the floor, and collect all the garbage. A day's work happens in less than 20 minutes.

This is how God's church is supposed to work.

When Nehemiah realized how heavy the workload of rebuilding Jerusalem would be, he didn't put on a tool belt and start mixing mortar. He recognized the different gifts God had given to each person in Judah, and he invited and allowed them to use their gifts to work together, making the load lighter than it would have been with fewer people.

Of course, the key to the success of any group endeavor is *the group*. And the group wouldn't exist without each individual participating. Are you a participator or a bystander? God wired you up to participate, not to sit on your hands. How are you helping to make the load lighter in your home, church, or school?

JUNE 20

Crows Don't Kill Eagles

SANBALLAT WAS VERY ANGRY when he learned that we were rebuilding the wall. He flew into a rage and mocked the Jews, saying in front of his friends and the Samarian army officers, "What does this bunch of poor, feeble Jews think they're doing? Do they think they can build the wall in a single day by just offering a few sacrifices? Do they actually think they can make something of stones from a rubbish heap—and charred ones at that?" Tobiah the Ammonite, who was standing beside him, remarked, "That stone wall would collapse if even a fox walked along the top of it!" **NEHEMIAH 4:1-3, NLT.**

What I saw was shocking. In fact, it was gruesome. I was driving in northern Canada and watching a large number of bald eagles, seagulls, and crows flying over a body of water. I had pulled over to take in the awesomeness of the sight, when I saw one of the most vicious acts of aggression I'd ever witnessed.

An eagle was being tormented by a crow. The crow kept flying above the eagle and dive-bombing its head. I'm not sure what the eagle had done to deserve all this negative attention, but it was clearly irritated with the crow. In a split second the eagle flipped on its back in midair, grabbed the crow in its talons, killed it, and then dropped its lifeless body into the water. Pestering an eagle isn't a smart idea!

When God's people are called to a task, you can be sure they'll encounter people who question their motives and put stumbling blocks in their way. Anytime anyone wants to make progress for the Lord, somebody will attempt to shoot them down.

Nehemiah was commissioned to rebuild his beloved city. As soon as he started, the crows came out to heckle the eagles. It would have been easy for Nehemiah and his workers to get discouraged and give up as the insults poured in. But they didn't. They worked through the insults and the intimidation, and they finished the wall so the returned exiles could have a safe home.

There are two things to think about here. 1. Are you a crow or an eagle? Do you give people a hard time because you aren't on board with their projects? 2. When the crows start to heckle you, remember that you are an eagle, called by God. Let the crows heckle. They'll be eating their lunch out of a dumpster while you soar on the heights of God's blessings.

JUNE 21

What to Do on a Holy Day

THEN NEHEMIAH THE GOVERNOR, Ezra the priest and teacher of the Law, and the Levites who were instructing the people said to them all, "This day is holy to the Lord your God. Do not mourn or weep." For all the people had been weeping as they listened to the words of the Law. Nehemiah said, "Go and enjoy choice food and sweet drinks, and send some to those who have nothing prepared. This day is holy to our Lord. Do not grieve, for the joy of the Lord is your strength." **NEHEMIAH 8:9, 10.**

Acommon question I get as an Adventist pastor is "What is OK and not OK to do on the Sabbath?" I hate that question. In my opinion it's not even a good question.

One of the problems I've noticed is that as Seventh-day Adventists we often segment our time into "sacred time" and "secular time." In other words, we dedicate some time to God and the rest to ourselves and to the world. I wonder how God feels about that? It would be like me saying to my wife, "One day a week I'll act like I'm married to you, but the other six days I'll just do what I want." Every day should be dedicated to living in God's will and in His presence.

But what about special days? holy days? What about the Sabbath? Isn't that supposed to be different? Well, yes, actually, it is. In fact, in chapter 13 of his book Nehemiah really gets on the Jews about opening their businesses on the seventh day and replacing Sabbath with greed. He tells them to knock it off!

So how am I supposed to "keep" the Sabbath? I'd like to refer you to the above text for a clue. Nehemiah informed the people that the day on which this story took place was a holy day and that their response to that day was inappropriate. They were mourning and weeping when they were supposed to be celebrating. This gives us our first clue as to how to "keep" Sabbath.

Holy days are for celebration. They are for eating and drinking and being with friends and family. The Sabbath is a holy day that is to be celebrated in such a way. (I think that's where potlucks come from!)

So this Sabbath, ignore the world, set aside your need for greed, and celebrate with family and friends. Celebrate what the Lord has done for you!

JUNE 22

Fermented Minds

ON THE SEVENTH DAY OF THE FEAST, when King Xerxes was in high spirits because of the wine, he told the seven eunuchs who attended him—Mehuman, Biztha, Harbona, Bigtha, Abagtha, Zethar, and Carcas—to bring Queen Vashti to him with the royal crown on her head. He wanted the nobles and all the other men to gaze on her beauty, for she was a very beautiful woman. But when they conveyed the king's order to Queen Vashti, she refused to come. This made the king furious, and he burned with anger. **ESTHER 1:10-12, NLT.**

If you could eliminate one thing from the world so that it would be a better place, what would you eliminate? I've posed this question to dozens of people. They have come back with such answers as cancer, diabetes, fast food, people who drive too slow in the fast lane—all good answers, to be sure. The thing I would eliminate from the world would be alcohol. I hate what alcohol does to people.

Watch any half-hour newscast, and you will see that a large proportion of child abuse cases, spousal abuse cases, and car crashes involve somebody under the influence of alcohol. Alcohol lowers a person's inhibitions so that they will do things that they would never do without the poison fogging their brain. It contributes to unwanted pregnancies, unnecessary regrets, and untimely deaths. It pulls in more than $100 billion in sales each year in the United States. People pay for misery.

I don't mean to be too over-the-top here, but this is a soapbox I feel compelled to stand on. I've had people say, "The Bible doesn't say that you should never drink alcohol." My response is "I don't need the Bible to tell me that to know I should stay away from alcohol. The Bible definitely warns us about the effects of alcohol. So why try your luck?"

King Xerxes (or as I like to call him, King Jerkses) was drunk and tried to take advantage of his wife. I admire her for being a strong woman, resisting the urge to parade around in front of a bunch of drunk men. Good for her.

As for you? The sooner you realize that God has called you to a clear-thinking, sober life, the better. Stay away from the poison and fill your mind and body with good things. If you do, you will have fewer regrets.

JUNE 23

For Such a Time as This

ESTHER'S MESSAGE WAS GIVEN TO MORDECAI. Then Mordecai sent back word to Esther: "Just because you live in the king's palace, don't think that out of all the Jewish people you alone will escape. If you keep quiet at this time, someone else will help and save the Jewish people, but you and your father's family will all die. And who knows, you may have been chosen queen for just such a time as this." **ESTHER 4:12-14, NCV.**

Have you ever tried to pound a nail with a water balloon? Have you ever tried to light a fire with a wet sponge and an old shoe? Have you ever tried to swat a fly with a piano? Of course not. Water balloons are not made for pounding nails. Wet sponges are made for cleaning, not for lighting fires. Pianos are for making music, not killing flies.

The million-dollar question is What are *you* made for? Why did God see fit to have you living on this earth at this point in history? Are you a random accident that just happened when your mom and dad fell in love, or were you planned for? The Bible would suggest that you were planned for. Somehow, some way, you have been especially designed and called to fit into God's plan for His world. It may be through the occupation He leads you to pursue. It may be through your place in your family or your neighborhood or your church.

The fact is that you may never know in this life how God used you to do what He needed you to do. Just as the people in the parable of Matthew 25 did, you may someday ask the Lord, "When did I ever see You and help You out?"

When we get to heaven, one of the joys we will experience is seeing how God used His faithful children on this earth and what impact it had on the world. But one thing I know: you are here on purpose.

Esther's message from her cousin Mordecai made an impression. He alerted her to the possibility that God had chosen her to act bravely *in such a time as this.* And even though she acted reluctantly, she did act, and God used her in a powerful way.

What's your level of willingness to be used by God? Show that willingness by choosing a daily life of faithfulness. Wait and see what the Lord will do!

JUNE 24

Serves Him Right!

SO HAMAN CAME IN, and the king said to him, "What should be done to the man whom the king delights to honor?" And Haman said to himself, "Whom would the king delight to honor more than me?" And Haman said to the king, "For the man whom the king delights to honor, let royal robes be brought, which the king has worn, and the horse that the king has ridden, and on whose head a royal crown is set. And let the robes and the horse be handed over to one of the king's most noble officials. Let them dress the man whom the king delights to honor, and let them lead him on the horse through the square of the city, proclaiming before him: 'Thus shall it be done to the man whom the king delights to honor.'" Then the king said to Haman, "Hurry; take the robes and the horse, as you have said, and do so to Mordecai the Jew who sits at the king's gate. Leave out nothing that you have mentioned." **ESTHER 6:6-10, ESV.**

I love this story as much as any in Scripture. There is something delicious about a story in which a bad guy is humiliated in front of all the people he tried to impress. It illustrates a truth that flows through every major religion—the idea that your actions will come back to you, for good or for bad.

In the story of Esther, Haman is driven by greed, a lust for power, and ethnic prejudice. The worst thing about allowing oneself to be driven by such heinous character traits is that they are so unfulfilling. Greed cannot be satisfied. Lust for power can never be quenched. Racial prejudice cannot be placated by the death of those one hates. Having these character traits in the driver's seat of one's life would mean choosing to live in a perpetual state of purgatory or hell on earth.

People who are driven by hate, jealousy, and revenge can sometimes disguise their putrid character, but in the end their true colors will be revealed. Haman thought he was getting the best of Mordecai and the Jews. What he didn't know was that God always honors the honorable. And doesn't it make the story even better that Haman had to honor the one he despised so much?

What drives you? Strive to be like Jesus. Let love and service be your guide. Ask Jesus to take away any malice you have in your heart and replace it with love and forgiveness.

JUNE 25

History Will Repeat Itself

ON THIS SECOND OCCASION, while they were drinking wine, the king again said to Esther, "Tell me what you want, Queen Esther. What is your request? I will give it to you, even if it is half the kingdom!" Queen Esther replied, "If I have found favor with the king, and if it pleases the king to grant my request, I ask that my life and the lives of my people will be spared. For my people and I have been sold to those who would kill, slaughter, and annihilate us...." "Who would do such a thing?" King Xerxes demanded. "Who would be so presumptuous as to touch you?" Esther replied, "This wicked Haman is our adversary and our enemy." Haman grew pale with fright before the king and queen. Then the king jumped to his feet in a rage and went out into the palace garden. Haman, however, stayed behind to plead for his life with Queen Esther, for he knew that the king intended to kill him. In despair he fell on the couch where Queen Esther was reclining, just as the king was returning from the palace garden. The king exclaimed, "Will he even assault the queen right here in the palace, before my very eyes?" And as soon as the king spoke, his attendants covered Haman's face, signaling his doom. Then Harbona, one of the king's eunuchs, said, "Haman has set up a sharpened pole that stands seventy-five feet tall in his own courtyard. He intended to use it to impale Mordecai, the man who saved the king from assassination." "Then impale Haman on it!" the king ordered. So they impaled Haman on the pole he had set up for Mordecai, and the king's anger subsided. **ESTHER 7:2-10, NLT.**

Have you ever noticed the startling similarities between the story of Esther and the story of God's people as depicted in Daniel, Revelation, and other parts of the Bible?

Think about it: God's people are held captive in a place that is not their home. An accuser stands up, says horrible things about them, and condemns them to death. As their execution date approaches, a hero stands up in defense of his people and enlists the help of a woman (in prophecy a woman represents a church) to fend off the enemy. The enemy has prepared punishment and death for God's people, but what the enemy had planned for God's people actually happens to him. The end.

The story of Esther is the story of God's last-day people. And because we know the story, we can live in these last days without fear. The enemy will be defeated, and we will stand victorious because of God's grace toward us.

One Weird Story

NOW THERE WAS A DAY when the sons of God came to present themselves before the Lord, and Satan also came among them. The Lord said to Satan, "From where do you come?" Then Satan answered the Lord and said, "From roaming about on the earth and walking around on it." The Lord said to Satan, "Have you considered My servant Job? For there is no one like him on the earth, a blameless and upright man, fearing God and turning away from evil." Then Satan answered the Lord, "Does Job fear God for nothing? Have You not made a hedge about him and his house and all that he has, on every side? You have blessed the work of his hands, and his possessions have increased in the land. But put forth Your hand now and touch all that he has; he will surely curse You to Your face." Then the Lord said to Satan, "Behold, all that he has is in your power, only do not put forth your hand on him." So Satan departed from the presence of the Lord. **JOB 1:6-12, NASB.**

OK, I admit it. This is one weird story. Some think that Job is a parable for us to learn from. Others think that Job was a literal person and that the events in this story happened just as written. For sure, the book of Job is unusual. It's one of only three books in the Old Testament that mention Satan by name. Many theologians think the Israelites didn't know much about Satan, so God got all the credit and all the blame for supernatural events. (Kind of explains some of the stories about God in the Old Testament.)

Then there is the part about God and Satan striking a deal over Job to test his faith. God gives Satan permission to strike Job's possessions (including Job's children) and even Job's health. This seems to fly in the face of what the rest of the Bible says about God, the devil, and God's people. So how are we to read the book of Job?

As we go through this story and focus on some of its verses together, I would like to suggest that we discover the beauty and power of God and learn what it means to live a life of faith in a world full of the devil's schemes.

The first lesson I'd like us to focus on is in Job 1:21, 22. Through all his pain Job decides to remain faithful and not curse God because of his problems. Instead, even in his agony, he blesses the Lord. That, my friend, takes great faith. God is not the author of pain and trouble. He is our Redeemer from it.

JUNE 27

Pick Wisely

THEN HIS WIFE SAID TO HIM, "Do you still hold fast your integrity? Curse God and die!" **JOB 2:9, NASB.**

When I was a chaplain for Mount Pisgah Academy in the late 1990s, I invited an elderly African-American pastor to share his wisdom with our student body. I'll never forget the sermons he delivered. One of his most poignant messages was whittled down to one catchphrase that he repeated throughout the talk. Looking over his glasses at the audience, he said, "Young people, I want you to hear me! You lie down with da dogs, you gonna get fleas!"

In other words, you can't choose your family, but you can choose your friends and your spouse. I can't tell you how many times I've had tearful parents in my office saying, "My son/daughter is really a good person. They just started hanging around the wrong people, and now we don't know if they will ever be OK."

Job was surrounded by negativity and naysayers. His wife told him to curse God and die. His friends had God figured out according to their worldly philosophy. They probably thought they were saying the right things, but they didn't understand what was going on and just made matters worse. I feel sorry for Job. He didn't have anybody on earth to lean on during his personal time of trouble.

There are two things we can learn from the book of Job here: (1) pick your friends wisely and (2) be a good resource for your friends when they go through hard times.

When you choose your friends and your spouse, remember, character matters. Choose to hang around people who have a strong moral fiber. Don't lie down with the dogs, or you're gonna get fleas.

And when your friends go through hard times, do them a favor: don't try to "explain" why bad things are happening in their life. Just be there for them. Lighten their mood appropriately. Go for a walk. Let them talk. Listen. Pray with them and let them know that you are on their side. You can also let them know that God will never leave them or forsake them.

No-Good,
Down-in-the-Dumps Blues

"LET THE DAY OF MY BIRTH BE ERASED, and the night I was conceived. Let that day be turned to darkness. Let it be lost even to God on high, and let no light shine on it. Let the darkness and utter gloom claim that day for its own. Let a black cloud overshadow it, and let the darkness terrify it. Let that night be blotted off the calendar, never again to be counted among the days of the year, never again to appear among the months. Let that night be childless. Let it have no joy. **JOB 3:3-7, NLT.**

When my niece was 3 years old, she would sometimes walk out of her bedroom in dramatic fashion, with a look of utter depression on her face, and declare, "I have no clothes, and nobody loves me!" Then she'd stand there and cry until her grandma swooped her up in her arms, kissed her, and dressed her for the day. Grandma had a way of making everything better. That's a mild case of being down in the dumps.

One night recently I ate supper with some friends. During our meal they detailed a list of circumstances that had left them down in the dumps. One of them had a heart condition that had landed him in heart surgery. A real estate deal had gone sour, leaving them with a massive debt—and to add insult to injury, the person who had benefited from the deal was a friend who they felt had allowed greed to rule the day at their expense. To top it all off, their first grandbaby had been stillborn. It was painful to hear my friend speak of holding that lifeless little baby in his arms for four hours after the delivery. They both looked at me and said, "Mark, we've decided that we are not blessed people." My friends were depressed, for sure.

What do you do when you feel cursed and not blessed? What do you do when you feel like a "not blessed person"?

I can suggest a couple of things to keep in mind: 1. You can't earn blessings from God. They are already yours. Don't believe the lie that God is cursing you for something you've done or not done. 2. You *are* blessed; you just can't see it right now because you are in the middle of a battle for your faith.

Hold on to Jesus. Remember, on Friday Jesus thought God had forsaken Him, but Sunday was coming. Your Sunday is coming.

JUNE 29

God Speaks

Let's hear the Lord Himself speak today. This is from Job 38. It's Hebrew poetry. Brace yourself.

WHERE were you when I laid the foundation of the earth?
TELL ME, if you have understanding,
WHO set its measurements? Since you know.
OR WHO stretched the line on it?
ON WHAT were its bases sunk?
OR WHO laid its cornerstone,
WHEN THE MORNING stars sang together
AND ALL the sons of God shouted for joy?

OR WHO enclosed the sea with doors
WHEN, bursting forth, it went out from the womb;
WHEN I made a cloud its garment
AND THICK DARKNESS its swaddling band,
AND I PLACED boundaries on it
AND SET a bolt and doors,
AND I SAID, 'Thus far you shall come, but no farther; . . .'

HAVE YOU ever in your life commanded the morning,
AND CAUSED the dawn to know its place,
THAT IT MIGHT take hold of the ends of the earth,
AND THE WICKED be shaken out of it?
IT IS CHANGED like clay under the seal;
AND THEY STAND forth like a garment.
FROM THE WICKED their light is withheld,
AND THE UPLIFTED arm is broken.

HAVE YOU entered into the springs of the sea
OR WALKED in the recesses of the deep?
HAVE THE gates of death been revealed to you,
OR HAVE YOU seen the gates of deep darkness?
HAVE YOU understood the expanse of the earth?
TELL ME, if you know all this. (verses 4-18, NASB).

He is God. We are not. 'Nuff said.

JUNE 30

The Power of a Song

HOW BLESSED IS THE MAN who does not walk in the counsel of the wicked, nor stand in the path of sinners, nor sit in the seat of scoffers! But his delight is in the law of the Lord, and in His law he meditates day and night. He will be like a tree firmly planted by streams of water, which yields its fruit in its season and its leaf does not wither; and in whatever he does, he prospers. The wicked are not so, but they are like chaff which the wind drives away. Therefore the wicked will not stand in the judgment, nor sinners in the assembly of the righteous. For the Lord knows the way of the righteous, but the way of the wicked will perish. **PSALM 1, NASB.**

There is something powerful about music. It can change our moods. It can bring us to tears. It can ramp us up and make us hyper. Music has a unique ability to help us memorize words and concepts. Music is a gift from God that King David and others in Bible history fully appreciated.

The word *psalm* means "a song sung to a stringed instrument." The Hebrews called them praise songs. The book of Psalms is the longest book of the Bible, containing 150 psalms, composed over a period of roughly 1,000 years. Psalm 117, having only two verses, is the shortest. Psalm 119, with 176 verses, is the longest. The book of Psalms is one of the parts of the Old Testament that Jesus quoted from most frequently.

More important than the facts about the book of Psalms is the raw emotion that King David and the other psalmists expressed in the songs they wrote—honest, passionate cries of praise, hurt, and anger spoken directly to God.

Take a look at Psalm 1. This psalm (like many others) comes across as a proverb. It gives great advice to every reader that could make their life more successful.

Imagine what kind of world we could live in today if we just took those words of advice. The "counsel of the wicked" is everywhere. It's on TV, in music, and in just about every public square. It's easily accessible. It's a rare person who decides not to walk in the counsel of the wicked.

Make a commitment today to root yourself in God's Word so that you will flourish in this life, bearing fruit and prospering in everything you do.

JULY 1

The Church That Became a Swimming Pool

THE KINGS OF THE EARTH PREPARE TO FIGHT, and their leaders make plans together against the Lord and his appointed one. They say, "Let's break the chains that hold us back and throw off the ropes that tie us down." But the one who sits in heaven laughs; the Lord makes fun of them. **PSALM 2:2-4, NCV.**

When I was an undergraduate student at Seattle Pacific University, I took a class called "The Soviet Union." It was a survey course that covered the history of that nation up through contemporary times. It was one of my favorite classes. During this class the professor told us a story that still makes me smile.

Joseph Stalin was the ruler of this Communist country during its darkest and most brutal time. Under his iron rule the Soviet Union persecuted religious institutions and jailed people who dared to stand up for their Creator. During this time Stalin, to make a statement, tore down a church in Moscow and began construction of the world's tallest skyscraper on that spot. However, his grand project never made much headway, and shortly after his death a huge public swimming pool was built where the church had once stood.

What Stalin and the other Communist leaders didn't know is that churches are not made up of bricks and mortar. Churches are made up of faithful believers. Often, because the pool was heated (I don't remember if it was artificially heated or fed by natural hot springs), a thick mist would hover over the water so that passersby couldn't even see the pool. During these times of thick mist, Christians would descend into the waters of the great pool that used to be a church and baptize new converts—right under the noses of their atheist dictators.

The evil forces of this world will do everything they can to thwart the work of God. They might as well try to stop the tide from coming in or try to keep the sun from rising. God's church is a living, breathing entity that is not confined to buildings and subcommittees. God's church is filled with people like you and me—people who are listening for that still small voice to lead us to our next mission.

Remember, as dark and godless as your surroundings might be, there are always a faithful few out there who are doing their best to follow Jesus, even amid severe persecution.

Crushing Pain

MY GOD, MY GOD, why have you forsaken me? Why are you so far from saving me, from the words of my groaning? . . . All who see me mock me; they make mouths at me; they wag their heads; "He trusts in the Lord; let him deliver him; let him rescue him, for he delights in him!" . . . I am poured out like water, and all my bones are out of joint; my heart is like wax; it is melted within my breast; my strength is dried up like a potsherd, and my tongue sticks to my jaws; you lay me in the dust of death. For dogs encompass me; a company of evildoers encircles me; they have pierced my hands and feet . . . they stare and gloat over me; they divide my garments among them, and for my clothing they cast lots. **PSALM 22:1-18, ESV.**

Some of the psalms contain prophecy. They point to Jesus, foretelling the future of the coming Messiah. Psalms 22, 23, and 24 seem to depict the Crucifixion, Jesus' Sabbath rest in the grave, and then Jesus' triumphant entry into heaven after the Resurrection.

Have you ever felt surrounded by the enemy? Jesus felt the crush of evil pressing against Him so severely that it caused Him to think His Father had forsaken Him.

I have suffered a broken nose, a dislocated kneecap, fingers slammed in a car door, and a couple of root canals. All of these caused me some pretty acute physical pain. But no physical pain can compare to the emotional pain I've felt during times of rejection, disappointment, and loss.

Many people think that Jesus died because of the physical toll crucifixion took on His body. That's not what took Jesus' life. Jesus died because He was crushed by sin and rejection. And because of His death, my sin will not crush me.

The Bible says that Jesus died for the sins of the world. That's everybody! And that's good news for everyone who decides they don't want the weight of their sin to crush them anymore. In the end, those who occupy heaven will have gladly accepted that forgiveness. Those who decide to live with their sin and guilt will ultimately be crushed by it, just as Jesus was on the cross.

I thank Jesus every day for showing me the love of the Father on that cross. And I invite you to accept His forgiveness today. Let your guilt stay on the bottom of the ocean, where it belongs.

JULY 3

Rest in Peace

THE LORD IS MY SHEPHERD; I shall not want. He maketh me to lie down in green pastures: he leadeth me beside the still waters. He restoreth my soul: he leadeth me in the paths of righteousness for his name's sake. Yea, though I walk through the valley of the shadow of death, I will fear no evil: for thou art with me; thy rod and thy staff they comfort me. Thou preparest a table before me in the presence of mine enemies: thou anointest my head with oil; my cup runneth over. Surely goodness and mercy shall follow me all the days of my life: and I will dwell in the house of the Lord for ever. **PSALM 23, KJV.**

What was the best sleep you've ever had? Let me tell you about mine.

I'd been having some knee problems, and it was time to get them fixed. One of my church members, Dr. Kaarsten Lang—who happens to be an orthopedic surgeon—was going operate on my knee and hopefully take care of the pain I'd been experiencing.

I remember lying on the operating table as the anesthesiologist put a little cup on my face and said, "Count backward from 10." I think I got to eight before I was out.

When I woke up, it seemed as if only a millisecond of time had passed. I looked at Dr. Lang and asked, "What's the matter? Aren't you going to operate on me?"

She smiled and said, "We're all done! You slept well!"

I was so knocked out I had no idea that someone was probing my knee with medical instruments. I wasn't worried about my family, my job, or the bills I needed to pay that month. When I was asleep, I didn't care if I needed to lose 20 pounds. I wasn't concerned about what I would eat for my next meal. When I was asleep, all was well.

The twenty-third psalm sounds to me like a prophetic description of Christ's experience in the tomb. It is also a reminder that we have no fear in death. When we are asleep, all is well because the Lord is our Shepherd.

When one of our loved ones dies, we are appropriately sad. We hate to experience loss. But we need to remember one thing: that person, whoever it is, doesn't have any worries or pain. The very next thing they will see is the face of Jesus. What a great thing to wake up to!

JULY 4

Independence Day!

LIFT UP YOUR HEADS, O GATES, And be lifted up, O ancient doors, That the King of glory may come in! Who is the King of glory? The Lord strong and mighty, The Lord mighty in battle. Lift up your heads, O gates, And lift them up, O ancient doors, That the King of glory may come in! Who is this King of glory? The Lord of hosts, He is the King of glory. **PSALM 24:7-10, NASB.**

I love Independence Day as it's celebrated in the United States. I love the fireworks, I love the barbecues, I love the sunshine, and I love having a day off to celebrate my freedom!

When my family and I lived in Wenatchee, Washington, the Fourth of July was typically a sunshiny day with 90-degree weather. We'd spend the day with friends, swim in their pool, eat all kinds of delicious food, and then make our way down to the river to watch the fireworks display.

Freedom is worth celebrating, don't you think?

Once a year the Jews have an Independence Day celebration. It's called Passover. They celebrate their release from the bondage of Egypt with a day off and good food.

The biggest freedom thief in the world is death. Death steals our ability to breathe, love, buy, sell, play, work, and eat good food. Dead people don't have freedom to do anything . . . because they're dead. Death is the ultimate prison. So it stands to reason that if someone were to conquer death, it would be worth celebrating, right?

The celebration described in Psalm 24 is just that. All of heaven is celebrating Jesus' triumph over death and His entrance back into the heavenly courts. Can you imagine the party? I'm pretty sure there was singing and dancing and eating of good food! I don't know if they have fireworks in heaven, but if they do, I'll bet it's quite a display.

Independence Day for Jesus happened after He rose from the dead. Oh, by the way, that marks our Independence Day too!

When Jesus conquered death, He did it for you and for me. Because of His resurrection, sin and death can no longer steal our freedom. Now that's worth celebrating, isn't it?

JULY 5

Rat-free Existence

BLESSED IS THE ONE WHOSE transgression is forgiven, whose sin is covered. Blessed is the man against whom the Lord counts no iniquity, and in whose spirit there is no deceit. For when I kept silent, my bones wasted away through my groaning all day long. For day and night your hand was heavy upon me; my strength was dried up as by the heat of summer. I acknowledged my sin to you, and I did not cover my iniquity; I said, "I will confess my transgressions to the Lord," and you forgave the iniquity of my sin. **PSALM 32:1-5, ESV.**

We had mice in our house. It was disgusting. We would find evidence of them behind our cereal boxes or spy a hole chewed into a sleeping bag. Sometimes when I'd walk barefoot down the stairs at midnight, I'd step on a freshly killed mouse that my cat had left like a land mine. But even with two cats doing their duty, the mice kept coming.

One night my wife and I were in bed reading when a mouse scampered across my chest. I never did catch that brave little critter.

I had had enough! So I bought mousetraps. That didn't work. So I did the most sensible thing I could do: I bought a huge bottle of rat poison with a skull and crossbones prominently placed on its label.

I brought that poison home and showed my wife. We both agreed that this would do the trick. We had found the solution to our mice problems! So we took the lid off the bottle and drank all of the rat poison. OK, no, we didn't.

It's been said that not forgiving people who offend you is like trying to kill the mice in your house by drinking rat poison.

Forgiving us is in God's nature. He forgave us before the foundation of the world, so we should forgive each other. And we should forgive ourselves.

When we don't accept forgiveness, we feel the way the psalmist describes above: as if our bones are being crushed. Conversely, when we accept and offer forgiveness, we gain a guilt-free conscience and experience peace in our lives.

It takes a big person to forgive. When we forgive, we give up the right to return hurt to the person who hurt us. That's not easy, but it is what God calls us to do.

The Right Delight

TAKE DELIGHT IN THE LORD, and he will give you the desires of your heart.
PSALM 37:4.

When I first saw her, I thought she was pretty. But I had been a Christian for only a year, and I wanted to keep my eye on the ball. I didn't need to complicate things with pretty girls.

The next weekend in church I saw her again . . . with someone. That confirmed it. I was not going to allow myself to get sucked in by her beauty. And then . . . then I heard her sing.

It happened during tryouts for an Easter play. There was a whole line of girls auditioning for a solo. When Wendy started singing, all the other girls just stepped away. She had a voice drenched in heavenly honey. I was hooked. The problem I faced? She had a boyfriend.

We met. I started the battle to win her affections. During that time I acquired a picture of her. Guess where I put that picture? In my Bible right next to the above verse. This was serious business. This was my future wife! So, just as the Bible declared, I put my delight in the Lord, having faith that He would give me the desires of my heart.

Somewhere along the way my faith in Jesus attracted this cute little blond, and she ended up giving me her heart. We were married in the same church where I had first heard her sing.

Notice the order of things as stated above. My delight was in the Lord. This kept my priorities straight. Everybody has desires—some of them holy, some of them unholy. If you want to ensure that your desires are right desires, delight yourself in the Lord. Make Him the center of your focus and attention, and He will give you gifts that will bring you more happiness and fulfillment than you could ever create for yourself.

JULY 7

David Comes Clean

CREATE IN ME A CLEAN HEART, O God, and renew a steadfast spirit within me. Do not cast me away from Your presence, and do not take Your Holy Spirit from me. Restore to me the joy of Your salvation, and uphold me by Your generous Spirit. **PSALM 51:10-12, NKJV.**

Repentance comes from a broken heart. Forgiveness is not a casual request. We ask for forgiveness because we have broken a covenant, messed up a relationship, or let down a friend.

King David was a man after the Lord's heart. He loved God with a ferocity that one seldom sees. He slew a giant, beat the Philistines into submission, and grew the kingdom of Israel into a world power. David was a man of deep passion. Unfortunately, that deep passion got him into trouble from time to time.

A sleepless night, a stroll onto the rooftop, a wandering eye, and an unchecked craving all took their toll. In one night David became an adulterer. In the next few days or weeks he added deception, bribery, and murder to his sin list. And just when he thought he would get away with it—God intervened.

You see, God doesn't let a believer blow off sin as if it's no big deal. God pursues His children, knowing that confession and forgiveness are the only means to repair a broken relationship.

The above psalm is David's response to his conviction. When he was confronted with his sin, it broke his heart. He couldn't bear letting his dirty little secret separate Him from God any longer.

I'm sure he wept as he composed this psalm. I'll bet he shed tears the first time he sang it in front of people. But as he expressed himself to God, as he poured out his heart with pen and paper (or whatever they wrote with back then), he was released from the chains that bound him, and he became free again.

Think about your life. Take a moment, open a Bible, and read this psalm aloud. Let it be your prayer for a clean heart today.

JULY 8

Leap of Faith

THE FOOL SAYS IN HIS HEART, "There is no God." They are corrupt, doing abominable iniquity; there is none who does good. **PSALM 53:1, ESV.**

You have to have faith in something. Faith is unavoidable. The only part of faith that you can control is what you decide to place your faith in. In regard to God, here are two of your options:

1. You can believe that at one time in the history of the universe nothing existed. What is nothing? I don't know that I can grasp what nothing is, because as far as I can tell, there is no such thing. So I would have to have faith that nothing exists. And then one day a zillion years ago nothing collided with nothing, and something came out. That something had no life, but it was something. That something began to expand into something bigger. At some point on our little planet a bit of that lifeless something started to breathe. It grew arms, legs, and a head and evolved into something mobile enough to crawl out of the ocean. It self-divided and then started coupling and mating to make new somethings. Billions of years later, here we are. A huge accident of the universe. Or . . .

2. You can look around and conclude that there is an intelligent design to everything you see. You can conclude that there is a Prime Mover that set the universe in motion. You can conclude that good and evil exist in the world because good and evil exist in the universe. You can believe that we are born destined to a purpose in life greater than selfish gain or survival of the fittest. You can trust in the idea that God is love and that He desires our company in this universe. You can read prophecy in the Bible and see that God knows the beginning and the end and has shared much of this knowledge with His children.

So what have you decided to put your faith in? Either way, you are not going to have indisputable evidence. Both choices are going to include some doubt. I cannot disprove God. I cannot prove God, either—with the exception of one powerful personal proof: I've seen Him work in my life and in the lives of others. My experience with God is real. I couldn't conjure up a lie as powerful as the truth about what Jesus has done for me. That's my proof. And that's where I've decided to place my faith.

Where have you decided to place your faith in this great debate?

JULY 9

Shout to the Lord!

SHOUT FOR JOY TO GOD, all the earth; sing the glory of his name; give to him glorious praise! Say to God, "How awesome are your deeds! So great is your power that your enemies come cringing to you. All the earth worships you and sings praises to you; they sing praises to your name." **PSALM 66:1-4, ESV.**

I'm not a shouter. My wife and I have been married for 27 years, and I've shouted at her only one time—and I wasn't even mad. I was trying to warn her about something. I'm just not a shouter.

I bring this up because there's one prevalent theme in the Psalms that I just don't know how to handle. Over and over the psalmist invites us to *shout* to the Lord! I've never done this. I've never once shouted to or at the Lord.

Now, I know there are a couple kinds of shouting. There's happy shouting, and there's mad shouting. I've happily shouted, just not to God. I went to a Seattle Seahawks professional football game with my friend Ira. During the game in the football stadium I shouted. So did the 67,000 other people there. It was so loud that I could yell with all my strength at Ira (who was standing right next to me) and he couldn't hear me. The shouting in that stadium ruffles the visiting teams; the Seahawks draw their opponents into false-start penalties (because they can't hear their quarterback calling plays) more often than any other team in the NFL. Those are happy shouts.

I've heard my share of mad shouts too. I grew up in a home with lots of shouting. I prefer the happy shouts.

So if the Bible tells us a billion times to "shout to the Lord," why don't we do it? Why don't we shout to the Lord in church? Why don't we shout to the Lord during our devotional time or while we're driving down the road?

I've thought about it, and here's the only way I can see doing this. What would happen if you gave God a good round of applause for His blessings and yelled, "Hey, God, You are awesome! Yeah, God!" Maybe this would qualify as shouting to the Lord! Why not give it a try?

JULY 10

Music to His Ears

SING FOR JOY TO GOD our strength; shout aloud to the God of Jacob! Begin the music, strike the timbrel, play the melodious harp and lyre. **PSALM 81:1, 2.**

I know that pastors aren't supposed to have favorites in our ministry, but we do. My favorite time speaking for an academy Week of Prayer happened at Columbia Adventist Academy in southern Washington State. Now, keep in mind, I had been the guest speaker at dozens of academies, camp meetings, and colleges throughout the years, so I kind of knew what to expect when I pulled in to the small academy campus. Song service would start, the musicians would kind of be into it, but the kids sitting in the chapel would be looking at their schoolbooks, talking, texting, and doing almost anything but singing to Jesus. Most kids are just too cool to sing to Jesus and mean it. My experience on this campus was a little different from that.

I walked in about a half hour early and stood by myself. I saw a group of students from the academy up toward the stage in a tight little circle, praying for the meetings and praying that their music would be pleasing to God. Then a bell rang, and all the students and teachers filed into the room and sat down. Meanwhile a group of musicians walked up front and picked up guitars, sat at a keyboard, and sat behind a little trap set. *Here we go again*, I thought.

Not so. As soon as the band struck a note, the whole student body stood up and started singing joyfully to their God. A dozen or so lifted hands as they sang. It seemed that everybody had a look of joy on their face as they sang their guts out to God. I had never seen anything like it. It was pure joy and unbridled worship for the King. It brought me to tears.

Somehow that school had made worship a part of their culture. They didn't just sing. They sang to Jesus. They didn't just repeat words out of a songbook. They sang with heart and passion to the God they loved.

As I observed this anomaly, I couldn't help thinking how God must be enjoying hearing His children sing so sincerely of their love for Him. I'll never forget that Week of Prayer. Neither will God. God loves it when we sing to Him.

JULY 11

The Place I Want to Go

BETTER IS ONE DAY in your courts than a thousand elsewhere; I would rather be a doorkeeper in the house of my God than dwell in the tents of the wicked. For the Lord God is a sun and shield; the Lord bestows favor and honor; no good thing does he withhold from those whose walk is blameless. **PSALM 84:10, 11.**

I've been around the world a few times speaking, vacationing, and participating in mission trips. I love traveling. I love seeing the different cultures and landscapes and experiencing the different sights, smells, and sounds of places I do not call my home.

I recently had one of the kids in my church ask, "Pastor Mark, of all the places you've been in the world, what's your favorite?"

I didn't even have to think about my answer. "Kenya!" I exclaimed. I love Kenya. I've been there seven times on mission trips, and each time I've gotten lost in the magic of the Masai Mara. The specific part of Kenya that I have fallen in love with is in the Great Rift Valley, where elephants, cheetahs, rhinos, and hippos dwell in their natural habitat. I love sleeping in a tent and hearing the distant roar of a lion, listening to an elephant breaking down trees in the middle of the night on the outskirts of camp, and having to worry about a monkey stealing food off my plate if I don't pay attention.

The mystery and beauty of Africa have captured my heart and my imagination. I love the people, the sights, the smells, the flora, and the fauna.

If you could choose to spend a couple of weeks anywhere in the world, where would it be? Australia? Hawaii? Europe? The Great Wall of China?

If you were to pose this question to whichever one of the sons of Korah wrote Psalm 84, his answer would be "I'd like to go to church." Well, they didn't have churches in that day, but the Temple is where he'd want to go. Why? Because he sensed the presence of God there. He loved the secure feeling of being wrapped up in God's presence.

Like this psalmist, I yearn to be in God's presence. And even though I know God is with me and in me through the Holy Spirit, I can't wait to see Jesus face to face. I long for that day. How about you? What's the part of heaven you most look forward to?

Don't Mess With the Most High

THOSE WHO LIVE IN THE SHELTER of the Most High will find rest in the shadow of the Almighty. This I declare about the Lord: He alone is my refuge, my place of safety; he is my God, and I trust him. For he will rescue you from every trap and protect you from deadly disease. He will cover you with his feathers. He will shelter you with his wings. His faithful promises are your armor and protection. Do not be afraid of the terrors of the night, nor the arrow that flies in the day. Do not dread the disease that stalks in darkness, nor the disaster that strikes at midday. Though a thousand fall at your side, though ten thousand are dying around you, these evils will not touch you.
PSALM 91:1-7, NLT.

Ofa Langi is intimidating. He's a large Tongan man who rides a bright-red Harley-Davidson. He also happens to be my associate pastor.

Right after college Pastor Ofa worked as a youth/young adult pastor in Kirkland, Washington. One evening he was at a church member's home, where a bunch of youth and young adults were hanging out to eat and worship together. Pastor Ofa was in the kitchen eating (something he is very good at—I think it's his spiritual gift) when somebody shouted, "Hey, Pastor Ofa! Somebody just stole your helmet off your motorcycle!"

Without thinking, Pastor Ofa dropped his food, ran out the side door of the kitchen, and dashed down the driveway toward the road. As he ran, he saw a car parked on the street with two people in the front seat. He also saw his helmet on the lap of one of the thieves.

Pastor Ofa ran right toward the vehicle of the now-startled young people, jumped into the air, and landed with his knees on the front windshield, breaking through to retrieve his helmet.

The young man in the driver's seat opened the door and ran down the road. His pregnant girlfriend sat in the passenger seat screaming and crying, fearing the wrath of the Tongan man kneeling on her dashboard.

This is my associate pastor. I always feel safe when we're together!

The psalmist felt like this in the presence of God. He could walk into any situation and feel secure, because God is a great bodyguard.

JULY 13

New Songs

OH SING TO THE LORD A NEW SONG; sing to the Lord, all the earth! Sing to the Lord, bless his name; tell of his salvation from day to day. Declare his glory among the nations, his marvelous works among all the peoples! **PSALM 96:1-3, ESV.**

Music may well be the most divisive issue in church. I have received more heated e-mails, listened to more opinions, and seen more angry outbursts about the kind of music played and sung in church than on any other topic.

Music is personal. It moves the soul and influences emotion as nothing else does. I can be driving down the road in my car and hear a song on the radio that, in a split second, brings me back to my old neighborhood with my old friends and puts a smile on my face—all from a song.

When it comes to music in church, I am no expert. Some say we should sing only hymns out of the hymnal with a piano and/or organ accompanying. Others say we should sing the new songs with a full band accompanying. Here's what I think:

1. The Bible tells us to sing a *new song* to the Lord. So sometimes we should sing new songs.

2. The Bible tells us that we should sing *to the Lord*. I've that noticed many songs, new and old, sing *about* spiritual things. I prefer to sing *to* the Lord. I like to tell Him how I feel about Him as I sing.

3. When people say that some music comes from "the world," my response is "Show me music that hasn't come from the world." Organs have been used in taverns as well as in churches. Pianos are used in rock concerts and chapels. Guitars are used to praise God and to tear Him down. The Bible says that if we use our gifts and talents to glorify God, we're on the right track. To discount a song because it's new or because it's played with a different rhythm doesn't make biblical sense to me.

My preference? I love a huge pipe organ and majestic hymns. My preference, your preference, and God's preference may be worlds apart. I just know He loves it when His children praise His name. So let's not wound each other over music. Let's use all our energies to tell the world the wonders of our God.

JULY 14

Thanks a Lot!

SHOUT WITH JOY TO THE LORD, all the earth! Worship the Lord with gladness. Come before him, singing with joy. Acknowledge that the Lord is God! He made us, and we are his. We are his people, the sheep of his pasture. Enter his gates with thanksgiving; go into his courts with praise. Give thanks to him and praise his name. For the Lord is good. His unfailing love continues forever, and his faithfulness continues to each generation. **PSALM 100, NLT.**

I just had the most marvelous day. It was my son's fifteenth birthday. All week I'd been two hours away from home working at camp meeting, so birthday plans had kind of been made on the fly. I found out that some of my son's classmates were staying out at the campgrounds all week, so we made plans for my wife and son to meet us about a half hour away at the Old Spaghetti Factory for a birthday lunch.

There were five teens, plus my wife and me, and we ate like kings. Afterward we went to a family fun park, and I paid for the teens to race go-carts, go on rides, and play laser tag. We had a marvelous time and spent a lot of money.

At the end of the day, when we all got back to where we were going, of the five young people who were there only one (besides my son) said thank you. Now, I know they all had a good time. I know they were probably all thankful to spend the day eating good food and doing fun things, but only one of them said thank you. I noticed that.

Think of the things God has given you in your life. I know everything's not perfect, but think of all the things you have and the experiences you get to enjoy. Think of your family, a marvelous sunset, your most recent meal. I know you're thankful. But have you said thank you to the One who gave you life?

Here's a spiritual chore I'd like you to complete. Find a notebook and keep it next to your bed. Call it your "thank-you book." Each night before you fall asleep, spend a couple minutes reviewing the day you spent with God, and write down the things you are thankful for. Let the list pile up. Tell Him thank you for all the things He treated you to that day. I think it will make Him smile.

JULY 15

Pants on Fire

NO ONE WHO PRACTICES DECEIT will dwell in my house; no one who speaks falsely will stand in my presence. **PSALM 101:7.**

I hate it when people lie to me. I really do. Even if I don't want to hear what the truth actually is, I'd rather hear hard truth than a smooth lie.

Sometimes I lie. Or at least I have in my history. The first time I remember lying, I was about 3 years old. I lied about an ice-cream cone. I got caught and received a memorable spanking.

One of the most disappointing lies I've ever experienced occurred on a Halloween night. I was taking my 4-year-old son around to a bunch of church members' houses to get free candy. He was dressed as a little ninja and was enjoying all the attention. My church members were all expecting him and were having a good time giving candy away to all the little beggars that night.

After we hit all the houses on my list, we saw that we were next to a house where one of my prominent church members lived. It was in a neighborhood with lots of families, and the street was crowded with moms, dads, and little ones going from door to door. We pulled alongside the curb in front of their house and approached the door of this church member. On the door was a sign that said, "Sorry, we aren't home tonight. Have a happy Halloween!" As we were leaving the driveway to get into our car, I met a group of families with their children and introduced myself. They had all been to the door and had seen the posted sign.

Just then a light went on in the kitchen. The blinds were up, so we could clearly see the wife grab a big bowl of popcorn, turn the light off, and scurry up the stairs to a room above the garage, where we could clearly see the light emanating from a television.

Now, none of the people in the neighborhood knew these folks, since they had moved in recently, but suffice it to say, the people in the neighborhood were not impressed. One of the fathers said, "Why would you have to lie to avoid giving candy to kids?" Ouch.

Don't be a liar. The devil is a liar. You don't want to be like him. You want to be like the Truth, Jesus. Liars are . . . well, just liars.

JULY 16

Tippy the Lawless

O HOW I LOVE YOUR LAW! It is my meditation all the day. Your commandments make me wiser than my enemies, for they are ever mine. I have more insight than all my teachers, for Your testimonies are my meditation. I understand more than the aged, because I have observed Your precepts. I have restrained my feet from every evil way, that I may keep Your word. I have not turned aside from Your ordinances, for You Yourself have taught me. How sweet are Your words to my taste! Yes, sweeter than honey to my mouth! From Your precepts I get understanding; therefore I hate every false way.
PSALM 119:97-104, NASB.

When I was young, I fell in love with a female in my life. I was just 8 years old, but I knew she was the one I had been waiting for all my life. Her name was Tippy. She was a dog.

Tippy, a mutt we got from the pound, loved her family more than life itself. She was amazingly smart and knew lots of tricks. Her one bad habit surfaced each time our family got in the car and drove off. She'd try to follow us. She'd barrel down the road after us and end up running in front of cars on a busy street. So my dad built a fence.

However, Tippy, as it turned out, was an escape artist. She defied my dad's best attempts at making a chicken-wire fence that would hold her. Each time she escaped, my dad would figure out how she had gotten out and fix the weak point. Finally, we thought we had the fence Tippy-proofed enough to hold her.

One sunny Sunday morning we put Tippy in her cage, got in the car, and went to IHOP for breakfast. On our way home, as we pulled off the busy road into our neighborhood, my dad applied the brakes and said, "Oh, no!" Yup, it was Tippy lying on the side of the road, lifeless. Somehow she had gotten out of her cage and tried to follow us. We had a little burial in the backyard. Lots of tears.

God's law is a lot like Tippy's fence. He's given it to us for a purpose. When we stay inside the confines of God's law, we are safe, secure, and happy. But when we seek our freedom outside of God's law, we risk everything. In fact, true freedom is found in obedience to God's law. Perfect joy is found in living a life with no regrets.

JULY 17

Unseen Protector

I WILL LIFT UP MY EYES TO THE MOUNTAINS; from where shall my help come? My help comes from the Lord, who made heaven and earth.
He will not allow your foot to slip; He who keeps you will not slumber. Behold, He who keeps Israel will neither slumber nor sleep. The Lord is your keeper; the Lord is your shade on your right hand. The sun will not smite you by day, nor the moon by night. The Lord will protect you from all evil; He will keep your soul. The Lord will guard your going out and your coming in from this time forth and forever. **PSALM 121, NASB.**

For most of our journey through the Psalms I've used snippets of a chapter to give the flavor of a psalm or to illustrate a lesson. I didn't do this with Psalm 121, because I couldn't. It's just too beautiful to read only a portion of it. And it reminds me of one of my favorite memories.

When my son was 2 years old, we lived on the side of a hill near Asheville, North Carolina. Behind our house was a wide trail that went for miles up and around a wooded wonderland. There were deer, wild turkeys, and all kinds of exciting things to view up there. There were also copperheads—poisonous snakes that could do quite a bit of damage to a 2-year-old. There was also plenty of poison ivy.

I always enjoyed watching my 2-year-old son and his dog, Bob, wander out of the backyard and up the hill together. They would go on a wonderful adventure, my son not knowing that his dad was always behind them, keeping them in view. I was never so far away that my son could fall into peril. I was the unseen protector of the one I loved.

I can imagine the Lord getting great amounts of enjoyment as we navigate life. There are dangers and perils in this world that we aren't even aware of. As I look back on my life, I can now see numerous times that an unseen hand has saved my life.

Now that my son is older, I can't hide in the shadows and protect him anymore. I've had to hand that task over to God. Letting go of being my son's stalker isn't easy, but as I read the psalm for today, I have confidence that my God will be a great caretaker for my boy.

Take a moment and thank God for the times He has intervened in your life.

It Takes Everybody

HOW WONDERFUL IT IS, HOW PLEASANT, for God's people to live together in harmony! It is like the precious anointing oil running down from Aaron's head and beard, down to the collar of his robes. It is like the dew on Mount Hermon, falling on the hills of Zion. That is where the Lord has promised his blessing—life that never ends. **PSALM 133, TEV.**

One of the best illustrations of this psalm happened when I was a boys' dean at a little school up in Bella Coola, British Columbia. The staff and students had been backpacking and canoeing for more than a week. On the last day of our trip we had made it back to the trailhead in one piece and were eager to get back to the dorms to shower and eat food that wasn't cooked over a campfire.

Our journey from the trailhead was a treacherous one. We had to navigate our vehicles over bumpy roads, through a couple of creeks, over some suspect old wooden bridges, and over some huge rocks left by a landslide. It was about an hour's drive to the paved road, and we were eager to get home.

About halfway up the road all the vehicles stopped. A rock half the size of a VW Beetle was in the middle of the road. A cliff to our left dropped about 500 feet. A cliff to our right went up another 1,000 feet. No way to drive around.

All the boys got out of the vehicles and tried to move the rock. It wouldn't budge. All the girls laughed. "Do you need our help, boys?" All the girls *and* all the boys tried to move the rock. It wouldn't budge. Some of the boys found part of an old telephone pole and tried using it for leverage. The rock budged! Not far, but it budged! Then one of the boys, who was skinny and loved math, said, "I have an idea! Use the jacks in the vehicles to move the rock!" Brilliant! All the girls and all the guys and all the staff worked together to move that rock an inch at a time until finally we sent it tumbling down the cliff and into the river below.

This never could have happened had not all of us worked together. Father, Son, and Holy Spirit work together for our good, just as we should work together for the good of the church and this world. What kind of church would we have if we stopped fighting and started working together? I'd like to see that kind of church; wouldn't you?

JULY 19

Not an Accident

YOU MADE MY WHOLE BEING; you formed me in my mother's body. I praise you because you made me in an amazing and wonderful way. What you have done is wonderful. I know this very well. You saw my bones being formed as I took shape in my mother's body. When I was put together there, you saw my body as it was formed. All the days planned for me were written in your book before I was one day old. **PSALM 139:13-16, NCV.**

I don't know how old I was when my mom first told me I was adopted, because it seems like I've always known. I was a ward of the state of California when my parents adopted me at 5 weeks old. Somewhere along the line my mom became a Seventh-day Adventist. My dad gave it a shot but decided church wasn't for him.

As I grew up, I experienced the polarization of a husband and wife who were not on the same page. My mom wanted to raise my sister and me as happy little Adventists. My dad just wanted to keep their old life intact.

As I grew up, I ended up making choices that compromised my mind, my body, and my soul. In academy my peers knew I was doing things that, if I were caught, would get me kicked out.

It wasn't until I was 22 years old that I yielded to the Holy Spirit's call and gave my heart to Jesus. It was the most eventful and wonderful time of my life. Jesus became real to me. I devoured the Bible and grew in faith. It wasn't long before I was preaching, and eventually I began working for the church as a pastor. Life was good.

Then one Friday night I received a phone call from a stranger. "I'm your birth mother!" she told me. I came to discover that she had grown up an Adventist but had become disillusioned and had left the church. When she had me, she wasn't married, and she adopted me out in secret. Her family hadn't even known of her pregnancy!

When she called me that fateful Friday night and found that I was a Seventh-day Adventist pastor, it took her breath away.

Friends, God has a plan for you. You aren't an accident in this universe. God wants to use you to make a difference. He knows you inside and out!

JULY 20

An Energetic Ending

PRAISE THE LORD! Praise God in his sanctuary; praise him in his mighty heaven! Praise him for his mighty works; praise his unequaled greatness! Praise him with a blast of the ram's horn; praise him with the lyre and harp! Praise him with the tambourine and dancing; praise him with strings and flutes! Praise him with a clash of cymbals; praise him with loud clanging cymbals. Let everything that breathes sing praises to the Lord! Praise the Lord! **PSALM 150, NLT.**

I can't think of a better way to end our time in the Psalms than with the last psalm. What a powerful description of unbridled worship! Nothing held back. Nobody self-conscious. Just celebratory worship. Why don't people do this more often?

Second Samuel 6 tells the story of the ark of the Lord returning to Jerusalem. As the ark entered the city, something sudden and unusual happened. David, the king, "danced before the Lord with all his might" (verse 14, NKJV).

Now, I'm not a dancer. I'm six feet six inches and slightly uncoordinated, so I'm pretty sure that even if I attempted to dance I'd sprain an ankle. What would it look like for someone to dance with all their might? It seems that it would be vigorous. It seems that one would break a sweat. I've never seen someone praise God by dancing with all their might, but I imagine it would be an odd and beautiful thing.

Interestingly enough, when David's wife saw the king leaping and dancing with all his might, she got upset and embarrassed at the spectacle. Can you imagine?

A lot of people think that the only way to properly worship God is to sit still, listen to a sermon, and occasionally say amen. As we read the last psalm of the Bible, it occurs to me that worship can (and maybe should) be more lively than that.

When we get excited about something, we react. Whether with laughter or tears, applause or reverent silence, shouts or gasps, we react to things that move us. When was the last time you allowed yourself to be moved in worship to God?

Once upon a time Jesus said, "If these people kept quiet, the rocks would cry out!" (see Luke 19:40). I pray that when I worship, God isn't tempted to make rocks cry out.

JULY 21

Knowing Stuff

THE FEAR OF THE LORD is the beginning of knowledge, but fools despise wisdom and instruction. **PROVERBS 1:7.**

Everybody seems to know everything nowadays. Any information you could ever desire is a mouse click away. Need an introduction to astrophysics? No problem—Google it. Want to know how to change the brakes on a 2009 Honda Accord? Someone demonstrates it on YouTube. Having problems with moles in your lawn? Find six ways to kill them on Ask.com. Knowledge is highly accessible in our day and age. Wisdom, on the other hand, seems like a rare commodity.

One of my favorite quotes on wisdom is "Knowledge is knowing that a tomato is a fruit; wisdom is knowing not to put it in a fruit salad." Here are some of my other favorites about wisdom:

- Do not argue with idiots. They will drag you down to their level and beat you with experience.
- Light travels faster than sound. This is why some people appear bright until you hear them speak.
- The early bird might get the worm, but the second mouse gets the cheese.
- Better to remain silent and be thought a fool than to speak and remove all doubt.
- You do not need a parachute to skydive. You only need a parachute to sky-dive twice.
- Always borrow money from pessimists. They won't expect it back.
- You're never too old to learn something stupid.
- To be sure of hitting the target, shoot first and call whatever you hit the target.

These are little nuggets of "wisdom" gleaned off the World Wide Web. The wisdom found in the book of Proverbs, on the other hand, is Spirit-filled and reliable. Some of the verses in Proverbs are funny, some thought-provoking, and others seemingly contradictory. One thing is for sure: if you use these wise sayings as a rule of life, you will prosper in all ways. In the following pages we will look at several of these spiritual nuggets and find wisdom to apply to our lives.

JULY 22

Shut Up and Listen

THE WISE IN HEART accept commands, but a chattering fool comes to ruin.
PROVERBS 10:8.

I've been a guide for whitewater rafting adventures since the 1980s. It's one of my great joys in life. There is nothing quite as fun as getting in an inflated rubber boat with a bunch of friends and paddling through 12-foot rapids together.

One of my responsibilities as a guide is to have "the talk" with all my rookie rafters. In the talk I tell them how to paddle, what commands to expect on the river, and what to do in case of an emergency. I always end my talk by saying, "If you listen to your guide, you will have a successful and fun trip down the river. If you don't listen to your guide, you will be taking your life into your own hands."

I have had occasions when people in my rafts thought they knew better than their guide. The boat landed upside down, and everybody got a bath. They listened after that.

From the time we are small we refuse to listen to counsel. "I can do it by myself!" we say as we button our shirt all askew. We don't want to listen to our parents, our teachers, or any authority, for that matter. We are all born with a stubborn pride that says, "I don't have to listen to you!"

Solomon the wise says differently. He says it's smart to stay silent and listen to commands. Notice that he calls someone who can't be silent a fool. People who chatter their opinions over the quiet instruction of their elders are, for lack of a better word, idiots! I call them "yeah buts," as in "Yeah, but what about this and what about that?"

In my ministry I've worked with people who really needed good advice. As I'd give them the words they needed to hear to make better decisions and go in a better direction, they would say, "Yeah, but . . ." They'd developed a habit of making excuses to get out of listening to lifesaving advice.

The wisdom of Solomon tells us to stop, listen, and learn. Take commandments to heart. Don't be a yeah but.

JULY 23

Hey, Did You Hear About . . . ?

A GOSSIP BETRAYS A CONFIDENCE, but a trustworthy person keeps a secret. **PROVERBS 11:13.**

My first year of college was quite an experience for a variety of reasons. I had many frustrations, most of them brought on by my own bad choices. But there was one incident during my freshman year that still has me scratching my head.

I was sitting in the cafeteria eating supper when a friend came up to me and asked, "Hey, what's up with you and Marie?" Marie was a friend I had made there at Walla Walla. The only time I ever saw her was in a group of friends; nothing exclusive.

"What do you mean, 'what's up'?" I asked.

"Paul said you and Marie were sitting on her couch and kissing."

I went to Paul. He confirmed the story. Jesse had told him. I went to Jesse. He also knew the story. Each person was kind enough to tell me who had told them. Finally, I got to Stuart. Stuart wouldn't tell me who had told him, but he was sure it was true. He seemed to think he had the inside scoop.

The problem with the story, of course, was that I had never kissed Marie. I had never even been alone with Marie long enough to ask what her middle name was!

I remember how frustrating this was for both Marie and me as we tried to dig to the bottom of the rumor. Everyone we spoke to seemed to know the story and had shared it with someone in their circle, but nobody would confess to starting the rumor.

I once knew a person who had a great habit. Anytime anyone came to her with gossip to share, she would stop the person and inform them that any story they told her would be repeated directly to the person it was about—with appropriate credit as to who had shared it, of course! So ended the gossip.

May we be gossip enders and not people who fan the flames of bringing others down.

JULY 24

Mike and Bonkers

THE RIGHTEOUS CARE for the needs of their animals, but the kindest acts of the wicked are cruel. **PROVERBS 12:10.**

As I've mentioned before, it's very possible that my wife likes animals more than she likes people. When I met Wendy, she had an unusual cat named Bonkers. My wife loved him as if he were her firstborn. She would pick him up, sling him over her shoulder, and let him suck on her earlobe (which absolutely disgusted me).

After we got married, we lived in an apartment off the dorm where I was boys' dean. There was a boy named Mike in my dorm who liked to tease people to the point of annoyance. He was a nice kid, but sometimes he would get into mischief over his head. One evening Wendy and I were sitting in our apartment with our window open. We could hear the kids talking out on the deck. Mike was laughing and bragging about something he had done to Bonkers. The prank he described made my wife furious. She got up and was ready to march out the door to read him the riot act when I stopped her. "Let's be creative in the way we teach him this lesson, shall we?"

That night after all the boys were in bed, we snuck up the stairs to Mike's room. The door was open, and he was lying on the bottom bunk with a blanket hanging down from the top as a curtain between himself and the rest of the room. Wendy had a pitcher of ice-cold water in her hand. In a split second the curtain was peeled back, the water was delivered, and we were down the stairs. He didn't know what hit him.

Mike came marching down to my apartment and started banging on the door to complain about the mystery assailant. As he started to vent, he saw Wendy sitting on the couch behind me with a grin on her face. He blurted out, "I didn't do anything to Bonkers. I was lying, I promise!" He knew before we even said a thing.

Few things get me riled up like animal cruelty. What kind of character qualities would someone have to possess in order to harm or torture an animal? God gave us the animals to manage and enjoy. Let's treat our furry friends with love and respect. If you don't, beware of ice-cold water.

JULY 25

A Well-placed Rod

HE WHO SPARES HIS ROD hates his son, but he who loves him disciplines him promptly. **PROVERBS 13:24, NKJV.**

If you ever want to do research on effective parenting, don't go to Walmart at 10:00 p.m. I was in South Carolina at Nosoca Pines Ranch when I realized I had forgotten my toothbrush and toothpaste. I hopped into the car, drove around the lake to the Walmart Supercenter, and went hunting for an Oral-B. As I passed the toy section, I heard what sounded like a wild animal caught in a snare. Looking down the aisle, I saw what was causing the commotion. It was a huge power struggle between a 4-year-old girl and her mother.

When I first spotted them, the mom had the little girl in her arms as the young one shrieked at the top of her lungs and violently tried to pry herself loose from her bear-hugging mom. I stopped to see what would happen. This was good entertainment on a Saturday night in South Carolina.

The little girl's anger turned into rage, and she started pounding on her mother's face with both fists. The mother closed her eyes and tried to move her face from side to side to lessen the pain of the blows, all the while yelling, "ONE! TWO! . . . ONE! TWO! . . . ONE! TWO!" She never did get to three.

That was several years ago. I can only imagine what that little girl has grown up to be, if she's still alive.

This young mother was afraid to discipline. What people don't realize is that discipline is a good thing! People discipline their bodies to make them strong. Is there pain involved? Yes. But the results are great.

Just like a bodybuilding trainer, parents can discipline their children into strong, godly teens and adults. But discipline isn't just something that other people provide for you. You can practice spiritual disciplines to make your faith stronger. Daily prayer, Bible study, service, Sabbathkeeping, fasting, and many other spiritual training exercises can help grow you into a strong person of faith.

Are some of these things painful? Yes. But is it worth the pain? Definitely.

The Wrong Way

THERE IS A WAY THAT appears to be right, but in the end it leads to death.
PROVERBS 14:12.

My favorite place in the world to backpack is in Tweedsmuir Provincial Park in the coastal mountains of British Columbia, Canada. The park has a nice 30-mile hike and a five-lake canoe trip. When I worked in Bella Coola, each year we began our school year with all the students taking this trip. Each year at the trailhead our principal would instruct the kids on how to stay safe in the bear-infested woods by hiking together and staying on the trails. He would specifically tell the kids not to cut the switchbacks (trails that zigzag back and forth to make the hike less steep). Taking shortcuts across the zigzags damages the trails and, if you misjudge where you are, can get you very lost.

On the next-to-last day of our trip we hiked 10 miles down the side of a mountain. We were sitting around a campfire making supper, when somebody spoke up. "I haven't seen Kora [name changed to protect the innocent]. Have you?" Nobody had. In fact, the last time anyone had seen Kora was when we left the top of the mountain. This was a problem.

We all started calling her name. No response. Finally the staff sent three older boys who would rather hike than eat to run up the trail and see if they could find any sign of her.

About three miles up the trail they heard her calling. She thought she had figured out a shortcut down the mountain and had ended up lost, sitting by a river full of salmon and an occasional grizzly bear.

Some people in this life follow their instincts rather than their values. I've seen it a hundred times with young people and their choices in relationships. I've heard, "But at the time he seemed so right for me!" Tears. Snot. More tears.

Just because something "seems" right doesn't make it right. If you have any doubt, check the Word; ask trusted, godly, older friends; and let God speak.

JULY 27

Spilled Coffee, Lost Dignity

WHOEVER OPPRESSES THE POOR SHOWS contempt for their Maker, but whoever is kind to the needy honors God. **PROVERBS 14:31.**

I was taking classes at Seattle Pacific University while living in Bothell, a city about 30 miles out of Seattle. My car was in the shop, so I had to rely on public transit to get to school every day. I actually enjoyed the ride. It gave me time to read my homework and do assignments. I also enjoyed the 15 minutes I had to spend on the street in the middle of Seattle's downtown skyscrapers, waiting for my connecting bus. I'd squat on the sidewalk next to a building and watch the strange and wonderful people that such urban centers as Seattle can produce.

One day I was sitting and watching the line of people purchasing coffee from a mobile coffee cart. One by one the people would purchase their coffee. As they turned to leave the cart, a raggedy-looking homeless woman would hold out an empty coffee cup to beg for coins. Most people ended up putting their change in the cup. The woman was making quite a haul. And then it happened.

A well-dressed woman talking on a cell phone, holding a briefcase, and balancing her newly purchased wake-up juice didn't see the homeless woman holding out her cup. She bumped into the arm of the homeless woman, stopped abruptly, and spilled some of her coffee on the lapel of her jacket. Two amazing things happened as a result of this little encounter: 1. The businesswoman went off on the homeless woman. She started screaming and swearing at the poor, confused homeless woman so violently that I thought she was going to hit her. By the time the businesswoman was done ranting, she had thrown her coffee into a waste bin and marched down the road. 2. When the businesswoman left, the rest of the people near the bus stop came over to the now-crying homeless woman and stuffed her cup with a lot of paper money. They tried to soothe her hurt feelings with words of affirmation.

I think the words "pick on someone your own size" fit here. As God's children we have a responsibility to reach out and help the poor when we have the opportunity. Jesus tells us that when we do, we are doing it to Him.

JULY 28

Be Careful What You Say

A GENTLE ANSWER TURNS AWAY WRATH, but a harsh word stirs up anger.
PROVERBS 15:1.

Words pack more power than a right cross to the jaw. Carefully placed words can either bring peace or start a war. Rarely does a serious brawl begin without provocation. Taunting, verbal jabs, and insults can stir up anger and passion in any person and invite reactions that can turn violent in a split second.

Jim Rome got attacked on live TV because of harsh words. In 1994 Rome, a talk-show host who interviews sports stars for a living, was interviewing the quarterback for the New Orleans Saints, a fellow named Jim Everett. Everett had experienced a rough season that year but was still a proud athlete. Early in the interview Jim Rome said, "Chris Everett, good to have you on the show," taunting the quarterback by comparing him to Chris Evert, a female tennis player. Jim Everett let Rome know that he didn't appreciate the comment.

But Rome wasn't about to let up. He kept referencing the female tennis player with the similar last name until Jim Everett basically said, "You better not call me Chris Everett to my face one more time."

Rome thought for a moment and said, "Chris . . ."

At that point Jim Everett pushed over the interview table and clocked the provocative TV show host on live television. You can see all of this on YouTube. It's kind of hilarious in a sad way.

I'm guessing Jim Rome had not spent much time reading the book of Proverbs. If he had, he would have realized that a gentle answer turns away wrath. Provoking people to anger is not something that the Bible would consider a godly thing to do. In fact, Jesus said, "Blessed are the peacemakers" (Matthew 5:9).

I'm the first to admit that it can be fun to verbally poke people to produce a reaction. But I have to remind myself to be careful. I need to remember to use my words to build people up and not tear them down. Put this into practice today. See if you can find five people to lift up with your words today, and monitor their reactions.

JULY 29

Big Fall

PRIDE GOES BEFORE DESTRUCTION, a haughty spirit before a fall. **PROVERBS 16:18.**

I know the things that I don't do well. I don't ski well. I don't swim well (I can float forever, but I can't win a swim race to save my life). I can't sailboard. I have a problem when math gets too complicated. There are lots of things I'm not good at.

Conversely, there are things that I'm better at than most people. I'm not saying that I'm better at anything than all people; I'm just saying that I'm better at certain things than *most* people. One of those things is ping-pong. I'm a really good ping-pong player. I won first place in both my high school and my college ping-pong tournaments. I could beat you in ping-pong.

One day at church an elderly member told me that her son was in town. "I'd like you to connect with my son," this church member said. "He hasn't attended church regularly in years. I thought maybe you could go over to his house and play some ping-pong with him." I thought that was a good idea, so I called him up. He told me he played ping-pong with a few friends every Sunday morning and would love to have me over.

I entered the house that day very proud of my ping-pong skills. This person I was going to play was about 20 years my senior, so I thought I'd take it a little easy on the poor old guy. He beat me 21–6. We played 10 times that morning. I won one game. I was completely humiliated (if one can be humiliated from losing a ping-pong match). My pride walked into that house that morning. I left a humble man.

I once heard a story about an arrogant young preacher who thought he was all that and a bag of chips. He walked up to the pulpit and delivered a horrible sermon that did not resonate with the congregation. When he was done, he sat back down next to an old elder, humiliated. The old elder said, "Young man, if you had walked up to the pulpit the way you walked away from the pulpit, you would have done just fine."

Nothing good comes from a proud heart. In fact, many people believe that pride was the original sin. God calls His children to a life of humility, not pride.

JULY 30

Don't Get Your Exercise by Jumping to Conclusions

IN A LAWSUIT THE FIRST to speak seems right, until someone comes forward and cross-examines. **PROVERBS 18:17.**

She stomped into my office with a red face, tear-stained eyes, and a set jaw. She was angry, and I could tell I was in for a severe tongue-lashing. She started in, "I can't believe you did that! I can't believe you actually said those things about me! I will never trust you again!"

I was stunned. "What did I say about you that has angered you like this?"

"Mindy told me that you told her that . . . " She detailed the nasty particulars.

When she was done screaming at me, I was shaken but not particularly sorry—because all the misdeeds she was sure I was guilty of had never happened.

The red-faced young woman was sure she was right, so I decided to pop her bubble by calling in the young woman who had told her the things I had said and done.

When Mindy came in, she confessed that she had made everything up to get attention and that none of the things she had said about me were true.

We can be so sure we're right until we find out we're wrong. It happens all the time. The news will report one side of a story and get everybody all riled up until the other side of the story comes to light.

We do this with God, too. Throughout history people have assumed things about God, not knowing that there are two sides to His story. Religion paints God to be a kind of tyrant who runs hot and cold in His feelings toward humanity.

Jesus came to tell the other side of the story about God. He said, "If you've seen Me, you've seen the Father." (Yup, I've mentioned this before—it's one of my favorite Bible texts!) If we want to know the truth about God, we need to know Jesus. When we have questions about who God really is, we can look for those answers in the life, death, and resurrection of Jesus.

Oh, and when it comes to stories—any stories—always listen to both sides of an argument before you make a judgment on it. According to Solomon the wise, looking at both sides of a story will serve us well.

JULY 31

Bonkers, the Lazy Cat

A SLUGGARD BURIES HIS HAND IN THE DISH; he will not even bring it back to his mouth! **PROVERBS 19:24.**

When I first met my wife-to-be, I quickly realized that she did not live alone. She owned a large black-and-white cat named Bonkers. When I say large, I'm talking 25-plus pounds of lard. This cat was so fat that when he ran (which wasn't often), his belly would bounce off the ground.

After we married, we lived in a little place that was plagued with mice. At that time we had two cats: my cat and my wife's cat. I would watch as my cat (svelte as a cat should be) chased a mouse right over Bonkers' lethargic body. Bonkers would look only mildly interested in the chase—too much work.

I once saw Bonkers actually lying down with his head in the cat dish so he could eat with one side of his mouth and sleep at the same time. Bonkers was the laziest animal I've ever seen.

The only consequences Bonkers suffered for his fat, lazy slothfulness were a large belly and an early grave. These consequences can also result from laziness in the human race. I'm not sure there is anything more unattractive than laziness.

I had a stepfather who didn't work, didn't clean, didn't mow the lawn, didn't take the trash out, and didn't take care of his body. Yes, he went to an early grave, but before that he lost his dignity, his spark of life, and his neighborhood friends. His slothfulness left him with nothing, and I'm not talking just about material things; I'm talking about soul things. Laziness cost him his freedom. It trapped him in a house filled with junk, it trapped him in bad health, and it trapped him in a mind-set of self-defeat.

God did not create us to be lazy. Now, that doesn't mean the occasional mid-afternoon hammock nap is off-limits. But neglecting your mind, body, and soul because you choose not to exercise them is not the way to honor your Creator.

So do something! Exercise your mind! Work out your body! Train your soul! Do all these things to the glory of God, and you will be happy and strong.

Terror in a Hotel Hallway

WINE IS A MOCKER and beer a brawler; whoever is led astray by them is not wise. **PROVERBS 20:1.**

I'm sure he was normally a nice guy. I hear he was a traveling businessman staying in the same hotel as we were. He looked normal. But he didn't act normal.

I was in the city of Zaporozhye, Ukraine, with 25 young people, teaching English during the day and holding evangelistic meetings in the evening. It was a thrilling experience to bring the gospel to a country that only three years earlier had been clouded by atheistic Communism. People were more open to the gospel than I've ever seen before.

Each night our team would gather in the upper lobby of the hotel to sing, worship, and pray together. It was a magical time.

One night as we were worshipping together, a petite teenage girl from our team excused herself to run down to her room for something she needed. As she walked down the hallway toward her room, I heard a scream. I looked up and saw a large middle-age man dragging our team member into his room.

I jumped up and ran down the hall to the room, catching the door just before it slammed. I pushed the door open and started yelling at the large Russian man. I didn't know the language, so I just yelled, *"Nyet! Nyet!"* He slurred some words in my general direction and wouldn't let go of the girl.

I actually had to knock the big drunk man over to make him let go of the terrified student. As we hurried down the hall to the rest of the group, the police were running up the stairs to arrest our drunk friend.

The Bible is not silent about how damaging alcohol can be to a person's life. Alcohol inhibits the character, causing people to do things they would never think of doing when sober. Just look at the statistics: alcohol has a huge effect on the frequency of child sexual abuse, child physical abuse, spousal abuse, and emergency room visits.

No wonder God includes stern warnings in the Bible to stay away from the stuff. You don't need to tell me twice!

AUG 2

Nothing Like It

BETTER TO LIVE IN A DESERT than with a quarrelsome and nagging wife.
PROVERBS 21:19.

I was nervous. I knew I wanted to marry Wendy, but I needed some good advice before turning my intentions into a genuine proposal. So I went to one of the men I most admired in life. His name was Ron. He had been married for 20-plus years already, and he was the best husband and father I had ever seen.

When I sat down with Ron, my question was simple: "Ron, I think I want to ask Wendy to marry me. Do you have any advice for me so that I can know if I'm doing the right thing?"

Ron sat back, thought for a moment, and then answered, "Mark, if you find the right wife, there's nothing like it." I smiled and was about to respond, but he continued: "And if you find the wrong wife, there's nothing like that, either!" Well, now, *that* was reassuring.

My friend was right. Wendy and I have been married for 27 years, and there's nothing like it (in a good way!). But I know some people who have married poorly and have been miserable in their marriages. Many times their marriages have become divorces. So the question is How do you find a spouse who will make you happy instead of miserable? I don't have all the answers to this question, but I do have a couple of ideas that may help down the road:

- Find some trusted people in your life and give them permission to speak candidly about your potential spouse. Pay attention to the red flags they raise.
- Make sure you note how your potential spouse treats their family, especially their mother and father. This will someday be how they treat you.
- Look at what you and your future spouse have in common when it comes to ministry. Working as a team for a higher purpose often cements a deeper relationship.

God invented marriage as an illustration of who He is. Remember that God created humans in His own image, male and female. Much as Father, Son, and Holy Spirit are one, a man and woman are one, reflecting His image, when they marry. Satan will do everything he can to destroy the image of God, so choose wisely!

You're Fired!

LIKE AN EARRING OF GOLD or an ornament of fine gold is the rebuke of a wise judge to a listening ear. **PROVERBS 25:12.**

It was toward the end of my first year as a dean and Bible teacher at Bella Coola Adventist Academy. I was having the time of my life—until the principal of the school called me into her office. The words she shared hit me like a two-by-four. "Mark, I want you to know that we are not going to renew your contract next year. You are unorganized, late to everything, and unprofessional."

I wanted to fight back. I wanted to tell her that she didn't know what she was talking about. But she did. I was late to everything. I was unorganized. I was sloppy. *Rats!* Her words were hurtful, but they were the most helpful things anyone had ever said to me. I needed to hear the wise words of that insightful woman.

There were about two months left in the school year, and I decided that I needed to turn a corner in my life and prove her wrong. For the next two months I was early for everything. I was as organized as a soldier and as neat as a pin.

One more time, at the end of the school year, I was summoned to Mrs. Harris's office. "Mark, I don't know what has happened to you these past two months, but we like what we see. We've changed our minds and would like you to work here another year—if you continue to be the kind of person you've become in these past two months."

How do you respond to criticism? When people deliver words that are hard for you to hear, do you take them in with wisdom and discernment? Or do you give a knee-jerk reaction and walk away offended, not learning a thing from the experience?

King Solomon would suggest that instead of getting all bent out of shape, we ought to listen to our critics, especially the ones who are older and wiser than we are. They may be speaking lifesaving words.

I will be forever grateful to Diane Harris for speaking hard words to me—words I really needed to hear.

AUG 4

Zip Your Lip

LIKE ONE WHO TAKES AWAY a garment on a cold day, or like vinegar poured on a wound, is one who sings songs to a heavy heart. **PROVERBS 25:20.**

One of the thorns I've had to live with most of my life is that sometimes I speak and then think. I've been known to say things that were not appropriate for the moment. This comes from my natural defense mechanism of humor. I tend to try to lighten things up when it would be better just to keep silent.

When our 20-year-old daughter, Meghan, drowned in the Wenatchee River in a tragic accident, I felt as if my whole world had been turned upside down. The giant gouge in my soul seemed as if it would never heal. I had no words. I just felt as if I needed to sit in silence for a long, long time.

During this time there was a young woman named Sarah Norton, a friend of Meghan, who would come over to the house. She wouldn't ring the bell; she'd just open the door and let herself in, walk through the entryway and the kitchen, and come out to our back deck, where I'd be sitting on a swinging chair meant for two. Sarah would come and sit next to me and look over the river into the valley and hills of East Wenatchee. She didn't ever really say anything. She didn't lament out loud how much she missed Meghan. She just sat with me. It was nice. She and many others provided this gift of their presence without words. It was healing.

I learned a lot from Sarah and the others who comforted me this way. I learned that levity has its place, but so does silence. Sometimes a heavy heart needs to be heavy for a time. Attempting to pull somebody out of mourning too early can backfire.

During this time I had people who would come over and try to make sense of the tragedy. They'd say things like "God is in control" and "Maybe it was just Meghan's time."

Here's my advice: In the face of tragedy, don't say stupid things that make God look uncaring and that trivialize a bad situation. Just go sit with your friends and *shhh*. Let them know you love them and are with them in their pain.

Let There Be Light

WHOEVER CONCEALS THEIR SINS does not prosper, but the one who confesses and renounces them finds mercy. **PROVERBS 28:13.**

Sometimes people think hurt and pain should be avoided at all costs. But just because something hurts doesn't mean it's bad. In fact, much of the time pain brings opportunities and gains that can make us more into the image of Jesus than we ever thought possible.

In one of my churches a man sat in my office sobbing because his marriage was falling apart. His wife had caught him (for the third time in five years) viewing pornography on his computer. She had kicked him out of the house.

I asked the tearful young man, "When did pornography start to be a problem for you?" He told me he had been keeping it a secret since he was an early teenager. For 20-plus years this person had tried to keep his ugly secret in the dark. Now light was shining brightly on it, and it hurt. He didn't yet realize that when darkness is exposed by light, it may hurt for a while, but that's the only way the darkness can be replaced by truth-revealing light. That's the only way a person who is living in the dark can be healed.

The Bible tells us that Jesus came to chase away the darkness that people have in their minds about God. Jesus is the Light that reveals to the world who God really is. This bright light hurt the Pharisees, who had painted God into a corner. They believed all kinds of lies about God.

As God's children we are called to share the truth (light) about God with a world that has been duped into believing all kinds of lies (darkness) about Him. Of course, this can happen only if we know Jesus as our friend.

During the process of getting to know the Light, sometimes our darkness will be exposed. This will hurt. But once we let the light of Jesus soak in, confess our sin, and stop hiding it from God and from the people around us, we will be free indeed.

AUG 6

Rich Man, Poor Man

TWO THINGS I ASK OF YOU; deny them not to me before I die: remove far from me falsehood and lying; give me neither poverty nor riches; feed me with the food that is needful for me, lest I be full and deny you and say, "Who is the Lord?" or lest I be poor and steal and profane the name of my God. **PROVERBS 30:7-9, ESV.**

The burden of riches is something I've never had to suffer. I was raised in a middle-class family that had enough money for a house and a couple of cars. We never owned a vacation home or a car for every driver. We had food on the table and were able to pay our rent. We didn't have a ski boat and a cabin on the lake. I don't know what it's like to have money to burn.

On the other side of that coin, I also don't know what it's like to be financially destitute. I've always had a bed to sleep in, food to eat, and clothes to wear. I've never had to beg for anything. I've been employed in some kind of work since I was 14 years old. I've always had money in my pocket if I needed it.

Agur, the man who wrote this proverb, asks God to protect him from poverty, which isn't too unusual. But he also asks for something that you don't hear very often: He asks God not to make him rich. He just wants to be middle-class.

Agur the proverb writer knew that riches are a snare for most people. Later, in the New Testament, Jesus said that it's hard for rich people to be believers. I think He said this because rich people don't know (or have forgotten) what it's like to have to depend on others, and if you can't depend on God, you will likely not be a very devout Christian.

On the other hand, Agur knew that extreme poverty can cause a person to compromise their values out of a sense of self-preservation. Lying and stealing are no way to live life.

Jesus picks up on this proverb when He instructs us to ask God each day for our daily bread—no more and no less. It's not wrong to be rich. It's not wrong to be poor. But whether you have a lot or a little, strive to serve God and honor His Word. And be content with the daily bread He provides you.

How to Stop Being Bored

THESE ARE THE WORDS OF THE TEACHER, King David's son, who ruled in Jerusalem. "Everything is meaningless," says the Teacher, "completely meaningless!" What do people get for all their hard work under the sun? Generations come and generations go, but the earth never changes. The sun rises and the sun sets, then hurries around to rise again. The wind blows south, and then turns north. Around and around it goes, blowing in circles. Rivers run into the sea, but the sea is never full. Then the water returns again to the rivers and flows out again to the sea. Everything is wearisome beyond description. No matter how much we see, we are never satisfied. No matter how much we hear, we are not content. History merely repeats itself. It has all been done before. Nothing under the sun is truly new. Sometimes people say, "Here is something new!" But actually it is old; nothing is ever truly new. We don't remember what happened in the past, and in future generations, no one will remember what we are doing now. **ECCLESIASTES 1:1-11, NLT.**

I don't know about you, but when I read the above verses this morning I just wanted to reach through the Bible and give King Solomon a big hug! What a downer this guy was when he wrote this! In order to get into Solomon's mind-set, it's important to know a little bit about him before we continue with a few thoughts on this book of Scripture.

None of the statements or thoughts in Ecclesiastes are outside of the truth. King Solomon experienced every aspect of life. He lived an amazingly righteous and good life, *and* he swung hard to the other side, living a licentious and selfish life. King Solomon really did see and do it all. Some of the things he did almost became his undoing.

It seems that Solomon had a bent for experiencing life and then got bored with it. I fear that one of the things the king missed out on was what it felt like to serve others and make their lives better because of the choices he made. I say this because each time I try serving others, I experience something new and fresh.

Do you ever feel like Solomon? Has your life become a ho-hum daily ritual? If so, start serving others and helping where you can. You'll never be bored with that.

AUG 8

Build It Up and Knock It Down

THE BEST THAT PEOPLE CAN DO IS EAT, drink, and enjoy their work. I saw that even this comes from God, because no one can eat or enjoy life without him. If people please God, God will give them wisdom, knowledge, and joy. But sinners will get only the work of gathering and storing wealth that they will have to give to the ones who please God. So all their work is useless, like chasing the wind. **ECCLESIASTES 2:24-26, NCV.**

One of the joys of being principal of a K-12 school was having a large preschool and daycare center on the same campus. The preschool/daycare was a thriving ministry—more than 180 families from the community used our services. I would go up once a week for staff meetings and then walk around the facility and speak with the staff, watch the kids, and check out any needs the facility might have.

One day when I was sitting and watching, I saw a small child playing all by himself with some plastic building blocks. There were lots of kids doing other things in the room while the little architect carefully assembled his masterpiece. Just as he was getting done with his first attempt at a mini Taj Mahal, two little boys came over and kicked his blocks into a pile of rubble.

My little friend cried for a minute, then starting building again. Once again, just as he was finishing, the same two little boys (I'm pretty sure this wasn't an accident) came over and destroyed his work. This time blocks were thrown, words were shouted, tears were shed, and adults intervened.

One of the great pearls of wisdom in the book of Ecclesiastes is the reminder that everything we do on this earth is meaningless if we don't have a relationship with God that will give significance to our lives. If at the end of our life all we can do is look back on the things we have built and accumulated, if all we can do is look back at how good our food and drink were, we will look back and say, "It was all meaningless."

The old saying goes, "You can't take it with you." And it's true; the only things you can take to heaven are yourself and the people you've influenced for Christ when He's given you that opportunity.

What Time Is It?

FOR EVERYTHING THERE IS A SEASON, and a time for every matter under heaven: a time to be born, and a time to die; a time to plant, and a time to pluck up what is planted; a time to kill, and a time to heal; a time to break down, and a time to build up; a time to weep, and a time to laugh; a time to mourn, and a time to dance; a time to cast away stones, and a time to gather stones together; a time to embrace, and a time to refrain from embracing; a time to seek, and a time to lose; a time to keep, and a time to cast away; a time to tear, and a time to sew; a time to keep silence, and a time to speak; a time to love, and a time to hate; a time for war, and a time for peace. **ECCLESIASTES 3:1-8, ESV.**

In 1965 a music group called The Byrds released a song that rose to number one on the pop charts. The name of the song? "Turn! Turn! Turn! (to Everything There Is a Season)." The lyrics? They were taken right out of the Bible, from Ecclesiastes 3. As far as I know, it's the only time Bible verses ever became number one on the Billboard Hot 100. In fact, the lyrics for this song were probably the oldest lyrics ever recorded to sell so many records! I think that's pretty cool.

When we read the verses above, we see a list of ways people react to the different situations they find themselves in on this earth. Solomon seems to be telling us that these are the ingredients of the lives of human beings: being born, embracing, speaking, loving, hating, dancing, and dying. And for everything there is a season. At some point in your life you will feel compelled to do each of these things. You will love. You will hate. You will embrace. You will refrain from embracing. You will see times of war and peace. Your life will be made up of all these things.

Take a quick inventory just now. Solomon lists 28 things that there is a time for. How many of the 28 have you participated in?

The key to happiness in this life, of course, is not simply to do the 28. The key is to do them at the right time. The key is to embrace a God-life, to let Him breathe these things into your life as He wills, and then to react to all these situations with grace and humility.

From the list above, what "time" is it in your life right now? Whatever that time is, let God be at the center of it and celebrate Him!

AUG 10

Confronting Evil

AGAIN I SAW ALL THE OPPRESSIONS that are done under the sun. And behold, the tears of the oppressed, and they had no one to comfort them! On the side of their oppressors there was power, and there was no one to comfort them. And I thought the dead who are already dead more fortunate than the living who are still alive. But better than both is he who has not yet been and has not seen the evil deeds that are done under the sun.
ECCLESIASTES 4:1-3, ESV.

For several years now I've taken short-term mission trips to Kenya to work with the Masai Development Project. You can learn more about this group at www.4mdp.org.

These wonderful people rescue young girls out of the nastiest situations you could imagine. The Masai people are a male-dominated society in which polygamy, child physical and sexual abuse, forced female circumcision, and other horrors are the reality of daily life.

From the hearts of two ordinary but wonderfully gifted women came this organization with the mission to rescue young Masai girls from the evils they might otherwise endure. They house them, feed them, bathe them, teach them, and let them know that there is a God of love who has motivated them to do all this. I'm way impressed with their organization and their work.

One of the thrills of my life is to see people like this become the Mother Teresas of the world, touching and relieving human suffering in the name of Jesus. It seems that suffering in this world is almost matched by people who are willing to stick their necks out and be the hands and feet of Jesus.

Solomon correctly describes how true suffering afflicts people in this world. Our challenge is to do something about it when we have a chance. The Bible says that just praying for someone who is suffering is not enough. If we can add hands-on compassion to our prayers, we have a responsibility to help.

Oh, and next time you feel like pitching a hissy fit because your iPod isn't working the way it's supposed to, remember, you have an iPod. The Masai people live in huts made of mud and cow manure. Count your blessings; pray for the less fortunate; and when you have the opportunity, lend a helping, merciful hand.

Words Be Few

GUARD YOUR STEPS WHEN YOU go to the house of God. Go near to listen rather than to offer the sacrifice of fools, who do not know that they do wrong. Do not be quick with your mouth, do not be hasty in your heart to utter anything before God. God is in heaven and you are on earth, so let your words be few. **ECCLESIASTES 5:1, 2.**

There's a praise song that I have liked for a long time. Matt and Beth Redman wrote it, and the lyrics come from this chapter in Ecclesiastes. The title is "Let My Words Be Few," and the song is a simple expression of love and awe to our Savior.

Do you know the song? Why not sing it or play it right now? If you don't know it, find a video of it on YouTube and listen to the message. But don't just sing or listen—let the song be an act of worship from your heart to God's.

This song captures the heart of what Solomon seemed to be trying to express in the verses above. God is God, and I am not. When I walk into His presence, I am not to be flippant about it. Churches dedicated to His worship are sacred places; they should be treated as such. And when you are in the presence of God, you don't need to speak much. Listen. What does God have to say to you while you are in His presence?

The Redmans' song has it right: when it boils down to the nitty-gritty of our faith, it boils down to Jesus. Jesus is the Author and Finisher of our faith. He is the revelation of God. He came to this earth to explain the Father, because people have been unable to "get" Him since the Garden of Eden.

Jesus came to live and die for us, even when we were far from any inkling of caring about Him. King Jesus is what it's all about. So, as the author of Ecclesiastes says: "Let your words be few."

AUG 12

Spread the Wealth

I HAVE SEEN ANOTHER EVIL under the sun, and it weighs heavily on mankind: God gives some people wealth, possessions and honor, so that they lack nothing their hearts desire, but God does not grant them the ability to enjoy them, and strangers enjoy them instead. This is meaningless, a grievous evil. **ECCLESIASTES 6:1, 2.**

Mr. Campbell is now in his 90s. I've known him for about 10 years. And he and his wife are remarkable.

I first met Mr. and Mrs. Campbell when I became a pastor in Wenatchee, Washington. I was told by several church members that it was the Campbells' generosity that had placed the church and the school on such solid financial footing.

The first time I walked into Mr. Campbell's office, I didn't notice anything unusual about him. He was wearing a suit that he must have purchased in 1974. He didn't have his office decorated extravagantly. He just seemed like a normal person. He was very friendly and asked me to sit down and chat with him.

As he and his wife told me their story, I began to realize that Mr. and Mrs. Campbell weren't just a little bit rich. The Lord had blessed them through the years to the point that they had become an empire of sorts. Yet they were some of the least pretentious and most generous people I had ever met.

One day I was with Mr. Campbell around Christmastime as he went from charity to charity to hand out Christmas checks. As we drove, he said, "Mark, I have a lot of money, but I've learned that it's only money and I can't take it with me. I didn't live my life and do the things I did with the intention of making all this money—I just enjoyed living my life and helping other people get a start in life. The Lord has really done the rest."

I have never been tempted with riches, but if I were to be, I'd like to think that I'd have the same attitude as my friends Carl and Betty Campbell. I'd like to think that I would use my money to bless others and grow God's kingdom.

In the meantime it's my job to take my pastoral salary and my wife's teaching salary and bless God with them. As you begin to acquire things and make money, keep your focus on blessing God. Don't let the bling blind you to His desires.

God Is Better Than You Think

FOR THE LIVING KNOW that they will die, but the dead know nothing; they have no further reward, and even their name is forgotten. Their love, their hate and their jealousy have long since vanished; never again will they have a part in anything that happens under the sun. **ECCLESIASTES 9:5, 6.**

One evening I was in a hospital visiting with the family of a church member who had just come out of surgery. The news was good, and it looked as if things were going to turn out well for the patient and the family.

As I exited the room, a young nurse took me aside and asked, "Are you a pastor?"

"Yes. Is there something I can help with?"

She told me about a woman in a room close by who was in a lot of distress. The woman knew she was going to die soon, but was fighting it and was very afraid. The nurse asked if I could look in on the patient and pay her a visit. So I did.

When I walked into the room, I saw an elderly woman lying in bed. She was the color of death. I could tell she didn't have long. But she was lucid and noticed when I came into the room.

I introduced myself as a pastor, and after some small talk I asked her if she was ready to die. "No, I'm not!" she exclaimed, and then started crying.

When I asked why she was upset, she told me that she didn't want to go to heaven without her husband. I offered to call her husband and have him come in. She said, "No, you don't understand; my husband has been dead for 10 years, and he's in hell. I don't want to live for eternity in heaven while my husband has to spend his eternity in hell."

I asked if I could share some things in the Bible that might relieve her mind. As I shared what the Bible says about death and sleep and resurrection, she started to cry again. Then she gasped out this amazing statement: "God is a lot better than I thought He was."

There are texts all over the Bible that make it clear that death is nothing to fear. It's as scary as a quiet afternoon nap.

AUG 14

Get the Good Life Now

REMEMBER ALSO YOUR CREATOR in the days of your youth, before the evil days come and the years draw near when you will say, "I have no delight in them." **ECCLESIASTES 12:1, NASB.**

My dad turns 80 years old two weeks from the writing of this chapter. Eighty years old! That's old. And I can't believe he's made it to 80! Even though he takes care of his body now, he smoked for 50 years, which left him with a pretty bad case of emphysema. He's got an oxygen hose that stretches all over our house so he can breathe while he putters around. Abusing his body at a young age is one of his great regrets.

Almost every day my dad looks at me and colorfully expresses how much he dislikes getting old. I keep telling him that it beats the alternative! It's hard to know how his health would be now if he hadn't smoked for so many years, but I'm guessing it would be much better.

The writer of Ecclesiastes had been around the block once or twice. He was full of wisdom that came from years of observing the joys and the absurdities of life. And after writing all of his observations and musings, he ended with this sage advice for the young: Don't wait to turn your heart to God. Don't think that at some ripe old age you can finally follow His will for your life. Why waste time? Serve God now, and you will have a fuller life than you could otherwise live on your own.

I've seen too many people try to live a party life, thinking, *One day, someday, I'll start to live what I believe is right.* All too often that's their intention in the beginning. Then, as they acclimatize to life without faith, they drift off to the point where they just don't care anymore.

Contrast that with young people who live a vibrant lift of faith while they are young. They end up going on mission trips, participating in church, and loving their family instead of cultivating negative, self-destructive behavior.

In the chapter just before this one, Solomon challenges his young readers to take life by the horns. Have a great time and party your socks off! Just do this with the knowledge that there is a God who loves and judges.

Mushy Stuff

HOW BEAUTIFUL YOU ARE, my darling, how beautiful you are! Your eyes are like doves behind your veil; your hair is like a flock of goats that have descended from Mount Gilead. Your teeth are like a flock of newly shorn ewes which have come up from their washing, all of which bear twins, and not one among them has lost her young. Your lips are like a scarlet thread, and your mouth is lovely. Your temples are like a slice of a pomegranate behind your veil. Your neck is like the tower of David, built with rows of stones on which are hung a thousand shields, all the round shields of the mighty men. **SONG OF SOLOMON 4:1-4, NASB.**

One of my all-time favorite movies is *The Princess Bride*. In it a grandfather reads a book about "true love" to his sick grandson. The kid is sick in bed but doesn't hesitate to interrupt the story and completely gross out any time there is kissing. Little boys don't like romance. And I suppose romance is a touchy topic for a youth devotional too.

As mushy and romantic as the Song of Solomon is, I challenge you to read it and see that it has a deeper meaning.

In this book Solomon and his true love exchange "love notes" written so vividly and with such passion that this book almost didn't make it into the Old Testament. But the intimacy that these two lovers project toward each other is the intimacy that God projects toward us, no matter what we've done.

What if archaeologists somehow dug up a picture of Solomon's bride only to find that she was about as attractive as an old saddlebag? What if she was, as they say, facially challenged? Would you find it strange that he wrote all these things about her? So would I.

Yet this wonderful book in the Bible is the story of God and us. God is crazy about you and me. I don't know about you, but when I look in the mirror I don't see flock-of-goat hair and sheared-sheep teeth. I see a tall, slightly overweight guy with a big nose. Yet God doesn't see me the way I see myself. He sees the one in whom He places all His delight! When God looks at you, He sees someone He would rather die for than live without.

233

AUG 16

Stiff-necked and Forgetful

LISTEN, O HEAVENS, AND HEAR, O earth; for the Lord speaks, "Sons I have reared and brought up, but they have revolted against Me. An ox knows its owner, and a donkey its master's manger, but Israel does not know, My people do not understand." **ISAIAH 1:2, 3, NASB.**

Isaiah is a wonderful book of prophecy that has a lot to say about a lot of topics. In this book Isaiah, a prophet in the country of Judah (remember, Israel and Judah had split into two countries shortly after Solomon's reign), speaks God's feelings toward, His prophecies against, and His redemptive heart for His people.

The children of Israel were supposed to be a light to the world. They were supposed to show who God truly is to a world that was far from Him. God had given the Israelites everything they needed to be the most wonderful revelation of His character that had ever been.

The problem was that every time Israel got anywhere near another nation, instead of influencing that nation for good they got sucked into the evil practices of those pagan nations. So instead of being a light to the world, Israel became a stench in the nostrils of the very One who had chosen them and loved them.

The book of Isaiah is one of God's last appeals to His people to repent and turn from their evil ways before suffering the consequences. As we survey this book, we will run into some great stories, some heart-wrenching appeals, and some amazing prophecies about the coming Messiah.

One thing to keep in mind as you read this book is that being a prophet, especially in this time of turbulence in Israel's history, was a thankless and dangerous job. Isaiah was called to speak to a people who didn't want to hear what he had to say. But he did it anyway. He obeyed God even when it was unpopular and hard to do.

Think about your life. Has God ever called you to speak a word of warning to a friend or a loved one? How did you handle the task? Sometimes God moves us to say unpopular things to people so they have a chance to turn and walk with God again. This kind of response to God takes a courageous person.

Snow White and the Seven . . . Pardons?

"COME NOW, AND LET US reason together," says the Lord, "though your sins are as scarlet, they will be as white as snow; though they are red like crimson, they will be like wool." **ISAIAH 1:18, NASB.**

One of the best things about Christianity is that it's a religion of forgotten mistakes. In fact, God had forgiveness in His heart toward you even before you were born.

My first year in college was a complete disaster. I was not prepared to be a responsible self-starter, and I was very distracted by all the naughty things I could do with my newfound freedom. As a consequence, my grades suffered a slow, meaningless death. (Just to give you an idea, my highest grade was a C. In tennis.)

One of the classes I took was called Ministry of Jesus. It was taught by one of the most wonderful, kind-spirited men I've ever met. When he handed out grades just before the end of the quarter, I saw that I had a flaming F because of my daily absences. I panicked and told this wonderful, godly man a lie. I told him that my mom had been in the hospital and that I'd had to miss class because of it. I felt bad about lying, but he changed my grade to a D, apparently because he felt sorry for me.

Years later, after my conversion, I saw this professor along the street. The memory of my deception flooded back into my brain, and I felt the urge to go and confess my sin to him.

When I approached him, he smiled. I reintroduced myself and told him that I was sorry for lying to him. I also told him that since that time I had given my life to Jesus and was now a preacher.

This kind, wonderful man looked at me and said, "Oh, Mark, I knew you were lying at the time. I just felt that if you had to lie about getting a grade in Bible, you must have a pretty good reason. I've never thought of it since. You were forgiven as soon as you lied to me."

What a relief! This is similar to the way God looks at you and me when we come to confess our sins. Revelation 13 says that the Lamb was slain from the foundation of the world. Forgiveness was in the heart of God before we ever sinned.

AUG 18

Send Me!

IN THE YEAR OF KING UZZIAH'S DEATH I saw the Lord sitting on a throne, lofty and exalted, with the train of His robe filling the temple. Seraphim stood above Him, each having six wings: with two he covered his face, and with two he covered his feet, and with two he flew. And one called out to another and said, "Holy, Holy, Holy, is the Lord of hosts, the whole earth is full of His glory." And the foundations of the thresholds trembled at the voice of him who called out, while the temple was filling with smoke. Then I said, "Woe is me, for I am ruined! Because I am a man of unclean lips, and I live among a people of unclean lips; for my eyes have seen the King, the Lord of hosts." Then one of the seraphim flew to me with a burning coal in his hand, which he had taken from the altar with tongs. He touched my mouth with it and said, "Behold, this has touched your lips; and your iniquity is taken away and your sin is forgiven." Then I heard the voice of the Lord, saying, "Whom shall I send, and who will go for Us?" Then I said, "Here am I. Send me!" **ISAIAH 6:1-8, NASB.**

What a remarkable section of Scripture! Can you imagine how Isaiah felt when God opened up a glimpse into heaven? I guess we don't have to imagine—the Bible tells us. Isaiah felt unworthy. He felt dirty when he stood in the presence of pure holiness.

But notice what God did to assure Isaiah that everything was OK. He had an angel take a live coal from the altar of incense in the heavenly sanctuary and place it on Isaiah's lips. Now, you might think that a live coal on your lips would hurt; maybe it would create painful blisters! Not these coals. These coals are different. These coals do something strange and wonderful: they provide atonement.

When two people or two groups of people have a breach in their relationship, atonement is needed to bring the two back into mutual understanding, love, and acceptance. In our case (and Isaiah's) we need atonement between God and us. It's not that God has anything against us or has distanced Himself from us; it's that we have distanced ourselves from God by believing the enemy's onslaught of lies about Him.

Those coals from that altar are the unending love of God. When we realize God is love and we live that truth, atonement happens. We become more like Him, and we want to be used by Him. Our prayer becomes "Lord, send me."

Dark Versus Light

THE PEOPLE WHO WALKED IN darkness have seen a great light; those who dwelt in a land of deep darkness, on them has light shined. You have multiplied the nation; you have increased its joy; they rejoice before you as with joy at the harvest, as they are glad when they divide the spoil. . . . For to us a child is born, to us a son is given; and the government shall be upon his shoulder, and his name shall be called Wonderful Counselor, Mighty God, Everlasting Father, Prince of Peace. Of the increase of his government and of peace there will be no end, on the throne of David and over his kingdom, to establish it and to uphold it with justice and with righteousness from this time forth and forevermore. The zeal of the Lord of hosts will do this. **ISAIAH 9:2-7, ESV.**

This prophecy is one of Isaiah's many poetic and powerful statements about the coming Messiah. We could dwell on several statements in the above text for today's devotional, but I'd like to focus on just one: "The people walking in darkness have seen a great light."

Almost always when light and dark are used as a metaphor in Scripture, you can substitute truth and lies for light and dark. Light equals truth and dark equals lies. When we read about dark and light, we need to ask the question "Who is spreading lies, what are those lies, and whom are those lies about?" We should also ask, "Who is spreading truth, what is that truth, and whom is that truth about?"

In this case we know who the truth spreader is, because the whole prophecy is about the coming Messiah, Jesus. Jesus is the light bearer. Jesus is the truth teller. But whom is He telling the truth about? He is telling the truth about His Father. He is telling the truth about God!

The devil has been spreading lies—some blatant, some subtle—about God since before the creation of the world. By the time Jesus came to earth to live the truth about the Father, even the religious people believed all kinds of things about God that weren't true. That's why they were so upset at what Jesus said and did. The religious people of Jesus' day didn't recognize God in Jesus. They were so convinced by the lies of the devil that they crucified the very God they thought they were serving.

If you want to know the truth about God, study Jesus. He is the light.

AUG 20

The Way It's Supposed to Be

THE WOLF SHALL DWELL WITH THE LAMB, and the leopard shall lie down with the young goat, and the calf and the lion and the fattened calf together; and a little child shall lead them. The cow and the bear shall graze; their young shall lie down together; and the lion shall eat straw like the ox. The nursing child shall play over the hole of the cobra, and the weaned child shall put his hand on the adder's den. They shall not hurt or destroy in all my holy mountain; for the earth shall be full of the knowledge of the Lord as the waters cover the sea. **ISAIAH 11:6-9, ESV.**

I woke up one morning and realized it was garbage day. That meant I had to go out my front door, get my garbage and my recycling bins, and drag them up the driveway so Waste Management could empty them for my next week of throwing things away.

As I walked outside, I heard an unusual noise. It was a high-pitched chattering that sounded both agitated and angry, as if a small creature of some kind was very upset. I looked up and saw a gray squirrel on the very top of a telephone pole next to our property. The squirrel was having a fit. It was yelling and screaming, jumping around and letting the whole world know that it was mad at something. Since I don't speak squirrel, I hauled my garbage up to the curb and went back into the house.

About 10 minutes later my son, Cole, came up the stairs for breakfast. He came into our sitting room, but instead of sitting down to watch the news with me, he opened the door to go out onto the deck. "Whoa!" he exclaimed.

I jumped up and looked to see what had startled him. Evidently my cats had killed a squirrel and had left the corpse in front of the door. And then I remembered the upset little squirrel on the telephone pole. I took my wife and Cole out to see it. The squirrel was still having a fit. Now I knew why. My cats had attacked and killed its friend/relative. This little squirrel was upset because it knew that this was not the way things were supposed to be.

The above text from Isaiah 11 reminds us of how things *are* supposed to be. Wolf, lamb, leopard, cow, human, and lion are all supposed to get along. Snakes aren't supposed to bite. Peace is supposed to reign. I look forward to that day.

Rebellious Cherub

"HOW YOU HAVE FALLEN FROM HEAVEN, O star of the morning, son of the dawn! You have been cut down to the earth, you who have weakened the nations! But you said in your heart, 'I will ascend to heaven; I will raise my throne above the stars of God, and I will sit on the mount of assembly in the recesses of the north. 'I will ascend above the heights of the clouds; I will make myself like the Most High.' Nevertheless you will be thrust down to Sheol, to the recesses of the pit." **ISAIAH 14:12-15, NASB.**

Sometimes prophecy points forward. Sometimes prophecy points backward. Sometimes prophecy speaks truth about a current situation. This prophecy in Isaiah points backward to the origins of sin in the universe, before earth was created. This prophetic utterance gives us a small peek into what happened in the heart of one who was once celebrated in heaven.

When Satan is first described, it almost sounds like a description of Jesus, doesn't it? If I were to ask you who the morning star or the son of the dawn is in the Bible, who would come to mind? Yet these are the very names ascribed to Lucifer. So what happened to this spectacular creature? How was this once-exalted angel brought down?

It's literally the oldest story in the book. Lucifer was guilty of breaking the tenth commandment. He thought so much of himself that he became filled with pride. His favorite piece of art in heaven was a mirror. He loved himself more than he loved his Creator. He started to covet the place of God.

When pride is fostered, it becomes an ugly thing. Pride distorted Lucifer's perception of a loving God. He started to think that God was controlling and unfair. His discontent spilled out into his language as he spread his poison among the angelic host, who trusted and adored him.

It wasn't long before Lucifer's name would change from "morning star" to "accuser." He was somehow able to spread his lies and convince a third of heaven to see things his way. And it all started with pride. It's no wonder the Bible spends so many verses focusing on the need of God's people to humble themselves as Jesus humbled Himself when He came to earth.

AUG 22

Giving Birth

BUT YOUR DEAD WILL LIVE, their bodies will rise—let those who dwell in the dust wake up and shout for joy—your dew is like the dew of the morning; the earth will give birth to her dead. **ISAIAH 26:19.**

The Old Testament doesn't speak of future resurrection very often. I think God just hadn't informed most of the writers about the option of eternal life or about heaven and the new earth. But this promise in Isaiah captures the hope we all have—hope to see our loved ones again in a better place and in perfect health.

I love the imagery that Isaiah chooses here: "The earth will give birth to her dead." I know this will come as a surprise to my readers, but I've never once been pregnant, so I won't pretend to understand all the nuances of what it takes to have a baby. But I have studied biology, and I have seen people and animals give birth, so let me wax eloquent for a moment on this wonderful subject.

From my limited experience in the delivery room, I've concluded that pregnancy isn't painless. In fact, I understand that a woman holding her husband's hand during the birth process has the strength of 10 men—at least that's what her husband's hand thinks. Maybe it would be a good idea for a hand surgeon to set up an office right next to the OB-GYN clinic.

On this earth we suffer. Jesus even called all the trials and tribulations we endure "birth pangs." Life can leave us hurting in ways that go beyond physical pain. When we lose loved ones to the sting of death, it's all we can do to bear the ache.

Last year alone I conducted 11 funerals. Eleven times I had to witness the pain of families who didn't want to say goodbye so soon. Eleven times we stood by a casket in a cemetery while people laid flowers and notes on it in the hope that someday they would see their father, brother, mother, or sister again.

Living on this earth has its share of birth pangs, but remember, at the end of the pain there is a reward, and that promised reward is the greatest reunion in the history of this universe. The earth will give up her dead, and there will be joy.

AUG 23

Mental GPS

WHETHER YOU TURN TO THE right or to the left, your ears will hear a voice behind you, saying, "This is the way; walk in it." **ISAIAH 30:21.**

Boston, Massachusetts, confuses me. I think the streets of the city must have been laid out according to the horse trails that already existed, turning those haphazard trails into roads. While most cities have some semblance of square blocks to help a person navigate their roads, Boston seems to be a winding mass of circles.

I was speaking at some meetings in Lancaster, Massachusetts, over a Father's Day weekend. In one of these meetings I met a young man whom I really came to enjoy. He was about 19 years old and had no father, so he lived with his mom. His name (at least the name he used when he introduced himself to me) was Sparky. Sparky was about six feet tall and weighed 300 pounds—and he could dunk a basketball.

With Father's Day coming up, I thought it would be cool to drive into Boston with Sparky and see a Red Sox game. Now, this was before the days of GPS and cell phones that can tell a person when to take a right or a left.

Somehow Sparky and I found the stadium and had a grand time at the game. The game finished early enough for us to drive back to the college campus where I was speaking in time for that evening's meeting.

Sparky and I hopped in the car and tried to retrace our steps to get out of the city and onto the interstate that would take us to our destination. About a half hour into our trip, we noticed the stadium ahead of us. Knowing that the Red Sox didn't have two stadiums in Boston, I came to the quick conclusion that we were lost. We tried for another half hour to find our way out of the city, until finally I just gave a cab driver $20 to lead me to the right on-ramp so we could get home safely.

It's easy to get lost in this life. I know people who have made so many wrong turns in their lives that they think they will never find their way home. God's promise to all His children is that when we hide our life in Him, the Holy Spirit will gently whisper directions into our lives to keep us on the straight and narrow.

AUG 24

In the Presence of the Fire

THE SINNERS IN JERUSALEM SHAKE with fear. Terror seizes the godless. "Who can live with this devouring fire?" they cry. "Who can survive this all-consuming fire?" Those who are honest and fair, who refuse to profit by fraud, who stay far away from bribes, who refuse to listen to those who plot murder, who shut their eyes to all enticement to do wrong—these are the ones who will dwell on high. The rocks of the mountains will be their fortress. Food will be supplied to them, and they will have water in abundance. **ISAIAH 33:14-16, NLT.**

For centuries the majority of the Christian church has been teaching that hell is a place somewhere in the universe where God puts wicked people so they can suffer for their sins forever and ever and ever. And ever.

The Bible says something different. First of all, we are promised in several passages that there will be a day that sin is wiped from the universe. Second, the Bible, in both the Old and New Testaments, talks about the total destruction of the wicked. Third, God clearly does not want to destroy anyone at all. I do believe people will be destroyed, but they will be destroyed because of who they have chosen to be, not because God gets angry and wrathfully zaps them. Look again at the above verse. There is a reference made there to everlasting burning. Heard of that before?

The Bible talks about a place of everlasting burning that will destroy the wicked. But did you know that the everlasting burning is a place where the saved will stand also? Look again at the verse! The everlasting burning is wherever God is! But why doesn't it affect the saved?

Here's the principle: in the Bible fire is sometimes equated with love. Romans 12:20 says that treating our enemies with love is like burning them with hot coals. Song of Solomon 8:7 says that unquenchable fire can't snuff out love. Hebrews 12 says that God is a consuming fire. Yet John says that God is love.

Standing in the presence of God's love at the end of time will be heaven for the saved and hell for the lost. Sin cannot survive in the presence of God's unmasked love. If a person holds on to their sin at the end of time, they will be consumed by their sin. I'm so glad Jesus took our sin so we can stand in the presence of God's love.

We Have This Hope

You will notice that this page looks different from most of the other pages in this book. Some chapters in the Bible just need to speak for themselves. This one is **ISAIAH 35, NCV**. I didn't want to comment on it. Instead, I want you to read it and meditate on it. I changed the font up so it would be worthy of such words. As you read about our blessed hope, you'll see what I mean. God has graced us with this promise—let's hold on to it with all our might.

THE DESERT AND DRY LAND WILL BECOME HAPPY; the desert will be glad and will produce flowers. Like a flower, it will have many blooms. It will show its happiness, as if it were shouting with joy. It will be beautiful like the forest of Lebanon, as beautiful as the hill of Carmel and the Plain of Sharon. Everyone will see the glory of the Lord and the splendor of our God. Make the weak hands strong and the weak knees steady. Say to people who are frightened, "Be strong. Don't be afraid. Look, your God will come, and he will punish your enemies. He will make them pay for the wrongs they did, but he will save you."

Then the blind people will see again, and the deaf will hear. Crippled people will jump like deer, and those who can't talk now will shout with joy. Water will flow in the desert, and streams will flow in the dry land. The burning desert will have pools of water, and the dry ground will have springs. Where wild dogs once lived, grass and water plants will grow. A road will be there; this highway will be called "The Road to Being Holy." Evil people will not be allowed to walk on that road; only good people will walk on it. No fools will go on it. No lions will be there, nor will dangerous animals be on that road. They will not be found there. That road will be for the people God saves; the people the Lord has freed will return there. They will enter Jerusalem with joy, and their happiness will last forever. Their gladness and joy will fill them completely, and sorrow and sadness will go far away.

AUG 26

All to Jesus

HE GREW UP LIKE A SMALL PLANT before the Lord, like a root growing in a dry land. He had no special beauty or form to make us notice him; there was nothing in his appearance to make us desire him. He was hated and rejected by people. He had much pain and suffering. People would not even look at him. He was hated, and we didn't even notice him. But he took our suffering on him and felt our pain for us. We saw his suffering and thought God was punishing him. But he was wounded for the wrong we did; he was crushed for the evil we did. The punishment, which made us well, was given to him, and we are healed because of his wounds. We all have wandered away like sheep; each of us has gone his own way. But the Lord has put on him the punishment for all the evil we have done. He was beaten down and punished, but he didn't say a word. He was like a lamb being led to be killed. He was quiet, as a sheep is quiet while its wool is being cut; he never opened his mouth. Men took him away roughly and unfairly. He died without children to continue his family. He was put to death; he was punished for the sins of my people. He was buried with wicked men, and he died with the rich. He had done nothing wrong, and he had never lied. **ISAIAH 53:2-9, NCV.**

Once again we see Isaiah's prophecies pointing to Jesus in a powerful way. I wonder what it was like for Jesus to read and memorize these scriptures as a young child. I wonder what it was like when it first dawned on Him that Isaiah's predictions were pointing to Him. It must have brought a heavy, sinking feeling to know that all the awful things this prophecy said were going to happen to Messiah applied to Him. Yet He didn't run away from His calling, His choosing. Instead He embraced His fate because of love.

Some people have taught that God more or less forced Jesus to come down to live, suffer, and die. That can't be further from the truth. Remember, Jesus is God. As a part of the Trinity He chose His destiny before the creation of the world. He knew that if we were to bring disaster on the universe, He would do whatever it took to redeem us.

Fulfilling the prophecies that spoke of Him, Jesus lived the kind of life that would show us the Father. When He died, He paid the wages of sin. He died a horrible death so we wouldn't have to. And He did all this because He loves us, not because He was forced to. I can live for that kind of love.

Time to Rest

"IF YOU KEEP YOUR FEET from breaking the Sabbath and from doing as you please on my holy day, if you call the Sabbath a delight and the Lord's holy day honorable, and if you honor it by not going your own way and not doing as you please or speaking idle words, then you will find your joy in the Lord, and I will cause you to ride in triumph on the heights of the land and to feast on the inheritance of your father Jacob." For the mouth of the Lord has spoken. **ISAIAH 58:13, 14.**

Sabbathkeeping has gone through all kinds of interpretations throughout the centuries and from denomination to denomination. At one time Jews were so strict about observing the Sabbath that they wouldn't even dare to pick up a few sticks for their fire on that day. If they did and were seen, they could be stoned to death.

Of course, the Sabbath as described in the Bible is the seventh day of each week from sundown Friday to sundown Saturday. As Christianity became established in the world, and as the Catholic Church became the world leader in all things Christian, the day of worship gradually changed from the seventh day to the first day of the week. Then other denominations formed out of the Catholic Church, and eventually people all over the world generally regarded the Sabbath as Sunday.

It's interesting that even with the day change, many of these denominations (until recently) treated their "Sabbath" as a special day. Many people would avoid work or sports. Most states had towns that would completely close down on Sunday. It wasn't until recent times that Christians had little to no regard for any kind of Sabbath rest.

Israel had more than one Sabbath. They had the weekly Sabbath, and then they had the festival Sabbaths that God asked them to observe. But instead of observing these Sabbaths, they went about their own business. The streets of Jerusalem were filled with vendors buying and selling their goods. They had no regard for what God deemed holy.

This prophecy in Isaiah is a call to God's people to come back to relationship with Him in Sabbath rest. It's a call to come apart from the world for a weekly appointment to focus on and rest in His salvation. God still calls His people into a time of "Ahhh . . ." He's given you a day off—why not take it?

AUG 28

New Jerusalem Fairway

"FOR BEHOLD, I CREATE NEW heavens and a new earth; and the former things will not be remembered or come to mind. But be glad and rejoice forever in what I create; for behold, I create Jerusalem for rejoicing and her people for gladness. . . . There will no longer be heard in her the voice of weeping and the sound of crying. No longer will there be in it an infant who lives but a few days, or an old man who does not live out his days; for the youth will die at the age of one hundred and the one who does not reach the age of one hundred will be thought accursed. They will build houses and inhabit them; they will also plant vineyards and eat their fruit. They will not build and another inhabit, they will not plant and another eat; for as the lifetime of a tree, so will be the days of My people. . . . The wolf and the lamb will graze together, and the lion will eat straw like the ox; and dust will be the serpent's food. They will do no evil or harm in all My holy mountain," says the Lord. **ISAIAH 65:17-25, NASB.**

I like to imagine what life will be like in the new earth. I know my imagining is futile, because I'm pretty sure I can't comprehend what things are going to look, taste, sound, and smell like. But my mind wanders.

Besides all the peace and love and joy we'll experience there, I'd like to think there are going to be a lot of golf courses. I know, I'm sick in the head, but it's my head, and I can do what I want with it! People often ask me, "Why would there be golf in heaven? It won't be a challenge there, because we'll do everything right the first time!"

I'm not so sure about that. I think heaven will contain challenges, physical and mental. I think we'll always be learning more in heaven. After all, there will still be only one omniscient Person in the universe, and it won't be me.

What's your picture of the new earth? I asked some students that question, and a girl raised her hand and suggested, "The new earth is going to be a place where I can eat all the food I want and never get full and never gain a pound." I kind of like that view of the new earth too.

Whatever your idea of what our eternal future is going to be like, I know God's plans are more radically awesome than anything we could ever think up on our own. And I don't know about you, but I can't wait to tee off!

Young and Called

THE LORD GAVE ME THIS message: "I knew you before I formed you in your mother's womb. Before you were born I set you apart and appointed you as my prophet to the nations." "O Sovereign Lord," I said, "I can't speak for you! I'm too young!" The Lord replied, "Don't say, 'I'm too young,' for you must go wherever I send you and say whatever I tell you. And don't be afraid of the people, for I will be with you and will protect you. I, the Lord, have spoken!" **JEREMIAH 1:4-8, NLT.**

When I lived in Canada, there was a big meeting at the university where I worked. The meeting was full of pastors and church administrators from across Canada, and the discussion was about the alarming rate at which young people were leaving the church. Someone made a suggestion that churches should get young people more involved, that young people should serve on church boards and participate up front more often. At this an elderly church administrator got up and said, "I will not have a young person serve on my board or stand up and speak in my church! They are not old enough to have that kind of responsibility!" The discussion really got interesting after that statement.

I once toured a United States battleship. It was huge and intimidating. As impressive as the physical structure of that floating city was, I was even more struck by the knowledge that it was being run by a bunch of 18- to 20-year-olds. Young people are powerful when they are pointed in the right direction.

In this opening chapter of the book of Jeremiah we get a glimpse of how God does things in His universe. Notice first that God creates us with intention. There are no accidents. We are chosen and planned for before we are even born.

Then notice how the youngster, Jeremiah, expresses how inadequate he thinks he is for the job at hand. He thinks that because he's young he can't do great things for God.

I love God's response. In essence God says, "You're going to be great, because I made you to be great. Now get out there and make Me proud!"

When God calls us to do a job, He will equip us to do that job. He's really good at that. So remember, God created you with intention, and He intends to use you!

AUG 30

Another Bad Job

"JEREMIAH, GET READY. Stand up and tell them everything I command you to say. Don't be afraid of the people, or I will give you good reason to be afraid of them. Today I am going to make you a strong city, an iron pillar, a bronze wall. You will be able to stand against everyone in the land: Judah's kings, officers, priests, and the people of the land. They will fight against you, but they will not defeat you, because I am with you to protect you!" says the Lord. **JEREMIAH 1:17-19, NCV.**

As I mentioned before, I've done some pretty horrible jobs in my life. I've worked in fast-food restaurants. I've decided that grumpy hungry people aren't very nice sometimes. I've dug up a septic tank and its drain field. That was perfectly disgusting. I've been the principal of a school. Trying to please students, parents, and teachers all at the same time is impossible. I've had lots of jobs that I didn't like much. But I would do any of these jobs for an eternity before I would choose the life of a prophet.

When you're a prophet, chosen by God to speak to His people, you almost always end up in a lose-lose proposition. I don't know of a time when God chose a prophet to deliver news to a king or the nation of Israel and it ended up being a pleasant task. In fact, it seems that much of the time prophets were either getting killed or running from people who wanted to kill them.

In Jeremiah's case he had the horrible responsibility of telling his people that they were naughty and that God was going to lift His protection from them and that they would all be killed or captured by a foreign king and that this nationwide abduction would send God's kids into a foreign land for the next 70 years. (Was that a mouthful or what?) All of these tasks placed on the shoulders of a young person. Who would want that job?

Yet Jeremiah faithfully did what the Lord had asked him to do. He became the most unpopular guy in the kingdom because he was chosen to point the finger of condemnation. Jeremiah's calling left him with few friends. But he stood up and proclaimed the word of the Lord anyway. How would you respond if God called you to say things that people didn't want to hear?

Emergency God

"WILL YOU STEAL, MURDER, and commit adultery and swear falsely, and offer sacrifices to Baal and walk after other gods that you have not known, then come and stand before Me in this house, which is called by My name, and say, 'We are delivered!'—that you may do all these abominations? Has this house, which is called by My name, become a den of robbers in your sight? Behold, I, even I, have seen it," declares the Lord. **JEREMIAH 7:9-11, NASB.**

Pastors see odd things and deal with situations that can sometimes be frustrating. And while I want to be compassionate to people in their times of need, sometimes I just want to jump across the table and wring people's necks for making life decisions that get them into bad situations in the first place.

Case in point: There were a couple of young people who grew up in church and plainly knew the difference between right and wrong. They went to Christian schools, attended church regularly, and were baptized when they were in their early teens. God's desires and expectations for them were no mystery. But after graduating from high school, they both wandered to the "far country" in public universities and started to hang out with people who hadn't grown up with the same values as they had. It wasn't long before the two young people fell in love and moved in together.

They also picked up drinking habits that became the culture of their life. Then the young man got in trouble with the law. He got a DUI (driving under the influence of alcohol) and was also charged with a hit-and-run.

As soon as this happened, the young couple made an appointment with me, their church pastor. While in my office, they both asked for my prayers and for the church's financial help to get them out of this horrible situation. All of a sudden they needed God.

Jeremiah is dumbfounded as he writes these prophecies against Israel. He sees their history. They live their lives far from God until they get themselves in a bind, and then they run back to Him and expect Him to bail them out of the problems that came from their unfaithfulness.

I think God deserves better than that. If my friends called me only when they were in trouble, I'd be tempted not to answer the phone. Aren't you glad I'm not God?

SEPt 1

The Potter's Hand

THIS IS THE WORD THE LORD spoke to Jeremiah: "Go down to the potter's house, and I will give you my message there." So I went down to the potter's house and saw him working at the potter's wheel. He was using his hands to make a pot from clay, but something went wrong with it. So he used that clay to make another pot the way he wanted it to be. Then the Lord spoke his word to me: "Family of Israel, can't I do the same thing with you?" says the Lord. "You are in my hands like the clay in the potter's hands. There may come a time when I will speak about a nation or a kingdom that I will pull up by its roots or that I will pull down to destroy it. But if the people of that nation stop doing the evil they have done, I will change my mind and not carry out my plans to bring disaster to them. There may come another time when I will speak about a nation that I will build up and plant. But if I see it doing evil by not obeying me, I will change my mind and not carry out my plans to do good for them." **JEREMIAH 18:1-10, NCV.**

You have limited control of some things. You can control the kind of toothpaste you use. You can control whether you do your homework and hand it in on time. You can even control what your body looks like by what you eat and whether you exercise. But . . .

You had no control over what part of the world you would be born in or who your parents would be. As you drive down the highway, you have no control over the oncoming cars that pass you at 50-plus miles per hour. You have no control (or at least you shouldn't) over the actions of your family members, your classmates, and your friends.

The control you do have is the ability to choose God or reject God. You can choose to do the right thing or to ignore what you know is right and go your own way. We all have that ability. But we need to remember that with our choices come consequences, for good or for bad.

Bob Dylan sang a song entitled "Gotta Serve Somebody." In the song he says, "It may be the devil or it may be the Lord, but you're gonna have to serve somebody."

When we choose to serve God, we give Him permission to mold our characters the way a potter molds and shapes a piece of clay. We can be cooperative clay or stubborn clay; we have control over that. When we yield to the Potter, He promises to make us into something beautiful.

To the Far Country

JEREMIAH THE PROPHET SAID TO all the people in Judah and Jerusalem, "For the past twenty-three years . . . the Lord has been giving me his messages. I have faithfully passed them on to you, but you have not listened. Again and again the Lord has sent you his servants, the prophets, but you have not listened or even paid attention. Each time the message was this: 'Turn from the evil road you are traveling and from the evil things you are doing. Only then will I let you live in this land that the Lord gave to you and your ancestors forever. Do not provoke my anger by worshiping idols you made with your own hands. Then I will not harm you.' But you would not listen to me," says the Lord. "You made me furious by worshiping idols you made with your own hands, bringing on yourselves all the disasters you now suffer. And now the Lord of Heaven's Armies says: Because you have not listened to me, I will gather together all the armies of the north under King Nebuchadnezzar of Babylon, whom I have appointed as my deputy. I will bring them all against this land and its people and against the surrounding nations. I will completely destroy you and make you an object of horror and contempt and a ruin forever. . . . This entire land will become a desolate wasteland. Israel and her neighboring lands will serve the king of Babylon for seventy years." **JEREMIAH 25:2-11, NLT.**

This is one tough section of the Bible, because in it you see God resorting to what He didn't want to have to do. In this prophecy God tells His people that they've had many chances to turn around, to step up, but they haven't listened. So now He will withdraw His mighty presence from their nation and allow His "servant" Nebuchadnezzar, a pagan king, to come and carry His children off to a far country.

This is not God's desire. As you have read in the book of Jeremiah, God's desire is that His people repent and start acting like princes and princesses of heaven. Instead, God sees His children acting more and more like servants of hell.

Sometimes—not always, but sometimes—God has to let His children go to Babylon so they can eventually come to their senses. I know that sounds strange, but it's true. God's plan for Israel was *not* to give up on them, but to hand them over for a time so that maybe, just maybe, He could still redeem them.

SEPt 3

Big Plans

"FOR THUS SAYS THE LORD: When seventy years are completed for Babylon, I will visit you, and I will fulfill to you my promise and bring you back to this place. For I know the plans I have for you, declares the Lord, plans for wholeness and not for evil, to give you a future and a hope. Then you will call upon me and come and pray to me, and I will hear you. You will seek me and find me. When you seek me with all your heart, I will be found by you, declares the Lord, and I will restore your fortunes and gather you from all the nations and all the places where I have driven you, declares the Lord, and I will bring you back to the place from which I sent you into exile." **JEREMIAH 29:10-14, ESV.**

In the middle of today's reading is one of the most overused but one of the most beautiful texts in the Bible. " 'For I know the plans I have for you,' declares the Lord, 'plans to prosper you and not to harm you, plans to give you hope and a future.' "

This text eloquently captures the heart of God for His people. It shows us a God who, even though His children seem to be in a constant state of rebellion, has always had good intentions toward them. In other words, God believes in you and has amazing plans for you, even if you aren't interested in Him.

I think the most frequent concern I deal with in the lives of teens is self-esteem. Maybe they feel unloved and unwanted by parents, they've had some sort of breakup with their not-so-significant other, or they just don't like how they look. I've seen everything from self-abuse (cutting, carving, eating disorders) to suicidal thoughts. All this because when they look in the mirror, they see failure. They see someone who's fat, ugly, and unimportant. If only every young person could see what God sees.

When God looks at you, He smiles. He sees in you what you can't possibly see in yourself. He sees your future with Him. He sees your every gift and ability being used to make this world a better place. He sees you living in joy. God is so excited about you that He can hardly wait to speak with you each and every day.

So what are your plans? Do you have it all figured out? Do you know what you're going to do in this life? Whether you do or don't, I hope you have rooted yourself in Christ and are open to His leading. He may lead in a different direction than you have in mind. God's got big plans for you! Enjoy!

Really, Really Sad

THIS IS WHY I WEEP and my eyes overflow with tears. No one is near to comfort me, no one to restore my spirit. My children are destitute because the enemy has prevailed. **LAMENTATIONS 1:16.**

When I see the title of this poetic, emotionally charged book of the Bible, I remember that the root of Lamentations is the word *lament*. Lament: to feel, show, or express sorrow or regret; to mourn deeply.

Have you ever mourned deeply for anything?

When I married my wife, her best friend was a cat—a 25-pound cat named Bonkers. When Wendy came home, that huge black-and-white cat would run to her and end up in her arms. He would put his paws around her neck and suck on her ear. Gross, right? This cat was everything to my wife.

One of the unfortunate consequences of owning a pet is having to eventually say goodbye to it. About a year after we married, Bonkers got an infection of some kind and died. My wife cried such a deep cry that day. And her mourning didn't subside in a day or even a week. My wife was grief-stricken for a month because her cat had died!

The book of Lamentations is full of poetic grief and mourning. Jeremiah is heartbroken over the overthrow of his beloved city. He's also grief-stricken over the fact that his people wouldn't listen to God's pleading on their behalf.

As you read this book, you will gain a sense of how devoted Jeremiah was to God's cause and how he had a finger on the very pulse of God. Jeremiah's lament is God's lament.

The lament that God and His prophet expressed for their people is the same lament that God must feel about His children who choose to rebel today. He laments because He knows what they are missing out on. He laments because He knows the joy that escapes those who reject His love.

Conversely, the Bible tells us that all of heaven rejoices when even one person repents. Why not use this day to give God reason to rejoice?

SEPt 5

Fathers Aren't Bosses

BECAUSE OF THE LORD'S GREAT love we are not consumed, for his compassions never fail. They are new every morning; great is your faithfulness.
LAMENTATIONS 3:22, 23.

I've had times in my life when I promise God that I'll never commit a particular sin again. For weeks I'm strong in my resolve. And then something happens, and before I know it, I'm caught in the same sin again. Whenever this happens, I feel horrible about letting God down. I want to run away from God and not come to Him with my failures. And then I remember that He's not my boss—He's my Father.

When I was 16, my mom used her influence as the president's secretary to get me a summer job at the corporate offices of a large insurance company. I worked in an office that processed people's insurance claims. The job wasn't difficult. There was a system of checks and balances that I had to go through for each claim. And then I ran into a difficulty. I had a couple of claims I didn't know how to process correctly. Instead of asking for help, I put them in a drawer in my desk.

It wasn't long before people discovered that something had gone wrong with those claims, and they started asking questions. When my boss finally quizzed me on the whereabouts of the missing papers, I lied and said I didn't know where they were.

My boss was upset. He fired me. I deserved it.

Growing up, I did similar things in my family. It drove my father crazy. Why wouldn't I just tell the truth when I did something wrong?

But in all the times my dad caught me doing something wrong, never once did he threaten to adopt me out or disown me. My dad never fired me from the family.

Fathers don't act like bosses. Bosses dock your pay. Bosses write you up. Bosses fire you. Fathers correct, discipline, and nurture you into a better way. Fathers keep your best interest in mind. Fathers love you. Fathers let you know that your performance has no bearing on your relationship with them.

It's not *my* faithfulness that saves me. My faithfulness is filled with holes. I've had too many times when my faithfulness has faltered—but not God's. His faithfulness never fails. He's always cheering us on. He's always willing to guide us into a better way.

Speechless

This is another case of "too awesome to comment on." **EZEKIEL 1:4-28, NASB.**

AS I LOOKED, BEHOLD, a storm wind was coming from the north, a great cloud with fire flashing forth continually and a bright light around it, and in its midst something like glowing metal in the midst of the fire. Within it there were figures resembling four living beings. And this was their appearance: they had human form. Each of them had four faces and four wings. Their legs were straight and their feet were like a calf's hoof, and they gleamed like burnished bronze. . . .

As for the form of their faces, each had the face of a man; all four had the face of a lion on the right and the face of a bull on the left, and all four had the face of an eagle. Such were their faces. Their wings were spread out above; each had two touching another being, and two covering their bodies. . . . In the midst of the living beings there was something that looked like burning coals of fire, like torches. . . . And the living beings ran to and fro like bolts of lightning.

Now as I looked at the living beings, behold, there was one wheel on the earth beside the living beings, for each of the four of them. The appearance of the wheels and their workmanship was like sparkling beryl, and all four of them had the same form, their appearance and workmanship being as if one wheel were within another. Whenever they moved, they moved in any of their four directions without turning as they moved. As for their rims they were lofty and awesome, and the rims of all four of them were full of eyes round about.

Whenever the living beings moved, the wheels moved with them. And whenever the living beings rose from the earth, the wheels rose also. . . .

Now over the heads of the living beings there was something like an expanse, like the awesome gleam of crystal, spread out over their heads. . . .

Now above the expanse that was over their heads there was something resembling a throne, like lapis lazuli in appearance; and on that which resembled a throne, high up, was a figure with the appearance of a man. Then I noticed from the appearance of His loins and upward something like glowing metal that looked like fire all around within it, and from the appearance of His loins and downward I saw something like fire; and there was a radiance around Him. As the appearance of the rainbow in the clouds on a rainy day, so was the appearance of the surrounding radiance.

Such was the appearance of the likeness of the glory of the Lord. And when I saw it, I fell on my face and heard a voice speaking.

SEPt 7

From Ezekiel to Revelation

THEN HE SAID TO ME, "Son of man, eat what you find; eat this scroll, and go, speak to the house of Israel." So I opened my mouth, and He fed me this scroll. He said to me, "Son of man, feed your stomach and fill your body with this scroll which I am giving you." Then I ate it, and it was sweet as honey in my mouth. **EZEKIEL 3:1-3, NASB.**

Bible students will notice that the book of Ezekiel is similar in content to the book of Revelation. The opening vision in chapter 1 of Ezekiel is very similar to the throne-room scene in Revelation 4. In both books there are creatures covered with eyes surrounding the throne of God. God is pictured enthroned in power with flashes of lightning and peals of thunder.

These creatures that the prophets see have interesting faces. Their faces are like a human, a lion, an ox, and an eagle. The significance of this lies in the way the Old Testament sanctuary was laid out. The sanctuary in the wilderness was surrounded by the 12 tribes of Israel, three on each side. The leading tribe in each group of three had a banner that symbolized their group. According to Jewish tradition, these four banners posted around the sanctuary in the wilderness portrayed a man, a lion, an eagle, and an ox. Remember, the sanctuary on earth was patterned after the sanctuary in heaven.

Another similarity between Ezekiel and Revelation involves a scroll that the prophet is instructed to eat. (Talk about eating your words!) To both Ezekiel and John the scroll tastes delicious. In both cases the scroll represents the revealing of the true character of God and how His plan will unfold for His people.

In the book of Ezekiel God calls His people to repentance and lets them know that after a period of time He will call them out of Babylon, and Jerusalem will be restored for them. In the book of Revelation God calls His people out of "Babylon" and promises a New Jerusalem for those who love Him. God's promise for you and me is a new heart, a new life, and eventually a New Jerusalem! Let's always look to Jesus to know the truth about God and avoid any trips to Babylon!

SEPt 8

You Want Me to Do What?

AND YOU, SON OF MAN, take a brick and lay it before you, and engrave on it a city, even Jerusalem. And put siegeworks against it, and build a siege wall against it, and cast up a mound against it. Set camps also against it, and plant battering rams against it all around. And you, take an iron griddle, and place it as an iron wall between you and the city; and set your face toward it, and let it be in a state of siege, and press the siege against it. This is a sign for the house of Israel. **EZEKIEL 4:1-3, ESV.**

As I've noted before, being a prophet is not a job that anyone in their right mind would ever apply for. In this case Ezekiel is asked to do some pretty bizarre stuff.

In order to illustrate what is going to happen to the city of Jerusalem, God tells Ezekiel that He is going to have him tied up with ropes so that he has to lie on his left side in front of a small model of Jerusalem. He is to do this for the sin of Israel. And he has to lie there in the street in front of this model for a year and a month.

When this time period is up, Ezekiel is to roll over and lie on his right side for the sin of Judah for another 40 days. So for 430 days Ezekiel is to lie on one side or the other and serve as a visual demonstration of the prophecy against Israel and Judah.

Added to Ezekiel's humiliation is his eating assignment. God gives Ezekiel instructions on exactly what and how much he is to eat and drink during this weird time of prophecy. And to make matters worse, God actually tells Ezekiel to use his own body waste as fuel for his cooking fire. This is where Ezekiel speaks up and protests. "God, I've never been unclean. Cooking with stuff scraped out of the toilet would make me unclean!"

God considers Ezekiel's protest and says, "OK, you can use cow manure."

It would be easy to get caught up in how outrageous this prophetic exhibit from Ezekiel must have looked (or smelled). But the big message here is that God will do anything to get His people's attention. He loves us so much that He won't let us simply die in our sin. He'll even use the outrageous to win us back.

SEPt 9

What Are You Here For?

THIS IS WHAT THE SOVEREIGN Lord says: This is Jerusalem, which I have set in the center of the nations, with countries all around her. Yet in her wickedness she has rebelled against my laws and decrees more than the nations and countries around her. She has rejected my laws and has not followed my decrees. **EZEKIEL 5:5, 6.**

When I was 20 years old, I worked for some people who owned three restaurants. One of the restaurants was located in Mercer Island, an affluent community on an island in the middle of Lake Washington between Seattle and Bellevue, Washington. I was hired to manage the restaurant, hire and fire employees, keep the food supply fresh, and make sure that customers had a wonderful dining experience.

One night we were just slammed with customers. Everybody was working hard and running to keep up with customer demand. In the middle of the fray one of my waitresses stomped up to me with a scowl on her face and said, "If it wasn't for all these customers, I could get some work done!" Then she stomped off.

The irony of this statement, of course, is that without customers the waitress wouldn't have a job at all!

In the above text God announced a truth that hadn't seemed to dawn on Israel. He proclaimed that He had set Jerusalem in the middle of the world—the part that was known to them, anyway. Right in the middle of Egypt, Assyria, and Babylon stood Jerusalem, the city of God. Well, at least it was supposed to be the city of God. Instead, it became the city of all kinds of gods. It ceased to honor God with its existence. Just like my waitress friend, Jerusalem didn't seem to realize why God had put it there.

Have you ever realized that you are where you are, created to be who you are, for a reason? Did you know that God has placed you on this earth for a purpose? Your faithfulness and your allegiance to your Creator can be a testimony to the people around you who desperately need to know His love.

Don't be like Jerusalem and get caught up in the things of this world. The Israelites got distracted and left their calling for a life that eventually led them to disaster. Our calling is to honor God, lift Him up, and let the world know that we are His.

Day of the Living Dead

THE HAND OF THE LORD was upon me, and He brought me out by the Spirit of the Lord and set me down in the middle of the valley; and it was full of bones. He caused me to pass among them round about, and behold, there were very many on the surface of the valley; and lo, they were very dry. He said to me, "Son of man, can these bones live?" And I answered, "O Lord God, You know." Again He said to me, "Prophesy over these bones and say to them, 'O dry bones, hear the word of the Lord.' Thus says the Lord God to these bones, 'Behold, I will cause breath to enter you that you may come to life. I will put sinews on you, make flesh grow back on you, cover you with skin and put breath in you that you may come alive; and you will know that I am the Lord.'" So I prophesied as I was commanded; and as I prophesied, there was a noise, and behold, a rattling; and the bones came together, bone to its bone. And I looked, and behold, sinews were on them, and flesh grew and skin covered them; but there was no breath in them. Then He said to me, "Prophesy to the breath, prophesy, son of man, and say to the breath, 'Thus says the Lord God, "Come from the four winds, O breath, and breathe on these slain, that they come to life."'" So I prophesied as He commanded me, and the breath came into them, and they came to life and stood on their feet, an exceedingly great army. Then He said to me, "Son of man, these bones are the whole house of Israel; behold, they say, 'Our bones are dried up and our hope has perished. We are completely cut off.' Therefore prophesy and say to them, 'Thus says the Lord God, "Behold, I will open your graves and cause you to come up out of your graves, My people; and I will bring you into the land of Israel. Then you will know that I am the Lord.'" **EZEKIEL 37:1-13, NASB.**

To Israel this vivid prophecy of Ezekiel was a promise of hope. God could heal them. He could breathe life into their dead spiritual souls. He could even unite Judah with Israel once more and give His people another chance to be the light of the world.

But more than a prophecy about Israel, this text gives us a glimpse into our very near future. Just as God breathed the breath of life into the first man, the Spirit of God will one day breathe life into the dead bones of millions of His children.

That's a literal resurrection of the dead. But what about a spiritual resurrection? Do you need new life breathed into your relationship with God? Your Creator is waiting and willing to give you resurrection power. Just ask Him!

SEPt 11

Veggie Tales

DANIEL THEN SAID TO THE GUARD whom the chief official had appointed over Daniel, Hananiah, Mishael and Azariah, "Please test your servants for ten days: Give us nothing but vegetables to eat and water to drink. Then compare our appearance with that of the young men who eat the royal food, and treat your servants in accordance with what you see." So he agreed to this and tested them for ten days. **DANIEL 1:11-13.**

Knowing the difference between right and wrong is important. Doing the right thing when wrong is begging you to concede is important. Doing the right thing when nobody is around is amazing! We call that integrity.

All of Daniel's life his parents had taught him the difference between right and wrong. There were more than 600 laws in the Torah (the first five books of our Bible) that Daniel had taken to heart, and to the best of his ability he had kept them his whole life.

Now, as a young man (probably a teenager), he has been forcibly removed from his homeland of Judah and taken to Babylon. The Babylonians had an interesting way of dealing with their captives. Instead of making them into slaves who did menial labor, they recruited the best and brightest for the service of the king.

The test for this labor was based on physical and mental ability, so the young Israelites were fed the best food from the king's table. Much of this food was unclean according to the Torah and unfit for these boys to eat. They knew that they were not supposed to eat pepperoni pizza and that clams were not on God's menu for them. So all four boys abstained from what was wrong and stood up for the right. (How many others came from Israel but didn't stand up for what they believed in?)

The coolest thing about this story is that the four guys found strength in one another to do the right thing. That's how it's supposed to be. We're supposed to encourage one another toward good things. Together we can be stronger than when we're alone. In fact, that's why God gave us church. God knew that when believers come together in faith, that faith can encourage others to be bold for Jesus.

SEPT 12

Can't Wait for the Rock

DANIEL REPLIED, "No wise man, enchanter, magician or diviner can explain to the king the mystery he has asked about, but there is a God in heaven who reveals mysteries. He has shown King Nebuchadnezzar what will happen in days to come. Your dream and the visions that passed through your mind as you were lying in bed are these." **DANIEL 2:27, 28.**

Nebuchadnezzar's dream in Daniel 2 is an iconic reminder that God has a plan for this world and that He's willing to share it with His children.

In this dream the king sees a great image whose head is made of gold, its upper body of silver, its waist of bronze, its legs of iron, and its feet of iron and clay. Then from out of nowhere a boulder comes hurtling through space, strikes the statue, and obliterates it. The debris blows away like dandelion seeds, and the rock that broke the statue grows as big as a mountain and fills the whole earth.

The funny thing is that the king doesn't remember what he dreamed; he just knows it was something important and that it troubled him. After a bit of drama involving the other wise men, Daniel volunteers to interpret the dream for the pagan king.

The interpretation of this dream gives the king—and us—a glimpse into the future. Daniel plainly tells the king that each section of the statue represents a new kingdom that will rise up and rule the earth. We know from history that Babylon gave way to Persia, which gave way to Greece, which gave way to Rome, which eventually split into 10 powers that ultimately became Europe.

But what about the ending? Who or what is the rock that smashes the great statue in the dream? That rock is Jesus. As you will see later in the book of Daniel, each kingdom that rises does more damage to the name and character of God. Each kingdom becomes more like Satan and less like Jesus. This defaming of God's character will continue until the cup of this world's sin is filled to the brim and Jesus comes before this world destroys itself.

According to this prophetic dream, we are standing in the toenails of history. The Rock that smashes the statue is sure to roll this way any time now. I don't know about you, but I'm ready for the Rock to do His work. I'm ready to go home.

SEPt 13

Three Amigos

SHADRACH, MESHACH AND ABEDNEGO REPLIED to him, "King Nebuchadnez-zar, we do not need to defend ourselves before you in this matter. If we are thrown into the blazing furnace, the God we serve is able to deliver us from it, and he will deliver us from Your Majesty's hand. But even if he does not, we want you to know, Your Majesty, that we will not serve your gods or worship the image of gold you have set up." **DANIEL 3:16-18.**

The king should have known that these three amigos weren't going to bow down to the idol when the music played. They hadn't eaten his food because they knew that was wrong. But, like most politicians, the king was so full of himself that he just couldn't resist the opportunity to get some self-glory.

How easy would it have been for these three young men, at just the right time, to bend down to tie their shoes? How easy would it have been for them to say to one another, "We all know that we don't really believe in this stuff, but why stick out like a sore thumb?"

But they didn't. They refused to follow the crowd. Instead, they did what they knew was right. And their reward? A fiery furnace.

I want you to notice something in this story, because it's a principle in Scripture that separates God from Satan. Satan and his minions threaten you with words and thoughts similar to this: "Worship how we want you to, or we'll burn you up!" God and His followers say, "Worship God and follow Him because it will give you a full life, but if you choose not to, God will not force you to."

The religion of Babylon threatens, uses force, and coerces with fear. The religion of Jesus uses love, kindness, and free will. Satan would like us to use threats of fire and hell to motivate people to serve God out of fear. This isn't God's way. The Bible says that it's God's kindness that leads us to repentance.

It is true that in the end there will be fire. But that fire is meant to purify the earth of sin's devastation. And like the three friends in today's text, God's children will not be destroyed by that fire, because that fire is His love and glory. God's kids will stand in that fire like the three amigos, because Jesus will stand there with them.

Spit in His Eye

KING BELSHAZZAR MADE A GREAT FEAST for a thousand of his lords and drank wine in front of the thousand. Belshazzar, when he tasted the wine, commanded that the vessels of gold and of silver that Nebuchadnezzar his father had taken out of the temple in Jerusalem be brought, that the king and his lords, his wives, and his concubines might drink from them. Then they brought in the golden vessels that had been taken out of the temple, the house of God in Jerusalem, and the king and his lords, his wives, and his concubines drank from them. They drank wine and praised the gods of gold and silver, bronze, iron, wood, and stone. **DANIEL 5:1-4, ESV.**

There are some things you just shouldn't profane. As an American I have a hard time seeing people misusing our national flag. I find it difficult to place anything on top of a Bible. I can tolerate swearing and profanity for a while, but I can't stand it when people use God's name in their crass slang.

In today's reading we see an arrogant king who thumbs his nose at God. King Belshazzar was aware of God's workings in the life of Nebuchadnezzar. He had heard of God's presence in the fiery furnace and His hand in the humbling of the proud king. He knew of the strange dream that predicted the end of the Babylonian empire. In spite of all this knowledge, King Belshazzar spit in the eye of God by using holy articles for his party guests to get drunk from.

God has His limits. In one of the coolest stories in the Bible, a mysterious hand appears out of nowhere and starts writing on the wall of the party hall. It's a message to the king: "You have been weighed and measured, and you have been found lacking."

What a horrible thing to hear from God. It's such a contrast to what we want to hear: "Well done, My good and faithful servant."

As the history of the world begins to testify to the goodness and love of God, people will find themselves either praising and honoring God or profaning Him and misrepresenting Him. The big danger we need to avoid is the danger that brought down Belshazzar—being so self-absorbed that we lose sight of God's sovereignty and glory. It's when we keep our eyes on Jesus that we can keep ourselves in perspective.

SEPt 15

Daniel the Lionhearted

THE NEXT MORNING KING DARIUS got up at dawn and hurried to the lions' den. As he came near the den, he was worried. He called out to Daniel, "Daniel, servant of the living God! Has your God that you always worship been able to save you from the lions?" Daniel answered, "O king, live forever! My God sent his angel to close the lions' mouths. They have not hurt me, because my God knows I am innocent. I never did anything wrong to you, O king." King Darius was very happy and told his servants to lift Daniel out of the lions' den. So they lifted him out and did not find any injury on him, because Daniel had trusted in his God. **DANIEL 6:19-23, NCV.**

The closest I've ever come to being eaten by an animal happened in Bella Coola, British Columbia. It was a warm, sunny afternoon. Classes were out for the day, and I was sitting with a bunch of students out on the lawn in front of the dormitories. I was lying on a blanket in the sun, almost asleep, when one of the students said, "I'm bored. Can we go to the zoo?"

I knew what he was asking. Bella Coola didn't have an actual zoo. But the kids in the dorms lovingly referred to the local dump as "the zoo" because of the bears that went there looking for a free meal.

I thought that was a fun idea, so we loaded up the van and drove down to the entrance of the dump. We all piled out of the van (about 14 of us) and started walking down the road. Suddenly one of the girls said, "Hey! Look at the cute little bear cubs!" I turned around and saw two little cubs scampering off the road behind us. Then I heard it. *Wooof!* I turned to see a mama bear standing on her haunches, making threatening noises.

I yelled for all the kids to gather together in a tight group as mama bear started running toward us at an alarming speed. Fifty feet from us she changed her mind and ran off the road toward her babies.

Daniel took a sudden trip to the zoo. He was cast into the lions' den because he wouldn't compromise his spiritual convictions. He stood up for Jesus even though his life was threatened. Dare to be a Daniel. Dare to stand alone. God bless you today as you face opportunities to stand up for your faith.

Little Braggart

WHILE I WAS THINKING ABOUT the horns, there before me was another horn, a little one, which came up among them; and three of the first horns were uprooted before it. This horn had eyes like the eyes of a human being and a mouth that spoke boastfully. **DANIEL 7:8.**

In the book of Daniel, chapters 1 through 6 (other than Daniel 2) are prophetic stories that parallel what will happen in the last days of this earth's history. They predict that politics and religion will join hands and start to legislate how people worship. The chapters from Daniel 7 to the end of the book use symbolic images to detail what will happen on earth until Jesus comes to take us home.

Daniel 7 parallels Daniel 2 in describing the world powers that rise and fall as history unfolds. The animals/beasts represent, in succession, Babylon, Persia, Greece, and Rome. But in Daniel 7 something different happens. Out of the 10-horned fourth beast (Rome) rises a little horn that tears out three other horns. This horn is different from the other horns because it has a face and a mouth that speaks boastful things. This little horn (world power) also attempts to change God's law and His set times, and it wages war against God's holy people, who dare to follow God in a different way than it prefers.

The big hint that the angel gives to Daniel (and to us) for identifying this little horn is the time frame when the little horn is allowed to rule on earth without opposition. In Daniel 7:25 we are told that the little horn runs roughshod for "a time, times and half a time." By comparing with other similar prophecies, we can determine that this means three and a half years. I'll talk about time prophecies later in more detail, but for today I want you to notice something that comes up quite frequently in prophecy.

Notice how long the little horn enemy of God gets to spread its lies about God. Now think about how long Jesus spent in ministry to show this world the true character of the Father. That's right: three and a half years. In other words, the devil and his allies get a chance to show the world who they think God is for three and a half years (in symbolic numbers), and Jesus comes to earth to show us the Father for three and a half years. Comparing the two and their track record, I choose to view God through the lens of Jesus!

SEPt 17

Church, Rise Up

AND HE SAID UNTO ME, Unto two thousand and three hundred days; then shall the sanctuary be cleansed. **DANIEL 8:14, KJV.**

In Daniel 8 animals are again used to portray Persia and Greece as world powers that receive authority but that increasingly trample the name of God. After them Rome tramples the earth and does even more damage to the name of God and to His people.

Daniel 7 and 8 talk explicitly about how God's enemy uses earthly political and religious powers to pollute the very sanctuary of God. This is a problem. God's sanctuary becomes polluted, not with actual litter or exhaust from cars, but with the lies and misrepresentations that the devil spreads about who God is.

On a surface level we can easily see the success of the little horn's attacks on God. When a tornado or hurricane devastates life and property, what does the local news call that devastation? An "act of God," right? Who came up with the idea that God is the destroyer? Not God. That's not what Jesus taught about God.

The enemy of God has the whole world, even the religious world, believing that God has a dark side and will send you to everlasting punishment and hellfire if you don't love Him as He wants you to. They teach that Father God is some monster who needs to be held back by Jesus so He doesn't destroy His children because they've been so naughty.

The enemy has polluted the sanctuary. But that's not the end of the story. The angel tells Daniel that after a period of time (2,300 days) the sanctuary would be cleansed of the lies that have polluted it. Here's where it gets exciting: You and I are invited to be a part of the cleanup that needs to happen in the sanctuary.

In the Israelite sanctuary the cleansing happened on the Day of Atonement. "Atonement" means bringing God and people back together, and we have a role in that process. Daniel 8:14 is God's prophetic call to His church to rise up and dispel the lies about Him so that people will want a relationship with Him. That's our job. We can help clean up the pollution in the sanctuary by telling the truth about the love of God.

Won't you join God's team to fight the lies of the devil? Remember, if you've seen Jesus, you've seen the Father.

Messiah Predicted

SEVENTY WEEKS HAVE BEEN DECREED for your people and your holy city, to finish the transgression, to make an end of sin, to make atonement for iniquity, to bring in everlasting righteousness, to seal up vision and prophecy and to anoint the most holy place. So you are to know and discern that from the issuing of a decree to restore and rebuild Jerusalem until Messiah the Prince there will be seven weeks and sixty-two weeks; it will be built again, with plaza and moat, even in times of distress. Then after the sixty-two weeks the Messiah will be cut off and have nothing, and the people of the prince who is to come will destroy the city and the sanctuary. And its end will come with a flood; even to the end there will be war; desolations are determined. And he will make a firm covenant with the many for one week, but in the middle of the week he will put a stop to sacrifice and grain offering; and on the wing of abominations will come one who makes desolate, even until a complete destruction, one that is decreed, is poured out on the one who makes desolate. **DANIEL 9:24-27, NASB.**

Did you know that the book of Daniel foretold Jesus' appearing on this earth as the Messiah? In fact, the beginning and end of Jesus' three and a half years of ministry were predicted to the very year.

In the Bible, time prophecies are often given in days. In Numbers 14:34 and Ezekiel 4:6 Scripture sets a precedent indicating that when you substitute a day for a year, you can accurately apply time prophecies to actual periods in history.

In Daniel 9 we have a 70-week prophecy that starts with the decree to rebuild Jerusalem. We know from history that this decree went out in 457 B.C. If you add 69 weeks, or 483 years in a day/year substitution, you come out to A.D. 27 (remember that there's no zero year in the B.C.–A.D. time line). A.D. 27 was when Jesus was baptized by John in the Jordan.

Later the prophecy says Messiah will be cut off midweek, or three and a half years after He begins His ministry. Jesus died just when it was foretold.

God shared His plan with Daniel almost 500 years before it happened. God gave these prophecies so we can have confidence in Him. Jesus is the truth. He invites you and me to join that proclamation of the truth, otherwise known as the everlasting gospel!

SEPt 19

God Wins When You Shine

NOW AT THAT TIME MICHAEL, the great prince who stands guard over the sons of your people, will arise. And there will be a time of distress such as never occurred since there was a nation until that time; and at that time your people, everyone who is found written in the book, will be rescued. Many of those who sleep in the dust of the ground will awake, these to everlasting life, but the others to disgrace and everlasting contempt. Those who have insight will shine brightly like the brightness of the expanse of heaven, and those who lead the many to righteousness, like the stars forever and ever. **DANIEL 12:1-3, NASB.**

When my wife, Wendy, was a small child, she had some medical issues that landed her in a hospital bed for several weeks. As with any child, at some point in between family visits she got bored. There were no nurses around, so she slipped out of bed and wandered down to the waiting room to see if her family was there. They weren't, so she wandered around a little more until she found herself in the waiting room again. She got tired, crawled under one of the couches in the waiting room, and fell asleep.

In the meantime a nurse went in to check on her little patient. The girl was nowhere to be seen. Panic. A call was made to Wendy's mother. She raced down to the hospital and spent the next couple of hours searching for her daughter.

Finally, exhausted and discouraged, Wendy's parents sat down in the waiting room. Wendy's little sister had a doll, which she dropped on the ground. Imagine their surprise when a little hand reached out, grabbed the doll, and pulled it under the couch! The wait to find their little girl was excruciating, but in the end it was worth it.

Listening to and recording this great book of prophecy was quite hard for Daniel. At one point he became physically sick over the description of the horrible power that would dare to drag God and His people through the mud. Can you imagine how Daniel's mood must have lightened at the end of his angelic visit as he came to understand that in the end God will reign, and He will rescue His people?

God showed Daniel that there will be great times of trouble. Prophecy says that we will have to wait for our Lord to come again. But in the end it will be worth it.

SEPt 20

Kinesthetic Learners

I WILL PLANT HER FOR MYSELF in the land; I will show my love to the one I called "Not my loved one." I will say to those called "Not my people," "You are my people"; and they will say, "You are my God." **HOSEA 2:23.**

My wife is a really smart elementary school teacher. She told me that a great teacher will teach to every kind of learning need. I had no idea what she was talking about, so she explained: "Some kids can hear something, and they learn it well. Other young people can read something and learn it on the spot. Other kids need to touch and feel something to understand it. And still others need to see something acted out to understand it."

I think I fall into the last category. For some reason I can remember movies I've seen—lines and scenes—better than most people do.

I'm sure that God understands learning styles. Maybe that's why He had prophets speak to His children, write to His children, and give His children things to touch and feel (Thomas had to touch Jesus' scars). God also had His prophets enact scenarios that illustrated a message He wanted to get across to His kids. The book of Hosea shows us one of these living examples.

God approaches the prophet Hosea and asks him to marry a prostitute. Can you imagine? Hosea obeys God and marries Gomer the harlot. He does. But the whole time she's married to him, she's off sleeping with other men. It's just a horrible life for the poor prophet. They have kids. Who knows who the dad really is?

All the while all of Israel is seeing this weird and disturbing marriage relationship between the prophet and the prostitute. And then it hits them: this adulterous relationship is the same relationship that God's people have with God. God's people have been cheating on Him for centuries.

This object lesson serves us in the twenty-first century, too. Any of us who have been baptized are "married" to God. We stood in the water and publicly pledged our faithfulness to Him. How faithful have we been?

The beauty of the book of Hosea is that even when God's people are unfaithful, He is faithful. He will never file for divorce. He will always take us back.

SEPt 21

Unwanted Gift

THEN, AFTER DOING ALL THOSE things, I will pour out my Spirit upon all people. Your sons and daughters will prophesy. Your old men will dream dreams, and your young men will see visions. In those days I will pour out my Spirit even on servants—men and women alike. And I will cause wonders in the heavens and on the earth—blood and fire and columns of smoke. The sun will become dark, and the moon will turn blood red before that great and terrible day of the Lord arrives. But everyone who calls on the name of the Lord will be saved, for some on Mount Zion in Jerusalem will escape, just as the Lord has said. These will be among the survivors whom the Lord has called. **JOEL 2:28-32, NLT.**

In the middle of all the minor prophets' warnings to the people of Israel we keep finding these wonderful yet cataclysmic promises. This one from Joel is one of the most quoted.

Notice that at some point the Lord is going to pour His Spirit on *all* people on earth. This is key to our understanding of what kind of God we serve. Let me explain.

When I was younger, I had a friend who was (in my opinion) spoiled with rich parents and an unending supply of money. Don't get me wrong—I really liked my friend and would have hung out with him whether he was rich or poor. But through the years I noticed that he was taking things more and more for granted.

When I was a junior in high school, my friend drove up to my parents' place in a brand-new Mercedes-Benz sport convertible. I couldn't believe it. "Man, you are so lucky! I can't believe your parents got you a new Benz!"

My friend's response: "Yeah, I don't think I want it. I'd rather have a new Camaro."

My friend was given a gift that anyone would celebrate, and he didn't want it! In the end God is going to pour His Spirit out on all humankind. Every breathing person is going to be given that precious gift, but as it turns out, there will be many who don't want it. They would rather live the way they want to live, leaving the gift of God unopened.

God loves all His children and wants all of them to have a full life. He extends His invitation to all. That's the kind of God we serve.

SEPt 22

That's Not Fair!

SEEK GOOD, NOT EVIL, that you may live. Then the Lord God Almighty will be with you, just as you say he is. Hate evil, love good; maintain justice in the courts. Perhaps the Lord God Almighty will have mercy on the remnant of Joseph. **AMOS 5:14, 15.**

We all have a built-in sense of justice. We want things to be fair. In 1989 my wife and I traveled from Seattle to Bella Coola, British Columbia, to spend some time with her parents. To get there we had to drive north to Williams Lake, B.C., and then due west toward the coast for about 250 miles. The road west is pretty barren, especially in the winter.

On our way back to Seattle we were driving about 50 miles per hour on the high plains back toward Williams Lake. As I drove around a snowy corner, I saw two horses in the middle of the road. I didn't think we'd survive going off either side of the road, and I certainly didn't want to slam on my brakes in the slippery snow, so I decided to do my best to drive between the two horses. I missed. We slammed right into the back of one of them.

The owners flew out of their house. The father of the family was spitting mad at his 8-year-old son for leaving the gate open. They had to shoot the horse. And they might as well have shot our car, since it was pretty smashed up too.

The owner of the horse sued me for hitting his horse. That's right—he sued me. In the courtroom he lied and said that only one horse was out and that it was because his fence had been broken about a mile down the road.

I told my side of the story (the truth), and the judge rendered the verdict. My insurance company had to pay half the cost of the dead horse. It was an expensive horse.

It was so frustrating to sit there in that courtroom and listen to the man lie through his teeth. There was nothing I could do about it.

God hates injustice. I know the word *hate* is a strong word, but when it comes to injustice, I think it's the only word that can describe how He feels. That's why it's so important for His children to act in a just manner as they deal with one another and with the world.

SEPt 23

The Unmerciful Prophet

THIS CHANGE OF PLANS GREATLY UPSET JONAH, and he became very angry. So he complained to the Lord about it: "Didn't I say before I left home that you would do this, Lord? That is why I ran away to Tarshish! I knew that you are a merciful and compassionate God, slow to get angry and filled with unfailing love. You are eager to turn back from destroying people. Just kill me now, Lord! I'd rather be dead than alive if what I predicted will not happen." **JONAH 4:1-3, NLT.**

I've always had a love–hate relationship with the book of Jonah. On the one hand, I love the story. It's such a good story that the people at VeggieTales actually made a full-feature movie out of it.

On the other hand, this is a story of a prophet who behaves badly. As a man called by God and expected to represent God and His mercy, Jonah gets an F– on his report card. Unlike God, Jonah seeks justice long before he extends mercy.

When Jonah gets his call to go to Nineveh, God isn't asking him to preach to his own people. The people God is calling to repentance here aren't Jews; they're a bunch of heathens—people whom Jonah has been trained to avoid all of his life. They're the kind of people who are the problem with the world. Jonah may have had the opinion that all these Ninevites should be put on an island and nuked. That's why he was overjoyed to hear that God was going to destroy them for their naughtiness.

This attitude is a sickness that can also invade God's people today. We can be so focused on being right that we look down on other people. Different religions around the world make it their business to proclaim that only they reside in God's favor; everybody else is on God's naughty list. In essence, what many religions say is "If you don't believe all the things we believe, God can't save you." When we do this, we condemn billions of people to hell with our attitudes and our actions. This kind of attitude makes us huddle into little religious groups, meeting together and proclaiming the truth among ourselves instead of doing what Jesus asked us to do and acting how Jesus asked us to act.

Jesus is in the business of transforming and saving, not judging and condemning. Jonah didn't get that. And it's too bad—he missed out on making some really cool Ninevite friends.

SEPt 24

Life in Three Words

HE HAS SHOWN YOU, O MORTAL, what is good. And what does the Lord require of you? To act justly and to love mercy and to walk humbly with your God. **MICAH 6:8.**

I love this verse. In it we have God's most basic desire for how His people are supposed to act on earth. Three words: justice, mercy, and walking.

Justice is defined as getting what you deserve or giving others what they deserve. If you go over the speed limit and get a ticket, that's justice. If you get a job because of your abilities and not because of your skin color or who your parents are or what school you went to, that's justice. God wants us to be just and fair with the people around us.

Mercy is defined as *not* getting or giving what's deserved. Justice says, "You deserve that punishment, so that's what you get." Mercy says, "You deserve that punishment, but I'm going to cut you some slack and give you a break."

I can't tell you how many times I've received mercy from friends, family, and state troopers. Our God always extends mercy before judgment. That's His nature. He wants all to respond to mercy, grace, and kindness. Justice (the not-so-pleasant kind) falls on us when we reject God's mercy and accept the natural consequences of our sin.

But what about the walking? I had been in hot pursuit of my wife for a couple months. It was a battle between me and a guy she'd been seeing for a couple of years. We had been on some dates and had spent enough time together that I knew this was the girl I wanted to marry. But for some reason I couldn't seal the deal. We still had some things to discuss, divulge, and settle on.

It was on a walk that this all finally happened. We were in Victoria, British Columbia. We finished dinner and walked along the bay for about an hour. It was on that walk that we fell irrevocably in love. It was on that walk that I got my first kiss.

Walking with God is similar. During your walk with Him you will share the intimate details of life that only a friend could be privileged to hear. Walking with God will also produce a closeness that can come only with trust. Take some time each day to walk with God; you'll fall in love all over again.

SEPt 25

I Got Your Back

THE LORD IS GOOD, A refuge in times of trouble. He cares for those who trust in him, but with an overwhelming flood he will make an end of Nineveh; he will pursue his foes into the realm of darkness. **NAHUM 1:7, 8.**

Whom would you want on your team? LeBron James? Kobe Bryant? Maybe Felix Hernandez or Tom Brady? How about Bill Gates? I suppose the person you would want on your team would depend on what your team was trying to achieve. You wouldn't choose LeBron James to strengthen your golf team. You wouldn't choose Bill Gates to be the captain of your hockey team. Having the right teammate on the right team makes all the difference in the world.

A few years back I was invited to assemble a team to participate in a fund-raising event to benefit a local fire department. It was an all-day event that covered three sports: trapshooting, golf, and bowling. The team that ended up with the average top score in all these events won the tournament.

I'm a pretty competitive person, so I called the friends I thought would give us the best chance at winning. When my team showed up at the event, everybody looked at one of my team members and wondered how he could give us any kind of advantage. His name was Ron Knutson. He had white hair and was about 70 years old. What they didn't know was that Ron was my ringer in golf and trap-shooting.

When it came time for trapshooting (which I had never tried in my life), Ron opened the back of his vehicle and took out four guns that were the top of the line for the event. Then he proceeded to shoot perfect scores for our team. He's also a very good golfer.

Looks can be deceiving. We won the tournament easily.

Having the right person on your side can give you a distinct advantage in life. That's why it's imperative to have God on our team. With God on our side, who can stand against us?

How Sasha Got Healed

LORD, I HAVE HEARD OF your fame; I stand in awe of your deeds, Lord. Repeat them in our day, in our time make them known; in wrath remember mercy. **HABAKKUK 3:2.**

Most of the time when God shows up, I'm not expecting it. I think there's a precedent for that in the Bible. The vast majority of people did not expect Jesus to show up in Bethlehem when He did. Nobody expected the mighty blast from the nostrils of God at the Red Sea. And Jesus made it very clear that everybody will be surprised at the Second Coming. God shows up when we don't expect Him to. And this is a good thing.

Back in the early 1990s my wife and I went with a team of young people to the Ukraine to teach English and hold evangelistic meetings. It was an amazing experience that came at a time when Communism had fallen and many people in that part of the world were hearing about God for the first time. The meetings were packed, the people were gracious, and God was in that place.

It was during this amazing experience that God showed up in an unexpected way. A young mother brought her 10-year-old son, Sasha, to my wife. Sasha had been sick for months (he hadn't been to school in a year) and appeared to be on his last legs. He was listless and barely had enough energy to eat. The doctors had told the family that Sasha had a matter of months to live. His mom had almost given up hope, but her simple request was that our group pray for her son.

At 10:00 that night our group got together to lift Sasha up in prayer. We were earnest, but no more earnest than we had been hundreds of times before when praying for people who didn't get well.

The next morning Sasha's mother ran into the room we were prepping for our next meeting. She was tearful (in a good way) and speaking Russian at 100 miles an hour. Our translator explained that at 10:00 the night before, Sasha had been lying on the couch, when all of a sudden the color ran back into his face. He jumped up and started running around the room and shouting, "I don't feel sick anymore!"

God showed up. I wasn't really expecting it, but in the end I had to agree with the prophet Habakkuk: "I stand in awe of your deeds." I love it when God shows up.

SEPt 27

Love Ballad

THE LORD YOUR GOD IS with you, the Mighty Warrior who saves. He will take great delight in you; in his love he will no longer rebuke you, but will rejoice over you with singing. **ZEPHANIAH 3:17.**

My wife is the most creative person I've ever met. She can sit across the table from anybody or anything and sketch what she sees with speed and accuracy. She plays the keyboard, guitar, flute, and cello. She paints beautifully. And she composes music. I can barely tie my shoes.

Given my wife's extensive talents, it seemed perfectly natural that she would write a song to be sung at our wedding. It was a love song about us. I wasn't surprised that she had written the song. I *was* surprised when she informed me that we would be singing the song to each other.

We practiced the song over and over until we pretty much had it memorized. It was a great song, with piano and flute as instrumental accompaniment. The words were poetic and adequately described our growing love for each other. No surprises. Everything was set for the ceremony. And then came the wedding day.

After all the wedding attendants were standing in their places, after the flower girl and the Bible boy marched up, after the candles were lit, it happened. The wedding march started to play over the huge pipe organ, the doors swung open, and there she stood. Radiant. Beautiful. And she was walking toward me. I panicked. And then I started to cry. I completely lost it.

Wendy was now standing in front of me with two microphones: one for her and one for me. And I was crying like a newborn baby. I tried to sing, but I was all choked up and my nose was dripping on the microphone—all because of love.

The Bible says that God is so in love with you and with me that He rejoices over us with singing. Can you imagine what that sounds like? No crying will mess up the melody of that song. That song—our song—is sung on our behalf with fervent passion and perfect pitch. Can you imagine God singing over you? Well, He does. He's thrilled with you and sees all of your potential.

SEPt 28

Holey Pockets

NOW THIS IS WHAT THE Lord Almighty says: "Give careful thought to your ways. You have planted much, but harvested little. You eat, but never have enough. You drink, but never have your fill. You put on clothes, but are not warm. You earn wages, only to put them in a purse with holes in it." **HAGGAI 1:5, 6.**

Haggai is a book dedicated to motivating the children of Israel to rebuild a house where God can be worshipped. The above description reminds me of how hard it is to give to the cause of the Lord when your own financial life has mixed-up priorities.

My mom and stepfather were a mess. My mom had suffered from a brain tumor, which had left her with a completely different personality than she'd had when I was a child. My stepfather possessed about a seventh-grade education and had spent 18 years in a federal penitentiary. All of this added up to two people who had no idea what to do with money when they had it.

Once I went to their house to work on a budget for them to live by. I explained to them that when they received money, they needed to first return a tithe to God, then make sure their obligations to the government were met (taxes), then pay their bills, then use the leftover money for other things they needed. My stepfather said, "We can't afford to pay tithe." I didn't argue with him.

Later that day, when I was going through their financial papers, I found that the Social Security Administration had sent them a back payment check for $11,000 because of some errors they had made on my mom's checks. I asked them what they had done with the money. "We went to Vegas for a weekend and lost it all," they told me. And they couldn't afford to pay tithe?

Haggai calls God's people to get their priorities straight. Take care of your commitment to God's work first, and then use your money for the things you want and need to make your life more comfortable.

God has blessed us with all kinds of unexpected riches. Why not remember Him with a part of what He has seen fit to bless us with?

SEPt 29

Painted Ponies

DURING THE NIGHT I HAD A VISION. I saw a man riding a red horse. He was standing among some myrtle trees in a ravine, with red, brown, and white horses behind him. I asked, "What are these, sir?" The angel who was talking with me answered, "I'll show you what they are." Then the man standing among the myrtle trees explained, "They are the ones the Lord sent through all the earth." Then they spoke to the Lord's angel, who was standing among the myrtle trees. They said, "We have gone through all the earth, and everything is calm and quiet." **ZECHARIAH 1:8-11, NCV.**

I don't have a great love for horses. First of all, I don't think it's smart to climb on and ride anything that is alive and bigger than I am. Second, I discovered early on that horses have teeth that leave bite marks on one's arm. And third, horses don't have brakes.

Once when I was in high school I went over to Barb Douglas's house to ride horses. The horse she gave me was not a nice horse. I think it may have been possessed. I got on it, and it started to gallop down the street at a breakneck pace toward a very busy intersection. I ended up having to jump off the possessed horse while it was going at full gallop, leaving me with a bump on my head and some serious road rash.

In Zechariah we see God using horses as His emissaries to do a task around the world. As you can probably figure out, there weren't literal horses zooming to and fro to investigate what was going on throughout the whole world. These were just symbols of God's watchful eye.

Horse symbols are also used in the book of Revelation. God chooses four colored horses to symbolize the church and its relationship to the world and to Him. These four horses have infamously been called "the four horsemen of the Apocalypse." Of course, these aren't literal horses either. They symbolize the church after Jesus' resurrection. These horses get progressively more horrible (as the church of the Middle Ages did) and misrepresent God and His kingdom in treacherous ways.

And then there is a white horse in Revelation that carries a victorious King who rides to rescue His bride. This is a horse I can appreciate. And its rider is True.

The Day I'm Waiting For

"SURELY THE DAY IS COMING; it will burn like a furnace. All the arrogant and every evildoer will be stubble, and that day that is coming will set them on fire," says the Lord Almighty. "Not a root or a branch will be left to them. But for you who revere my name, the sun of righteousness will rise with healing in its rays. And you will go out and frolic like well-fed calves. Then you will trample on the wicked; they will be ashes under the soles of your feet on the day when I act," says the Lord Almighty. **MALACHI 4:1-3.**

I look forward to it every year. I know it makes me look like a big dumb man, but I really look forward to the start of the NFL season. The sights and sounds of football players and whistles and commentators on Sunday afternoons help me know there's something right in the world today.

This football season was no different. I had been waiting for the first Sunday of football season all summer long. I'd listened to the radio to know what all the teams were up to. I had cleared my schedule so I wouldn't have any conflicts pulling me away from my basement TV. I had purchased chocolate-covered almonds and other snacks to set on the table in front of me. I had my remote batteries changed. I was ready. And finally, it came. Opening day of the NFL.

And then it went. I sat all day watching football, eating snacks, working on my exercise machine (to counter the snacks), and then watching more football. And to tell you the truth, at the end of the day I wondered why I'd wasted the day.

There is another day that I'm looking forward to. It's described in the Bible as the culmination of justice, mercy, and grace. It's a day when God will be vindicated and finally seen for who He is: a God of perfect love who gives grace and desires that all of His children be saved.

Malachi the prophet describes this day as a day of justice. He has watched evil people run roughshod over Israel and its people for too long. Malachi longs for the day when those who thumb their noses at everything good and holy will get their just deserts. He longs to see an end to pain, suffering, and hate. So do I. I can't wait for that day. Oh, and at the end of that day I'm pretty sure I will have no regrets!

OCt 1

You Can't Pick Your Relatives

THE BOOK OF THE GENEALOGY OF JESUS CHRIST, the son of David, the son of Abraham. Abraham was the father of Isaac, and Isaac the father of Jacob, and Jacob the father of Judah and his brothers, and Judah the father of Perez and Zerah by Tamar, and Perez the father of Hezron, and Hezron the father of Ram, and Ram the father of Amminadab, and Amminadab the father of Nahshon, and Nahshon the father of Salmon, and Salmon the father of Boaz by Rahab, and Boaz the father of Obed by Ruth, and Obed the father of Jesse, and Jesse the father of David the king.
MATTHEW 1:1-6, ESV.

The New Testament starts in the book of Matthew with Jesus' family tree. Most people skip this part of the Bible and go on with the story of Jesus' birth. Not me. No way. There's far too much intrigue and great soap opera material here to just skip right over! And then there's the odd part at the end of the genealogies, where Matthew (a tax collector—maybe he'd be a CPA in our culture) seems not to count correctly. He says there are three sets of 14 generations from Abraham to Jesus. Take time to count and see how many you see! Can you figure out how he got that number?

The best part of the genealogies is who gets included in them. This is a scandalous group! Rahab the prostitute. Judah the adulterer. Tamar the widow who sleeps with her father-in-law. Bathsheba, not named but referred to as Solomon's mom and Uriah's wife (not David's). And then there's a list of kings that would make anybody who knew their story turn red. What a family! You could write a book about all the things this motley crew said and did. Oh, that's right—there *was* a book written about Jesus' relatives' exploits. It's called the Old Testament.

I'm an adopted person who has had the privilege to meet and know my birth family. It was uncanny to me how much I had in common with this wonderful group of people whom I hadn't even met until I was 29 years old.

When Jesus came to earth as a human being, He had in Him the genetic predispositions of all His ancestors. Can you imagine? He had all the noble traits but also all those other traits that dragged some of His ancestors down bad roads. Yet Jesus, in His humanity, never sinned. Jesus' example shows us that even though we can't pick who came before us, we can pick whom we will follow!

OCt 2

A Righteous Man

NOW THE BIRTH OF JESUS the Messiah took place in this way. When his mother Mary had been engaged to Joseph, but before they lived together, she was found to be with child from the Holy Spirit. Her husband Joseph, being a righteous man and unwilling to expose her to public disgrace, planned to dismiss her quietly. **MATTHEW 1:18, 19, NRSV.**

This is a scenario that is sacred, comical, and unbelievable, all in one God-led event. Imagine what it would be like to be a 15-year-old girl (marrying age in Jesus' time) pledged to be married to a decent guy, only to find out that you are pregnant. Not only are you pregnant, but God caused the pregnancy. And how do you know this? An angel told you.

For those young women who are reading this devotional, if you were to wake up tomorrow morning having dreamed that you were going to become pregnant without ever having been with a man, what would you think? (In the book of Luke Gabriel appears "live" to Mary, but in Matthew the angel always comes in a dream.) Would you announce it to your family at the breakfast table? If you had a boyfriend, would you tell him?

Guys, if you had a girlfriend and found out she was pregnant, and up till then you had made honorable choices with her, what would you do? What if she were to tell you that she had never been with a man, but she was pregnant with God's Son and the pregnancy was His doing? Would you believe her?

I think one of the best parts of the story of Jesus' birth is Joseph's initial reaction to Mary's announcement. He could have freaked out and reported her to the town elders. If she were found to be pregnant out of wedlock, she could have been dragged out of the city and stoned to death. Instead, he decided just to walk away quietly. And then he got his dream.

The angel in the dream must have been convincing, because Joseph took Mary as his wife and nurtured her along until the birth of Jesus. That must have been quite an exercise of faith for Joseph. He must have been a godly man. And I love how the above verse says that a righteous man doesn't bring anybody into public disgrace. We need more righteous men in the world today.

OCt 3

The New Moses

[JOSEPH] GOT UP, TOOK THE child and his mother during the night and left for Egypt, where he stayed until the death of Herod. And so was fulfilled what the Lord had said through the prophet: "Out of Egypt I called my son." **MATTHEW 2:14, 15.**

Each Gospel writer frames Jesus in a different light. This is to be expected, because each writer wrote to a different audience and had a different point to get across. In the book of Matthew the author writes to the people of Israel and portrays Jesus as the new Moses.

To a Jew in Jesus' day Moses was a hero of, well, biblical proportions. Moses was the one who had led God's people out of slavery and had given them their freedom. Moses was the one who had gone up the mountain and received the sacred law. Moses was the one who had directed the building of the tabernacle in the wilderness, a place where God would reside. Moses was as good as it gets.

Matthew highlighted all the aspects of Jesus life' that were God's way of saying, "Hey, everybody! There's a new deliverer in town, and it's My Son!" Look at the similarities:

* Moses is born, and a king tries to kill him.
* Moses comes out of Egypt to save his people.
* We have no details about Moses' childhood.
* Moses spends 40 years in the wilderness to prepare for ministry.
* Moses goes up on a mountain and receives the law.
* Moses goes up on a mountain and comes down with a shining face.

* Jesus is born, and a king tries to kill Him.
* Jesus flees to Egypt, then comes out of Egypt to save His people.
* We have no details about Jesus' childhood.
* Jesus spends 40 days in the wilderness to prepare for ministry.
* Jesus goes up on a mountain and gives the new law (the Sermon on the Mount).
* Jesus goes up on a mountain and is transfigured. His face glows like the sun.

There are many more parallels between the two, but the difference is that Moses delivered his people out of literal slavery. Jesus came to deliver us from something that goes much deeper—sin.

Total Submission

AT THAT TIME JESUS CAME from Galilee to the Jordan River and wanted John to baptize him. But John tried to stop him, saying, "Why do you come to me to be baptized? I need to be baptized by you!" Jesus answered, "Let it be this way for now. We should do all things that are God's will." So John agreed to baptize Jesus. As soon as Jesus was baptized, he came up out of the water. Then heaven opened, and he saw God's Spirit coming down on him like a dove. **MATTHEW 3:13-16, NCV.**

Baptism is a real trip. I was baptized when I was 22 years old. The pastor who baptized me was about five feet seven inches tall and weighed about 150 pounds. I am six feet six inches tall and weigh . . . more than that. Let's just say it was a struggle getting me out of the water.

Nobody really knows where the tradition of baptism came from. The apostle Paul equates it with Israel going through the Red Sea from bondage to freedom. In another place he compares it to death and resurrection.

When I study with people for baptism, I tell them that the closest thing we have to it on earth is marriage. When people get married, they stand up in front of a whole bunch of people in a ceremony and pledge to be faithful to someone for the rest of their lives. Then they have the rest of their lives to prove their fidelity.

Baptism is kind of the same thing. Baptism is a public ceremony in which a person stands up in front of a bunch of people to pledge their fidelity to God. Baptism is a promise to the One you love that you will never cheat on Him and will be a good spouse until you die or until the Bridegroom comes back for you.

So why did Jesus need to be baptized? What sin did He commit that needed the waters of baptism to make it clean? Something to think about: baptism is not about having sins washed away as much as it is about submitting to the will of another.

When you give someone the power to hold you underwater, you assume a vulnerable and submissive posture. Baptism is the ultimate expression of submission to God, exemplifying your desire for Him to assume complete control over your life. This is what Jesus was showing us at His baptism. He was saying, "Father, I humbly submit My whole life, everything, to You."

Oct 5

Salt and Light

"You are the salt of the earth, but if salt has lost its taste, how shall its saltiness be restored? It is no longer good for anything except to be thrown out and trampled under people's feet. You are the light of the world. A city set on a hill cannot be hidden. Nor do people light a lamp and put it under a basket, but on a stand, and it gives light to all in the house. In the same way, let your light shine before others, so that they may see your good works and give glory to your Father who is in heaven. **MATTHEW 5:13-16, ESV.**

I love this text because it is true. Jesus doesn't say "You *should* be salt" or "You *should* be light." He says you *are* these things.

Salt is an interesting mineral. When used well, it can really enhance food. When used improperly, it can cause sour looks on otherwise cheerful faces. Light is the same way. When light is used properly, it can create a pleasant experience. When light is used improperly, it can cause people to wince and turn their heads away.

I don't eat eggs very often, but when I do, I like them scrambled. And I like to put just the right amount of salt on them to give them the perfect taste. Eggs without salt are bland. They need salt. But it has to be just the right amount of salt.

One morning while I was in college, my friend thought it would be funny to loosen the cap on the saltshaker at the table in the cafeteria. I came over with my tray, sat down, and attempted to sprinkle salt on my scrambled eggs. Of course, the lid came off, and my eggs got "assaulted." I tried to eat what I could, but it was almost unbearable.

Something similar happened when I would sleep out in the tree house with my friends as a child. Our flashlights came in handy when we needed them, but they were annoying and overwhelming when my friends shone them directly in my eyes in the middle of the night.

Being salt and light can be a good thing or a bad thing. Salt and light used properly can advance God's cause well. But salt and light used improperly can drive people away. Let's season the earth with grace and lighten it with truth in ways that will make God look great.

The Crime That
Was Never Committed

"YOU HAVE HEARD THAT it was said to our people long ago, 'You must not murder anyone. Anyone who murders another will be judged.' But I tell you, if you are angry with a brother or sister, you will be judged. If you say bad things to a brother or sister, you will be judged by the council. And if you call someone a fool, you will be in danger of the fire of hell. . . . You have heard that it was said, 'You must not be guilty of adultery.' But I tell you that if anyone looks at a woman and wants to sin sexually with her, in his mind he has already done that sin with the woman. If your right eye causes you to sin, take it out and throw it away. It is better to lose one part of your body than to have your whole body thrown into hell. If your right hand causes you to sin, cut it off and throw it away. It is better to lose one part of your body than for your whole body to go into hell." **MATTHEW 5:21-30, NCV.**

Some of the most striking words that Jesus shares during the Sermon on the Mount have to do with the intentions of the heart. In the scripture above Jesus is saying that people suffer guilt if they even *desire* to do a horrible thing.

Some friends of ours had a little dog that hated me. I'm not sure what kind of dog it was, but it would bark, charge at me, and try to bite me every time I entered their house. It was the kind of dog that needed to go on a one-way hunting trip, if you know what I mean.

That dog never bit me. But it wanted to. Now, the fact that the dog didn't bite me was a good thing—for me. But I could clearly see what was in the dog's heart and mind. It wanted to take a healthy chunk of skin off the back of my calf muscle. It may not have actually committed the crime, but its heart was right there as if it had.

If you get preoccupied with a sin in your heart, if you keep playing evil things over and over in your mind, you have surrendered yourself to the barbs of that sin just as if you had participated in it. Rehearsing those things in your mind will do damage. And, if you are a human being, beholding something and relishing it for a length of time will eventually change your behavior to mirror your mind. Dwell on good things, and your actions will follow your heart.

OCt 7

The Opposite of Human Nature

"YOU HAVE HEARD THE LAW THAT SAYS, 'Love your neighbor' and hate your enemy. But I say, love your enemies! Pray for those who persecute you! In that way, you will be acting as true children of your Father in heaven. For he gives his sunlight to both the evil and the good, and he sends rain on the just and the unjust alike. If you love only those who love you, what reward is there for that? Even corrupt tax collectors do that much. . . . But you are to be perfect, even as your Father in heaven is perfect." **MATTHEW 5:43-48, NLT.**

Adolf Hitler. Osama bin Laden. Timothy McVeigh. Joseph Stalin. John Wilkes Booth. These are some of the most reviled men in American history. All of them are famous for doing things that make the normal human's blood boil. If anybody on earth has earned the right to be on a list of hated people, these men have earned their spot.

And then along comes Jesus with words that just don't make sense to a normal human being. "Love your enemies and pray for those who persecute you." Are you kidding me? If I were a Jew in Germany during World War II, Jesus would want me to "love" Adolf Hitler? Is that even possible?

Let me ask you a question. Did God love Adolf Hitler? If the answer is yes, then we have to ask the question "Why did God love Adolf Hitler?" The only answer I can think of is that God loves all of His children.

My next-door neighbors had nine kids. Eight of them turned out to be good, responsible citizens. One of them turned out to be an adulterer, a drug addict, a crack dealer, and a thief. The things he did on a daily basis in no way represented the family. In fact, he brought shame to the family name. He fathered children whom he didn't care for. His final act on this earth was to take an accidental overdose of an illegal drug. He died in disgrace on the front-room carpet of a mutual friend.

It's been about 12 years since his death. His mom still misses him and still loves him with the fierce love of a mother. Her love knew no condition.

I think that's God's goal for us. We are to love without condition. We may not like what a person is doing, but treating them with love and praying for them is our calling. Hate is not an option for us as believers.

Listen!

EVERYONE WHO HEARS MY WORDS and obeys them is like a wise man who built his house on rock. It rained hard, the floods came, and the winds blew and hit that house. But it did not fall, because it was built on rock. Everyone who hears my words and does not obey them is like a foolish man who built his house on sand. It rained hard, the floods came, and the winds blew and hit that house, and it fell with a big crash. **MATTHEW 7:24-27, NCV.**

When I lived in Bella Coola, British Columbia, I became acquainted with two brothers, John and Stanley Edwards. Both of them were hermits who lived out in the wilderness up by a place called Lonesome Lake. Every once in a while they would both end up in town for supplies and would catch up with each other. Both were hard of hearing, so one day when I walked into John's little cabin near my in-laws' property, I saw something quite entertaining. John and Stanley were sitting at the table chattering to each other. Both of them were talking about different subjects, but neither of them was listening!

Every once in a while I'll turn on a political news show on FOX, CNN, or one of those networks that really don't give you the news, because they're more focused on telling you what to think about the news. As soon as I do, I regret it, because the Democrats and Republicans are talking over each other and not listening to each other.

Listening—not hearing, but listening—seems to be a dying art in America. How many times have we heard but not listened? How many times have we had to say, "Boy, I wish I had paid more attention to [fill in the blank]"?

Our listening disability translates even to our spiritual lives. Many of us pray and pray and pray, but how many of us take time to listen to the voice of God? We're like Stanley and John. Maybe while we're talking to God, He's trying to talk to us. We can't hear, because we're not listening. But God wants us to hear Him.

God's most radical attempt to get us to hear Him, to listen to Him, was to come in human flesh and dwell among us. At the end of the Sermon on the Mount Jesus reminds us that when we hear His words and do them, we'll be wise followers instead of foolish wanderers.

OCt 9

Meet Jesus' Friends

AS JESUS PASSED ON FROM THERE, he saw a man called Matthew sitting at the tax booth, and he said to him, "Follow me." And he rose and followed him. And as Jesus reclined at table in the house, behold, many tax collectors and sinners came and were reclining with Jesus and his disciples. And when the Pharisees saw this, they said to his disciples, "Why does your teacher eat with tax collectors and sinners?" But when he heard it, he said, "Those who are well have no need of a physician, but those who are sick. Go and learn what this means, 'I desire mercy, and not sacrifice.' For I came not to call the righteous, but sinners." **MATTHEW 9:9-13, ESV.**

Pastor Ira Bartolome is just like Jesus. Well, at least in one respect he is just like Jesus. When I first started at the church I currently pastor, Ira was an associate who had been here for three years. I valued Pastor Ira for lots of reasons, but the thing that impressed me most was his knowledge of the back stories of hundreds of people in our church.

The church I serve is full of medical professionals—eye surgeons, dentists, medical doctors, physical therapists, and others who have been in school longer than most people would ever want to be. Money is not a problem, yet driving by the church and looking in the parking lot would not give an outsider the indication that the attendees are anything but ordinary, average Americans. It's a group of down-to-earth people.

Mixed in with these people who make a good living is a smattering of people who don't. These people struggle with joblessness, chronic illness, substance abuse, or personality quirks that keep them on the fringe of the mainstream. These are the people whom Pastor Ira introduced to me as his friends. These are the people Pastor Ira had a heart for. Often I didn't observe a lot of return on the time he invested in them, yet he loved them and considered it a privilege to minister to their needs—just like Jesus.

When Jesus was in town, He didn't hang out with big money; He usually chose to hang with the people whom society either didn't notice or didn't like. His mission wasn't to the folks who didn't need help; His mission was to touch those who did. He wasn't interested in popularity contests; He was interested in touching the lives of those whom the world had cast aside.

Snooty Christians

JESUS SENT OUT THESE TWELVE men with the following order: "Don't go to the non-Jewish people or to any town where the Samaritans live. But go to the people of Israel, who are like lost sheep. When you go, preach this: 'The kingdom of heaven is near.' Heal the sick, raise the dead to life again, heal those who have skin diseases, and force demons out of people. I give you these powers freely, so help other people freely. Don't carry any money with you—gold or silver or copper. Don't carry a bag or extra clothes or sandals or a walking stick. Workers should be given what they need. When you enter a city or town, find some worthy person there and stay in that home until you leave." **MATTHEW 10:5-11, NCV.**

My friend Paul Dybdahl has a great theory about why Jesus sent the 12 disciples out with no money, no change of clothes, and no food. He thinks that if the disciples walked into a town with none of these things, they would be totally reliant on the generosity of strangers for their well-being. And when we are totally dependent on strangers, we tend to be nicer, less judgmental, and more tolerant.

Conversely, when we have the upper hand, when we think we have the truth that everybody else should be desperate to know, we can act snooty about it. Sometimes we even draw theological lines in the sand and start to think we are better than other people because we are the possessors of golden truth in the midst of a dying world.

When we start to perceive others as less than we are because of what we know or possess, we don't act the way Jesus wanted His disciples to act when He sent them out. Jesus wants us to have a servant mentality when it comes to interacting with those around us. He wants us to be nicer, less judgmental, and more tolerant. When we treat other people as if they are valuable and as if their life and opinions matter to us, they begin to open up and willingly exchange ideas and dialogue.

Nothing shuts an opportunity to dialogue more than a theological know-it-all. People who bring religious superiority to a potential relationship often find themselves wondering where all their friends are.

So here you are. Jesus is sending you out to be the salt of the earth. Why not approach the world with ears to listen and kindness to show? Just like Jesus.

OCL 11

A Day to Do Good

THEN JESUS WENT OVER TO THEIR SYNAGOGUE, where he noticed a man with a deformed hand. The Pharisees asked Jesus, "Does the law permit a person to work by healing on the Sabbath?" (They were hoping he would say yes, so they could bring charges against him.) And he answered, "If you had a sheep that fell into a well on the Sabbath, wouldn't you work to pull it out? Of course you would. And how much more valuable is a person than a sheep! Yes, the law permits a person to do good on the Sabbath." Then he said to the man, "Hold out your hand." So the man held out his hand, and it was restored, just like the other one! Then the Pharisees called a meeting to plot how to kill Jesus. **MATTHEW 12:9-14, NLT.**

Your reading today is dated October 11. That's exciting to me, because it means the fourth weekend in October is coming up! And why does this excite me? Because the fourth weekend in October is the time for national Make a Difference Day! What? You've never heard about Make a Difference Day?

More than 20 years ago a national newspaper, *USA Weekend*, got the idea of challenging Americans to make a difference in their community on the fourth Saturday of October. Their idea has grown into the largest one-day community service event in the United States. Three million people contribute time, money, and effort to making their part of the world a better place on Make a Difference Day each year.

My church takes part in Make a Difference Day too. We don't just participate on Saturday (Sabbath); we take the whole weekend. It's a blessing for our church members and our community. We have groups that bake goodies for our local firefighters and police, people who help the local women's shelter, a group that buys groceries for a single mother and her kids, a group that works with the local animal shelter, a woman who provides a harp concert for a nursing home—all this to become the hands and feet of Jesus in our community, in partnership with everyone else who wants to make a difference.

Jesus made a difference one Sabbath in a man's life when He healed his withered hand. This upset the religious leaders so much that they plotted to kill Him because of it. I want to make a difference in the world just like Jesus, even if it upsets people.

Weeds Get Their Due

JESUS PRESENTED ANOTHER PARABLE to them, saying, "The kingdom of heaven may be compared to a man who sowed good seed in his field. But while his men were sleeping, his enemy came and sowed tares among the wheat, and went away. But when the wheat sprouted and bore grain, then the tares became evident also. The slaves of the landowner came and said to him, 'Sir, did you not sow good seed in your field? How then does it have tares?' And he said to them, 'An enemy has done this!' The slaves said to him, 'Do you want us, then, to go and gather them up?' But he said, 'No; for while you are gathering up the tares, you may uproot the wheat with them. Allow both to grow together until the harvest; and in the time of the harvest I will say to the reapers, "First gather up the tares and bind them in bundles to burn them up; but gather the wheat into my barn."'" **MATTHEW 13:24-30, NASB.**

When I was a kid, I hated weeding more than I hated anything else that a kid could hate. I hated weeding more than I hated spinach. I hated weeding more than I hated having to say "I'm sorry" to my sister. I loathed weeding. Why? Because I have really bad hay fever.

Every time I had to go out and weed, my eyes would water and itch so terribly that I would dig at them and scratch them with my dirty fingers trying to get relief. And then the sneezing would commence. Sometimes I would sneeze 15 times in a row, spraying the weeds with whatever comes out of a 10-year-old's nose. It was awful.

That's why I like Jesus' parable about the weeds. Finally, weeds get what they deserve! I figure I won't have hay fever in heaven, because the weeds are all going to be bundled up and burned at the end of time. No more weeds, no more sneezing, right?

This parable is really a story that tells us that justice is going to be done. Justice is defined (by me) as people getting what they deserve. In this case I suppose it's people getting what they *desire*. In the end some people are going to welcome the Lamb, and some are going to resist His invitation to enjoy eternal life. Those who don't want God's love and presence in their lives are going to hang on to their sin and be consumed with it. Everybody gets what they want in the end. Justice will be served. God will be glorified, and His children will be brought home.

OCT 13

Get Out of the Boat!

ABOUT THREE O'CLOCK IN THE MORNING Jesus came toward them, walking on the water. When the disciples saw him walking on the water, they were terrified. In their fear, they cried out, "It's a ghost!" But Jesus spoke to them at once. "Don't be afraid," he said. "Take courage. I am here!" Then Peter called to him, "Lord, if it's really you, tell me to come to you, walking on the water." "Yes, come," Jesus said. So Peter went over the side of the boat and walked on the water toward Jesus. But when he saw the strong wind and the waves, he was terrified and began to sink. "Save me, Lord!" he shouted. Jesus immediately reached out and grabbed him. "You have so little faith," Jesus said. "Why did you doubt me?" When they climbed back into the boat, the wind stopped. Then the disciples worshiped him. "You really are the Son of God!" they exclaimed. **MATTHEW 14:25-33, NLT.**

The part of this story that I think is the most misunderstood is when Jesus chastises Peter for not having enough faith to keep from sinking. Peter kind of gets a bad reputation for this.

I've decided that Peter isn't the goat but the hero of this story. Can you imagine being tossed around by the whitecaps of the Sea of Galilee, wondering if you'll make it to the other side of the lake, when all of a sudden you look up and see what appears to be a ghost? For the disciples this had to be both confusing and frightening, so much so that they screamed in terror, "Ahhh! It's a ghost!"

And then the ghost speaks. "Hey! It's Me!" This is where my admiration for Peter hits an all-time high.

Peter says, "If it's You, call me out to where You are on the water." See, this is where I have difficulty. I've played too many practical jokes on people. My mind says, "Yeah, but what if it isn't Jesus? What if it's a demon or something? If you step out of the boat and it's not Jesus, you're sunk!"

But Peter acts on his faith and gets out of the boat. The other 11 disciples didn't even try. Sometimes Jesus calls us out of our comfortable boat and into the raging sea. Do you have faith like Peter? When Jesus calls you to step out of your comfort for Him, what will you do?

Fish Food

THE COLLECTORS OF THE TWO-DRACHMA temple tax came to Peter and asked, "Doesn't your teacher pay the temple tax?" "Yes, he does," he replied. When Peter came into the house, Jesus was the first to speak. "What do you think, Simon?" he asked. "From whom do the kings of the earth collect duty and taxes—from their own children or from others?" "From others," Peter answered. "Then the children are exempt," Jesus said to him. "But so that we may not cause offense, go to the lake and throw out your line. Take the first fish you catch; open its mouth and you will find a four-drachma coin. Take it and give it to them for my tax and yours." **MATTHEW 17:24-27.**

Fish eat weird things. In 2010 shark fishermen off the Bahamas caught a large tiger shark. When they gutted it, they found Judson Newton, a novice sailor who had gone missing days earlier.

In 2008 scientists in Greenland were performing an autopsy on a shark and were surprised to find part of a polar bear inside.

In 2012 Suseela Menon went to a Malaysian market to buy a small shark for some stew. When she got home and started to filet it, something hard and shiny fell out. It was a Portuguese medallion, several hundred years old. How this medallion got from the neck of a Portuguese sailor in the 1500s to the stomach of this baby shark, nobody knows.

When I go camping and backpacking, I enjoy throwing a line in the water. Never once have I found anything in the mouth of a fish (other than my hook). It must have been some sight for Peter, a professional fisherman, to find a coin that was worth just enough to pay for Jesus' and Peter's Temple contribution.

I think Jesus' discussion with Peter about the Temple tax is interesting. He made it clear that He would be in the right if He didn't pay the Temple tax to support the work of the priests in the sanctuary. After all, wasn't the whole sacrificial system fulfilled in Jesus?

Jesus could have thumbed His nose at the Temple tax collectors. Instead, He had Peter go and find the money in the most bizarre of places—in the mouth of a fish.

I like *why* Jesus did this miracle. He did it so He wouldn't offend the tax collectors. Jesus never acted selfishly. He always thought of others' needs first.

OCt 15

Plenty of Stuff

JESUS ANSWERED, "IF YOU WANT to be perfect, go, sell your possessions and give to the poor, and you will have treasure in heaven. Then come, follow me." When the young man heard this, he went away sad, because he had great wealth. **MATTHEW 19:21, 22.**

Being rich would be really, really fun. When I was a kid, we used to play a little daydreaming game. Someone would ask, "If you got three wishes from a magic genie, what would you wish for?"

The smart answer, of course, would be to wish for an infinite number of wishes that the genie had to fulfill! But I wasn't that smart. My first answer to that little game was "I would want an endless bank account, so I could never run out of money!" Now, you have to admit, that would be pretty cool!

Possessions have become very important in our society. Actually, they've probably always been important. I mean, from the beginning we've had to protect our belongings with "thou shalt not steal" rules: "Leave my stuff alone or I'll throw you in jail!" We like the things our money has purchased. But then we want more things. After a while, the things we have aren't good enough or new enough to be as cool as other people's things.

Americans are so attached to their things that they spend $22 billion each year on storage units so they can keep all the stuff they don't have room for in their homes or garages!

Some people would describe the American dream as the drive to get an education so that they can get a job so that they can make money so that they can get stuff so that they can play with their stuff—or store it in a big orange building and keep it safe. This may be the American dream, but, as I read the Bible, it doesn't seem to be God's dream for His children.

God has blessed different people with different gifts. Some people are really good at making money. There's nothing wrong with owning stuff. Let's just make sure our priorities are aligned with God's will so that we can use our stuff to glorify Him. Take an inventory of your stuff. How are you using it to enhance your relationship with Him?

Wrecked

JESUS ENTERED THE TEMPLE COURTS and drove out all who were buying and selling there. He overturned the tables of the money changers and the benches of those selling doves. "It is written," he said to them, "'My house will be called a house of prayer,' but you are making it 'a den of robbers.'"
MATTHEW 21:12, 13.

Have you ever witnessed something so unjust that you just had to do something about it?

Dian Fossey was an American zoologist who had an obsession with studying the mountain gorillas in Rwanda, Africa. Her book *Gorillas in the Mist* is still the best-selling book on primates that has ever been written.

When Dian entered the forests of Rwanda to study the gorillas, she soon discovered that people were killing these majestic creatures for profit. Poachers were brutally breaking up the families of these intelligent animals.

Dian decided she needed to take action. It tore her heart out to see this cruelty. The murders of some of her favorite gorillas caused Dian to go militant in preventing poaching. Dian became more radical in protecting the gorillas and devoted less time to studying them: she and her staff cut animal traps; frightened, captured, or embarrassed unsuspecting poachers; took their cattle for ransom; and burned their camps.

Dian Fossey saw an injustice and felt compelled to act. Her actions made some people so mad that they murdered the champion of the gorillas. Her efforts to stop the poachers' cruelty ended up costing Dian her life.

When Jesus walked into the Temple area and saw the money changers taking advantage of the poor and underprivileged, He couldn't keep silent. In a rare display of force, Jesus kicked over tables and chased crooks away. To see His Father's house being used to take advantage of people, to cheat people in the name of God, was too much for Him to take. He stood up to bring justice to an unjust situation. Jesus' actions ended up costing Him His life.

I believe Jesus calls His children to bring justice to an unjust world. What do you see that wrecks you? How can you make a difference in that situation?

OCt 17

Love God, Love Humans

WHEN THE PHARISEES LEARNED that the Sadducees could not argue with Jesus' answers to them, the Pharisees met together. One Pharisee, who was an expert on the law of Moses, asked Jesus this question to test him: "Teacher, which command in the law is the most important?" Jesus answered, "'Love the Lord your God with all your heart, all your soul, and all your mind.' This is the first and most important command. And the second command is like the first: 'Love your neighbor as you love yourself.' All the law and the writings of the prophets depend on these two commands." **MATTHEW 22:34-40, NCV.**

Six hundred thirteen. This is the number of laws that Jews have found in the first five books of the Bible that God's children need to obey. Six hundred thirteen. That's a lot. Some of those laws are obscure: A teenager who curses at their mom or dad is to be dragged out of camp and stoned to death; if you beat your slave so badly that they have to stay in bed for a couple days, it's OK because they are your property; if a woman gives birth to a girl instead of a boy, her time of separation from the community is doubled. These 613 laws were given to a large group of people in the wilderness so they could maintain order in their society and keep physically healthy.

Then Jesus comes to earth and is questioned about the greatest of the 613 laws. Which one is His favorite? I imagine He ponders the question for a moment and then says, "Love God and love your neighbor. All of the 613 hang on these two laws."

I love this answer. It's as if Jesus takes the grand intention for all 613 laws and draws them into a powerful bundle of goodness and love.

As I think of all the laws in the Old Testament that I'm familiar with, the one law that seems to come the closest to Jesus' statement above is the Sabbath law found in the Ten Commandments. It's the perfect union between love for God and love for your fellow humans. The first part of the commandment sets aside time for human beings to recognize God's creative power and worship Him for who He is. The second part of the commandment asks you to give anyone within your sphere of influence the chance to do the same. Loving God and loving others enough to give them the chance to love Him too is the heart of the fourth commandment. No wonder the Bible describes the Sabbath as a special sign between humans and God.

OCT 18

What Makes Jesus Angry

WOE TO YOU, TEACHERS OF THE LAW and Pharisees, you hypocrites! You shut the door of the kingdom of heaven in people's faces. You yourselves do not enter, nor will you let those enter who are trying to. Woe to you, teachers of the law and Pharisees, you hypocrites! You travel over land and sea to win a single convert, and when you have succeeded, you make them twice as much a child of hell as you are. **MATTHEW 23:13-15.**

Strong words. When we read them, they're almost shocking. In the Gospels we don't see Jesus speaking to people this way very often. Did He wake up on the wrong side of the bed that particular morning? Was He just having a bad day at the office?

As you look at Jesus' life, you'll notice that there were some things that got under His skin. There were situations that upset Him and caused Him to react in, shall we say, more passionate ways than He did in normal life circumstances.

Jesus got upset when He saw religion taking advantage of people who were trying to be near God. It just wrecked Him to see religious people treat His lambs as if they were a nuisance. He couldn't handle it when God's children were made to feel guilty and abandoned by the very religion that was supposed to lead people to the Father and clarify His love for them.

This was the very thing Jesus witnessed when He entered the Temple and saw the money changers (robbers) stealing from the poor, making them somehow buy their way into God's graces. That injustice caused Him to go ballistic with the whip, kicking over tables and clearing the place that was meant for people to come together in peace to pray. And in today's verses, when confronted by the pastors and teachers of His day, He rebuked them for misrepresenting God by the way they were treating His people. The names that Jesus painted them with were highly offensive and meant to be that way. He wanted them to know that they had no business kicking people to the curb because they weren't as "holy" as the leaders thought they should be. They had turned religion from a pathway to peace and joy into a burden that people had to bear.

As ambassadors for Jesus, may we always use religion to lead people to Jesus.

OCt 19

The End According to Jesus

BUT IMMEDIATELY AFTER THE TRIBULATION of those days the sun will be darkened, and the moon will not give its light, and the stars will fall from the sky, and the powers of the heavens will be shaken. And then the sign of the Son of Man will appear in the sky, and then all the tribes of the earth will mourn, and they will see the Son of Man coming on the clouds of the sky with power and great glory. **MATTHEW 24:29, 30, NASB.**

When my mom started taking church really seriously, she became enamored with all things end of the world. She loved prophecy and wanted to know as much as she could about it. Consequently, she would tell my sister and me dramatic stories about how the world around us was going to collapse and we would have to run for our lives from the bad people who wanted to harm God's people. She said we'd have to flee into the hills and hide in caves to avoid being captured and killed by those who didn't like how we were worshipping. She even bought a book on how to eat in the wilderness and survive in any type of weather.

This kind of stuff fascinated me when I was a little tyke. Like many young boys, I loved the thought of outsmarting the bad guys, living off the land, and sneaking through the woods. So it didn't dawn on me that the little friend I made on a beach vacation wouldn't be thrilled at the thought of the time of trouble.

As we walked on the beach, I was telling him all about it, when I noticed he was crying. I asked him what was the matter. In tearful tones he said, "I don't want Jesus to come back! All this stuff scares me!"

I'm pretty sure that was *not* the effect Jesus intended to have on His listeners as He talked about the end of all things. As we study what He said, we realize that Matthew 24 parallels the seven seals of Revelation. Jesus was describing how the church would go downhill so drastically that it would actually start persecuting those who didn't fall in line with its erroneous ways. And He predicted that this misrepresentation of the Father would continue until Jesus comes back to rescue His own.

The prophecies in the Bible shouldn't scare us. They should give us hope. Remember, it's Jesus who's coming back to get us. We don't ever have to fear Him.

Wise Young Women

THEN THE KINGDOM OF HEAVEN will be comparable to ten virgins, who took their lamps and went out to meet the bridegroom. Five of them were foolish, and five were prudent. **MATTHEW 25:1, 2, NASB.**

I know some pretty wise people. I try to rely on them for life direction and good advice when I need it.

In this parable there are five wise virgins and five foolish virgins. So the question we've got to ask is What makes the wise virgins wise and the foolish virgins foolish? Did the foolish virgins put tomatoes in their fruit salad?

As we look at this parable, we see that the wise virgins make it into the wedding party, and the foolish ones end up gnashing their teeth (something I really want to see someone do before I die) and having a really bad day on the outside of a closed door. Why? What did the foolish virgins do wrong, and what did the wise virgins do right?

A look into the story reveals the fact that five of the virgins had extra oil, and five of the virgins didn't. They all had oil in the first part of the parable, but after having to wait a long time, five of them ran out. Were they foolish because they ran out of oil? After all, people surely ran out of oil for their lamps all the time back in the day.

When you think about it, all 10 virgins were doing the same thing: they were all waiting for the Bridegroom. The difference was that five of the virgins thought He was going to come really soon. Five of the virgins thought He *might* come soon, but just in case He didn't, they should prepare for the long haul.

Jesus is coming soon. I hope He comes *very* soon. But I'd better be prepared to be here for the long haul just in case. Wise people concentrate on their relationship with Jesus each day as if it were their last day on earth. Wise people don't try to predict when He's coming back, because they are too busy serving Him today. Foolish people get burned out and run out of patience. Don't be a foolish virgin.

OCt 21

Afraid of the Master

AND THE ONE ALSO WHO had received the one talent came up and said, "Master, I knew you to be a hard man, reaping where you did not sow and gathering where you scattered no seed. And I was afraid, and went away and hid your talent in the ground. See, you have what is yours." **MATTHEW 25:24, 25, NASB.**

Doug Bing is one of my bosses in my church organization. When pastors on my staff are called to work in another district, he's the person who finds a replacement to recommend to my church and to the governing body that operates the churches in our conference. Doug is good at what he does, and I like him a lot.

Doug is also a naughty man. Well, at least he was for a moment. We were in the process of looking for a new associate pastor, and Doug had given me the name of a guy he was going to contact and give the thumbs up to move into our district. According to protocol, Doug would meet with an executive committee and affirm the call. Doug would call the new pastor and tell him the news, and then I'd call the pastor and welcome him into our church.

I was overexcited about the new hire, so I called and told him all the stuff Doug was supposed to tell him before Doug called. When Doug found out that I had jumped ahead of the game, he called me and ripped into me for about two minutes on the phone. I felt so embarrassed and horrible until Doug started laughing and said, "Just kidding. You give me a hard time all the time, so I figured it was my turn." Whew! What a relief.

This was the man I knew him to be. I'm glad that the guy I admired and respected turned out to be the guy I admired and respected!

In the parable in Matthew 25 the man with one talent projected qualities onto the Master that just weren't true. Often when we make God out to be something He's not, we end up with everything we projected Him to be, not because He is those things, but because we suppose Him to be those things. There's a danger that we could become like the people in the book of Revelation who are afraid of the wrath of the Lamb. Can you imagine being afraid of a lamb?

The Goat Hole

BUT WHEN THE SON OF MAN comes in His glory, and all the angels with Him, then He will sit on His glorious throne. All the nations will be gathered before Him; and He will separate them from one another, as the shepherd separates the sheep from the goats; and He will put the sheep on His right, and the goats on the left. **MATTHEW 25:31-33, NASB.**

I pastor the best church in the whole world, period. There is no argument that anyone can make to disprove this fact. OK, I admit I may be a little bit biased. But I have good reason!

The other day I was sitting in an office with two administrators of a community action organization that serves our whole county. The sole purpose of this organization is to feed, clothe, house, and otherwise minister to the needs of the poor in our community. And they are really good at what they do.

As I sat there in the office with these two administrators, they said, "We are so thankful for your church. Your community outreach team has their hands in almost everything we do in this community. If your church ever went away, we wouldn't be able to serve the community the way we do."

Hearing that from these saintly women made me smile. It made me smile because if I were to judge whether the people in my church were sheep or goats, I'd choose sheep—at least based on this parable.

When I was a principal, we had to cut down a huge tree in our school courtyard so we could expand our building to accommodate growth. One of the teachers was in love with that tree. The day before we cut it down, she took a picture of it, framed it, and gave it to me with a note: "You will go to the goat hole for cutting down this tree!" Of course, she was joking . . . I hope.

According to Jesus, the goat hole is reserved for the devil and his angels—and those people on this earth who are so self-centered that they don't give a hoot about their fellow humans. Goat-hole people walk past suffering humanity without a thought.

Sheep people, on the other hand, become the hands and feet of Jesus. They make it their business to show the Father by offering His gentle touch—just like Jesus.

OCt 23

Passover Lamb

ON THE FIRST DAY OF THE FESTIVAL of Unleavened Bread, the disciples came to Jesus and asked, "Where do you want us to prepare the Passover meal for you?" "As you go into the city," he told them, "you will see a certain man. Tell him, 'The Teacher says: My time has come, and I will eat the Passover meal with my disciples at your house.'"

So the disciples did as Jesus told them and prepared the Passover meal there. When it was evening, Jesus sat down at the table with the twelve disciples. . . . As they were eating, Jesus took some bread and blessed it. Then he broke it in pieces and gave it to the disciples, saying, "Take this and eat it, for this is my body." And he took a cup of wine and gave thanks to God for it. He gave it to them and said, "Each of you drink from it, for this is my blood, which confirms the covenant between God and his people. It is poured out as a sacrifice to forgive the sins of many. Mark my words—I will not drink wine again until the day I drink it new with you in my Father's Kingdom." **MATTHEW 26:17-29, NLT.**

Did you know that Jesus knew the exact date and time of His death? How did He know? Jesus knew His Bible. He knew that every significant teaching in the Old Testament pointed to Him. He knew that He was the Passover Lamb. He knew the year He was going to die based on the prophecies in Daniel 9 (which gave the exact year that Messiah would be "cut off"), and He knew that He would likely die at the same time that the Passover lamb was killed in Jerusalem.

So what did Jesus leave with His followers as a last message before He died? He used an amazing and beautiful object lesson to show His disciples who He is. He held up the bread and said, "This is my body given for you" (Luke 22:19). He held up the cup and said, "This is my blood of the covenant." In other words Jesus said that He is our Passover Lamb. When we believe in Him, we have passed from death to life. He is the blood on the doorposts of our hearts.

He asked the disciples to remember this fact whenever they ate the bread and drank from the cup. In our tradition we call it the Lord's Supper or Communion. When we eat and drink it, we celebrate Jesus as our Passover Lamb.

Mental Anguish

THEN JESUS WENT WITH THEM to a place called Gethsemane, and he said to his disciples, "Sit here, while I go over there and pray." And taking with him Peter and the two sons of Zebedee, he began to be sorrowful and troubled. Then he said to them, "My soul is very sorrowful, even to death; remain here, and watch with me." And going a little farther he fell on his face and prayed, saying, "My Father, if it be possible, let this cup pass from me; nevertheless, not as I will, but as you will." And he came to the disciples and found them sleeping. And he said to Peter, "So, could you not watch with me one hour?. . . Again, for the second time, he went away and prayed, "My Father, if this cannot pass unless I drink it, your will be done." And again he came and found them sleeping, for their eyes were heavy. So, leaving them again, he went away and prayed for the third time, saying the same words again. **MATTHEW 26:36-44, ESV.**

There is no greater pain than mental anguish. Give me physical pain before mental anguish any day of the week. The death of a family member, rejection from a lover, betrayal by a friend, being a Seattle sports fan . . . all these things produce an ache in the heart that is deeper than any physical pain.

It seems like a millennium ago that I was 19 years old and crying on my old bed in my mother's house. Why was I crying? Because a girl named Ruth had broken my heart. I was sure I was in love with her. I had our futures planned out. It was a relationship made in heaven! And then she dumped me. While we were in South Dakota. For an ex-boyfriend. I went home, cried deep tears, and felt like dying.

Jesus was going through more than mere rejection from someone He was infatuated with. Jesus was taking on the sins of the world, your sins and mine, and He faced the threat that those sins would separate Him from the Father. This struck terror into the heart of the Son of God. He begged for the cup to pass from Him.

But He knew that He and the Father had a task. They must rescue us from the one who had kidnapped humanity way back in the Garden of Eden. Jesus was willing to face this mental torment for us because He would rather die than live without us.

OCt 25

Living a Double Life

NOW PETER WAS SITTING OUTSIDE in the courtyard, and a servant-girl came to him and said, "You too were with Jesus the Galilean." But he denied it before them all, saying, "I do not know what you are talking about." When he had gone out to the gateway, another servant-girl saw him and said to those who were there, "This man was with Jesus of Nazareth." And again he denied it with an oath, "I do not know the man." A little later the by-standers came up and said to Peter, "Surely you too are one of them; for even the way you talk gives you away." Then he began to curse and swear, "I do not know the man!" And immediately a rooster crowed. And Peter remembered the word which Jesus had said, "Before a rooster crows, you will deny Me three times." And he went out and wept bitterly. **MATTHEW 26:69-75, NASB.**

When I was in high school, I had a friend who had the ability to turn God on and off in his life in the blink of an eye. When I first got to know him, I had the distinct impression that he was a conservative (even prudish) religious person who was sold out on what he believed in. He was always up front leading out in religious programs and was generally regarded as a young person who loved God and wasn't afraid to show that love in front of others.

Then one Saturday evening I was with some neighborhood friends who didn't attend the Christian school I was attending. These friends wanted to go to a party. I knew this was the kind of party that my parents and teachers wouldn't approve of, but I didn't have a very good moral compass at the time, so I went along.

When we got to the party, I was stunned to see the young man from my school who was such a spiritual icon participating in things that flew directly in the face of who he professed to be. This young man acted one way in front of one group of people and another way in front of another group. He was what we call two-faced.

Peter wanted to be brave and stand up for Jesus, but because of the people around him, he changed his behavior to reflect his surroundings instead of ac-knowledging Jesus. This ended up causing him much pain. How much better would it be for us to stay true to the One we believe in on all occasions?

Rescue From the Kidnapper

AT NOON, DARKNESS FELL across the whole land until three o'clock. At about three o'clock, Jesus called out with a loud voice, "Eli, Eli, lema sabachthani?" which means "My God, my God, why have you abandoned me?" Some of the bystanders misunderstood and thought he was calling for the prophet Elijah. One of them ran and filled a sponge with sour wine, holding it up to him on a reed stick so he could drink. But the rest said, "Wait! Let's see whether Elijah comes to save him." Then Jesus shouted out again, and he released his spirit. **MATTHEW 27:45-50, NLT.**

The Crucifixion is one of the most misunderstood events in the history of the universe. Many of my Christian friends see the cross as a way to pay off an angry God and prevent Him from killing His children for having broken His divine law. Instead of viewing the cross and God in this light, imagine with me another scenario . . .

You are the parent of a beautiful young daughter who is the apple of your eye. You love her more than you love your own life. In your house you have some rules: clean your room, put away your messy dishes, and don't talk to strangers—reasonable commandments for the household, to be sure.

One day your daughter is outside a local gas station while you are paying for your fuel inside. While she waits, a man engages her in conversation, eventually luring her into his van. He kidnaps her and does unspeakable things to her.

At the moment you realize this has happened, what are your thoughts about your daughter? Do you think, *My daughter has broken one of the rules that I set in my house. When I find her and get her back, I'm going to punish her for her disobedience!* Or would your thoughts be more accurately described as *Someone has kidnapped my daughter! I will go through hell and high water to get her back, and when I find her, I'll nurture her and heal her from the pain she has experienced at the hands of her kidnapper!*

The cross is God's ultimate expression of love and forgiveness. It is God's way of reclaiming this world and its inhabitants. God's forgiveness preceded the cross, and His love was magnified for us on the cross.

Oct 27

The Undead

THE DAY AFTER THE SABBATH DAY was the first day of the week. At dawn on the first day, Mary Magdalene and another woman named Mary went to look at the tomb. At that time there was a strong earthquake. An angel of the Lord came down from heaven, went to the tomb, and rolled the stone away from the entrance. Then he sat on the stone. . . . The soldiers guarding the tomb shook with fear because of the angel, and they became like dead men. The angel said to the women, "Don't be afraid. I know that you are looking for Jesus, who has been crucified. He is not here. He has risen from the dead as he said he would. . . . The women left the tomb quickly. They were afraid, but they were also very happy. They ran to tell Jesus' followers what had happened. Suddenly, Jesus met them and said, "Greetings." The women came up to him, took hold of his feet, and worshiped him. Then Jesus said to them, "Don't be afraid. Go and tell my followers to go on to Galilee, and they will see me there." **MATTHEW 28:1-10, NCV.**

Hollywood is infatuated with movies about zombies and the undead. Usually these movies have gory images of people fresh out of the grave walking around all decayed, looking menacing and threatening. There are whole video game series dedicated to eradicating the undead from the earth. I believe Satan has done everything he can to turn the thought of resurrection into something scary and gory.

The Bible never pictures resurrection as anything to be afraid of. In fact, resurrection is linked to our only hope of getting out of this world alive! The zombie apocalypse is going to happen, but on a much grander scale than Hollywood could ever dream up! The Bible says that when we come out of our graves, we will receive new bodies that will never decay and that will experience eternal life, not eternal death. We won't be limping around the world to consume our living neighbors; we will be lifted to heaven in glory to be with our best Friend!

All this is possible, of course, because of God's unending love for His children and because of Jesus' resurrection as the firstfruits of what is yet to come.

Jesus' resurrection caught everyone by surprise. The soldiers ended up like dead men, the women who came to the tomb were startled by the announcing angel, and the disciples were all in disbelief—and this after Jesus had told them time after time that He would rise again. Jesus promises us new, resurrected bodies one day soon. We can bank on that promise.

OCt 28

Not So Scary Anymore

AFTER HE SAID THIS, he was taken up before their very eyes, and a cloud hid him from their sight. They were looking intently up into the sky as he was going, when suddenly two men dressed in white stood beside them. "Men of Galilee," they said, "why do you stand here looking into the sky? This same Jesus, who has been taken from you into heaven, will come back in the same way you have seen him go into heaven." **ACTS 1:9-11.**

first saw Holden when he was just 1 year old. Now he's 4, and until last weekend in church he was afraid of me.

Every time I tried to speak with Holden, he'd look at me with frightened eyes and hide behind his mother. Every time I tried to tease him, he'd cry. Once I tried to pick him up, and he started to scream, wriggled from my hands, and ran the other direction. I couldn't figure out why Holden was afraid of me, because most of the kids in church think I'm a nice man. (Well, I am six feet six inches and 220 pounds.)

Last weekend everything changed. I was sitting at potluck with Holden's mom, Julie, enjoying a great meal and a meaningful conversation, when I felt something I wasn't expecting. Holden was holding my hand. And before I knew it, Holden was sitting on my lap.

We started to play and laugh together, and eventually Holden was kissing my cheek and giggling. I looked at Julie and said, "Where is all this coming from? This kid has been terrified of me for three years, and now I'm his best friend?"

Julie looked at me and said, "Well, once he got to know you, you weren't so scary anymore."

A lot of people are terrified of the Second Coming. They're afraid to face the One who they believe is coming back to this earth to exact judgment on fallen humanity. People who are afraid of the Second Coming can take solace in Acts 1:11. "This same Jesus" is the one who is coming back. It's the same Jesus whom the disciples saw every day, walking and talking, healing and restoring. This same Jesus is the one who is returning. When you get to know Him, He's not scary at all. In fact, you may want to crawl up on His lap and give Him a kiss.

OCt 29

The Gift of Gibberish?

WHEN THE DAY OF PENTECOST arrived, they were all together in one place. And suddenly there came from heaven a sound like a mighty rushing wind, and it filled the entire house where they were sitting. And divided tongues as of fire appeared to them and rested on each one of them. And they were all filled with the Holy Spirit and began to speak in other tongues as the Spirit gave them utterance. **ACTS 2:1-4, ESV.**

When I was in my early 20s, I went through a phase of church hopping. I hadn't yet settled on the church I wanted to be a part of, so I decided to visit lots of different churches to see what was out there. I had some pretty eye-opening experiences, but none of them more illuminating than my speaking-in-tongues experience.

I was sitting in a church with thousands of people as a popular speaker sermonized on the topic of speaking in tongues. It was a well-crafted and convincing sermon that basically said, "If you aren't speaking in tongues, you aren't born again."

I wanted to be born again, because I had fallen in love with Jesus. So I went up front after the meeting and found the preacher. I said, "I love Jesus very much, but I don't speak in tongues. Do you think Jesus wants me to have this spiritual gift?"

"Yes, I know He does," said the speaker. "Would you like to speak in tongues right now?" I told him that I did if Jesus wanted me to.

We knelt down, and he told me to start to pray, asking God to give me this spiritual gift. I did. In English. While I prayed the preacher started speaking in gibberish, pressing his hand on my forehead. Nothing happened. I didn't start to speak in gibberish as he did.

After several minutes of my failed attempt at speaking in tongues (as he would have defined it) we quit, and he said, "Go home, and instead of praying, practice running a bunch of consonants together. After a while you'll get used to it, and it will become your prayer language." I decided not to follow his advice.

Obviously, the gift of tongues in Acts 2 was different than my pastor friend suggested. Every spiritual gift is given to enhance our understanding of God's character and build the kingdom of God. Anything else may be a counterfeit.

OCt 30

Walking and Leaping and Praising God

BUT PETER SAID, "I have no silver and gold, but what I do have I give to you. In the name of Jesus Christ of Nazareth, rise up and walk!" And he took him by the right hand and raised him up, and immediately his feet and ankles were made strong. And leaping up he stood and began to walk, and entered the temple with them, walking and leaping and praising God. And all the people saw him walking and praising God, and recognized him as the one who sat at the Beautiful Gate of the temple, asking for alms. And they were filled with wonder and amazement at what had happened to him. **ACTS 3:6-10, ESV.**

I was walking through my church one day when one of the members, Kaarsten Lang, looked at my gait and said, "Why are you limping? What happened to you?"

I had been on a seven-mile hike the week before, and because of previous injuries to my poor, tattered knee, it was hyperextended and swelled up like a grapefruit. "I've dislocated my kneecap several times," I explained, "and now it gives me fits from time to time. It feels like something is stuck in the joint, and I can't move it freely."

Kaarsten is an orthopedic surgeon. And a former high school classmate. I knew I wasn't getting out of this situation without a knife to my knee! Sure enough, she offered, "Why don't you let me operate on it? I can clean all that stuff up for you!"

"Sure!" I said. "Let's get my knee fixed!"

Dr. Kaarsten ordered an MRI, looked at the pictures, and showed me all the little creepy-crawlies that were moving around in my 50-year-old knee. She said, "I can get in there and get all those bits and pieces out in no time flat."

She was right—the operation was easy. But the recovery was another story. I spent weeks limping around with a cane before I was able to walk without discomfort. All from a little, tiny outpatient robotic surgery.

It would have been so much easier to have Peter walk up to me and say, "Silver and gold have I none, but what I have I give you. In the name of Jesus Christ, be healed!"

Knowing Dr. Kaarsten's heart for hurting and injured people, I know she'd love to have the spiritual gift of instant healing. In the meantime her gifted touch allowed me to jump and leap and praise the Lord—it just took a few extra weeks.

OCT 31

From Wimp to Powerhouse

NOW WHEN THEY SAW the boldness of Peter and John, and perceived that they were uneducated, common men, they were astonished. And they recognized that they had been with Jesus. But seeing the man who was healed standing beside them, they had nothing to say in opposition. But when they had commanded them to leave the council, they conferred with one another, saying, "What shall we do with these men? For that a notable sign has been performed through them is evident to all the inhabitants of Jerusalem, and we cannot deny it. But in order that it may spread no further among the people, let us warn them to speak no more to anyone in this name." So they called them and charged them not to speak or teach at all in the name of Jesus. But Peter and John answered them, "Whether it is right in the sight of God to listen to you rather than to God, you must judge, for we cannot but speak of what we have seen and heard." **ACTS 4:13-20, ESV.**

What an amazing contrast we see here between Peter and, well, Peter. Just a few weeks earlier Peter was denying that he even knew Jesus! Just a few weeks earlier he heard that rooster crow and ran out of the courtyard weeping because he had denied the very One he thought he would die for.

And now? Now he's willing to go through brutal beatings, verbal ridicule, and even death for his Best Friend. What happened? What made the cowering, scared-for-his-life disciple bold enough to stand in the face of the rulers and say, "Which is right in God's eyes: to listen to you, or to him? You be the judges! As for us, we cannot help speaking about what we have seen and heard."

I'd like to suggest that Peter's power came from experiencing forgiveness. Do you remember the story? In John 21, after the Resurrection, Jesus summons Peter to walk on the beach with Him. During this painful conversation courage is kindled, a friendship is healed, and a leader is built. Jesus knows that Peter denied Him three times. So three times Jesus asks Peter to confirm his love for his Master. It's as if Jesus is trying to undo what Peter had done in denying Him.

Peter returned from that walk a forgiven man. Forgiveness gives people the power to live again. It gives people the courage to live up to their high calling. It takes off shackles and releases into ministry. Peter, the forgiven, was able to stand up to the religious bullies of his day and stand up for the Jesus he had previously denied.

310

Off to a Good Start

THE APOSTLES WERE PERFORMING many miraculous signs and wonders among the people. And all the believers were meeting regularly at the Temple in the area known as Solomon's Colonnade. . . . Yet more and more people believed and were brought to the Lord—crowds of both men and women. As a result of the apostles' work, sick people were brought out into the streets on beds and mats so that Peter's shadow might fall across some of them as he went by. Crowds came from the villages around Jerusalem, bringing their sick and those possessed by evil spirits, and they were all healed. **ACTS 5:12-16, NLT.**

I love the picture of how the church began to form. As you read these texts, can you feel the excitement? This was something new and refreshing, inventive and exhilarating. These were not the stale old religious traditions that had been a drudgery for years in Israel. Things were happening, people were being healed, the members of the community were looking out for one another, and people were stirred up about the fact that the Messiah had come.

Look at the ingredients that made the early church so cool:

1. They spent a lot of time together. Believers in Jesus had no church to meet in. They weren't welcome in the synagogues. Their homes weren't capable of handling large crowds, so they met on the east side of the Temple under Solomon's Colonnade—a kind of porch just outside the Temple courts. And they didn't meet just one day of the week as most Christians do; they met daily. What a concept for a church, huh?

2. They were generous. As you read these early chapters of Acts, you realize that nobody needed to pass the offering plate around. Everybody just came together and gave what they could to help the cause and take care of one another's needs.

3. They multiplied! Because of these factors, the early Christians added to their number daily.

What would happen if a church today sold all its buildings and properties and met in a public place to worship God every day? And what would happen if those believers, instead of taking up offerings for this or that, brought their possessions to advance the gospel and to help meet one another's needs? Would you go to a church like that?

NOV 2

Religious Killers

BUT STEPHEN WAS FULL OF THE HOLY SPIRIT. He looked up to heaven and saw the glory of God and Jesus standing at God's right side. He said, "Look! I see heaven open and the Son of Man standing at God's right side." Then they shouted loudly and covered their ears and all ran at Stephen. They took him out of the city and began to throw stones at him to kill him. . . . While they were throwing stones, Stephen prayed, "Lord Jesus, receive my spirit." He fell on his knees and cried in a loud voice, "Lord, do not hold this sin against them." After Stephen said this, he died. **ACTS 7:55-60, NCV.**

Jesus saw this coming. He told His disciples, "They will put you out of the synagogue; in fact, a time is coming when anyone who kills you will think they are offering a service to God" (John 16:2). What kind of religious people would get so riled up about their picture of God that they would actually want to do another person harm because of it? And what kind of picture of the Father do you suppose the Jewish leaders had that would cause them to get angry enough to kill in His name?

All too often we see in the news a story about a person in the Middle East strapping a bomb to his chest and walking into a crowded market. Often before he hits the trigger mechanism he will yell out, "For the glory of God!" Really? Your picture of God is so warped that you would actually kill people in His name?

Some people would ascribe this kind of sick behavior only to those in the radical Muslim world. But Christians have done their fair share of killing in the name of God too. In fact, the church of the Middle Ages persecuted and killed other Christians in the name of God.

But we would never do that, right?

Jesus in the Sermon on the Mount tells us that if we even hate someone else, we are guilty of murder. Ouch. I see it every day in churches and schools. People killing each other with hurtful words, gossip, and mean looks.

Stephen was the first of many martyrs to give up his life for what he believed. Is there anything you can think of that you believe in so much that you would actually lay down your life for it?

A Dip in the River

AS THEY TRAVELED ALONG THE ROAD, they came to some water and the eunuch said, "Look, here is water. What can stand in the way of my being baptized?" And he gave orders to stop the chariot. Then both Philip and the eunuch went down into the water and Philip baptized him. **ACTS 8:36-38.**

I love baptisms. I think baptism is one of the most meaningful rituals we observe in the Christian tradition. Through the years I've had people ask me to baptize them. My response to their request is always, "Why? Why do you want to be baptized?"

I've gotten various responses to my question. Some have said that they felt they were old enough to be baptized, and they just figured it was time to do it because of their age. I've had others tell me that they wanted to be baptized because their friends were getting baptized. These are not the answers I'm looking for.

Baptism and marriage have a lot in common. A marriage ceremony doesn't happen on the same day you meet your mate (unless you're in Vegas). Usually a person takes time to fall in love with the future husband or wife before the ceremony. Then two people stand up in front of friends and family and pledge their love to each other.

Baptism is the same idea. You meet and get to know and trust Jesus. At some point you discover He's proposed to you, and you say yes to Him. Then you stand with Him at your baptism and commit to follow Him and be faithful to Him as long as you shall live.

If we treated getting married the way we treat making a decision for baptism, things would be awkward. If my prospective wife were to ask me why I wanted to marry her, and my answer was "Because I figured I'm old enough to get married now" or "Well, all my friends are getting married, so I figured I should too," I'm pretty sure I wouldn't ever get married. At least not to my wife.

Baptism is the public sealing of a sacred romance between me and the God I love. The Ethiopian man fell in love with Jesus and wanted to be baptized as a sign of love and submission to the One he loved.

NOV 4

Deceived or Defiant?

BUT SAUL, STILL BREATHING THREATS and murder against the disciples of the Lord, went to the high priest and asked him for letters to the synagogues at Damascus, so that if he found any belonging to the Way, men or women, he might bring them bound to Jerusalem. Now as he went on his way, he approached Damascus, and suddenly a light from heaven flashed around him. And falling to the ground he heard a voice saying to him, "Saul, Saul, why are you persecuting me?" **ACTS 9:1-4, ESV.**

There are at least two kinds of sin. One kind of sin happens when you know something is wrong and you choose to do it anyway. The other kind of sin is committed by a person who has no idea that they are doing something against the will of God.

To illustrate, when my son was 2 years old, he quickly learned the meaning of the word *no*. If he reached out to touch something he wasn't supposed to touch, or if he looked as if he was going to throw the food on his highchair, a sharp "NO!" from his mother or me would curtail his evil intent. My son was not openly defiant at that early age, so a quick "NO!" usually did the trick.

One afternoon I was downstairs watching the news with my son. It was cold out, so we had the fireplace on. He held the remote control for the TV in his hand as he toddled around the room. Then I saw him stop and look at the fire, look at the remote control, look at the fire . . . the little wheels in his head were turning fast. He looked at me, and I said, "NO!" He squinted his eyes, turned around, and threw the remote in the fireplace. Open defiance!

I don't believe this was the case with Saul. I think Saul was just deceived. In his mind he was serving the Lord with all his heart. He was so zealous that he was willing to kill in the name of God. He was so zealous that God had to knock him off a horse to get his attention.

Being zealous in our beliefs can be a good thing. But any time we believe so zealously that we despise those who don't believe as we do—well, let's just pray that we can come to our senses before God has to knock us off our high horse.

The Lie of Prejudice

HE SAW HEAVEN OPENED AND something like a large sheet being let down to earth by its four corners. It contained all kinds of four-footed animals, as well as reptiles and birds. Then a voice told him, "Get up, Peter. Kill and eat." **ACTS 10:11-13.**

I grew up with a prejudiced mind. It was given me by my culture. I was born into a middle-class White neighborhood in the very early 1960s, when racial division was the norm. White people went to White places, and Black people went to Black places. Black people were not called African-Americans or Blacks or Negroes; the names I grew up with for folks with darker skin than I had were derogatory and mean-spirited.

And then I got into my junior high years and started playing a lot of basketball. On the outdoor basketball court I was the minority. I was lily-white, and when I ran hard, my cheeks would get red. All the Black kids called me Rosie. "Wooo! Rosie can jump! Look at that! Rosie can score!" I didn't mind the nickname.

Then I started college and became best friends with Marie. Marie and I were talking one day, and she mentioned that America was still prejudiced. I told her, "We live in the 1980s now. People aren't prejudiced anymore." She told me that I needed to watch the news through her eyes just one time. So we did.

Marie pointed out that each time the news anchor described a crime committed by a White man, the anchor referred to the perpetrator as "a man." But whenever the crime was committed by a Black man, the news anchor described the suspect as "a Black man." In other words, a normal man was White. This made an impression on me.

Peter had been told all his life that non-Jews were not his equals. He had been taught not to touch or associate with them. The Jews thought that only they could be saved.

Peter's vision should be our vision. Peter learned that God has called all people clean. The Bible says that Jesus "wants all people to be saved" (1 Timothy 2:4). For us to label any group of human beings as "less than" because of the color of their skin, their religion, or whom they may be attracted to would be to deny God's vision for our lives. God loves everyone, even you. Why not extend that love to everyone too?

NOV 6

Angels in the Flames

SUDDENLY AN ANGEL OF THE LORD appeared and a light shone in the cell. He struck Peter on the side and woke him up. "Quick, get up!" he said, and the chains fell off Peter's wrists. Then the angel said to him, "Put on your clothes and sandals." And Peter did so. "Wrap your cloak around you and follow me," the angel told him. Peter followed him out of the prison. **ACTS 12:7-9.**

Lee Price is my huggie buddy. I call him that because every weekend in church I walk up to him and make him give me a hug. I'm not sure he enjoys that part of his church experience, but I do, because I think I'm the only person he hugs. He's actually getting pretty good at it, too!

One day I asked my huggie buddy if he thought an angel had ever bailed him out of a dire situation. He had a quick answer.

Lee and his brother worked for the Great Northern Railway back in the 1960s. Lee was a section laborer. The two of them were assigned to help put out a fire that the railroad had accidently started on Blanchard Mountain near Bellingham, Washington.

They were following a bulldozer that was cutting a fire trail up the steep side of the mountain, when the fire jumped a barrier and crowned (spread into the treetops) right on top of Lee and his brother. They had no water left to shoot at the fire and nowhere to run. Suffocating from the smoke, they hunkered down behind a ridge to escape the flames. They were sure they were toast. But somehow the fire burned right over them and left them unscathed like Shadrach, Meshach, and Abednego. Lee has no explanation but to say his angels were watching over him.

Peter was in a bad way. He was in prison, not knowing his fate. Maybe he'd get a beating. They might even crucify him. But God still had plans for Peter. An angel appeared and saved him from a bad situation. Angels are really good at that.

I'm glad Peter was rescued from prison. I'm glad an angel rescued my huggie buddy, too. And I know my angels have rescued me time and time again. I can't wait to get to heaven and hear the rescue stories about situations I'm not even aware of where my angel intervened!

Singing for Your Enemies

AROUND MIDNIGHT PAUL AND SILAS were praying and singing hymns to God, and the other prisoners were listening. Suddenly, there was a massive earthquake, and the prison was shaken to its foundations. All the doors immediately flew open, and the chains of every prisoner fell off! The jailer ... drew his sword to kill himself. But Paul shouted to him, "Stop! Don't kill yourself! We are all here!" The jailer called for lights and ran to the dungeon and fell down trembling before Paul and Silas. Then he brought them out and asked, "Sirs, what must I do to be saved?" They replied, "Believe in the Lord Jesus and you will be saved, along with everyone in your household." And they shared the word of the Lord with him and with all who lived in his household. Even at that hour of the night, the jailer cared for them and washed their wounds. Then he and everyone in his household were immediately baptized. **ACTS 16:25-33, NLT.**

I've never been in prison. But I'm guessing that if I were thrown in prison in the United States of America, I would be treated more like a guest who isn't allowed to leave than a rented mule.

Paul and Silas were arrested and beaten to a pulp. The whips used to inflict punishment left deep cuts that were not bandaged or slathered with healing balm. The fiery sting from their wounds was fresh and got worse as the night went on. And their response? They sang hymns all night. Maybe that was their revenge on their jailers.

It was during their concert that the earthquake came. Doors swung open and chains dropped off. Anyone who wanted it had a "get out of jail free" card.

As Paul and Silas made their way to freedom, they saw the jailer ready to fall on his sword. At that moment Paul had a decision to make: Do I let my enemy fall on his sword, or do I attempt to save his life?

Paul's back was stinging from the beating he had received just hours before. He had reason to keep on walking. But he didn't. He stopped, turned, and saved a life. He treated his jailer the way Jesus treated the Romans when He was on the cross. Paul forgave these Romans and told them about the risen Christ. Hearts were broken, souls were saved, and families were baptized.

When Jesus said, "Love your enemies," this is what He meant. This is how we are to treat the people who hurt us. Easy to say, hard to do.

NOV 8

Unashamed at Taco Bell

FOR I AM NOT ASHAMED of the gospel, because it is the power of God that brings salvation to everyone who believes: first to the Jew, then to the Gentile. **ROMANS 1:16.**

Excuse me, sir. Do you love Jesus?"

I was sitting at Taco Bell minding my own business, happily chowing down my seven-layer burrito, when he approached me. He couldn't have been more than 6 years old. He had blond hair and freckles and a welcoming little grin on his face. At first he just came over and smiled at me.

"Hi, there!" I said, mouth full. "What's your name?"

"Blake."

"Well, hi, Blake. I'm Mark. How can I help you?"

"Excuse me, sir. Do you love Jesus?"

Before I could answer, Blake's mother rushed over and grabbed him by the hand, apologizing all over herself. I stopped her and asked why she was apologizing.

"Ever since we started attending church again, Blake can't stop asking people if they love Jesus. It's like it's in him and it has to get out. I'm so sorry—we didn't mean to make you feel uncomfortable."

I assured her that I didn't feel uncomfortable at all and, in fact, I do love Jesus.

Blake's childlike boldness for Christ amazes me. No inhibitions. Not one concern that a question so deep and personal could possibly embarrass the asker or the askee. Just bold, positive faith.

Jesus said that if we acknowledge Him before the people around us, He will acknowledge us before the Father. I want that. I want to be spoken well of in heaven. I want Jesus to brag about my boldness in the faith.

When we were little, we used to sing the song "This Little Light of Mine." One of the verses says, "Hide it under a bushel, NO! I'm gonna let it shine."

Little Blake hadn't grown up enough to learn how to hide his light. I hope I never grow up and learn how to hide my light. Lights are for shining, not hiding.

Bad Example

AS IT IS WRITTEN: "God's name is blasphemed among the Gentiles because of you." **ROMANS 2:24.**

Brennan Manning once wrote, "The greatest single cause of atheism in the world today is Christians who acknowledge Jesus with their lips, then walk out the door and deny Him by their lifestyle. That is what an unbelieving world simply finds unbelievable."

I know a multimillionaire who is a gracious, quiet man of God. He attends his local church each week, speaks kindly of his neighbors, and has managed to build a business empire. When I was principal of a school, he'd call me every once in a while and ask if I wanted to travel to such and such a place in the United States or Canada in one of his corporate jets, just for the fun of it. The first time I was able to go with him, I thought I had died and gone to heaven. What a cool experience to fly in a personal jet, have a car meet us at an airport, and feel as if I was important!

On that flight I said, "Carl, usually people with your kind of money have a lot of enemies. Why is it that you don't?"

He said, "Mark, I've found that if you treat people fairly and solve conflict by admitting you are wrong, usually people can get along."

One Christmas I went with Carl to visit all the community agencies. At each agency the staff received a hearty handshake, a word of appreciation for their contribution to the community, and a $10,000 check.

I know another person in another community who has all the money one could ever want, but he has a different reputation. He is always right, and everyone else is always wrong. He is contentious, angry, Scrooge-like with his money, and paranoid that everyone is out to get his riches. He treats people as if they were created for him to wipe his feet on. He goes to church every week, too. Folks don't like him much because of how he acts. In fact, he's given his local church a bad name in the community.

How we act matters. It reflects on the God we claim. Claiming Christ and acting like the devil is taking God's name in vain.

NOV 10

Sinner Man

FOR ALL HAVE SINNED and fall short of the glory of God, and all are justified freely by his grace through the redemption that came by Christ Jesus. **ROMANS 3:23, 24.**

I'll never forget the day this text took on real meaning to me. I was sitting in a seminary class learning more Greek. My teacher directed us to this text and showed us how some words were written in a way that suggested an event at a particular point in time, while others referred to something that happened at a point in time but would also always be true. He showed us that the Greek suggested that the text could read this way: "For all have sinned and will continue to sin, and all have fallen short of the glory of God and will continue to fall short of the glory of God, and all are justified freely by his grace."

This thought was revolutionary to me. It told me that God chose me in spite of what He knew I was going to do. God knows the evil that lurks in the dark parts of my heart. He knows what I have done in my shady past. And He knows that I will likely dishonor Him with my words and actions in the future.

But He also knows my heart. He knows I don't want to dishonor Him. And He knows that there will be times when I actually do the things He intended for me to do.

What hit me that day in that seminary class was that God loved, saved, and chose me knowing I have defects that will likely haunt me for the rest of my life.

Look at the cast of characters that God chose to represent Him on this earth: Noah the drunk, Samson the philanderer, David the adulterer, Peter the denier, Paul the murderer, you . . . are you seeing a pattern here?

God doesn't look at our defects when He chooses us. He looks at our possibilities. He sees in us kingdom potential. Noah saved life on earth from the Flood, Samson slew God's enemies, David ruled as a mighty king, Peter took the gospel to the world, and Paul wrote half of the books in the New Testament.

Within you is the possibility of good and evil. God chooses to dwell on and develop your positive attributes. He has chosen you to plug into His kingdom in just the right way. You can be sure that He knows your faults. You can also be sure that He has chosen you anyway.

Null and Void

SIN ENTERED THE WORLD THROUGH one man, and death through sin, and in this way death came to all people, because all sinned. . . . But the gift is not like the trespass. For if the many died by the trespass of the one man, how much more did God's grace and the gift that came by the grace of the one man, Jesus Christ, overflow to the many! **ROMANS 5:12-15.**

Some friends of mine purchased their first house a few years ago. They went through the whole process: they drove through neighborhoods looking for "for sale" signs, hired a real estate agent, found the house they thought they could afford, applied for a loan, got approved, closed on the purchase, and moved in.

What they didn't realize was that there was a sizable crack in the foundation, which created some problems that were going to be very expensive to fix. On further investigation they discovered that the sellers of the home had known about the defect in the foundation and had covered it up so they could sell the house.

My friends actually ended up taking the original owners to court. The judge saw the deception and ordered that the sale of the house be revoked and declared null and void. The sale was based on deception, and when it was proved so, my friends got their money back, and the original owners got their house back.

When this world was originally created, God gave humans dominion over it. Adam and Eve were the prince and princess of this world. Then a snake came along and deceived them. When Adam and Eve ate the fruit, they handed the title of this world over to the evil one. The Bible calls him the prince of this world. Satan is the ruler of this world . . . until . . .

Jesus realized that this world had been sold on false pretenses. Satan had lied about God's character and claimed things about Him that were just not true. Jesus came to rescue the first Adam (humanity) by becoming the second Adam and proving the devil to be the liar he is.

At the cross God's love was magnified so that the sale of this earth from humans to the devil was declared null and void. The sale of this world was nailed to the cross, and the kingdom of this world was handed over to its new owner, Jesus, the new Adam.

NOV 12

A Law You Should Break

THEREFORE, THERE IS NOW no condemnation for those who are in Christ Jesus, because through Christ Jesus the law of the Spirit who gives life has set you free from the law of sin and death. **ROMANS 8:1, 2.**

A word about the word *condemnation:* Jesus did not come to condemn but to save. Sometimes we condemn one another. That's not good. Maybe the worst condemnation is when we condemn ourselves. Self-condemnation happens when God forgives us, but we can't forgive ourselves. Now, about our text today . . .

The law of sin and death is a law that people live under when they choose not to accept God's way of escape from it. It's a law that is just as sure as gravity. What is the law of sin and death? It's actually spelled out earlier in the book of Romans. It goes like this: "The wages of sin is death."

Sin equals death. Sometimes death happens quickly; sometimes it happens over a long period of time. But the law of sin and death is sure. Sin separates us from the Lifegiver.

I had a friend in high school who chose the law of sin and death. He told me he had no desire to know anything about God. "I just want to live my life the way I want to live my life, and then I'll go to hell. I don't care," he said.

My friend chose this life. He did things that he knew were wrong by most moral standards. He's been in and out of relationships, in and out of jail. He's experiencing the law of sin and death as it eats away at his life. It's a sad thing to see.

If only my friend would realize that there is no condemnation for those who are in Christ. No condemnation from God, because He forgives our sins. No self-condemnation, because when we're living according to the Spirit, we're making choices we can feel good about. A life dedicated to good things that honor God is a life filled with promise.

The other part of this text that is so encouraging is that I'm secure in God's grace while I'm still growing in Him. There is no condemnation for me even though I still stumble and fall. My mistakes can't take me out of the hand of God.

The All-New Ofa

THEREFORE, I URGE YOU, BROTHERS and sisters, in view of God's mercy, to offer your bodies as a living sacrifice, holy and pleasing to God—this is your true and proper worship. Do not conform to the pattern of this world, but be transformed by the renewing of your mind. Then you will be able to test and approve what God's will is—his good, pleasing and perfect will. **ROMANS 12:1, 2.**

Ofa Langi grew up in southern California in a poor but happy family. Then his dad died quite suddenly of liver cancer. His father's death turned Ofa's life upside down, and he began to make some bad decisions. Ofa started hanging out with the rough kids in the neighborhood. By the time he was 14 he was learning how to abuse substances, steal, and do other things that drove his mother to her knees.

At 19 Ofa was still headed down a bad road in life. One morning Ofa was riding in a car with his brother-in-law, planning to help him with some things at work. Tired from an evening of partying the night before, Ofa fell asleep in the passenger seat. What he didn't know was that as he dozed off, so did the driver of the car. They hit a palm tree, and Ofa was rushed to the hospital.

In the hospital a doctor lectured Ofa, "If you want your leg to heal, you need to heal your life. Stop the drugs, alcohol, and cigarettes."

Ofa's family realized they needed to make a move to give him a new chance at life. They moved north to the Seattle area, praying the whole time for his healing. During this time Ofa recognized God's invitation in his life and gave his heart to Jesus.

Ofa had very little scholastic ability, yet he went to college and majored in theology. From there he went on and achieved a Master of Divinity degree. He's a tremendous preacher and a powerful man of God. He's also my associate pastor. Ofa is a new creation.

I don't know who you think you are, but if you are in Christ, you are a new creation. Every day the old is gone and the new has come. You may have lived a life to this point that you aren't proud of, but your transformation in Christ will shatter your past and bring you into God's glorious plan.

NOV 14

Hail to the Chief

LET EVERYONE BE SUBJECT TO the governing authorities, for there is no authority except that which God has established. The authorities that exist have been established by God. **ROMANS 13:1.**

As I'm writing this chapter, it's been four days since a national election in the United States. Based on some of the Facebook posts I've read after the election, you would think we're facing a worldwide zombie apocalypse. Many people believe that because the candidate they voted for lost, America is lost too.

Along with the mourning has come a torrent of hateful speech spreading all kinds of gloom and doom and half-truths about the current president. It's disheartening to read.

A couple days after the election I had a woman in my office who was afraid that her marriage was in trouble and that her husband was going into a depression. When I asked her about the patterns of her husband's life, she said, "Every day he spends countless hours watching a political network that is always critical of the other party. In the car he's always got political talk shows on that are constantly blasting away at politicians they disagree with."

And here it was the Thursday after the election. His wife was in my office worried that her husband was in a constant state of depression and lethargy. I wonder why!

A couple of lessons can be gained from my politically disappointed friend: **1. Don't place your hope and faith in any person.** To think that any candidate or political party is going to "save" your country or "doom" your country would be to place your hopes in something other than God's sovereignty. The Lord sets them up and the Lord takes them down. Blessed be the name of the Lord. **2. Surrounding yourself with negativity and criticism day in and day out will, by osmosis, change your character into one of negativity and criticism.** Turn off the news channels that tell you how wrong everyone else is. Turn off the radio programs that do the same.

Surround yourself with positivity. Pray for your leaders. And vote your conscience. Focus on Jesus and not the government.

Be Convicted in Your Own Mind

ACCEPT OTHER BELIEVERS who are weak in faith, and don't argue with them about what they think is right or wrong. For instance, one person believes it's all right to eat anything. But another believer with a sensitive conscience will eat only vegetables. Those who feel free to eat anything must not look down on those who don't. And those who don't eat certain foods must not condemn those who do, for God has accepted them. . . .

In the same way, some think one day is more holy than another day, while others think every day is alike. You should each be fully convinced that whichever day you choose is acceptable. Those who worship the Lord on a special day do it to honor him. Those who eat any kind of food do so to honor the Lord, since they give thanks to God before eating. And those who refuse to eat certain foods also want to please the Lord and give thanks to God. For we don't live for ourselves or die for ourselves. If we live, it's to honor the Lord. And if we die, it's to honor the Lord. So whether we live or die, we belong to the Lord. **ROMANS 14:1-8, NLT.**

I have a friend who says, "If you can't sin as I do, then you can't go to heaven!" In other words, my sins are OK with God, but yours aren't. Sounds ridiculous, doesn't it?

I have a friend who is a pastor. (Actually, I have lots of friends who are pastors!) This particular friend enjoys his food. There's not much he won't eat if it's set in front of him. I think eating is one of his spiritual gifts! My friend used to pastor a church that had in it some people who were convinced that true Christians should eat a specific diet and abstain from certain foods. Their convictions were not the same as my pastor friend's.

One day an emergency elders' meeting was called. The purpose was to discuss grave concerns about what some of the elders had seen my friend eating at an Applebee's restaurant one evening. It wasn't anything that had any biblical restrictions on it, but the elders who had their dietary convictions were projecting their convictions onto my friend. He didn't last at that church too much longer.

I think it's important for Christians to help one another along life's path. When we see a brother or sister in blatant violation of Scripture, I think attempting to correct that individual in love is the right thing to do. But please, to promote unity and to be like Jesus, don't let your convictions bully those around you. Your job is to build others up in Christ.

NOV 16

Now, Children, Let's Play Nice!

I APPEAL TO YOU, BROTHERS AND SISTERS, in the name of our Lord Jesus Christ, that all of you agree with one another in what you say and that there be no divisions among you, but that you be perfectly united in mind and thought. **1 CORINTHIANS 1:10.**

My wife is a grade school teacher. She's been teaching for close to 30 years (which is amazing, since she's only 29 years old!). I could never do this job, because if I did, I'd get put in jail. I don't understand how a group of little kids who have several opportunities each day to play outside on the playground can end up in tears because "Jonny said that" or "Susie pushed me" or "Linda won't share the ball with me!" I would just take them all and duct-tape them to their chairs. And then I would get arrested. That's why I'm not an elementary teacher.

But if you stop and think about it, these kids act just like adults. I have a friend who was pastoring a church full of members who behaved like kids on a playground. Their only job was to get along with one another and treat people with love. Instead, the church was full of backbiting and gossip. So the pastor did something out of the ordinary. He placed a huge banner above the pulpit that said "Criticism" in big red letters.

That weekend he preached his sermon, but he didn't preach about criticism. The folks wondered what was going on. Maybe he was leading up to that topic. But week after week the banner stayed and the sermon topics didn't match his prop.

Finally, during a church board meeting the longtime chair of the church board asked the pastor, "You've had that sign up above the pulpit for three weeks now, but you haven't preached about criticism. What's going on?"

The pastor replied, "Oh, the sign has nothing to do with the sermon series. When this church stops being so critical, I'll take the sign down."

Three months later the people finally got the message, and the sign came down.

As Christians we have a really cool opportunity. We have the opportunity to show the universe what it looks like to play nicely together. The world is our playground, and God's people are our classmates. Wouldn't it be a tragedy if we spent our time at one another's throats instead of playing nicely together?

Not So Smart

REMEMBER, DEAR BROTHERS AND SISTERS, that few of you were wise in the world's eyes or powerful or wealthy when God called you. Instead, God chose things the world considers foolish in order to shame those who think they are wise. And he chose things that are powerless to shame those who are powerful. . . . For our benefit God made him to be wisdom itself. Christ made us right with God; he made us pure and holy, and he freed us from sin. Therefore, as the Scriptures say, "If you want to boast, boast only about the LORD." **1 CORINTHIANS 1:26-31, NLT.**

I'd like to play a game with you. There's a sentence below this paragraph that I'd like you to read. Read it and close your eyes for 10 seconds. Then read it again and close your eyes for another 10 seconds. Then count the number of *f*s in the sentence.

Finished files are the result of years of scientific study combined with the experience of years.

How many *f*s did you count?

I once spoke at a faculty conference at a university and handed out this sentence to the faculty in attendance. There were probably 50 people in the room. I had the above sentence on 50 different pieces of paper. But I told them that they all had different sentences.

I had them read their sentence to themselves three times. Then I asked, "How many of you have only one *f* in your sentence?" Nobody raised a hand. "How many have two?" A few hands went up. "Three?" The majority of hands raised. "Four?" A few hands. "Five *f*s?" Just a couple of hands. "Six *f*s?" A smattering of hands.

When I announced that they all had the same sentence and that they all had 6 *f*s, everyone laughed—except for one Ph.D. He insisted that he had only three *f*s in his sentence. I insisted that he had six. He insisted that I was a moron. Then he told me he'd sing the national anthem in front of his colleagues if he had six *f*s.

He came up front, I pointed out that he was overlooking the *f* in the three occurrences of the word *of*, and he sang the national anthem. Sometimes being really smart is not the same thing as having wisdom. Ph.D.s come from years of school. Wisdom comes from God.

NOV 18

Master Architect

FOR WE ARE BOTH GOD'S WORKERS. And you are God's field. You are God's building. Because of God's grace to me, I have laid the foundation like an expert builder. Now others are building on it. But whoever is building on this foundation must be very careful. For no one can lay any foundation other than the one we already have—Jesus Christ Anyone who builds on that foundation may use a variety of materials—gold, silver, jewels, wood, hay, or straw. But on the judgment day, fire will reveal what kind of work each builder has done. The fire will show if a person's work has any value. If the work survives, that builder will receive a reward. But if the work is burned up, the builder will suffer great loss. The builder will be saved, but like someone barely escaping through a wall of flames. Don't you realize that all of you together are the temple of God and that the Spirit of God lives in you? **1 CORINTHIANS 3:9-16, NLT.**

'm a very poor builder. If you gave me a bunch of wood and asked me to build a box, it would likely end up being a triangle. I'm great at following directions, though. If you're a builder, and you stand over me and tell me what to do, I can build anything. But if you give me a pile of lumber and ask me to build a new deck . . . well, let's just say I wouldn't stand on that deck and expect it to hold my friends at a barbecue.

Yet I've been on dozens of mission trips where I helped build medical clinics, schools, and churches. I'm going to Kenya next summer to help build a cafeteria for a girls' rescue mission. When I get done, I know the structure will be sound and will look good, not because I'm an expert builder, but because I listened to the people who are expert builders. They'll give me direction, and I'll do my best to follow that direction.

Paul uses building a temple as an example of how we construct our life. Just like real-life building with lumber and bricks, I'm no expert on how to build the temple of God. I mean, I know the basics: surround myself with positive people; choose to do the right thing, even when it's not popular; get some exercise and fresh air; spend time with God on a regular basis. I know the materials I'm supposed to use to build a great temple of God. My problem is I'm not an expert builder.

Jesus is an expert builder. I've discovered that if I just listen to Him as He directs my life, this temple of God will end up just as He designed it. I don't have to worry anymore about my building skills; I can leave the blueprint of my life in His hands.

Captivated by This Privilege

FOR I RECEIVED FROM THE LORD what I also delivered to you, that the Lord Jesus on the night when he was betrayed took bread, and when he had given thanks, he broke it, and said, "This is my body which is for you. Do this in remembrance of me." In the same way also he took the cup, after supper, saying, "This cup is the new covenant in my blood. Do this, as often as you drink it, in remembrance of me." For as often as you eat this bread and drink the cup, you proclaim the Lord's death until he comes. Whoever, therefore, eats the bread or drinks the cup of the Lord in an unworthy manner will be guilty of profaning the body and blood of the Lord. Let a person examine himself, then, and so eat of the bread and drink of the cup. **1 CORINTHIANS 11:23-28, ESV.**

My mom says that as a young lad I was fascinated by the Communion service. We'd sit in the balcony of the church, and I'd watch with wide eyes as the pomp and ceremony of the Lord's Supper was played out.

Up front a linen-covered table was decorated with big, shiny silver trays with lids. On the lids were large silver crosses. The organ would play softly as the pastor and some church elders walked out and sat behind the table. Then, with military precision, two rows of deacons would walk up the aisle toward the table. The pastor and elders would take the lids off the trays and start handing them to the deacons. In the trays were broken pieces of unleavened bread and little cups of grape juice.

When all the deacons had a tray, they would turn around and march back up the aisle toward the congregation to serve them the emblems of Christ's body and blood.

At one point during a Communion service, my mom tells me, the drama of the moment so captivated me that when the deacons turned around with the trays and started marching toward the congregation, I stood up, pointed at them, and yelled, "Here they come, Mama! Here they come!" This, of course, brought levity to the whole service that day.

Taking the symbols of Christ's body and blood should be a reminder, whenever I do it, that Jesus took on my sin so that I wouldn't have to be a slave to it anymore. This is a privilege that is not to be taken lightly.

NOV 20

Body Parts

FOR THE BODY DOES NOT CONSIST of one member but of many. If the foot should say, "Because I am not a hand, I do not belong to the body," that would not make it any less a part of the body. And if the ear should say, "Because I am not an eye, I do not belong to the body," that would not make it any less a part of the body. If the whole body were an eye, where would be the sense of hearing? If the whole body were an ear, where would be the sense of smell? But as it is, God arranged the members in the body, each one of them, as he chose. If all were a single member, where would the body be? As it is, there are many parts, yet one body. **1 CORINTHIANS 12:14-20, ESV.**

I was walking with a friend around the track during evening recreation time at an academy I worked for in North Carolina. He was the business manager of the academy, and I was the chaplain. As we walked, he was telling me about his job. He had to crunch numbers all day long. He was also in charge of the work program at the school, which helped students raise money for their tuition so they could afford a private education. As he described his job, I started to get a weird feeling in my stomach. Finally I blurted out, "I would hate your job! How can you stand it?"

Bob looked right back at me and said, "Are you kidding? I'd hate *your* job! I can't imagine all that planning and creativity. And having to stand up in front of a group of people to speak? That would terrify me!"

We both got a good laugh as we realized that God had made us so different, yet He was still able to use both of us to better His kingdom.

In 1 Corinthians 12 Paul tells us that we are all body parts. As I get older, I find that when body parts start to fail me, I notice! I need all my body parts to work properly for me to live a happy, healthy life.

So it is with church. God has wired up all kinds of people all kinds of ways so they can come together and do kingdom work. In our churches there are noses and eyes, hands and feet, brains and spines. Yes, there are even armpits . . . you know who they are. But we need them! Jesus needs all the parts of His body to work together for the good of the kingdom.

Love

Usually this spot on your page is reserved for the text. Not today. Today we need to let one of the most significant chapters in all of Scripture speak for itself. Because in the end everything boils down to love. Thousands of songs have been dedicated to the topic of love. It seems that love is one of the great mysteries of the human experience. Yet God is love. And we should be love too. Here is **1 CORINTHIANS 13.**

IF I SPEAK IN THE TONGUES OF MEN OR OF ANGELS, but do not have love, I am only a resounding gong or a clanging cymbal. If I have the gift of prophecy and can fathom all mysteries and all knowledge, and if I have a faith that can move mountains, but do not have love, I am nothing. If I give all I possess to the poor and give over my body to hardship that I may boast, but do not have love, I gain nothing.

Love is patient, love is kind. It does not envy, it does not boast, it is not proud. It does not dishonor others, it is not self-seeking, it is not easily angered, it keeps no record of wrongs. Love does not delight in evil but rejoices with the truth. It always protects, always trusts, always hopes, always perseveres.

Love never fails. But where there are prophecies, they will cease; where there are tongues, they will be stilled; where there is knowledge, it will pass away. For we know in part and we prophesy in part, but when completeness comes, what is in part disappears. When I was a child, I talked like a child, I thought like a child, I reasoned like a child. When I became a man, I put the ways of childhood behind me. For now we see only a reflection as in a mirror; then we shall see face to face. Now I know in part; then I shall know fully, even as I am fully known.

And now these three remain: faith, hope and love. But the greatest of these is love.

NOV 22

Time to Wake Up

BUT LET ME REVEAL TO YOU a wonderful secret. We will not all die, but we will all be transformed! It will happen in a moment, in the blink of an eye, when the last trumpet is blown. For when the trumpet sounds, those who have died will be raised to live forever. . . . Then, when our dying bodies have been transformed into bodies that will never die, this Scripture will be fulfilled: "Death is swallowed up in victory. O death, where is your victory? O death, where is your sting?" For sin is the sting that results in death, and the law gives sin its power. But thank God! He gives us victory over sin and death through our Lord Jesus Christ. So, my dear brothers and sisters, be strong and immovable. Always work enthusiastically for the Lord, for you know that nothing you do for the Lord is ever useless. **1 CORINTHIANS 15:51-58, NLT.**

I used to pastor a church that had a children's room in back. That's a room where mothers and fathers with young children can sit, usually behind soundproof glass, to take care of their baby's needs and still take in the church service. In this particular church somebody with a clever sense of humor had put a sign on the outside of the soundproof glass that said, "We shall not all sleep, but we shall all be changed." I thought that was hilarious.

First Corinthians 15 means a lot to me, because it does a good job of clearing up several theological questions that people have. This chapter clears up what happens when a person dies. It calls death "sleep." It also makes clear that there's going to be resurrection, and resurrection will happen at the second coming of Jesus. If a person were to die and go to heaven right away, why would there be a need for resurrection day? Everyone who died in Jesus would already be in heaven, right?

But even more clarifying than that is the fact that Jesus won the victory over death. We don't have to worry about the afterlife. We don't have to worry about death anymore, because Jesus took the keys of this world from its old landlord, Satan, and has unlocked death, making resurrection a sure thing.

Paul finishes this part of his letter to the church in Corinth by reminding them that because we have resurrection to look forward to, we shouldn't give up on right living. A life lived for God, as challenging as it might be sometimes, will be worth it in the end.

Stones of Death

NOW IF THE MINISTRY OF DEATH, carved in letters on stone, came with such glory that the Israelites could not gaze at Moses' face because of its glory, which was being brought to an end, will not the ministry of the Spirit have even more glory? For if there was glory in the ministry of condemnation, the ministry of righteousness must far exceed it in glory. . . . For if what was being brought to an end came with glory, much more will what is permanent have glory. **2 CORINTHIANS 3:7-11, ESV.**

Have you ever heard the Ten Commandments referred to as "the ministry that brought death"? That's not how they were presented to me when I learned about them. I've heard them described as "the law of God" and "a transcript of God's character," but never as "the ministry of death."

What would possess Paul to refer to God's law in such a negative way? Did he suddenly become a Gentile? Did he just get tired of keeping the Ten Commandments and decide to do away with them? I don't think either of these things is true. So what was he up to?

First, it should be noted that Paul isn't talking about just the Ten Commandments here; he's talking about the whole of the old covenant. This would cover every law and every story in the first five books of the Bible. The Jews were intent on keeping each law perfectly so God wouldn't punish them. Maybe if they kept every law without a mistake, He would bless their nation. They held to the Isaiah text that spoke about the law and the prophets as being the test of what is true. Yet as hard as they tried, the people of Israel could never be perfect lawkeepers. It was impossible. The Law, rather than serving as a vehicle to a better knowledge of and relationship with God, became a mirror that condemned their behavior and showed that they deserved death.

Jesus came to fulfill the law. Everything in the law and the prophets came to perfection in Him. This was symbolized as He stood on the Mount of Transfiguration between Moses (the lawgiver) and Elijah (the chief of all prophets). Jesus doesn't condemn; the law does. Jesus forgives; the law can't do that. Jesus extends grace. Tablets of stone can't extend grace. Jesus is the fulfillment of the law and the way to salvation as the law never could be.

NOV 24

Metamorphosis

THEREFORE, IF ANYONE IS IN CHRIST, the new creation has come: The old has gone, the new is here! All this is from God, who reconciled us to himself through Christ and gave us the ministry of reconciliation: that God was reconciling the world to himself in Christ, not counting people's sins against them. And he has committed to us the message of reconciliation. **2 CORINTHIANS 5:17-19.**

When I was a kid, I lived at the end of a neighborhood that had, on the other side of a barbed-wire fence, a big pond with lots of frogs. Kids like frogs. Every year I'd go up during polliwog season, get a jar of those squirmy little tadpoles, and bring them home. I'd put them in my backyard in an old fish tank full of murky water and watch them go through their metamorphosis.

From day to day they would change from looking like fish to getting little legs and arms to finally losing their tails. When I was little, that change from a tadpole to a frog seemed miraculous to me. But that change is nothing compared to the change in a person from whose eyes the veil of sin is lifted so they can see God. That is a truly transforming change.

One of the great realizations of my life that helped transform me from a life of bad decisions to a life of better decisions was the knowledge that God wasn't counting my sins against me—a truth contained in today's verse. This was much different than I'd always thought. I thought God was up there somewhere with a heavenly ledger counting all the things I did wrong so at the right time He could nail me for being naughty.

Paul makes it clear that God doesn't pile our sins up against us; we do. When we live apart from Him and live in sin, that sin condemns us and crushes us. But God's desire is to free us from the weight of sin, not to see us crushed under it. Jesus came to make that clear. Jesus came to reconcile the Father with His children.

Reconciliation needs to happen, not because God left us, but because we left Him. The world has all kinds of misconceptions about God, because our eyes are veiled by sin. Jesus came to clear up those misconceptions and reconcile us to our Creator and Friend.

When I realized that God wasn't holding my sins against me, I felt that I could trust Him. And when I put my trust in Him, my life was transformed.

Thorn in the Flesh

BECAUSE OF THE SURPASSING GREATNESS of the revelations, for this reason, to keep me from exalting myself, there was given me a thorn in the flesh, a messenger of Satan to torment me—to keep me from exalting myself! Concerning this I implored the Lord three times that it might leave me. And He has said to me, "My grace is sufficient for you, for power is perfected in weakness." Most gladly, therefore, I will rather boast about my weaknesses, so that the power of Christ may dwell in me. . . . For when I am weak, then I am strong. **2 CORINTHIANS 12:7-10, NASB.**

My wife has a thorn in her flesh. No, it's not me. And shame on you for thinking that. It's her vision. My wife has nystagmus. Her eyes shake rapidly when she is tired or if her head is positioned wrong when she is looking at something. This became a challenge when she was taking piano lessons as a child.

My wife is an exceptional musician who can play keyboard, piano, guitar, cello, and flute. And my wife can read music, kind of. But because of her nystagmus she discovered that it's very difficult to read music that appears to be shaking back and forth at high speed. So God gave her a gift to make up for the thorn in her flesh.

One day Wendy's piano teacher gave her a particularly challenging piece to practice for the following week. Wendy asked her teacher to play it once so she would know how it was supposed to sound. The teacher did. And Wendy went home and practiced.

The next week Wendy brought out the music and played it. Wendy's teacher said, "That was played beautifully. But you played it in the wrong key." Wendy had practiced it from memory, not from the music! She learned at a young age to play by ear to compensate for her poor eyesight.

Paul had some sort of thorn in his flesh. We don't know if that thorn was a physical thorn, an emotional thorn, or an actual person who made his life hard. We do know that he asked God to take it away (just as my wife prayed about her poor eyesight), but, for reasons known only in heaven, God didn't. Paul chose to overcome his thorn with a positive attitude and God's grace. What's your thorn? Are you letting it prevent you from excelling in life?

NOV 26

The Gospel of Cutting?

I AM AMAZED THAT YOU are so quickly deserting Him who called you by the grace of Christ, for a different gospel; which is really not another; only there are some who are disturbing you and want to distort the gospel of Christ. But even if we, or an angel from heaven, should preach to you a gospel contrary to what we have preached to you, he is to be accursed! **GALATIANS 1:6-8, NASB.**

The book of Galatians is Paul's ferocious attack on a philosophy of the gospel that a group of "believers" had brought to the church in Galatia after Paul had left.

The church in Galatia was full of Gentiles (non-Jews) who didn't have a clear knowledge of the law of Moses. They were brought into belief in God through hearing about Jesus' crucifixion, His resurrection, and His reconciliation ministry. They were experiencing the joy of the Lord and worshipping God as He was revealed in the life, death, and resurrection of Jesus. And then came the group of believers who had labeled themselves "The Circumcision."

This group came in and taught that unless all the men of the church were circumcised, none of them could be right with God. This was the law according to Genesis 17. Their arguments were so convincing that the men of the church actually believed this "gospel" (which is supposed to mean "good news"). Some of them went ahead and got circumcised, and others were planning on it. *Now,* they thought, *we can be reconciled to God.*

The thinking that there is something we can do to our bodies to earn God's acceptance is no gospel at all. When Paul heard about what was happening, he wrote this scathing letter to correct their false thinking.

We don't have to have our skin pierced to reconcile us to God; Jesus was pierced so that we don't have to be. Jesus did the work of reconciliation so that we can know God as He is.

Satan will always try to convince us that there is something we need to do to convince God to save us. And Satan will always have religious people who will hold up flaming hoops for people to jump through so they can feel accepted by God. Don't fall for it! Remember: "Jesus loves me, this I know, for the Bible tells me so"!

I'm Not With Him

WHEN CEPHAS CAME TO ANTIOCH, I opposed him to his face, because he was clearly in the wrong. Before certain men came from James, he used to eat with the Gentiles. But when they arrived, he began to draw back and separate himself from the Gentiles because he was afraid of those who belonged to the circumcision group. The other Jews joined him in his hypocrisy, so that by their hypocrisy even Barnabas was led astray. **GALATIANS 2:11-13.**

When I was just starting college, I fell deeply in like with a girl about four years my senior. She was pretty, talented, and charismatic. She had an apartment in town, and I ended up in her living room just about every day. We got along so well that we decided that we would officially be boyfriend and girlfriend. I fell even deeper in like with her.

The weird thing about the relationship was that while we were alone, she was affectionate and warm toward me. But when we were out and about, she was distant and didn't seem to want her longtime friends to know that she and I were "a thing."

This all confused me. One night after we got back from a party, I asked her, "Why is it that you act differently toward me here in your apartment than when we're out with all of our friends?"

"Because you're just a freshman in college," she replied, "and I'm a little embarrassed about that."

We broke up.

After his "conversion" experience with Cornelius in Acts 10, Peter knew that God had extended the gospel to the Gentiles. He knew that the church was supposed to treat the Gentile Christians the same as the Jewish believers. Yet Peter had a hard time being seen with the Gentiles when the Jewish brethren were around.

It's easy to get caught up in the game of who's more popular than whom. It's easy to cease associating with some people because other people seem cooler or might look down on your old friends. It's easy, but it's not godly. God doesn't play favorites, and in most cases, neither should we.

NOV 28

Total Opposites

WHEN YOU FOLLOW THE DESIRES of your sinful nature, the results are very clear: sexual immorality, impurity, lustful pleasures, idolatry, sorcery, hostility, quarreling, jealousy, outbursts of anger, selfish ambition, dissension, division, envy, drunkenness, wild parties, and other sins like these. Let me tell you again, as I have before, that anyone living that sort of life will not inherit the Kingdom of God. But the Holy Spirit produces this kind of fruit in our lives: love, joy, peace, patience, kindness, goodness, faithfulness, gentleness, and self-control. There is no law against these things! **GALATIANS 5:19-23, NLT.**

Dark and light. Black and white. Love and hate. Oil and water. Cats and dogs. Boys and girls. Up and down. All of these things are contrasts. They are, in many ways, opposites. And some of them don't belong together.

When I was a kid, my mom would drop me off at Mrs. Nichol's house. Mrs. Nichol was my babysitter. Every morning when I went in, *Sesame Street* would be on. I can still remember the little game they would play on the picture board: "One of these things doesn't belong." They would have a banana, an orange, an apple, and a truck on the picture board. H'mmm, which one doesn't belong? Even at the age of 5 I was pretty sure I knew the answer. (The banana, right?)

If Paul were to play the *Sesame Street* game, he would put up pictures of love, gentleness, joy, and drunkenness. Then he would say to the church in Galatia, "One of these things doesn't belong. Can you guess which it is?"

The contrast in behavior between a person who is living a life for Jesus and a person who is living a worldly life is like the contrast between black and white, dark and light, or oil and water. Some things just don't mix. Jesus saw this and taught it very well. He saw that the Pharisees were self-professed holy people who engaged in behavior that bore the fruit of selfishness rather than the fruit of love. So He told His followers, "By their fruits you will know them" (Matthew 7:20, NKJV).

Followers of Jesus will be known by the way their character reveals more love, joy, peace, patience, kindness, goodness, faithfulness, gentleness, and self-control. If a person is not growing in these things, there is probably a problem with that person's faith in or view of God. True religion grows in good things.

Chosen

EVEN BEFORE HE MADE THE WORLD, God loved us and chose us in Christ to be holy and without fault in his eyes. God decided in advance to adopt us into his own family by bringing us to himself through Jesus Christ. This is what he wanted to do, and it gave him great pleasure. So we praise God for the glorious grace he has poured out on us who belong to his dear Son. He is so rich in kindness and grace that he purchased our freedom with the blood of his Son and forgave our sins. He has showered his kindness on us, along with all wisdom and understanding. God has now revealed to us his mysterious plan regarding Christ, a plan to fulfill his own good pleasure. And this is the plan: At the right time he will bring everything together under the authority of Christ—everything in heaven and on earth. Furthermore, because we are united with Christ, we have received an inheritance from God, for he chose us in advance, and he makes everything work out according to his plan. **EPHESIANS 1:4-11, NLT.**

There is nothing like the feeling of being valued, chosen, and wanted. And there is nothing worse than feeling rejected.

When I was in grade school, I loved a girl named Twila Jensen. We were in third grade at Crystal Springs Elementary School. Mike Brinkmeyer, Dennis Lehtinen, and I all loved Twila Jensen. Every day during lunch we would argue with one another about whom Twila liked more. We all had compelling arguments, but I thought I had an inside track on Twila's love, because every day at lunch I would give her part of my dessert.

One lunch period we had such a heated debate that we decided to approach the great Twila Jensen, our princess-in-waiting, and ask her whom she liked best. There she was, eating her lunch (and half of my candy bar) in all her splendor. I stepped up and ventured to ask the question that we all wanted her to answer. "Twila, we were wondering, which one of us do you like the most?"

Twila looked at us and dealt a crushing blow: "I hate all three of you." So ended our hopes and dreams of earning Twila's love. None of us were chosen.

You, however, are chosen. In fact, Ephesians 1 says that you were chosen before the creation of the world, picked by God Himself to play on His team. And this all happened way before you were even born. Long before He made the first human, God thought of you and smiled. You are chosen. Be happy about that today.

NOV 30

Skateboard Fiasco

BUT GOD, BEING RICH IN MERCY, because of the great love with which he loved us, even when we were dead in our trespasses, made us alive together with Christ—by grace you have been saved—and raised us up with him and seated us with him in the heavenly places in Christ Jesus, so that in the coming ages he might show the immeasurable riches of his grace in kindness toward us in Christ Jesus. **EPHESIANS 2:4-7, ESV.**

When I was young, I wanted a skateboard more than any other thing that I had ever seen or experienced. All my friends had skateboards. I didn't.

My two problems were (1) my dad didn't want to spend the money on a skateboard and (2) my dad knew that I was lanky and uncoordinated. A skateboard might contribute to my early death.

But after much begging and pleading on my part, Dad bought me a skateboard. His only rule was that I wasn't to ride it down Sprague Hill, a very steep hill in the neighborhood next to ours.

I obeyed this law of my dad's for a while. Then, of course, when I thought I had the skill to negotiate it, I tried to skate down Sprague Hill. And I crashed and burned. I was a bloody mess.

I walked up my driveway looking like a horror movie extra and thinking, *My dad is going to kill me!* I didn't know if he was going to spank me or ground me for life.

Dad was out fixing the car and looked up as I approached. When he saw me, the look on his face made it obvious that he noticed all the blood. He rushed over, and I thought, *This is it! I'm done for!* But instead of punishing me, my dad ushered me into the house, cleaned my wounds, and made me hot chocolate.

When I finally got the courage to ask him why he didn't punish me, he said, "I didn't ask you not to ride down that hill because I was trying to steal your fun. I was just concerned for your safety. I'm not going to punish you—you've already punished yourself. Son, I love you, and I just want the best for you."

This is how God sees you and me. He knows all the things we're going to do that misrepresent Him and fall short of our high calling, yet forgiveness was in His heart for us before we were even born. That's grace, and it's ours free of charge.

Represent

HIS INTENT WAS THAT NOW, through the church, the manifold wisdom of God should be made known to the rulers and authorities in the heavenly realms, according to his eternal purpose that he accomplished in Christ Jesus our Lord. **EPHESIANS 3:10, 11.**

When I was a principal, I had several opportunities to drive our bus on field trips to all kinds of interesting places. I enjoyed these trips because they got me out of the office and because I loved driving the big tour bus.

When we went on these trips, everyone knew which school we were from because all of our students wore school uniforms, which had the school crest embroidered on the left chest. Being so easily recognized, of course, could be a good thing or a bad thing.

Once I went to the Seattle Aquarium with our middle-school students. As we were loading the bus after our tour, an administrator from the aquarium came out to the curb and said, "These are the most well-behaved school-aged students we've had here in a long time." I beamed with pride.

That wasn't always the case, though. One day I was giving a tour to a pleasant young girl and her nice family. We were walking down the hallway halfway through the tour when the bell rang. Students started walking out of their classrooms. In the middle of the throng of students I saw the prospective student whisper in her mother's ear. The mother turned to me and said, "Thanks for showing us around. We've made up our mind."

The girl didn't end up attending our school. When I asked the parents what had settled the decision for them, they told me that one of our students was known in the community for partying and carousing. Later on that school year the student with this negative reputation was asked to leave for continually engaging in behavior that made him unfit to attend at our school.

Like it or not, we represent the families and organizations we associate with. People see us and make assumptions about us and those we hang with.

In Ephesians 3 Paul tells his church that they have an awesome responsibility. He suggests that the behavior of the church is supposed to be proof to the universe that God is who He says He is. What would people think about God from looking at you?

DEC 2

Potty Mouth

DO NOT LET ANY UNWHOLESOME talk come out of your mouths, but only what is helpful for building others up according to their needs, that it may benefit those who listen. And do not grieve the Holy Spirit of God, with whom you were sealed for the day of redemption. Get rid of all bitterness, rage and anger, brawling and slander, along with every form of malice. Be kind and compassionate to one another, forgiving each other, just as in Christ God forgave you. **EPHESIANS 4:29-32.**

One time I approached one of my favorite people in the world with some juicy gossip that I couldn't wait to share. I said, "Did you hear about [insert name here]?"

Before I could continue, she put her hand up and said, "Just a second. Before you continue, you need to know that no matter what you say about [insert name here], I'm going to go to them and tell them what you said, and I'm going to tell them that you said it. I'm going to quote you directly. OK, now you can tell the gossip."

I decided to forgo my gossip session and keep the juicy morsels to myself.

I learned a great lesson that day. In fact, I should have learned it long before.

When I was in high school, I went on one date with a girl who was a few years younger than I was. About a month after our date this young woman started telling some of the other girls in school some things that happened during our date that, by my recollections, never happened. Many of the girls believed her stories and started looking at me with scorn. I felt helpless. It was my word against hers.

OK, I admit that I've done plenty of things in my life worthy of scorn. And probably so have you. Even if the bad story is true, when you or I spread someone else's dirty laundry out for all to see, we are acting directly against Scripture's mandate: "Do not let any unwholesome talk come out of your mouths, but only what is helpful for building others up according to their needs, that it may benefit those who listen."

Christians are pretty good at attending church, paying tithe, and sorting through their theology. It seems the last thing they learn is how to love one another in action and in words. Let this be our goal, at least just for today.

My One-Step Solution to All Marriage Problems

FOR WIVES, THIS MEANS SUBMIT to your husbands as to the Lord. For a husband is the head of his wife as Christ is the head of the church. He is the Savior of his body, the church. As the church submits to Christ, so you wives should submit to your husbands in everything. For husbands, this means love your wives, just as Christ loved the church. He gave up his life for her to make her holy and clean, washed by the cleansing of God's word. He did this to present her to himself as a glorious church without a spot or wrinkle or any other blemish. Instead, she will be holy and without fault. In the same way, husbands ought to love their wives as they love their own bodies. For a man who loves his wife actually shows love for himself. **EPHESIANS 5:22-28, NLT.**

I've been a pastor for 27 years. I have not been a marriage counselor for 27 years. Yet somehow my office becomes a haven for couples with marriage problems and young couples who want to get married and need premarriage counseling. Again, I'm not a marriage counselor. In fact, I'm a lousy marriage counselor. I'm willing to listen, but after I'm done listening, I don't really know what to say.

Several years ago a couple came into my office and wanted marriage counseling. I explained to them that I'm not a licensed marriage counselor and that they should go to someone who knows how to counsel marriages. They insisted on having me help them out. After a couple hours of discussing their problems—some of which were pretty severe, including issues I'd never dealt with or even heard of—I looked at them and said, "OK, I think I know how to fix all this. You be nice to him, and you be nice to her. If you both could just be nice to each other, then you wouldn't have any of these problems." They both shook their heads, gathered their things, and found a professional counselor.

You may laugh at my advice, but you can't say it isn't true. If people would just choose to be nice to each other instead of choosing to be selfish about their wants and ambitions, most marriages would work out fine.

The above text lays it out as plain as it can be laid out. If a married couple would just do what the Bible says and have self-sacrificing love, respect, and submission toward each other, our divorce rate in the church would be a small percentage of what it is now. Practice these principles in your life now for future success.

DEC 4

Fighting the Wrong Fight

FINALLY, BE STRONG IN THE LORD and in his mighty power. Put on the full armor of God, so that you can take your stand against the devil's schemes. For our struggle is not against flesh and blood, but against the rulers, against the authorities, against the powers of this dark world and against the spiritual forces of evil in the heavenly realms. Therefore put on the full armor of God, so that when the day of evil comes, you may be able to stand your ground, and after you have done everything, to stand. **EPHESIANS 6:10-13.**

When I was in college, I read about a plan the Soviet Union devised to train dogs to help in the ground war during World War II. They developed harnesses for German shepherds that would hold specially constructed mines (bombs). They spent a lot of time training the dogs to run through a battlefield and under tanks so that the bomb would bump the bottom of the tank. This would activate the trigger mechanism, the bomb would go off, and the tank would be destroyed or disabled.

The day came for these dogs to put their training into practice. It wasn't too long before the Soviet dog trainers saw a number of flaws in their devious plan. One of them was that they had trained all their dogs with Soviet tanks. You guessed it—when they released the dogs, many of them ran underneath Soviet tanks on the field of battle. The term *backfired* isn't adequate to describe what happened. The dogs ended up fighting the wrong battle, or at least for the wrong side.

The book of Ephesians is replete with admonitions for us to get along with one another, love one another, and treat one another with respect. From our families to our friends to the church, our mandate is to love one another as Jesus has loved us. When we don't do this—when we fight with others—we are fighting the wrong battle.

You see, the battle we are to fight is not a battle with other people. Ephesians 6 makes it clear that the battle we engage in every day is a battle against the unseen. We fight the dark powers of the evil one. But the great scheme of the devil is to get God's children to fight the wrong battle. He wants us to fight among one another about stuff that doesn't matter. Don't give the devil a place like that in your life. Love is stronger than hate.

Just Like Jesus

COMPLETE MY JOY BY BEING of the same mind, having the same love, being in full accord and of one mind. Do nothing from rivalry or conceit, but in humility count others more significant than yourselves. Let each of you look not only to his own interests, but also to the interests of others. Have this mind among yourselves, which is yours in Christ Jesus, who, though he was in the form of God, did not count equality with God a thing to be grasped, but made himself nothing, taking the form of a servant, being born in the likeness of men. And being found in human form, he humbled himself by becoming obedient to the point of death, even death on a cross.
PHILIPPIANS 2:2-8, ESV.

I don't know that I could find in Scripture a more detailed prescription of what it would look like to be just like Jesus. Paul's heartfelt request to the members of the church in Philippi echoes my heart's ache for the church of today.

Some would say that the above description of the character of Christ was lived out in the person of Metropolitan Kirill. Never heard of him?

Metropolitan Kirill was an Orthodox priest in Bulgaria during World War II. Bulgaria, because of its desire to acquire land to add to the country, signed a deal with the Nazis to become a Nazi nation. Some time after this agreement came the orders to deport 20,000 Jews to an extermination camp.

As thousands of Jews were secretly being packed into railroad cars bound for death camps, out of the mist walked Metropolitan Kirill with about 300 church members. He barged his way through the Nazi SS soldiers and tried to enter a railroad car full of Jews. As he did he yelled, "Wherever you go, I will go! Wherever you lodge, I will lodge. Your people will be my people, and your God, my God." This, of course, is a passage from the book of Ruth.

When the SS soldiers dragged him off the railroad car, he ran and stood in front of the train and told them that if his Jewish friends had to go, the train would have to run over him first. Metropolitan Kirill's actions provide a great example of the self-sacrificing love of Jesus. This is our high calling—to think of others as better than ourselves and sacrifice for them.

DEC 6

The Gospel Truth

HE IS THE IMAGE OF THE INVISIBLE GOD, the firstborn of all creation. For by Him all things were created, both in the heavens and on earth, visible and invisible, whether thrones or dominions or rulers or authorities—all things have been created through Him and for Him. He is before all things, and in Him all things hold together. He is also head of the body, the church; and He is the beginning, the firstborn from the dead, so that He Himself will come to have first place in everything. For it was the Father's good pleasure for all the fullness to dwell in Him, and through Him to reconcile all things to Himself, having made peace through the blood of His cross; through Him, I say, whether things on earth or things in heaven. And although you were formerly alienated and hostile in mind, engaged in evil deeds, yet He has now reconciled you in His fleshly body through death, in order to present you before Him holy and blameless and beyond reproach—if indeed you continue in the faith firmly established and steadfast, and not moved away from the hope of the gospel that you have heard, which was proclaimed in all creation under heaven, and of which I, Paul, was made a minister. **COLOSSIANS 1:15-23, NASB.**

If I were to ask you to tell me what *the gospel* is, what would you say? I asked a Bible class that same question, and a smart-aleck tenth grader said, "Oh, that's easy: *the gospel* is *good news*." Very clever.

"I know that *gospel* means *good news*," I retorted, "but define it. What is the *good news*?" He didn't really have an answer.

Another person piped up: "The gospel means that Jesus died on the cross for me." Another student said, "Isn't a part of the gospel the fact that Jesus is coming back to take us home?"

After a good bit of discussion I had the whole class turn to Colossians 1, and we read the above passage. In one word, *Jesus* is the gospel. He is the good news. But why?

Jesus is the bridge that reconciles you and me to God. The gospel is God's attempt to reach out to us and say, "Hey! Look over here! I've been here the whole time! I haven't left you; you have left Me. Look at Jesus! If you've seen Him, you've seen Me! My character is defined by love. And because of Jesus you have a clear vision of who I am." Jesus is the gospel in flesh.

DEC 7

Global Popcorn

WE WHO ARE STILL ALIVE, who are left till the coming of the Lord, will certainly not precede those who have fallen asleep. For the Lord himself will come down from heaven, with a loud command, with the voice of the archangel and with the trumpet call of God, and the dead in Christ will rise first. After that, we who are still alive and are left will be caught up together with them in the clouds to meet the Lord in the air. And so we will be with the Lord forever. Therefore encourage one another with these words. **1 THESSALONIANS 4:15-18.**

When it comes to theology and doctrine, there are very few places in the Bible that outline a whole teaching in one place. For example, to do a Bible study on what happens to people after they die, one would need to give evidence from Genesis through Revelation to piece together the truth. Not so with the Second Coming.

If you wanted to show an interested party a chronology of the Second Coming, you could find things all over the Bible, but this one text tells us what's going to happen and in what order. Paul is very succinct. This text tells us several things:

1. On this old earth there will be people who are alive and people who have "fallen asleep" (died).
2. The Lord will come down with a *loud* command. (This tells us that it will be an audible event.)
3. His command will be accompanied by the voice of the archangel and the trumpet call of God. (I'm guessing that these will be loud, too—loud enough to wake the dead!)
4. The dead in Christ will rise first. (My friend refers to this part of earth's near future as "global popcorn.")
5. We and the newly raised dead will be caught up in the air with the Lord.
6. We will be with the Lord forever. (That's a really long time!)

Pretty simple, don't you think? A lot of people and churches have muddled the Second Coming into all kinds of things. Don't let the muddlers muddle things up for you. You can hang on to this very text as your anchor. And don't forget the last words of this passage: we are to encourage one another with the thought of the soon second coming of our Friend.

DEC 8

Lazybones

AND NOW, DEAR BROTHERS AND SISTERS, we give you this command in the name of our Lord Jesus Christ: Stay away from all believers who live idle lives and don't follow the tradition they received from us. For you know that you ought to imitate us. We were not idle when we were with you. We never accepted food from anyone without paying for it. We worked hard day and night so we would not be a burden to any of you. . . . Even while we were with you, we gave you this command: "Those unwilling to work will not get to eat." Yet we hear that some of you are living idle lives, refusing to work and meddling in other people's business. We command such people and urge them in the name of the Lord Jesus Christ to settle down and work to earn their own living. As for the rest of you, dear brothers and sisters, never get tired of doing good. **2 THESSALONIANS 3:6-13, NLT.**

I've been on a lot of short-term mission trips. I've taken students to the Ukraine, Mexico, Africa, and Central America. Each time we go on a mission trip, I can count on several things. I know that the majority of the kids will work hard. I also know that there will be at least one person who does not work hard. And I know that this one person will bug the ever-living daylights out of the rest of the group.

On one trip we were in Mexico working on an orphanage. This trip was a brutal trip because it was very hot, and we had a ton of digging to do. We had to dig trenches on each side of the quarter-mile-long driveway so that when it rained, the erosion wouldn't damage the road. The ground was hard and dry and full of rocks. The effort it took to get the job done was monumental. A couple of people using picks would loosen the dirt, and a lot of people with shovels would scoop it out. It was backbreaking.

Often in these trips the girls work as hard as or harder than the guys, and this trip was no exception. Each time I'd check on the girls' team, they'd be working hard—except for one girl. It seemed that every time I checked, she'd be taking a break or walking around picking wildflowers. But each time we'd break for a meal, she'd end up first in line for food.

This wore thin on the rest of the group, and they asked if I could sit down and speak with her. When I did, she cried and was offended. Oh, well.

Don't be idle. Pitch in and do your fair share, and maybe a little bit more. This will earn the respect of your peers and develop your character in good ways.

A Child Shall Lead Them

DON'T LET ANYONE LOOK DOWN on you because you are young, but set an example for the believers in speech, in conduct, in love, in faith and in purity. Until I come, devote yourself to the public reading of Scripture, to preaching and to teaching. Do not neglect your gift, which was given you through prophecy when the body of elders laid their hands on you. **1 TIMOTHY 4:12-14.**

My wife is an amazing person of faith. When she was 8 years old, she read a series of books that parallel the Bible. These books convicted her that she needed to be baptized. She was 8. When I was 8, I walked around amazed at the sound of a rock that I had dropped into a pop can. I don't know that I even read a book until I was 17. She was 8!

So at 8 years old Wendy approached her pastor and said, "I really love Jesus, and I think it's time for me to be baptized."

He laughed and patted her on the head. "I'll speak with your parents about it." This was his pastoral way of saying he thought she was too young to have such an idea.

After her mom and dad heard from the pastor, they suggested that maybe she should wait for a while before she was baptized. Wendy would have none of it. She insisted that this was what she wanted to do until they all finally gave in.

When the day of her baptism came, they had to put several strategically placed bricks in the baptistry so she could approach the pastor without having to swim. (She was a fairly small 8-year-old.) On that day she was baptized and has never regretted her decision. It wasn't too many years later that she was teaching the children's Sabbath school (even though she was barely older than the kids she was teaching) and taking her turn preaching in church.

As a pastor I have quite a few children approach me for baptism. I'm amazed at the number of parents who feel that they need to put off their child's fire and desire for baptism until a later date. Sometimes that later date never comes.

Paul encourages young Timothy not to let his youthfulness limit his calling in Jesus. And I encourage you to do the same. Don't let your youth prevent you from doing what God has called you to do.

DEC 10

Rich Man, Poor Man

FOR WE BROUGHT NOTHING INTO THE WORLD, and we can take nothing out of it. But if we have food and clothing, we will be content with that. Those who want to get rich fall into temptation and a trap and into many foolish and harmful desires that plunge people into ruin and destruction. For the love of money is a root of all kinds of evil. Some people, eager for money, have wandered from the faith and pierced themselves with many griefs. **1 TIMOTHY 6:7-10.**

Being rich is relative to one's circumstances. I'm a pastor, and my wife is a teacher. Two incomes with one child puts us in the upper middle class of society, as most figures go. We're not as wealthy as some, but not as poor as others. We have two cars and an old truck. We're trying to pay off a house. We have clothes and food and some inexpensive toys to keep us entertained. We aren't rich, but we feel comfortable.

On my first trip to Kenya we were out on the Masai Mara building a church and running a medical clinic. The Masai are a people group who herd cattle and live in houses made of gathered sticks, cow manure, and mud. They don't get a lot of water, and a favorite food is curdled milk and blood mixed in a hollowed-out gourd.

One day the chief of a group that lived near our building site approached me. He considered himself to be rich because he had many cows and five wives. He asked me what my house looked like. I actually had my cell phone with me on the trip (turned off and in my tent) and told him I'd share a picture with him if he wanted to see my house.

My house at the time was a 2,500-square-foot, two-story family home that was affordable for the salaries my wife and I were making. I showed my Masai friend the picture. He almost fell over. "Oh, you are a very wealthy man, Pastor Mark!"

No matter how I tried, I couldn't convince this man that I was not the multi-millionaire he thought I was. Rich is relative.

Paul's warning about desiring wealth in the above passage doesn't apply to just rich people or poor people; it applies to all of us. If the desire to gain wealth overwhelms your desire to serve God, you are going to be led to a bad end. Rich or poor or middle-class, our first duty is to honor God with everything we have.

Growing Up In Jesus

FLEE THE EVIL DESIRES OF YOUTH, and pursue righteousness, faith, love and peace, along with those who call on the Lord out of a pure heart. Don't have anything to do with foolish and stupid arguments, because you know they produce quarrels. And the Lord's servant must not be quarrelsome but must be kind to everyone, able to teach, not resentful. Opponents must be gently instructed, in the hope that God will grant them repentance leading them to a knowledge of the truth, and that they will come to their senses and escape from the trap of the devil, who has taken them captive to do his will. **2 TIMOTHY 2:22-26.**

Percy Davies, a church member of mine, was 90-plus years old. His bent back had endured years of working with iron—hard labor. Percy looked old, but he never acted old. He always had a twinkle in his eye and a witty comment on the tip of his tongue.

One day at a church potluck I noticed that Percy had taken a second dessert and was about to sink his dentures into it. I commented in a teasing way, "Percy, as your pastor, I just want you to know that eating one dessert is OK, but I'm pretty sure a second dessert is sinful."

Percy looked up at me, pie on his fork, and didn't miss a beat. "Pastor, at my age this is the only sin I have left that I still enjoy!"

Being young at heart is a gift from God. But being young in age is a challenge in this world. The evil desires of youth seem to be getting eviler (is that even a word?). Each generation seems more informed about perverse things that oppose the kingdom of God.

Once when I was driving my grandma into town, we passed a billboard that showed a provocative-looking woman advertising hard liquor. Grandma sighed and said, "This world is so evil." I asked her to explain. She told me that in her day people would have been arrested if they posted a sign along the road that had a scantily clad woman on it.

As we walked through the store, she pointed out magazine covers and opened my eyes to things that I had gotten used to but that she saw as symptoms of an ever-increasing openness to evil in our everyday world.

It's hard to live a Christian life when you're being barraged by evil from every side. Paul's advice is good: pursue righteousness, love, and peace.

DEC 12

Do Good

IN EVERYTHING SET THEM AN example by *doing what is good.* **TITUS 2:7.**

[JESUS] GAVE HIMSELF FOR US to redeem us from all wickedness and to purify for himself a people that are his very own, eager to *do what is good.* **TITUS 2:14.**

REMIND THE PEOPLE TO BE subject to rulers and authorities, to be obedient, to be ready to *do whatever is good.* **TITUS 3:1.**

THIS IS A TRUSTWORTHY SAYING. And I want you to stress these things, so that those who have trusted in God may be careful to devote themselves to *doing what is good.* These things are excellent and profitable for everyone. **TITUS 3:8.**

OUR PEOPLE MUST LEARN to devote themselves to *doing what is good,* in order to provide for urgent needs and not live unproductive lives. **TITUS 3:14.**

Let's see . . . if I were going to find a theme in the book of Titus, what would it be? Was the emphasis I added to the words from several passages in this book too subtle?

Taking on God's name and then acting poorly has been a problem for centuries. In fact, God tried to stem that tide a long time ago with the third commandment: "You shall not take the name of the Lord your God in vain, for the Lord will not hold him guiltless who takes His name in vain" (Exodus 20:7, NKJV).

The book of Titus says it this way: "*They claim to know God, but by their actions they deny him.* They are detestable, disobedient and unfit for doing anything good" (Titus 1:16). (Did you notice that phrase again?)

The book of Titus spends detailed time on how people who follow the Lamb should behave. Paul gives qualifications for church leaders and details the good qualities that believing men and women, both old and young, should possess. He describes such people as self-controlled, temperate, reverent, pure, kind, full of integrity, and busy doing good things. We do good things so that people will glorify God and see Him through us.

Ahhh . . .

THERE REMAINS, THEN, A SABBATH-REST for the people of God; for anyone who enters God's rest also rests from their own works, just as God did from his. Let us, therefore, make every effort to enter that rest, so that no one will perish by following their example of disobedience. . . . Nothing in all creation is hidden from God's sight. Everything is uncovered and laid bare before the eyes of him to whom we must give account.
HEBREWS 4:9-13.

As I write this chapter it is 7:49 p.m. on the day after American Thanksgiving, or, as those who are given to long lines and rabid shoppers know it, Black Friday. As is tradition in our home, my wife has set up a Christmas tree with all its glimmering lights, shiny ribbons, and colorful ornaments. There's soft music playing in the background, a cat on the floor, and a cat on my lap (making this chapter exceptionally difficult to write). In a word, I'm experiencing Sabbath.

My typical workweek starts off on Monday morning. (I try to take Sunday off, but because of church and school obligations, that doesn't always happen.) I drop my son off at school and am in the office by 8:00 a.m. I work in the office until about noon. I eat lunch and then do whatever needs to be done for the church until about 3:00. I pick up my son, and we usually do something together and end up at home. At 6:00 Monday through Thursday I prepare for and then leave for meetings, typically getting home about 9:30 p.m. On Fridays I usually work only from 8:00 a.m. till 2:00 p.m. And then there's Sabbath, the day we're all supposed to rest. I usually get to the church at 8:00 a.m. and leave around 1:30 p.m. This all adds up to a long week of work. I'm not complaining. I like my job. In fact, I love my job. It's just that sometimes I get tired.

God knows me. In fact, He knew me before I was even born. And He knew that I would need Sabbath rest, even from doing church work. Hebrews 4 reminds us that God rested from His work of creating, and we need to do the same.

But more than that, Hebrews 4 tells us that Jesus came to give us a deeper Sabbath rest from having to worry about saving ourselves. He came to give us rest in Him. There is no condemnation for us. We can rest now.

DEC 14

Perfect Yet?

DURING THE DAYS OF JESUS' life on earth, he offered up prayers and petitions with fervent cries and tears to the one who could save him from death, and he was heard because of his reverent submission. Son though he was, he learned obedience from what he suffered and, once made perfect, he became the source of eternal salvation for all who obey him. **HEBREWS 5:7-9.**

This is one of those verses in Scripture that people tend to skip over because they don't want to deal with it. It's worded in a way that makes devout followers of Jesus squirm in their seats. If you read it a little too fast at first, read it again, and this time notice what the words say about Jesus.

When the writer of Hebrews says "once made perfect," that would imply that there was a time Jesus wasn't perfect, right?

There is a secret about the word *perfect* as it is used in the Bible that not many people know. When we see the word *perfect*, we think *perfectly sinless*. But that's not what the word means, at least when it's used in Scripture. The word *perfect* simply means *completed mission*.

Noah was called perfect. Was he perfectly sinless? Nope. In one instance he was found drunk and naked in his tent. But did he complete his primary mission on earth? Yup, he saved the human race by building an ark and getting his family on it.

Again, Jesus was always sinless, but was He always perfect, in the way the Bible uses *perfect*? Well, no. Jesus' mission wasn't complete until the cross. When Jesus died on the cross, His mission was complete, and "he became the source of eternal salvation for all who obey him."

Will we ever be perfect as the Bible describes it? I hope so. Each one of us has a role to fill in God's kingdom on this earth. Some will have gigantic roles and some small ones. When we obey God's calling in our lives and fill those roles, we become perfect as described in the Bible. To do God's bidding is to complete our mission. Perfectly sinless? I don't see the evidence for that. Perfect in God's plan for us? I certainly hope so. Trust and obey, and He'll lead you where you need to be to do what you need to do.

Hall of Fame

BY FAITH ABEL OFFERED TO God a better sacrifice than Cain, through which he obtained the testimony that he was righteous, God testifying about his gifts, and through faith, though he is dead, he still speaks. By faith Enoch was taken up so that he would not see death; and he was not found because God took him up; . . . By faith Noah, being warned by God about things not yet seen, in reverence prepared an ark for the salvation of his household, by which he condemned the world, and became an heir of the righteousness which is according to faith. By faith Abraham, when he was called, obeyed by going out to a place which he was to receive for an inheritance; and he went out, not knowing where he was going. . . . By faith Isaac blessed Jacob and Esau, even regarding things to come. By faith Jacob, as he was dying, blessed each of the sons of Joseph, and worshiped, leaning on the top of his staff. By faith Joseph, when he was dying, made mention of the exodus of the sons of Israel, and gave orders concerning his bones. By faith Moses, when he was born, was hidden for three months by his parents, because they saw he was a beautiful child; and they were not afraid of the king's edict. . . . By faith the walls of Jericho fell down after they had been encircled for seven days. By faith Rahab the harlot did not perish along with those who were disobedient, after she had welcomed the spies in peace. And what more shall I say? For time will fail me if I tell of Gideon, Barak, Samson, Jephthah, of David and Samuel and the prophets, who by faith conquered kingdoms, performed acts of righteousness, obtained promises, shut the mouths of lions, quenched the power of fire, escaped the edge of the sword, from weakness were made strong, became mighty in war, put foreign armies to flight. **HEBREWS 11:4-34, NASB.**

Today's verse was a long one for a simple reason: each of the people listed in heaven's hall of fame should give you and me courage that we too can finish the race and end up with our names securely written in the book of life.

Just look at this cast of characters: murderers, prostitutes, warmongers, drunks, a guy who sacrificed his child to God, bad parents, a rapist . . . quite a motley crew, if you ask me. And they all get to go to heaven. Why?

Because God's faithfulness to His children is constant. That's why. We may be faithless at times, but He is always faithful. Be encouraged; you're on His team.

DEC 16

Why Are You Doing This to Me?

LET NO ONE SAY when he is tempted, "I am tempted by God"; for God cannot be tempted by evil, nor does He Himself tempt anyone. But each one is tempted when he is drawn away by his own desires and enticed. Then, when desire has conceived, it gives birth to sin; and sin, when it is full-grown, brings forth death. Do not be deceived, my beloved brethren. Every good gift and every perfect gift is from above, and comes down from the Father of lights, with whom there is no variation or shadow of turning. Of His own will He brought us forth by the word of truth, that we might be a kind of firstfruits of His creatures. **JAMES 1:13-18, NKJV.**

Have you ever looked up and said, "Why are You doing this to me, God?" or "Why am I going through this?" I have.

My first church was about 15 minutes from my house . . . or about a half hour, depending on how I hit the stoplights on the way there. There were times I'd leave the house late for church, praying that I'd hit all green lights. Of course, some of the time I would hit every red light and be stuck behind an elderly driver who went five miles per hour under the speed limit. I remember several times being mad at God for causing the red lights and putting that driver in front of me.

In reality, when it comes to temptation, the evil trials we find ourselves locked up in are not God-authored or God-initiated. In fact, most of the things we struggle with are things we've brought upon ourselves. God doesn't tempt us. He doesn't have any dark side that lures us into sin so that He can punish us for our naughtiness. James tells us that the only things we get from God are good things. Everything else we end up with—every not-good thing—comes from somewhere else.

James recognizes that there are those who think that God has a dark side—that God is fickle and runs hot and cold. James tries to dispel that image of God by explaining that God is light all the time. There are no shifting shadows in Him.

We need to get out of the habit of thinking that God is cursing us because of something we did or just out of sport. Our God has no dark side. No, every good and perfect gift comes from Him.

Tongues of Fire

CONSIDER WHAT A GREAT FOREST is set on fire by a small spark. The tongue also is a fire, a world of evil among the parts of the body. It corrupts the whole body, sets the whole course of one's life on fire, and is itself set on fire by hell. **JAMES 3:5, 6.**

The tongue is an amazing muscle. Consider these facts:

- Your tongue has about 10,000 taste buds.
- It is able to detect bitter, sour, salty, and sweet sensations.
- A single taste bud has between 50 and 150 taste cells.
- The heaviest tongue in the animal kingdom is found in the blue whale. Its tongue weighs as much as a small elephant!
- Israel's archenemies to the north, the Assyrians, sometimes cut out the tongues of their captives as punishment.
- The tongue, along with the lips, has caused more strife in this world between people than any other part of the body.

Jesus knew the tongue. Jesus knew and taught that what the tongue and lips produce doesn't originate there; it originates in the heart. But the damage to other people is done when the intentions of the heart come out through the tongue and the lips.

In the movie *The Help* there is an African-American maid working in the South for a White couple that has a chubby little daughter. The mother in this family is a horrible person who speaks degrading words to her daughter, leaving her in tears on a regular basis.

In the movie you see this wonderful nanny taking the little girl aside and saying over and over to her, "You is kind, you is smart, and you is important." Then she has the young girl repeat these things about herself. This nanny knew that positive, uplifting words make a difference in a person's life.

The words that came from the Father's tongue were uplifting and not degrading. "This is my beloved Son, in whom I am well pleased" (Matthew 3:17, KJV). We should use our tongues to bless those in our sphere of influence also.

DEC 18

How to End War

WHAT CAUSES FIGHTS AND QUARRELS among you? Don't they come from your desires that battle within you? You desire but do not have, so you kill. You covet but you cannot get what you want, so you quarrel and fight. You do not have because you do not ask God. When you ask, you do not receive, because you ask with wrong motives, that you may spend what you get on your pleasures. **JAMES 4:1-3.**

Did you know that some scholars have figured out that in recorded human history there have been only 292 years—in all of history—in which there has not been a war happening somewhere in the world? We are more used to war than we are to peace. God is all about peace. We are all about war. Maybe that's why Jesus made such a big deal out of being peacemakers. But peacemakers are rare these days.

We get all bound up in trying to force our will on one another. We intimidate each other with harsh words, we manipulate to get our own way, we hide things from the very people we should be honest with, and we end up with wars and battles. We have wars and battles in our homes; we have wars and battles in our churches; we have wars and battles in politics; and on a grander scale we have wars and conflicts among nations on a continual basis.

James 4:10 says, "Humble yourselves in the sight of the Lord, and He will lift you up" (NKJV). You see, at the root of every covetous desire are pride and control-seeking. I'm right and you're wrong. Why can't you see that I'm right and you're wrong? What are you, stupid? Are you just deceived? Now give me what I want, or I'll try to take it.

James knew that the antidote to every war is submission to God's desires for the human heart, and that's what he described in verse 10. Humility is the key to overcoming every battle that's fought in this world. Not bigger guns. Not more troops. Not a more convincing argument. Humility.

Look at how Jesus won the battle over sin and death. He didn't argue His way to victory. He didn't blast His enemies with more power. He didn't shout or hit. He healed sick people, He hung out with the lowest of society, He washed dirty feet, and He submitted to the cross. Humility.

Holy State of Mind

THEREFORE, WITH MINDS THAT ARE alert and fully sober, set your hope on the grace to be brought to you when Jesus Christ is revealed at his coming. As obedient children, do not conform to the evil desires you had when you lived in ignorance. But just as he who called you is holy, so be holy in all you do; for it is written: "Be holy, because I am holy." **1 PETER 1:13-16.**

I've noticed that a lot of people on this earth are who they think they are. I don't mean to sound silly here—I'm serious. Many people end up thinking their way into success or failure.

I've seen studies that said that most successful people had childhood influencers who spoke positively about them as they grew up, even when praise was unwarranted. These kids assumed that they were successful, so they were and continued to be successful.

When I was a kid, my mom and dad believed in me and expressed that belief in most areas of my life. But for a good while when I was young, I was absent-minded and would lose things, especially my dad's tools. From the time I was young I was reminded that I was not to touch his tools and that I wasn't mechanically inclined. And guess what? As I grew up I didn't know which end of a hammer to pound with. I became what I thought I was all along.

The apostle Peter reminds us that we need to "prepare our minds for action." I believe that one of the things he is talking about here is to project onto ourselves what Jesus has projected onto us: that we are holy by His grace, and holy people act a certain way.

We may not feel holy. We may not even act holy all the time, but if we adopt the attitude of being chosen by God, of being set apart for something special, of being a holy people, a royal priesthood, we will likely end up acting out who we think we are.

Conversely, if we adopt the attitude of a spiritually defeated person, of somebody who is always struggling with sin, of somebody who has to earn God's love, we will always struggle with acting in unholy ways.

If people could see themselves as Jesus sees them, I believe it would curb unholy behavior and produce an abundance of good things in believers' lives.

DEC 20

Powerful Evidence

WE ALSO HAVE THE PROPHETIC message as something completely reliable, and you will do well to pay attention to it, as to a light shining in a dark place, until the day dawns and the morning star rises in your hearts. Above all, you must understand that no prophecy of Scripture came about by the prophet's own interpretation of things. For prophecy never had its origin in the human will, but prophets, though human, spoke from God as they were carried along by the Holy Spirit. **2 PETER 1:19-21.**

One of the confirming truths that establishes our confidence in the Bible is found in prophecy. Prophecy is an otherworldly proof that Jesus is who He says He is and that we can rely on the Bible as it points to Jesus and His task on earth and in heaven.

Specifically, the prophecies of Daniel and Revelation increase our faith in the Bible as we understand the time frame in which they were delivered and how these prophecies unfolded over history.

The prophecy of the emerging kingdoms in Daniel 2 is an example. How could a person who lived during the Babylonian Empire have ever figured out that after Babylon would come Persia, then Greece, and then the iron rule of Rome? The answer, of course, is that no human could make this prediction, but God, who knows the end from the beginning, can and did.

Another wonderful prophecy is found in Daniel 9. How in the world could anyone have predicted the exact year that the Messiah would appear and the year He would die? Again, no person can do this, but God can.

We can be confident in God's prophets and in His prophecies. They are not always easy to decipher, but they are all true. And because we know that God's Word is true, we can be confident in the One to whom they all point: Jesus.

Peter isn't writing the above passage because of stuff he heard about Jesus. Peter actually walked and talked with the One about whom each of these prophecies spoke. Peter saw how every scripture from Moses through the prophets pointed to Jesus as the Savior and revealer of the Father's true character and love. Peter had confidence in the prophets, and so can we.

DEC 21

Light and Dark

ANYONE WHO CLAIMS TO BE in the light but hates a brother or sister is still in the darkness. Anyone who loves their brother and sister lives in the light, and there is nothing in them to make them stumble. But anyone who hates a brother or sister is in the darkness and walks around in the darkness. They do not know where they are going, because the darkness has blinded them. **1 JOHN 2:9-11.**

When I was a kid, I was deathly afraid of the dark. If you had asked me back then what it was about the darkness that scared me, I don't know whether I could have told you. I suppose it was the unknown.

My job as a youngster was to take out the garbage. This was no problem during daylight hours. But at night it was a terrifying proposition. Our garbage cans were located away from the safety of our porch light, around the corner, and behind a fence. The walk in the dark with a big bag of garbage was almost more than my young heart could take.

I remember several times as a youngster when I would walk with the garbage to the edge where the porch light stopped and the darkness began. I'd stand there and look into the void of darkness ahead of me. I was sure that when I lifted the lid of the garbage can, some hideous beast would jump out and grab me.

There's a reason we are afraid of the dark. When darkness clouds our vision, we can't see what's around us. Darkness obscures and twists, while light illuminates and allows for discovery.

In the Bible when you see light and dark, think truth and lies. When we shed light on a subject, we expose more of the truth about it. When we keep something in the dark, we try to hide the truth so it cannot be seen.

Jesus says that we are to be the light of the world. In other words, we are supposed to share the truth about God in a world of darkness (lies) every chance we get. We are to walk in the light (God's truth) and avoid the darkness (lies about God).

The apostle John reminds us of an essential truth: when we walk in the light (the truth about God), we love our brothers and sisters. If we don't love others, we are walking in the darkness (lies), because that's not how God acts.

DEC 22

God Is Love

DEAR FRIENDS, LET US LOVE one another, for love comes from God. Everyone who loves has been born of God and knows God. Whoever does not love does not know God, because God is love. This is how God showed his love among us: He sent his one and only Son into the world that we might live through him. This is love: not that we loved God, but that he loved us and sent his Son as an atoning sacrifice for our sins. Dear friends, since God so loved us, we also ought to love one another. **1 JOHN 4:7-11.**

There are a lot of words in the Bible that are used to describe God. All of them offer wonderful glimpses of His character and of who He is. But only one description encapsulates Him perfectly: love.

A lot of people try to describe what love is. I'd like to take a moment to describe what love isn't. Love is not control.

I get nervous when people say that God is "in control." I'm not sure what they mean by that, but I'm relatively sure that love and control cannot be exhibited by the same person.

If I said, "I love my wife," and then from the moment she woke up every morning I dictated everything she did—if and when she brushed her teeth, what she wore, what time she went to bed, what she ate, how she exercised—would you say I really loved her? Probably not. What would you call me? A control freak, right?

God is love, and love yields control so that a free moral agent can make a decision to love back or not.

If I were to define love, I'd say that love starts with me and ends up with someone else. Love cannot exist with just one person involved. Love always involves positive action toward another.

The definition and the very nature of love let us know that the Trinity is a reality. If love is always shared, and God has always existed, and God is love, then God has always shared love—Father, Son, and Holy Spirit have loved through eternity.

When we experience God's love, we are compelled to reflect that love to those around us; otherwise, what we are experiencing is not love.

Blessed Assurance

I WRITE THESE THINGS TO YOU who believe in the name of the Son of God so that you may know that you have eternal life. **1 JOHN 5:13.**

One of the most tragic yet all too frequent discussions I as a pastor have with church members is the discussion by a person's deathbed about their eternal destiny.

One would think that if people spent their life going to church, reading their Bibles, and following Jesus, death would be something they could nestle into quite comfortably, right? I mean, what could be more peaceful and anticipatory than slipping into a deep sleep with the excitement of knowing that the next face you're going to see is Jesus' face at the resurrection?

Yet time and time again I see believers fearing death. Why? Because many believers don't know if they are saved or not.

Once when I was sitting beside a wonderful man on his deathbed, he asked his family to leave the room so he could talk with me alone. In tears he confessed to me that he was fearful because he didn't know if he was saved. When I asked him why he wasn't sure, he told me, "I don't know. I'm just not sure."

I asked him if he believed in Jesus. He said, "Yes, I've believed all my life." Then I quoted John 3:16. I asked him, "Does the verse say, 'For God so loved the world that he gave his only begotten son, that whosoever believeth in him just might inherit eternal life if one catches God in a good mood that day'?"

He laughed and said, "No, that's not what it says. It says that if I believe, I get eternal life."

We talked some more, and I shared today's text in 1 John 5 with him. He smiled again and said, "Well, I guess that settles it. I get heaven. I get Jesus."

"Yep, you do."

My friend died in peace not too many days later. He died knowing that God would never leave him or forsake him.

Remember, if you are in Christ, there is no condemnation for you. The only way you won't be in heaven is if you don't want to be in heaven. Your salvation is secure.

DEC 24

Car Wash Religion

DEAR FRIENDS, ALTHOUGH I WAS very eager to write to you about the salvation we share, I felt compelled to write and urge you to contend for the faith that was once for all entrusted to God's holy people. For certain individuals whose condemnation was written about long ago have secretly slipped in among you. They are ungodly people, who pervert the grace of our God into a license for immorality and deny Jesus Christ our only Sovereign and Lord. **JUDE 3, 4.**

My wife and I were sitting and watching a program about a popular singer. I'm not sure why we were watching the program, because this particular singer is vulgar and uses language that neither of us use or appreciate. Maybe it was morbid curiosity.

In any case, we were watching the story about her day-to-day life and some of her performances. On stage she was overtly sexual and immoral. Her language seemed to originate in the gutter. We were not impressed. And then something happened in the show that floored us. This singer, just before she went out to entertain the masses in a huge stadium, gathered her band and her dancers behind the stage and prayed. That's right—this sexually lewd and vocally perverse person was asking Jesus to bless her performance. We changed the channel.

Jude's reminder to all believers is that Jesus' grace was never given so that we could become more like the devil and less like Jesus. Spending time with Jesus ought to make us more like Him. When we're walking with Jesus, we become less and less like the perverse world around us and more and more like Jesus, who showed us His example while He lived here on earth.

In college I had a friend who called his religion "the Sunday car wash." When I asked him to explain, he said, "Every Saturday night I go out drinking and messing around. On Sunday morning I go to confession, and a few Hail Marys and Our Fathers later, I'm as good as new!"

God's grace isn't a cover-up for bad behavior. God's grace is supposed to be transforming, changing us from the old person of sin to a new creation in Christ. Jude's reminder to all Christians is that we aren't slaves to sin anymore. Praise God for that!

The Revealing

THE REVELATION OF JESUS CHRIST, which God gave him to show his servants what must soon take place. He made it known by sending his angel to his servant John, who testifies to everything he saw—that is, the word of God and the testimony of Jesus Christ. **REVELATION 1:1, 2.**

The book of Revelation is one of the least-read books in the Bible, because it is one of the least-understood books in the Bible. And no wonder! Revelation is filled with all kinds of symbols that leave its reader wondering what, if anything, can be taken literally. There are weird-looking animals, lots of symbolic numbers, and some women of questionable character. There are flying scorpions, earthquakes, death horses, and a huge winepress with blood gushing out of it. Yikes! I can see why a lot of people freak out about the book of Revelation.

Before we spend the last seven days of this year in the book of Revelation, I would like to give you a word of caution and a word of encouragement. First, the word of caution.

I would submit to you that the images in the book of Revelation should be viewed as symbolic. The beasts, the churches, the women, the horses and their riders, the numbers—everything. In this book we will see Jesus portrayed as a white-haired man with fire in His eyes, a slaughtered lamb with seven eyes and seven horns, and a victorious rider of a white horse with a tattoo on His thigh. None of these visions represents what Jesus actually looks like, but all of them represent who He is or will be during that time of history. Get it? Not literal, symbolic.

My word of affirmation to you is this: the book of Revelation is all about Jesus revealing the true character of God by unveiling the future. This revelation will show the world once and for all that the devil is a liar and a murderer and a thief. Jesus will reveal to us that in the end He and the saints win, and the devil and his followers lose.

As we enter into the sacred pages of this great book, realize that as weird and scary as it can get, you and Jesus win, and heaven will be yours.

DEC 26

Open Up!

"TO THE ANGEL OF THE CHURCH IN LAODICEA WRITE: These are the words of the Amen, the faithful and true witness, the ruler of God's creation. I know your deeds, that you are neither cold nor hot. I wish you were either one or the other! So, because you are lukewarm—neither hot nor cold—I am about to spit you out of my mouth. You say, 'I am rich; I have acquired wealth and do not need a thing.' But you do not realize that you are wretched, pitiful, poor, blind and naked. I counsel you to buy from me gold refined in the fire, so you can become rich; and white clothes to wear, so you can cover your shameful nakedness; and salve to put on your eyes, so you can see. Those whom I love I rebuke and discipline. So be earnest and repent. Here I am! I stand at the door and knock. If anyone hears my voice and opens the door, I will come in and eat with that person, and they with me." **REVELATION 3:14-20.**

I used to pastor a church in a little touristy town in central Washington. In this church the organist did not like me at all. For the sake of anonymity, we'll call him Wayne.

Wayne would do things during the sermon that would irritate the daylights out of me. While I was preaching, he would fiddle with papers by the organ or "accidentally" hit one of the keys. Often he would grunt loudly and stomp off in the middle of a sermon. Finally I decided that Wayne and I needed to have a serious chat to see if we could work out our differences. So I went to visit him at his home.

When I approached Wayne's door (he was a single man), I could see that his windows were open and that he was watching television in his front room. I rang the doorbell. Wayne looked over his shoulder, saw that it was me, and turned the television up, not stirring from his seat. I rang the doorbell again. Nothing.

"Wayne, I can see you sitting there in your living room! I know that you know I'm at the door!" I yelled.

He yelled back, "And you know that I'm not going to answer it!" So ended my visit with Wayne.

Jesus knocks on the door of our heart just as obviously as I did on Wayne's. He wants to come in and share an intimate meal with us. Won't you let Him in?

DEC 27

A Glimpse Into Heaven

I WEPT AND WEPT because no one was found who was worthy to open the scroll or look inside. Then one of the elders said to me, "Do not weep! See, the Lion of the tribe of Judah, the Root of David, has triumphed. He is able to open the scroll and its seven seals." Then I saw a Lamb, looking as if it had been slain, standing in the center of the throne, encircled by the four living creatures and the elders. The Lamb had seven horns and seven eyes, which are the seven spirits of God sent out into all the earth. **REVELATION 5:4-6.**

In Revelation 4 and 5 we get to see directly inside the very power center of the universe. Admittedly, this is all symbolic, but it still sounds pretty cool. Some of the symbolism here is astounding. The 24 elders are reminiscent of the 24 divisions of priests that served in the Temple (see 1 Chronicles 24). The seven lamps burning before the throne remind us of the seven-branched lampstand in the holy place of the tabernacle. There is a lot of sanctuary symbolism in Revelation.

Most notable to me is the description of the One who sits with the Father on His throne. He is described as a Lamb that looks as if it has been slaughtered for sacrifice. I don't know if you've seen a slaughtered animal, but it's not a pretty sight. And who is the Lamb that was slaughtered? Jesus, of course.

This Lamb has seven eyes and seven horns—in other words, He sees all things and has all power. And from the Father's right hand (the hand of power) the Lamb takes a scroll that has writing on both sides. What is on this scroll? Interestingly, the contents of this scroll are important enough to bring the apostle John to tears. It must be important.

Again we see the symbols of the book of Revelation. There was another heaven-sent document that was written on both sides. Do you know what it was? The Ten Commandments, or as some have described them, the character of God. (You never heard that the Ten Commandments were written on both sides? Check out Exodus 32:15.)

The Lamb is about to disclose how the character of God will be revealed in contrast to the character of the dragon. The book of Revelation is all about the final revealing of God's character to a dying world. And you are a part of that plan.

DEC 28

The Four Horsemen

I WATCHED AS THE LAMB opened the first of the seven seals. Then I heard one of the four living creatures say in a voice like thunder, "Come!" I looked, and there before me was a white horse! Its rider held a bow, and he was given a crown, and he rode out as a conqueror bent on conquest. When the Lamb opened the second seal, I heard the second living creature say, "Come!" Then another horse came out, a fiery red one. Its rider was given power to take peace from the earth and to make people kill each other. . . . When the Lamb opened the third seal, I heard the third living creature say, "Come!" I looked, and there before me was a black horse! Its rider was holding a pair of scales in his hand. Then I heard what sounded like a voice among the four living creatures, saying, "Two pounds of wheat for a day's wages, and six pounds of barley for a day's wages, and do not damage the oil and the wine!" When the Lamb opened the fourth seal, I heard the voice of the fourth living creature say, "Come!" I looked, and there before me was a pale horse! Its rider was named Death, and Hades was following close behind him. **REVELATION 6:1-8.**

As the Lamb from Revelation 5 opens the seven seals on the scroll, we see the battle over God's character unfold before our very eyes. The four horsemen of the apocalypse reveal the battle between the Lamb's testimony of who God is and the testimony of the church that would arise some time after Jesus' resurrection.

The four horsemen show God's church turning against Him. The first horse is a white horse. White usually represents purity. However, it all goes bad when the first horse ends up with the intention of winning people over through conquest. Forcing people to follow God is never God's way. Unfortunately, the church fell into this trap early on.

As you read through the seven seals, you'll see a progression through world history that eventually ends in the second coming of Jesus. This will be the great climax of the great controversy over God's character.

One thing you may want to do is open two Bibles and compare Jesus' description of the end of all things in Matthew 24 with the seven seals of Revelation. You will see that Jesus' words in Matthew directly parallel His words to John in Revelation. The battle lines are being drawn. Those who follow the Lamb will prevail. Whom will you follow?

No Rest for the Restless

THEN I SAW ANOTHER ANGEL FLYING IN MIDAIR, and he had the eternal gospel to proclaim to those who live on the earth—to every nation, tribe, language and people. He said in a loud voice, "Fear God and give him glory, because the hour of his judgment has come. Worship him who made the heavens, the earth, the sea and the springs of water." A second angel followed and said, "'Fallen! Fallen is Babylon the Great,' which made all the nations drink the maddening wine of her adulteries." A third angel followed them and said in a loud voice: "If anyone worships the beast and its image and receives its mark on their forehead or on their hand, they, too, will drink the wine of God's fury, which has been poured full strength into the cup of his wrath. They will be tormented with burning sulfur in the presence of the holy angels and of the Lamb. And the smoke of their torment will rise for ever and ever. There will be no rest day or night for those who worship the beast and its image, or for anyone who receives the mark of its name." This calls for patient endurance on the part of the people of God who keep his commands and remain faithful to Jesus. **REVELATION 14:6-12.**

The three angels' messages in Revelation 14 are a powerful call to God's people; they serve as a *warning* that the false ideas about God are about to fall and as an *identifier* of the characteristics of God's people at the end of time.

The first angel's clarion call is to recognize God for who He is. Revelation 13 describes through symbolism a beast that looks like a lamb but speaks like a dragon—in other words, a group of people (or an entity) who claim to be followers of Christ but are really speaking and acting like the devil. The first angel calls God's people back to worshipping the Creator for who He really is.

The second angel's message announces the fall of all those who claim Christ but have lied about God and misrepresented Him to the masses.

The third angel through symbolic language lets us know that those who fall into the trap of believing lies about God will experience no rest. They will have no Sabbath. Their attempts at salvation through human effort will be fruitless.

A group in marked contrast to those described by the third angel appears at the end of today's reading. God's people will have rest because they obey Him and have faith that Jesus will sustain them through the end times. They will have listened to Jesus' words: "Come unto me, and I will give you rest."

DEC 30

The King Is Coming!

I SAW HEAVEN STANDING OPEN and there before me was a white horse, whose rider is called Faithful and True. With justice he judges and wages war. His eyes are like blazing fire, and on his head are many crowns. He has a name written on him that no one knows but he himself. He is dressed in a robe dipped in blood, and his name is the Word of God. . . . He treads the winepress of the fury of the wrath of God Almighty. On his robe and on his thigh he has this name written: KING OF KINGS AND LORD OF LORDS. **REVELATION 19:11-16.**

The climax to the great battle between God and Satan occurs at the second coming of Jesus. Revelation 19 uses spectacular language to describe this grand event. We see a white horse whose rider has eyes like blazing fire and a head that somehow can hold many crowns. He has a name that nobody knows, but then His name is given: "The Word of God." There's a tattoo on His thigh (not sure if it's permanent or in erasable ink . . . remember, no real tattoo—it's all symbolic). This is a pretty intimidating rider coming back for His people. I think in modern terms John might have had Him coming back on a Harley-Davidson!

This great event marks an end to the lies that the dragon has been spewing out about God for thousands of years. Jesus Himself described this event as "the coming of the Son of Man" (Matthew 24:27). Paul says that it will come "like a thief in the night" (1 Thessalonians 5:2) and will be accompanied by an ear-shattering trumpet blast and a great yell from the archangel. Peter says that the Second Coming will be so blazing hot that it will melt the elements. John says that some people will welcome this event, while others will get so freaked out that they will cry out for the mountains to fall on them.

One thing you should realize: those who fear the Second Coming don't know Jesus. In Revelation 6 they are described as being afraid of the wrath of the Lamb. What kind of people would be afraid of the wrath of a baby sheep? I suppose it would be people who don't know that you're not supposed to be afraid of a baby sheep.

Jesus is coming soon. He's not coming to intimidate you; He's coming to rescue you. You can look forward to that. There is no fear in love.

The Grand Finale

THEN I SAW "A NEW HEAVEN and a new earth," for the first heaven and the first earth had passed away, and there was no longer any sea. I saw the Holy City, the new Jerusalem, coming down out of heaven from God, prepared as a bride beautifully dressed for her husband. And I heard a loud voice from the throne saying, "Look! God's dwelling place is now among the people, and he will dwell with them. They will be his people, and God himself will be with them and be their God. 'He will wipe every tear from their eyes. There will be no more death' or mourning or crying or pain, for the old order of things has passed away." **REVELATION 21:1-4.**

This is it. This is what I'm looking forward to. More than anything else, I look forward to this day. Why?

This is the day that the disgusting mess of sin is finally wiped away. This is the day that my mom is in full health with no brain tumor. This is the day that my mother-in-law has no more pain. This is the day that my grandfather and I get to sit down for the first time and have a conversation about the amazing grace of Jesus and how He arranged our lives so that we could be together for the first time. This is the day of great reunion.

No more tears. Every painful memory, every foolish decision, every hurtful word, every feeling of rejection—gone.

No more death. Cancer—gone. AIDS—gone. War—gone. Old age—gone. Funeral parlors—gone. Cemeteries—empty. Hospital ventilators—remembered no more.

The old order of things has passed away. We no longer have a distorted view of God. We no longer, as Paul described it in 1 Corinthians 13, see through a glass darkly. Now we see face to face. We don't pray to an invisible God anymore. We see Him every day because He tabernacles (resides) with us.

The devil and his schemes are overthrown. Everyone who has fallen for and participated in the devil's lies has been destroyed by their own sin. The earth has been cleaned up by a purifying fire, and we are the new Adam and Eve. Eden is restored. Everything is as it should have been all along. This is our reward.

PRAYER REQUESTS

_____

_____

_____

_____

_____

_____

_____

_____

_____

_____

_____

_____

_____

_____

_____

_____

_____

_____

_____

ANSWERED PRAYER

_____

_____

_____

_____

_____

_____

_____

_____

_____

_____

_____

_____

_____

_____

_____

_____

_____

_____

NOTES:

Heather Thinks You're Ready for Some Good News

Cracked Glasses

Heather Thompson Day

Heather Thompson Day has some good news for those of us who think we've made too many mistakes. Sure, we have good intentions. But usually they lie shattered at our feet. What value could we possibly be to God in this condition? We're ruined. Useless.

In her newest book she explores myths that make us feel we're not good enough for God. She also points out those distractions that keep us from connecting with Him at a deeper level.

Heather is open about being a cracked glass herself. No real Christian is perfect, you know— just repaired. Regularly. 978-0-8280-2564-5

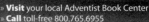

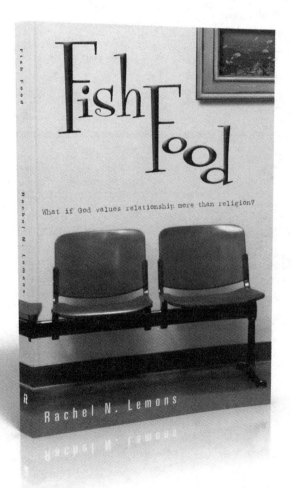